Lecture Notes in Mathematics

Edited by A. Dold and B. Eckmann
Series: Institut de Mathématique, Université de Strasbourg
Adviser: P. A. Meyer

712

Equations Différentielles et Systèmes de Pfaff dans le Champ Complexe

Edité par R. Gérard et J.-P. Ramis

Springer-Verlag
Berlin Heidelberg New York 1979

Editors

Raymond Gérard
Jean-Pierre Ramis
I.R.M.A.
7, rue René Descartes
F-67084 Strasbourg Cédex

AMS Subject Classifications (1970): 34 A 20, 34 A 30, 34 C 40, 34 E XX, 35 B 40, 35 C 10, 35 Q 15

ISBN 3-540-09250-1 Springer-Verlag Berlin Heidelberg New York
ISBN 0-387-09250-1 Springer-Verlag New York Heidelberg Berlin

Library of Congress Cataloging in Publication Data. Main entry under title: Équations de Pfaff différentielles et systèmes de Pfaff dans le champ complexe. (Lecture notes in mathematics ; 712) French or English. «Travaux...effectués dans le cadre de l'Action thématique programmée 'Internationale 1975', décision no. 2170 du Centre nationale de la recherche scientifique...[et] exposés au séminaire sur la théorie des équations différentielles dans le champ complexe, de l'Institut de recherche Mathématique avancée de Strasbourg.» Bibliography: p.
Includes index. 1. Differential equations--Addresses, essays, lectures. 2. Pfaff's problem--Addresses, essays, lectures. 3. Functions of complex variables--Addresses, essays, lectures. I. Gérard, Raymond, 1932-   II. Ramis, Jean Pierre. III. France. Centre national de la recherche scientifique. IV. Institut de recherche Mathématique avancée. V. Series: Lecture notes in mathematics (Berlin) : 712.
QA3.L28 no. 712 [QA372] 510'.8s [515'.35] 79-13782

© by Springer-Verlag Berlin Heidelberg 1979
Printed in Germany

Printing and binding: Beltz Offsetdruck, Hemsbach/Bergstr.
2141/3140-543210

Dans ce volume sont réunis des travaux qui ont été effectués dans le cadre de l'Action Thématique Programmée "Internationale 1975", décision n° 2170 du Centre National de la Recherche Scientifique .

L'objet de cette A. T. P. était de faire collaborer des spécialistes des fonctions de plusieurs variables complexes et des spécialistes de la théorie des équations différentielles et de Pfaff dans le champ complexe .

Les articles publiés ici sont originaux et ont été exposé au séminaire sur la théorie des équations différentielles dans le champ complexe, de l'Institut de Recherche Mathématique Avancée de Strasbourg .

R. GÉRARD et J. P. RAMIS
Responsables de l'A. T. P.

TABLE DES MATIERES

PARTIE A : Equations différentielles ordinaires dans le champ complexe .

PARTIE B : Systèmes de Pfaff dans le champ complexe .

INTRODUCTION TO THE ASYMPTOTIC THEORY OF

LINEAR HOMOGENEOUS DIFFERENCE EQUATIONS

by

Boele BRAAKSMA

1. INTRODUCTION.

We consider linear homogeneous difference equations

$$y(s+1) = A(s)y(s) , \tag{1.1}$$

where $A(s)$ is a given n by n matrix defined on a sector $S = \{s \in \mathbb{C} , \alpha_o \leq \arg s \leq \beta_o , |s| > r_o\}$. We look for solutions $y(s) \in \mathbb{C}^n$ in sectors S' of the same type as S . In particular, we are interested in the asymptotic behavior of solutions $y(s)$ as $s \to \infty$ in S' .

Equations (1.1) are among others useful in the theory of linear differential equations. There also is a similarity in the methods used in the asymptotic theory of linear difference and linear differential equations.

Complete knowledge of the asymptotics of (1.1) would imply that if $A(s)$ is holomorphic at ∞ then there are sectors $S_1,\ldots,S_k$ which cover a full neighborhood of $s=\infty$ such that in each sector S_j a fundamental set of solutions of (1.1) is known together with their asymptotic behavior as $s \to \infty$ in S_j .

We begin with the scalar case $n=1$. Suppose

$$A(s) = \sum_{j=0}^{\infty} A_j s^{-j} , \quad |s| > r_o . \tag{1.2}$$

Assume $A_o \neq 0$. We try a solution

$$y(s) = A_o^s \sum_{j=0}^{\infty} c_j s^{-j} . \tag{1.3}$$

Then we get

$$A_o \sum_{j=0}^{\infty} c_j(s+1)^{-j} = A_o \sum_{j=0}^{\infty} c_j s^{-j} \sum_{h=0}^{\infty} \binom{-j}{h} s^{-h} = \sum_{k=0}^{\infty} A_k s^{-k} \sum_{\ell=0}^{\infty} c_\ell s^{-\ell} . \tag{1.4}$$

Here $\binom{\beta}{j} = \dfrac{\beta(\beta-1)\ldots(\beta-j+1)}{j!}$.

Considering terms s^{-m} , $m = 0,1,2,\ldots$ on both sides of (1.4) we obtain

$$c_m + \sum_{p=1}^{m} c_{m-p} \binom{p-m}{p} = c_m + \sum_{p=1}^{m} c_{m-p} \tilde{A}_p \text{, where } \tilde{A}_p = A_o^{-1} A_p \text{ .}$$

So, for $m = 0$ we get $c_o = c_o$, for $m = 1$ we get $c_o \tilde{A}_1 = 0$ and for $m > 1$ we have

$$\text{(1.5)} \qquad c_{m-1}(1-m-\tilde{A}_1) = \sum_{p=2}^{m} c_{m-p} \{\tilde{A}_p - \binom{p-m}{p}\} \text{ .}$$

In case $A_1 = 0$ we may choose c_o arbitrary and then we determine $c_1, c_2, \ldots$ recursively. Hence if $A_o \neq 0$, $A_1 = 0$ we have a formal solution $y(s)$ given by (1.3) of (1.2) . However, in general this series diverges. The formal procedure above is also valid if $A(s)$ is represented by a formal series.

We will show that under certain assumptions on $A(s)$, which imply

$$\text{(1.6)} \qquad A(s) \sim \sum_{j=0}^{\infty} A_j s^{-j} \text{ , as } s \to \infty \text{ on } S \text{ ,}$$

there exists a solution $y(s)$ in a sector S' such that

$$\text{(1.7)} \qquad y(s) \sim \sum_{j=0}^{\infty} c_j s^{-j} \text{ , } s \to \infty \text{ on } S' \text{ .}$$

Here S and S' are certain sectors in $\mathbb{C}$, $S' \subset S$.

We shall assume for this purpose that $A(s)$ may be represented by a Laplace integral :

$$\text{(1.8)} \qquad A(s) = A_o + \int_0^{\infty} e^{-st} F(t)dt \text{ .}$$

Then we show that there exists a solution $y(s)$ which has a similar Laplace representation, if certain conditions are satisfied. The Laplace integrals for $A(s)$ and $y(s)$ may be expanded asymptotically like in (1.6) and (1.7) by means of Watson's lemma.

The next sections are organized as follows. In section 2 we collect properties of Laplace integrals which are useful for our purposes. Among others relations with factorial series are given. In section 3 we give some preliminary transformations for the difference equation (1.1). In section 4 we derive the integral equation which corresponds to (1.1) under the inverse Laplace transform and we show the existence of holomorphic solutions to the integral equation. After this we derive in Section 5 exponential bounds for these solutions and we obtain the solutions of the difference equation, if certain conditions are satisfied. In section 6 we consider a case where A_0 is singular. Concluding remarks on cases not treated here are made in section 7.

2. LAPLACE INTEGRALS AND FACTORIAL SERIES.

We consider Laplace integrals

$$f(s) = \int_0^\infty e^{-st} F(t)dt \,, \tag{2.1}$$

where the path of integration is some ray $\arg t = \theta$ in $\mathbb{C}$. We assume here that $F(t)$ is continuous on the path of integration and that there exists a positive μ such that

$$F(t) = O(e^{\mu|t|}) \,, \quad t \to \infty \tag{2.2}$$

on $\arg t = \theta$. Then $f(s)$ exists and is holomorphic for $\mathrm{Re}(s\, e^{i\theta}) > \mu$. We denote (2.1) also by $f = \mathcal{L}F$.

The Laplace transform is injective and the inverse Laplace transform can be represented by integrals of the type

$$F(t) = \frac{1}{2\pi i} \int_C e^{st} f(s)ds \,, \tag{2.3}$$

for a large class of functions (cf. Doetsch [4]). C is a suitable contour in the s-plane.

If $G(t)$ is another function continuous on $\arg t = \theta$ and satisfying (2.2) with F replaced by G, then

$$(\mathcal{L}F).(\mathcal{L}G) = \mathcal{L}(F*G) \,, \text{ where } (F*G)(t) = \int_0^t F(t-\tau)\, G(\tau)d\tau \,. \tag{2.4}$$

$F*G$ is the convolution of F and G.

A power series

$$(2.5) \qquad f(s) = \sum_{j=0}^{\infty} c_j s^{-j} , \quad |s| > r_o$$

is representable by a Laplace integral in half planes. For, (2.5) implies with Cauchy's formula for $f^{(j)}(s)$, that at any $\varepsilon > 0$ there exists a constant K such that

$$(2.6) \qquad |c_j| \le K(r_o + \varepsilon)^j , \quad j = 0,1,2,\ldots$$

Now

$$(2.7) \qquad f(s) = c_o + \sum_{j=1}^{\infty} c_j \int_0^{\infty} e^{-st} \frac{t^{j-1}}{(j-1)!} dt = c_o + \int_0^{\infty} e^{-st} F(t)dt ,$$

where

$$(2.8) \qquad F(t) = \sum_{j=0}^{\infty} c_{j+1} \frac{t^j}{j!} .$$

The path of integration in (2.7) is any ray $\arg t = \theta$. Then (2.7) may be verified using (2.6) for $\operatorname{Re}(s\, e^{i\theta}) > r_o$. In particular, (2.6) implies that $F(t)$ is an entire function of order r_o at most : for any $\varepsilon > 0$ we have

$$F(t) = O(e^{(r_o+\varepsilon)|t|}) , \quad \text{as} \quad t \to \infty .$$

The asymptotic behavior of the Laplace transform $f(s)$ as $s \to \infty$ is determined by the behavior of $F(t)$ at $t = 0$. This is clear in the case that $f(s)$ is holomorphic at ∞ from the relations (2.5) and (2.8). However, also in more general cases this is true. This is expressed by Watson's lemma (cf. Doetsch [4]).

LEMMA OF WATSON. Assume $F(t)$ is continuous for $\alpha \le \arg t \le \beta$, $t \ne 0$ and satisfies (2.2) as $t \to \infty$ on $\alpha \le \arg t \le \beta$. Suppose $F(t)$ is analytic for $\alpha < \arg t < \beta$ and

$$(2.9) \qquad F(t) \sim \sum_{j=0}^{\infty} a_j t^{\alpha_j - 1} , \quad t \to 0 \quad \text{for} \quad \alpha \le \arg t \le \beta ,$$

where $0 < \operatorname{Re} \alpha_1 < \operatorname{Re} \alpha_2 < \ldots$

Then

$$(2.10)\qquad f(s) = (\mathcal{L}F)(s) \sim \sum_{j=0}^{\infty} a_j\, \Gamma(\alpha_j) s^{-\alpha_j}\ , \text{ as } s \to \infty \text{ on}$$

$$(2.11)\qquad -\tfrac{1}{2}\pi + \delta - \beta \le \arg s \le \tfrac{1}{2}\pi - \alpha - \delta$$

for any $\delta > 0$.

Laplace transforms are closely related to factorial series. A factorial series is a series of the following type

$$(2.12)\qquad f(s) = A_0 + \sum_{j=0}^{\infty} \frac{A_{j+1}\, j!}{s(s+1)\dots(s+j)} .$$

If this series somewhere converges absolutely, then the region of absolute convergence is a halfplane $\operatorname{Re} s > \lambda$.

A useful property of factorial series in connection with difference equations is the following :

$$(2.13)\qquad f(s+1) - f(s) = -\sum_{j=0}^{\infty} \frac{A_{j+1}(j+1)!}{s(s+1)\dots(s+j+1)} .$$

A slightly more general factorial series is the so called generalized factorial series

$$(2.14)\qquad g(s) = A_0 + \sum_{j=0}^{\infty} \frac{A_{j+1}\, j!\, \omega^{j+1}}{s(s+\omega)\dots(s+j\omega)}$$

where $\omega \ne 0$. However, we see that $g(\omega s) = f(s)$. So only a transformation of the variable has been made. The series (2.14) converges absolutely if $\operatorname{Re}(s/\omega) > \lambda$.

The terms in the righthand side of of (2.12) contain beta-functions and may be represented by Laplace integrals.

$$\frac{j!}{s(s+1)\dots(s+j)} = B(j+1,s) = \int_0^1 (1-\tau)^j\, \tau^{s-1}\, d\tau = \int_0^\infty e^{-st}(1-e^{-t})^j\, dt .$$

This suggests for the factorial series in (2.12) the representation (1.8) where

$$(2.15)\qquad F(t) = \sum_{j=0}^{\infty} A_{j+1}(1-e^{-t})^j .$$

In fact we have the following theorem (cf. Doetsch [4]).

THEOREM. Suppose the factorial series (2.12) converges absolutely for $\operatorname{Re} s > \lambda$, where $\lambda \geq 0$. Let $F(t)$ be defined by (2.15). Then the series for $F(t)$ converges if $|1-e^{-t}| < 1$, and $F(t) = O(e^{(\lambda+\varepsilon)t})$, as $t \to \infty$ on $|\operatorname{Im} t| \leq \frac{1}{2}\pi - \delta$ for any positive δ and ε. The factorial series then may be represented by (1.8) with $A = f$, $\operatorname{Re} s > \lambda$. In (1.8) the path of integration is the positive axis.

Conversely, suppose $F(t)$ is analytic for $|1-e^{-t}| \leq 1$ except in $t = \infty$, and suppose $F(t) = O(e^{\mu t})$ as $t \to \infty$ in $|1-e^{-t}| \leq 1$. Here μ is a non-negative number. Then $f(s) = \mathfrak{L}(F)$ is representable as a factorial series for $\operatorname{Re} s > \mu$.

The extension of the theorem to generalized factorial series is immediate from the relation between (2.14) and (2.12) : $g(\omega s) = f(s)$.

This theorem implies for example that a power series in $\frac{1}{s}$ like (2.5) is representable as a factorial series, since it is representable by a Laplace integral. Furthermore, the asymptotic behavior of factorial series as $s \to \infty$ follows by combining this theorem with Watson's lemma, though it may also be found more directly. Sometimes one obtains as solutions of difference or differential equations functions with known asymptotic behavior. If these functions may be represented as Laplace integrals in certain strips, then they may be represented by convergent generalized factorial series.

The product of two generalized factorial series with a common half plane of absolute convergence is again a generalized factorial series (cf. convolution property of Laplace).

A factorial series (2.12) may also be represented as

$$f(s) = a_o + \sum_{j=0}^{\infty} \frac{b_j \, j!}{(s+\rho)(s+\rho+1)\dots(s+\rho+j)} \tag{2.16}$$

where ρ is some number. Here (2.16) holds in some half plane and the b_j may be explicitly given in terms of a_j. We use here $f(s-\rho) = \mathfrak{L}\{e^{\rho t} F(t)\}(s)$.

3. PRELIMINARY TRANSFORMATIONS OF THE DIFFERENCE EQUATION.

In this section we treat certain transformations which may reduce the difference equation (1.1) to a simpler one. We always assume that $A(s)$ is an n by n matrix defined in some sector $S: \alpha \leq \arg s \leq \beta$, $|s| > r_0$.

I. If

$$y(s+1) = s^c A(s)\, y(s), \tag{3.1}$$

where $c \in \mathbb{C}$ is a constant, then the transformation

$$y(s) = \{\Gamma(s)\}^c z(s) \tag{3.2}$$

reduces this difference equation to

$$z(s+1) = A(s)\, z(s). \tag{3.3}$$

II. If

$$y(s+1) = \lambda A(s)\, y(s), \tag{3.4}$$

where λ is a constant scalar, $\lambda \neq 0$, then the transformation

$$y(s) = \lambda^s z(s) \tag{3.5}$$

reduces the difference equation to (3.3).

III. If $\beta \in \mathbb{C}$ is a constant, then the substitution

$$y(s) = s^\beta z(s) \tag{3.6}$$

transforms (1.1) into

$$z(s+1) = \tilde{A}(s)\, z(s), \quad \text{where } \tilde{A}(s) = \left(1 + \frac{1}{s}\right)^{-\beta} A(s).$$

In particular, assume

$$A(s) = A_0 + \int_0^\infty e^{-st} F(t)dt, \tag{3.7}$$

where the path of integration is $\arg t = \theta$, and $F(t)$ is continuous and satisfies (2.2) on this path. Then

$$\tilde{A}(s) = A_o + \int_0^\infty e^{-st}\,\tilde{F}(t)dt \;, \tag{3.8}$$

where the path of integration is the same and

$$\tilde{F}(t) = F(t) + A_o\,\varphi(t) + (F * \varphi)(t) \tag{3.9}$$

with

$$\varphi(t) = \sum_0^\infty \binom{-\beta}{h+1} \frac{t^h}{h!} \;. \tag{3.10}$$

This easily follows using $(\mathcal{L}\varphi)(s) = (1+\frac{1}{s})^{-\beta} - 1$. We note that

$$\tilde{F}(0) = F(0) - \beta A_o \;. \tag{3.11}$$

In our example on page 2 we assumed that $A_1 = 0$ in (1.2). We see that if originally $A_1 \neq 0$ we may reduce (1.1) to this case by using (3.6) with $\beta = A_1 A_o^{-1}$ (note that in this example we have a scalar difference equation, so $A_1 \in \mathbb{C}$).

IV. By a constant transformation $y(s) = C\,z(s)$ we may reduce (1.1) with A given by (3.7) to the case that A_o is in Jordan form. Now assume

$$A_o = \operatorname{diag}\{A_{o,11}\,,\, A_{o,22}\} \tag{3.12}$$

where $A_{o,11}$ is a $p \times p$ matrix and $A_{o,22}$ is an $(n-p) \times (n-p)$ matrix. Assume $A_{o,11}$ and $A_{o,22}$ have no eigenvalues in common. We say that A_o has block diagonal form. Then there exists a transformation

$$y(s) = T(s)\,z(s) \tag{3.13}$$

such that (1.1) is transformed into

$$z(s+1) = \tilde{A}(s)\,z(s) \tag{3.14}$$

where $\tilde{A}(s)$ is given by (3.8) with $\tilde{F}$ satisfying

(3.15) $$\tilde{F}(0) = \text{diag}\{A_{1,11}, A_{1,22}\} .$$

$A_{1,11}$ is the first $p \times p$ block in $F(0)$ and $A_{1,22}$ is the last $(n-p) \times (n-p)$ block in $F(0)$. $\tilde{F}$ is continuous and satisfies (2.2) on the path of integration. Here $T(s)$ has the following form :

(3.16) $$T(s) = I_n + \frac{1}{s}\begin{pmatrix} 0 & Q_{12} \\ Q_{21} & 0 \end{pmatrix}$$

where Q_{12} is a constant $p \times (n-p)$ matrix and Q_{21} is a constant $(n-p) \times p$ matrix.

The proof of this statement is as follows (cf. Turrittin [8]). From (1.1), (3.13) and (3.14) we deduce

$$\tilde{A}(s) = T^{-1}(s+1)\ A(s)\ T(s) .$$

We may write $T(s) = I + \frac{1}{s} Q$ and hence $T^{-1}(s) = I + \frac{1}{s}\tilde{Q}(s)$, where $\tilde{Q}(s)$ is analytic at ∞ and $\tilde{Q}(\infty) = -Q$. These functions may be written as Laplace transforms : $T = I + \mathcal{L}Q$, $T^{-1} = I + \mathcal{L}R$, where $R(t)$ is an entire function with $R(0) = -Q$ (cf. (2.5), (2.7) and (2.8)). It easily follows then that

$$\tilde{A} = I + \mathcal{L}\tilde{F}$$

where $\tilde{F}(0) = A_oQ - QA_o + F(0)$.

In particular, using the block representation of A_o and Q (cf. (3.16)) we find for the corresponding blocks in $F(0)$ and $\tilde{F}(0)$: $\{\tilde{F}(0)\}_{jj} = \{F(0)\}_{jj}$, $j = 1,2$.

$$\{\tilde{F}(0)\}_{12} = A_{o,11}\, Q_{12} - Q_{12}\, A_{o,22} + \{F(0)\}_{12} ,$$

$$\{\tilde{F}(0)\}_{21} = A_{o,22}\, Q_{21} - Q_{21}\, A_{o,11} + \{F(0)\}_{21} .$$

Since $A_{o,11}$ and $A_{o,22}$ have no eigenvalues in common, we may choose Q_{12} and Q_{21} such that $\{\tilde{F}(0)\}_{12} = 0$, $\{\tilde{F}(0)\}_{21} = 0$ (cf. Wasow [9], ch. 2, sect. 4).

4. THE CORRESPONDING INTEGRAL EQUATION.

We assume from now on that $A(s)$ in (1.1) is given by (1.8) and that

$$A_o = \mathrm{diag}\{\lambda_o I_p , A_{o,22}\} \tag{4.1}$$

where $\lambda_o \neq 0$ and $A_{o,22}$ has no eigenvalue λ_o. Furthermore we assume for $F(t)$ either

i) $F(t)$ is defined on $\mathcal{D}_o = \{t \in \mathbb{C}, \arg t = \theta\}$, $F(t)$ is continuous and satisfies (2.2) on $\mathcal{D}_o$, and $F(t)$ has a directional derivative at $t=0$ in the direction $\arg t = \theta$,

or

ii) $F(t)$ is analytic in a closed star domain $\mathcal{D}_1$, with respect to 0, containing $\mathcal{D}_o$ for $\alpha_o \le \theta \le \beta_o$ and with the origin as interior point, and $F(t)$ satisfies (2.2) in $\mathcal{D}_1$.

In both cases we assume that $\mathcal{D}_o$ and $\mathcal{D}_1$ do not contain any of the numbers $2\pi i$, $-2\pi i$ and $-\log \gamma$, where γ is any non zero eigenvalue of $A_{o,22}$ and where all values of the log are taken.

Finally we suppose

$$F(0) = \mathrm{diag}\{A_{1,11} , A_{1,22}\} . \tag{4.2}$$

This is no loss of generality in view of sect. 3, IV. Moreover, we may assume $\lambda_o = 1$ in view of sect. 3, II.

If (1.1) has a solution in the form

$$y(s) = c_o + \int_0^\infty e^{-st} w(t)dt$$

with the same path of integration $\arg t = \theta$ as in (1.8), then we obtain after substitution in (1.1)

$$c_o + \mathcal{L}(e^{-t} w) = A_o c_o + \mathcal{L}(A_o w + F * w + F c_o) . \tag{4.3}$$

It follows that $A_o c_o = c_o$. Since $A_o = \mathrm{diag}\{I_p , A_{o,22}\}$ where $A_{o,22}$ has no eigenvalue 1, we have $c_o^T = (\tilde{c}_o^T , 0_{1,n-p})$ where $\tilde{c}_o$ is an arbitrary element of

$\mathbb{C}^p$. Now (4.3) reduces to

(4.4) $$(e^{-t} I_n - A_o)w = F * w + F c_o .$$

Substituting $t=0$ we see using (4.1) and the form of c_o that

$$A_{1,11} \tilde{c}_o = 0 .$$

Therefore we assume that $A_{1,11}$ has an eigenvalue 0 . This is no loss of generality as follows from sect. 3, III (use a preliminary transformation (3.6) with β equal to an eigenvalue of $A_{1,11}$, cf. (3.11)).

From the block diagonal form of A_o we derive

(4.5) $$(e^{-t} I_n - A_o)^{-1} = t^{-1} C(t) , C(t) = C_o + t C_1(t) , C_o = \mathrm{diag}(-I_p , 0) ,$$

where $C_1(t)$ is analytic in the star domain $\mathcal{D}$ with center 0 which arises from $\mathbb{C}$ by deleting halflines from $2\pi i$, $-2\pi i$ and $-\log \gamma$ to ∞ where γ runs through the non zero eigenvalues of $A_{o,22}$. Here all possible values of the logarithm are taken ; the cuts are chosen along rays arg t = constant , but the origin does not lie on a cut. Now we see $\mathcal{D}_o \subset \mathcal{D}$, $\mathcal{D}_1 \subset \mathcal{D}$.

Let

(4.6) $$F(t) = F(0) + t F_1(t) .$$

Then $F_1(t)$ is continuous on $\arg t = \beta$. Using (4.5) and (4.6) we may write (4.4) in the form

(4.7) $$tw(t) = C_o F(0) * w + t C_1(t) F(0) * w + C(t)\{(t F_1) * w + t F_1 c_o\} .$$

Here we have also used $F(0) c_o = 0$ (cf. (4.2)).
For the main term $C_o F(0) * w$ in the righthand side of (4.7) we may use

(4.8) $$C_o F(0) = \mathrm{diag}\{-A_{1,11} , 0\}$$

(cf. (4.2) and (4.5)).

We now distinguish two cases :

Case 1) : $A_{1,11} = 0$

Case 2) : $A_{1,11} \neq 0$.

We first consider case 1. This occurs for example if $p = 1$. Then $A_{1,11}$ is a scalar with eigenvalue 0, so $A_{1,11} = 0$. In case 1) the term $C_o\ F(0)$ in (4.7) is zero (cf. (4.8)).

We may now rewrite (4.7) as

$$(4.9) \qquad w(t) = t \int_0^1 f(t,\tau)\ w(t\tau)d\tau + C(t)\ F_1(t)\ c_o ,$$

where $f(t,\tau) = C_1(t)\ F(0) + C(t)(1-\tau)F_1(t-t\tau)$. This an integral equation which is similar to the integral equation used in the solution of the initial value problem for ordinary differential equations and the same technique may be applied.

Let $\mathcal{V}$ be the space of continuous functions on $\arg t = \theta$. Define the map T of $\mathcal{V}$ into $\mathcal{V}$ by

$$(Tw)(t) = t \int_0^1 f(t,\tau)\ w(t\tau)d\tau + C(t)\ F_1(t)\ c_o , \quad w \in \mathcal{V} .$$

Then for w_1 and w_2 in $\mathcal{V}$ and $|t| \leq R$, $\arg t = \theta$ we have

$$(4.10) \qquad |(Tw_1 - Tw_2)(t)| \leq K|t| \max_{\tau \in [0,t]} |w_1(\tau) - w_2(\tau)| ,$$

where K is an upper bound for $|f(t,\tau)|$ on

$$\{(t,\tau) : t \in \mathbb{C},\ \tau \in \mathbb{R},\ \arg t = \theta,\ |t| \leq R,\ 0 \leq \tau \leq 1\} .$$

Let $\mathcal{V}(R)$ be the space of continuous functions on $\{t \in \mathbb{C} : \arg t = \theta,\ |t| \leq R\}$, with sup norm. Here R is any positive number. It easily follows using (4.10) that there exists an integer N depending on R such that T^N is a contraction on $\mathcal{V}$. Then we may use the contraction principle to show that (4.9) has exactly one solution in $\mathcal{V}_R$, and so in $\mathcal{V}$.

If F is analytic in $\mathcal{D}_1$, we may prove in the same way that (4.9) has a unique solution which is analytic in $\mathcal{D}_1$.

Case 2). $A_{1,11} \neq 0$. The integral equation (4.7) now cannot be reduced to the form (4.9) with a continuous kernel $f(t,\tau)$. However, we may say that the integral equation now has a singularity of the first kind in $t=0$, similar to this notion for ordinary differential equations. For instance, if $F_1 \equiv 0$ and

$$u(t) = \int_0^t w(\tau)d\tau$$

we see that (4.7) is equivalent to

$$t\frac{du}{dt} = C(t)\ F(0)\ u(t)\ ,\ u(0)=0\ ,$$

which is a differential equation with a singularity of the first kind in the origin.

We assume here case ii), so that F is analytic in $\mathcal{D}_1$. Now we may use the same procedure in (4.7) as in the construction of solutions near a singular point of the first kind of ordinary differential equations. In this way we obtain a set of r solutions of (4.7) in the form

$$\sum_{j=0}^{r-1} \alpha_{j,r}(t)(\log t)^j\ ,$$

where r is the multiplicity of the eigenvalue 0 of $A_{1,11}$ and $\alpha_{jr}(t)$ have an algebraic singularity in 0.

Case 2) with $p=n$ and with $A(s)$ given as a factorial series has been treated by Harris [5]. He calls in this case ∞ a regular singular point of (1.1). He constructed directly by means of factorial series formal solutions which were then shown to be analytic solutions. Now (1.1) may be written as $y(s+1)-y(s) = \frac{1}{s}A_1(s)\ y(s)$, where A_1 is a factorial series, and (2.13) may be used.

5. EXPONENTIAL BOUNDS ON w ; SOLUTIONS OF (1.1).

In section 4 we obtained solutions of the integral equation (4.4). However, we need exponential bounds for these solutions as $t \to \infty$ in $\mathcal{D}_0$ or $\mathcal{D}_1$ in order that the function

$$y(s) = c_0 + \int_0^\infty e^{-st} w(t)dt \tag{5.1}$$

makes sense (the path of integration is $\arg t = \theta$, $\alpha_0 \le \theta \le \beta_0$). It follows from (4.1) with $\lambda_0 = 1$ that

$$(e^{-t} I_n - A_0)^{-1} = \mathrm{diag}\{(e^{-t}-1)^{-1} I_p, (e^{-t} I_{n-p} - A_{0,22})^{-1}\} \tag{5.2}$$

is bounded if $|t| \ge 1$, $t \in \mathcal{D}_0$ or $t \in \mathcal{D}_1$ except in the case that $A_{0,22}$ is singular and $\mathcal{D}_0$ or $\mathcal{D}_1$ contain points with arbitrary large real parts, since $(e^{-t})^{-1}$ is unbounded as $\mathrm{Re}\, t \to \infty$. We assume now that if A_0 is singular, then $\mathcal{D}_0$ and $\mathcal{D}_1$ lie in the left half plane.

From (2.2) and (4.4) we derive that there exists constants K_1 and K_2 such that

$$|w(\rho\, e^{i\theta})| \le K_1 \int_0^\rho e^{\mu(\rho-\sigma)} |w(\sigma\, e^{i\theta})| d\sigma + K_2\, e^{\mu\rho} \tag{5.3}$$

where $\rho \ge 0$ and $\rho\, e^{i\theta}$ on $\mathcal{D}_1$ or $\mathcal{D}_2$. Let $|e^{-\mu\rho}\, w(\rho\, e^{i\theta})| = \varphi(\rho)$. Then we have

$$\varphi(\rho) \le K_1 \int_0^\rho \varphi(\sigma) d\sigma + K_2 \,.$$

From Gronwall's lemma it now follows that

$$\varphi(\rho) \le K_2\, e^{K_1 \rho} ,$$

and consequently

$$|w(\rho\, e^{i\theta})| \le K_2\, e^{(\mu+K_1)\rho} , \quad \rho\, e^{i\theta} \in \mathcal{D}_0 \text{ or } \mathcal{D}_1 . \tag{5.4}$$

Hence the Laplace transform of $w(t)$ exists under the assumptions made above.

So we have the following result : assume (1.8), (4.1) with $\lambda_o \neq 0$, i) or ii) of sect. 4 and (4.2) with $A_{1,11} = \lambda_1 I_p$. If A_o is singular we assume $\mathcal{D}_o$ and $\mathcal{D}_1$ are in the left half plane. Then using (3.6) with $\beta = \lambda$, and choosing $c_o = e_j$ $(j = 1,\ldots,p)$ we get p solutions of (1.1) :

Then there exist p solutions

$$y_j(s) = \lambda_o^s \, s^{\lambda_1} \{e_j + \int_0^\infty e^{-st} \, w_j(t)dt\} \, , \; j = 1,\ldots,p \, , \tag{5.5}$$

where the path of integration is $\arg t = \theta$, $\alpha_o \le \theta \le \beta_o$. The integral converges if $\mathrm{Re}(s \, e^{i\theta}) > \mu + K_1$.

In case ii) different values of θ lead to analytic continuations of the same function $y_j(s)$.

In case i) $w_j(t)$ is continuous on $\mathcal{D}_o$ and in case ii) $w_j(t)$ is analytic in $\mathcal{D}_1$. In both cases

$$w_j(t) = O(e^{(\mu+K_1)|t|}) \quad \text{as} \quad t \to \infty \, .$$

The asymptotic behavior of the solutions $y_j(s)$ as $s \to \infty$ on

$$-\tfrac{1}{2}\pi + \delta - \beta_o \le \arg s \le \tfrac{1}{2}\pi - \delta - \alpha_o \, , \quad (\delta > 0)$$

may be derived from Watson's lemma (cf. sect. 2). Here $\alpha_o = \beta_o = \theta$ in case i).

If $\mathcal{D}_1$ contains the set $K_\omega = \{t \in \mathbb{C} : |1 - e^{-\omega t}| \le 1\}$ for some $\omega \neq 0$, then $A(s)$ and $y_j(s)$ are representable as generalized factorial series like (2.14) in the half plane $\mathrm{Re}(\frac{s}{\omega}) > \mu + K_1$.

In case 2 of section 5 we get similar, slightly more complicated results, now logarithmic terms may also appear. We omit the details. A complete treatment in the case $n = p$ and $A(s)$ given by factorial series has been given by Harris [5] .

6. A CASE WHERE A_o IS SINGULAR.

We now consider a case where A_o satisfies the assumptions of sect. 4 and A_o is singular. In sect. 5 we did not give an estimate for the solution w on rays in the right half plane in this case. The reason was that $(e^{-t} I_{n-p} - A_{o,22})^{-1}$ is not bounded at ∞ on such a ray. So we did not get a solution of (1.1) near the positive real axis. Suppose

(6.1) $$A_o = \operatorname{diag}\{I_p, B, 0\}$$

where B is a non singular $(n-p-1) \times (n-p-1)$ matrix with no eigenvalue 1. Now

(6.2) $$(e^{-t} I_n - A_o)^{-1} = \operatorname{diag}\{e^{-t}-1)^{-1} I_p, (e^{-t} I_{n-p-1} - B)^{-1}, e^t\} .$$

We see from (4.4) that the estimate for the last component w_n causes the difficulties. We cannot apply the method of sect. 5.

We assume that $A_o c_o = c_o$, $F(0)c_o = 0$,

(6.3) $$F(0) = \operatorname{diag}\{G, \sigma\}$$

where G is an $(n-1) \times (n-1)$ matrix and $\sigma \neq 0$. Then we deduce from (4.4) for w_n:

(6.4) $$e^{-t} w_n = \sigma \int_0^t w_n(\tau)d\tau + (t F_1 * w).e_n + (t F_1(t)c_o).e_n .$$

Now put $\int_0^t w(\tau)d\tau = u$. Then we may write (6.4) as an integrodifferential equation

(6.5) $$e^{-t} \frac{du_n}{dt} = \sigma u_n + (\tilde{F}_1 * u).e_n + \{t F_1(t)c_o\}.e_n , \text{ where } \tilde{F}_1 = \frac{d}{dt} (\tau F_1) .$$

Since $e^{-t} \frac{dv}{dt} = \sigma v$ has a solution $\exp(\sigma e^t)$, (6.5) may be transformed into

$$u_n(t) = \int_0^t [\exp\{\sigma(e^t - e^\tau) + \tau\}].[(\tilde{F}_1 * u)(\tau) + \tau F_1(\tau)c_o]d\tau.e_n .$$

Changing the order of integration we get

(6.6) $$u_n(t) = \{\int_0^t K(t,\tau) u(\tau)d\tau + K(t)c_o\}.e_n$$

where $K(t) = \int_0^t [\exp\{\sigma(e^t - e^\tau) + \tau\}]\ \tau\ F_1(\tau)d\tau$,

$$K(t,\tau) = \int_\tau^t [\exp\{\sigma(e^t - e^\xi) + \xi\}]\ \tilde{F}_1(\xi-\tau)d\xi \tag{6.7}$$

$$= -\frac{1}{\sigma}\tilde{F}_1(t-\tau) + \frac{1}{\sigma}\tilde{F}_1(0)\ \exp\sigma(e^t - e^\tau)$$

$$+ \frac{1}{\sigma}\int_\tau^t [\exp\sigma(e^t - e^\xi)]\ \tilde{F}_1'(\xi-\tau)d\xi\ .$$

We now estimate $u(t)$ on a path $\mathcal{L}$ which consists of the straight line segment $[0,t_0]$ and the half line $\arg(t-t_0) = 0$, where t_0 is chosen such that $\mathrm{Re}(\sigma e^{t_0}) \le 0$, and such that $\mathcal{L}$ lies in $\mathcal{D}_1$. We assume that we have case ii) of sect. 5 and $\mathcal{D}_1$ is such that there exists such a $\mathcal{L}$ in $\mathcal{D}_1$.

Then we see that for τ and t on $\mathcal{L}$, τ between 0 and t we have

$$|K(t,\tau)| \le k\ e^{\mu|t-\tau|}\ ,\ \text{and similarly}\ \ |K(t)| \le k\ e^{\mu|t|}\ .$$

Combining this with (6.6), (4.4) and (6.2) we get for the vector $(w_1(t),\ldots,w_{n-1}(t),u(t))^T$ an inequality similar to (5.3) on $\mathcal{L}$. From this we derive an exponential bound for this vector, and so for w , on $\mathcal{L}$. Hence we get now a solution

$$y(s) = c_0 + \int_{\mathcal{L}} e^{-st}\ w(t)dt\ ,$$

in a sector $|\arg s| \le \frac{1}{2}\pi - \varepsilon$. In this sector it may be expanded asymptotically as in Watson's lemma.

7. CONCLUDING REMARKS.

In the preceding sections we have only treated certain solutions which correspond to Jordan blocks in A_o which are a non zero multiple of an identity matrix. If this is not the case the situation is much more difficult. If A_o contains as first Jordan block $\lambda I_p + N_p$ where $\lambda \neq 0$, $N_p \neq 0$ and N_p nilpotent, then one uses a substitution

$$y(s) = \mathrm{diag}\{1, s^{-\frac{1}{p}}, \ldots, s^{-\frac{p-1}{p}}, I_{n-p}\} z(s)$$

in order to get

$$z(s+1) = \tilde{A}(s)\ z(s)$$

where $\tilde{A}(0) = \mathrm{diag}\{\lambda I_p, \tilde{A}_{o,22}\}$. So the first block in $\tilde{A}(0)$ has the right form, but we have now fractional powers in $\tilde{A}(s)$. A formal procedure for this case has been been given by Turrittin [8]. The corresponding analytic treatment may be given then in many cases by using a theorem on nonlinear difference equations of Harris and Sibuya [7].

The case that A_o is singular is also not treated completely (cf. also Braaksma and Harris [2] for another special case similar to the one in sect. 6).

The asymptotic theory of linear difference equations has many parallels with the theory of differential equations. In both theories the work of G.D. Birkhoff is fundamental. In Birkhoff's work one finds the most complete treatment of the asymptotic theory of difference equations. He uses different methods from those presented here (cf. [1], [2]). For a useful survey of the analytic theory of difference equations, see [6].

REFERENCES

[1] BIRKHOFF, G.D. Formal theory of irregular linear difference equations. Acta Math., vol. 54, 1930, p. 205.

[2] BIRKHOFF, G.D., and TRJITZINSKY, W.J. Analytic theory of singular difference equations. Acta Math., vol. 60, 1933, p. 1.

[3] BRAAKSMA, B.L.J., and HARRIS jr., W.A. On an open problem in the theory of linear difference equations. Nieuw Archief voor Wiskunde (3), vol. 23, 1975, p. 228.

[4] DOETSCH, G. Handbuch der Laplace Transformation I, II. Verlag Birkhäuser Basel, 1950 and 1955.

[5] HARRIS jr., W.A. Linear systems of difference equations. Contrib. to Diff. Equations, vol. 1, 1963, p. 489.

[6] HARRIS jr., W.A. Analytic theory of difference equations in Analytic theory of differential equations. Lecture Notes in Math., Springer Verlag, vol. 183, p. 46.

[7] HARRIS jr., W.A., and SIBUYA, Y. On asymptotic solutions of systems of non linear difference equations. Journ. reine angew. Math., vol. 222, 1966, p. 120.

[8] TURRITTIN, H.L. The formal theory of systems of irregular homogeneous linear difference and differential equations. Bol. Soc. Mat. Mexicana, vol. 215, 1960, p. 255.

[9] WASOW, W. Asymptotic expansions for ordinary differential equations. Interscience Publishers, New York, 1965.

FORMES CANONIQUES RATIONNELLES D'UN SYSTEME DIFFERENTIEL A POINT SINGULIER IRREGULIER

par

A. DABÈCHE

INTRODUCTION

Etant donné un système différentiel linéaire :

$$x \frac{d}{dx} \quad Y = A (x) Y \qquad (1)$$

où, A(x) est une matrice d'ordre n et à coefficients méromorphes au voisinage de l'origine de $\mathbb{C}$, on se propose de donner un moyen explicite permettant de reconnaître le "type" de singularité du système au point x = 0. Dans la littérature, ce problème a été traité par plusieurs auteurs. C'est ainsi que B. MALGRANGE (Cf[5]) en comparant les solutions holomorphes - solutions formelles (ou encore les solutions méromorphes - solutions à singularité essentielle), obtient une mesure de l'irrégularité en un point singulier d'un système différentiel D. Cette mesure est invariante par toutes les transformations rationnelles. Ceci lui permet de définir un indice {i (D)} dont la nullité caractérise les singularités régulières. On a un moyen de calcul explicite de cet indice lorsque le système différentiel provient d'une équation différentielle. D'autre part dans [3] R. GERARD et A.H.M. LEVELT (Cf[3]) définissent des critères mesurant l'irrégularité aux points singuliers des systèmes différentiels. Leur méthode consiste à étudier " le domaine + l'image modulo le domaine " d'un opérateur différentiel. Ce qui permet d'associer à tout point singulier d'un système différentiel, une suite d'entiers naturels (appelés invariants du point singulier) qui mesurent le degré de complication de la singularité. Mais on ne dispose pas d'une méthode de calcul de ces invariants pour un système donné sauf si la matrice du système considéré est de la forme :

$$\begin{bmatrix} 0 & 0 & \cdots & 0 & * \\ 1 & 0 & \cdots & 0 & * \\ 0 & 1 & & 0 & * \\ \cdot & \cdot & \ddots & \cdot & \cdot \\ \cdot & \cdot & & \cdot & \cdot \\ \cdot & \cdot & & \cdot & \cdot \\ 0 & 0 & & 1 & * \end{bmatrix} \qquad (2)$$

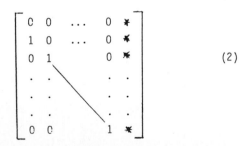

Par ailleurs, P. DELIGNE a démontré (Cf [2] lemme II.1.3.) qu'il existe une transformation Y = PZ, avec P méromorphe inversible en zéro, qui change le système différentiel (1) en un système différentiel de la forme :

$$x \frac{d}{dx} Z = B(x) Z \qquad (3)$$

où la matrice B(x) a la forme (2). Mais dans la pratique, on ne sait pas trouver (du moins à ma connaissance) cette transformation. C'est ce que nous avons essayé de faire dans cet article. Pour celà, on s'est inspiré de la décomposition bien connue des modules de type fini sur un anneau principal, en somme directe de modules monogènes [Bourhaki, Algèbre Chap. 7 th. 2 §4].

On montre d'abord qu'étant donné un espace vectoriel de dimension finie sur K [K étant le corps des fractions de $\mathbb{C}\{x\}$] et un opérateur différentiel ∇ : $V \to V$, alors V est somme directe de sous espaces vectoriels cycliques invariants par ∇. C'est l'objet du théorème 1, dont la démonstration donne les transformations permettant cette décomposition.

Ceci étant, on se sert de ce théorème pour décrire un algorithme permettant la construction effective d'un vecteur cyclique. C'est l'objet du théorème 2.

On peut dès lors calculer les invariants mesurant l'irrégularité du point singulier du système différentiel.

Notations :

On note :

$\mathcal{O} = \mathbb{C}\{x\}$ l'anneau des séries convergentes d'une variable x et à coefficients dans $\mathbb{C}$.

K le corps des fractions de $\mathcal{O}$

V un espace vectoriel de dimension n ($n \in \mathbb{N}^*$) sur K

∂ la dérivation $x\frac{d}{dx} : K \to K$

∇ un opérateur différentiel sur V, i.e. un $\mathbb{C}$-endomorphisme de V satisfaisant la relation :

$$\nabla(fv) = (\partial f)v + f\nabla v \text{ pour tous } f \in K \text{ et } v \in V$$

Définition

Soit W un sous-espace vectoriel de V, de dimension r. W est dit ∇-cyclique s'il existe un vecteur $w \in W$ tel que $(w, \nabla w, \ldots, \nabla^{r-1}w)$ soit une base de W.

Nous nous proposons de trouver des moyens de calcul explicites permettant de démontrer les deux résultats suivants :

Théorème 1 :

Soit $\nabla : V \to V$ un opérateur différentiel sur un espace vectoriel de dimension finie sur K. Il existe alors des sous-espaces ∇-cycliques $V_1, \ldots, V_k$ tels que l'on ait

$$V = V_1 \oplus \ldots \oplus V_k$$

Théorème 2 :

Soit $\nabla : V \to V$ un opérateur différentiel sur un espace vectoriel de dimension n sur K. Alors l'espace V est ∇-cyclique.

La démonstration de ces théorèmes repose sur plusieurs lemmes. Avant de les énoncer, introduisons les notions suivantes. Etant donnée une base $(e) = (e_1, \ldots, e_n)$ de V, on appelle réseau de V (et on le notera E), un sous $\mathcal{O}$-module libre engendré par les vecteurs $e_1, \ldots, e_n$. D'autre part, désignons par $M = (M_{ij})_{1 \leq i,j \leq n}$ la matrice de ∇ par rapport à la base (e) et par q l'entier ≥ 0 défini par :

$$q = \sup_{1 \leq i,j \leq n} \left[0, \; -\nu(M_{ij})\right]$$

(ν étant la valuation sur K). Cela étant, posons

$$\nabla_{q+1} = x^q \, \nabla.$$

On définit ainsi une application $\nabla_{q+1} : E \to E$, qui est $\mathbb{C}$-linéaire et qui vérifie la relation

$$\nabla_{q+1}(f\ v) = (x^{q+1} \frac{d}{dx} f)v + f\ \nabla_{q+1}v \qquad (\ f \in \mathcal{O} \text{ et } v \in E)$$

Il est clair que, si A désigne la matrice de ∇_{q+1} dans la base (e), alors $A \in M_n(\mathcal{O})$ et vérifie la relation

$A = x^q\ M$. où M désigne la matrice précedemment définie.

Enfin, notons θ la projection canonique de E dans le $\mathbb{C}$-espace vectoriel $\bar{E} = E/xE$ et $\bar{\nabla}_{q+1}$ le $\mathbb{C}$-endomorphisme de $\bar{E}$ défini par le diagramme commutatif.

$$\begin{array}{ccc} E & \xrightarrow{\nabla_{q+1}} & E \\ \theta \downarrow & & \downarrow \theta \\ E & \xrightarrow{\bar{\nabla}_{q+1}} & \bar{E} \end{array}$$

La matrice $\bar{A}$ de $\bar{\nabla}_{q+1}$ par rapport à la base $(\theta(e)) = (\theta e_1, \ldots, \theta e_n)$ n'est autre que $A(0)$.

On dira qu'un sous θ-module libre F de E, de rang r, est ∇_{q+1}- cyclique s'il existe $v \in F$ tel que $(v, \nabla_{q+1}v, \ldots, \nabla_{q+1}{}^{r-1}v)$ soit une θ-base de F.

Il est clair que si E est somme directe de sous-$\mathcal{O}$-modules libres $E_1, \ldots, E_k$, ∇_{q+1}-cycliques et de rangs respectifs $r_1, \ldots, r_k$, alors V est aussi somme directe de sous-espaces vectoriels $V_1, \ldots, V_k$, ∇-cycliques et de dimensions respectives $r_1, \ldots, r_k$.

De sorte qu'au lieu de démontrer les théorèmes 1 et 2 pour l'opérateur différentiel ∇, nous allons les démontrer pour l'opérateur différentiel ∇_{q+1}.

Nous pouvons maintenant énoncer le premier lemme :

Lemme 1

Soit $\bar{A} = (\bar{A}_{ij})_{1 \leq i,j \leq n}$ la matrice de $\bar{\nabla}_{q+1}$ dans la base $(\theta\ (e)\ )$ s'il existe un entier $r (1 \leq r \leq n-1)$, tel que $\bar{A}_{r+1,r}$ soit différent de zéro. Alors les vecteurs $e_1, \ldots, e_r, \nabla_{q+1}(e_r), e_{r+2}, \ldots, e_n$, forment une base de E.

Soit $A = (A_{ij})_{1 \leq i,j \leq n}$ la matrice de ∇_{q+1} par rapport à la base (e) et P la matrice définie par :

$$P = \begin{bmatrix} 1 & & 0 & A_{1,r} & 0 & 0 \\ 0 & & & & & 0 \\ & & & & & \\ & & 1 & & & \\ & & & A_{r+1,r} & & \\ & & & & 1 & \\ 0 & & 0 & A_{nr} & 0 & 1 \end{bmatrix}$$

dans laquelle la colonne (A_{ir}) occupe la $(r+1)^{\text{e}}$ place.

Il est clair que $P \in GL_n(\mathcal{O})$ puisque $P(0) = \text{diag}\,[1,\ldots, 1, \bar{A}_{r+1,r}, 1,\ldots,1]$ et que $\bar{A}_{r+1,r} \neq 0$

Soit alors $(e') = (e'_1,\ldots, e'_n)$ la base de E définie par :

$$(e'_1,\ldots, e'_n) = (e_1,\ldots, e_n)P.$$

Les vecteurs e'_i satisfont aux relations :

$$e'_i = e_i \qquad \text{pour } i \neq r$$

$$e'_{r+1} = \nabla_{q+1}(e_r).$$

ce qui démontre ce lemme.

Application

Supposons que le polynôme minimal de $\bar{\nabla}_{q+1}$ soit égal à son polynôme caractéristique. On sait alors qu'il existe une base (f) de E telle que la matrice de $\bar{\nabla}_{q+1}$ par rapport à la base (θf) ait la forme

$$\begin{bmatrix} 0 & & 0 & * \\ 1 & & 0 & * \\ & \ddots & & \vdots \\ 0 & & 1 & * \end{bmatrix} \qquad * \in \mathbb{C}$$

En appliquant le lemme 1 pour les valeurs successives de r : 1, 2,..., n-1, on obtient le résultat suivant :

Corollaire

Si les facteurs de similitude de l'endomorphisme $\bar{\nabla}_{q+1} : \bar{E} \to \bar{E}$ sont $(1,\ldots, 1, d_n)$ avec $d_n \in \{X\}$ alors le réseau E est ∇_{q+1}-cyclique.

Cela dit,

Lemme 2

Supposons que les facteurs de similitude de l'endomorphisme $\acute{\bar{\nabla}}_{q+1}$ soient $(1,\ldots,1,d_{s+1},\ldots,d_n)$ où $d_{s+1},\ldots,d_n$ sont des polynômes unitaires non constants tels que chacun divise le suivant. Il existe alors une base (e') de E telle que la matrice B de ∇_{q+1} par rapport à cette base soit de la forme :

$$B = (B_i^j)_{1 \leq i,j \leq n-s}$$

avec

$$B_j^j = \begin{bmatrix} 0 & & 0 & b_{j,1} \\ 1 & & 0 & b_{j,2} \\ & \ddots & & \vdots \\ 0 & & 1 & b_{j,n_j} \end{bmatrix} \qquad (1 \leq j \leq n-s)$$

$$B_i^j = \begin{bmatrix} 0 & \ldots & 0 & b_{i,1}^j \\ \ldots & \ldots & \ldots & \ldots \\ 0 & \ldots & 0 & b_{i,n_j}^j \\ 0 & \ldots & 0 & 0 \\ \ldots & \ldots & \ldots & \ldots \\ 0 & \ldots & 0 & 0 \end{bmatrix} \quad (i > j) \qquad B_i^j = \begin{bmatrix} 0 & \ldots & 0 & b_{i,1}^j \\ \ldots & \ldots & \ldots & \ldots \\ 0 & \ldots & 0 & b_{i,n_i}^j \end{bmatrix} (i<j)$$

où les $b_{j;k}$ appartiennent à $\mathcal{O}$ et les $b_{i,k}^j$ à $x\mathcal{O}$.

Exemple

Pour $n = 8$, $s = 5$ et $d°d_6 = 1$, $d°d_7 = 3$ et $d°d_8 = 4$, on obtient la figure suivante :

$$\left[\begin{array}{c|ccc|cccc} * & 0 & 0 & * & 0 & 0 & 0 & * \\ \hline * & 0 & 0 & * & 0 & 0 & 0 & * \\ 0 & 1 & 0 & * & 0 & 0 & 0 & * \\ 0 & 0 & 1 & * & 0 & 0 & 0 & * \\ \hline * & 0 & 0 & * & 0 & 0 & 0 & * \\ 0 & 0 & 0 & * & 1 & 0 & 0 & * \\ 0 & 0 & 0 & * & 0 & 1 & 0 & * \\ 0 & 0 & 0 & 0 & 0 & 0 & 1 & * \end{array}\right]$$

où les $*$ peuvent être différents de zéro.

Démonstration

Avec les hypothèses du lemme 2, on peut supposer que la matrice A de ∇_{q+1} dans la base (e), est de la forme $A = (A_i^j)$ $(1 \leq i, j \leq n-s)$ avec $A_i^j(0) = 0$ pour $i \neq j$ et

$$A_j^j(0) = \begin{bmatrix} 0 & & & 0 & a_{j,1} \\ 1 & \ddots & & 0 & a_{j,2} \\ & & \ddots & & \vdots \\ \Theta & & & 1 & a_{j,n_j} \end{bmatrix} \qquad (1 \leq j \leq n-s)$$

où les $a_{j,k}$ sont donnés par :

$$d_j = X^{n_j} - a_{j,n_j} X^{n_j-1} - \ldots - a_{j,1}$$

les d_j étant les facteurs de similitude non constants de $\bar{\nabla}_{q+1}$ et les n_j satisfaisant les relations :

$$1 \leq n_1 < \ldots \leq n_{n-s} \quad \text{et} \quad n = n_1 + \ldots + n_{n-s}$$

On peut ainsi appliquer le lemme 1 à la matrice A en commençant par la première colonne puis la deuxième et ainsi de suite jusqu'à la $(n-1)^e$ colonne. Ce qui permet de fabriquer une nouvelle base $(\tilde{e})$ par rapport à laquelle la matrice de ∇_{q+1} prend la forme :

$$\tilde{A} = (\tilde{A}_i^j) \qquad (1 \leq i,j \leq n-s)$$

avec

$$\tilde{A}_i^j = \begin{pmatrix} 0 & \cdots & 0 & \tilde{a}_{i,1}^j \\ \cdot & \cdots & \cdot & \cdot \\ 0 & \cdots & 0 & \tilde{a}_{i,n_i}^j \end{pmatrix} \qquad \text{pour } i \neq j$$

et A_j^j ayant la forme souhaitée du lemme 2.

Pour achever de démontrer le lemme 2, il suffirait alors de montrer qu'on peut éliminer dans les matrices $\tilde{A}_i^j (i > j)$ les termes $\tilde{a}_{i,n_j+1}^j, \ldots, \tilde{a}_{i,n_i}^j$ car pour ces matrices on a $n_i \geq n_j$. Soit P_{n-1} la matrice unité dans laquelle on a remplacé la (n-1) ligne par la n^e ligne de $\tilde{A}$ débarassee de l'élément $\tilde{a}_{n-s,\, n-s}$ (s'il est différent de zéro). Posons alors : $(\hat{e}) = (\tilde{e})^{P_{n-1}}$

La matrice $\hat{A} = (\hat{A}_i^j)$ de ∇_{q+1} par rapport à cette base a la même forme que la matrice $\tilde{A}$ sauf pour les $\hat{A}_n^j$ qui seront de la forme :

$$\hat{A}_n^j = \begin{bmatrix} 0 & 0 & 0 & \hat{a}^j_{n,1} \\ 0 & 0 & 0 & \hat{a}^d_{n,2} \\ 0 & 0 & \hat{a}^j_{n,ni} & \hat{a}^j_{n,ni-1} \\ 0 & 0 & 0 & 0 \end{bmatrix} \quad j \leq n-s)$$

Soit maintenant P_{n-2}, la matrice unité dans laquelle on a remplacé la (n-2) ligne pour la $(n-1)^e$ ligne de A debarassée des éléments non nuls situes à droite de la diagonale. Puis on continue comme précedemment. Au bout de (n-1) transformations du même type, on aura éliminé les termes $a^j_{i,k}$ pour lesquels $K > n_j$ et obtenu la forme indiquée par le lemme 2.

Lemme 3

Avec les mêmes hypothèses qu'au lemme 2, il existe un réseau E' de V et des sous-$\mathcal{O}$-modules libres $E'_1, \dots, E'_t$, ∇_{q+1}-cycliques tels que :

$$E' = E'_1 \oplus \dots \oplus E'_t \qquad (1 \leq t \leq n-s)$$

Démonstration

Par récurrence sur n = rang de E et sur s, le lemme 3 est évident pour n = 1.

D'autre part, le corollaire du lemme 1 montre qu'il est aussi vrai pour s =n-1.

Nous allons le prouver pour $1 \leq s < n-1$ et pour $n > 1$.

1) En utilisant les notations et le résultat du lemme 2, supposons que l'une des matrices $B^j_1 (j \geq 2)$ au moins, soit différente de zéro. Dans ce cas, posons

$$\mu = \inf_{\substack{2 \leq j \leq n-s \\ 1 \leq k \leq n_1}} \{ \nu (b^j_{1,k}) \}$$

$$P = \operatorname{diag} \left[x^{\mu} I_{n_1}, I_{n-n_1} \right] \qquad (I_k \text{ matrice unité d'ordre } k)$$

$$(f) = (f_1, \dots, f_n) = (e')P$$

$$\tilde{B} = P^{-1} BP + x^{q+1} P^{-1} \frac{dP}{dx} = \text{Matrice de } \nabla_{q+1} \text{ dans la base } (f)$$

Soit E le réseau de V engendré par $f_1, \dots, f_n$ et $\bar{\nabla}_{q+1}$ l'endomorphisme de $\tilde{E}/x\tilde{E}$ induit par ∇_{q+1} (de matrice $\tilde{B}$ (0) dans la base $\theta (f_1), \dots, \theta (f_n)$.

$$\tilde{B} = \left[\begin{array}{c|ccc} B_1^1 - \mu x^q I_{n_1} & x^{-\mu} B_1^2 & \dots & x^{-\mu} B_1^{n-s} \\ \hline x^{\mu} B_2^1 & B_2^2 & \dots & B^{n-s} \\ \dots\dots & \dots\dots & & \dots\dots \\ x^{\mu} B_{n-s}^1 & B_{n-s}^2 & \dots & B_{n-s}^{n-s} \end{array}\right]$$

$$\tilde{B}(0) = \left[\begin{array}{c|ccc} C_1^1 & C_1^2 & \dots & C_1^{n-s} \\ \hline & B_2^2(0) & & 0 \\ 0 & & 0 & B_{n-s}^{n-s}(0) \end{array}\right]$$

avec $C_1^1 = B_1^1(0) - \mu I_{n_1}$ si $q = 0$, $C_1^1 = B_1^1(0)$ si $q \geqslant 1$

et

$$C_1^j = \begin{bmatrix} 0 & \dots & 0 & \alpha_{1,1}^j \\ \vdots & & & \\ 0 & \dots & 0 & \alpha_{1,n_1}^j \end{bmatrix} \qquad (2 \leqslant j \leqslant n-s)$$

et l'un des $\alpha_{1,k}^j$ au moins est différent de zéro.

La matrice $\tilde{B}(0) - XI$ est <u>équivalente</u> à la matrice

$$\left[\begin{array}{c|ccc} D_1^1 & D_1^2 & \dots & D_1^{n-s} \\ \hline \bigcirc & D_2^2 & & \bigcirc \\ & \bigcirc & \ddots & D_{n-s}^{n-s} \end{array}\right]$$

avec $D_j^j = \mathrm{diag}\,[1, \dots, 1, \chi_j]$ $\qquad (1 \leqslant j \leqslant n-s)$

et

$$D_1^j = \begin{bmatrix} 0 & \dots & 0 & 0 \\ 0 & \dots & 0 & 0 \\ 0 & \dots & 0 & P_1^j \end{bmatrix} \qquad (2 \leqslant j \leqslant n-s)$$

où $\chi_1, \dots, \chi_{n-s}$ $P_1^2, \dots, P_{n-s}^{n-s}$ sont des polynômes en X tels que

a) $n_1 = d^\circ \chi_1 \leqslant \dots \leqslant d^\circ \chi_{n-s} = n_{n-s}$

b) $P_{1(X)}^j = \alpha_{1,n_1}^j X^{n_1 - 1} + \dots + \alpha_{1,1}^j$ $\qquad (2 \leqslant j \leqslant n-s)$

où les $\alpha_{1,k}^j$ ne sont pas tous nuls.

Ces relations montrent que :

$0 \leqslant d^\circ P_1^j \leqslant n_1 - 1 < n_1 = d^\circ \chi_1$ pour tout $j = 2, \ldots, n-s$

On en déduit que les facteurs de similitude de l'endomorphisme $\bar{\nabla}_{q+1}$:

$\tilde{E}/x\tilde{E} \to \tilde{E}/x\tilde{E}$ sont $(1,\ldots, 1, d'_{s+1},\ldots, d'_n)$ avec

$d^\circ d'_{s+1} \leqslant n_1 - 1 < n_1 = d^\circ d_{s+1}$.

En recommençant au besoin cette transformation un nombre fini de fois, on arrivera à remplacer un des facteurs de similitude au moins par 1, ce qui augmente l'entier s.

2) Toujours avec les notations du lemme 2, supposons que $B_1^j = 0$, pour tout $j \geqslant 2$ et qu'il existe i $(2 \leqslant i \leqslant n-s)$ tel que $B_i^1 \neq 0$, alors on pose

$$\nu = \inf_{\substack{2 \leqslant i \leqslant n-s \\ 1 \leqslant k \leqslant n_1}} \{v(b_{i,k}^1)\}$$

et $Q = \operatorname{diag}\left[x^{-\nu} I_{n_1}, I_{n-n_1}\right]$

Et en procédant comme au 1), on aboutira à la même conclusion.

3) Si $B_1^j = 0$ pour tout $j : 2 \leqslant j \leqslant n-s$ et $B_i^1 = 0$ pour tout i : $2 \leqslant i \leqslant n-s$, alors $E = E_1 \oplus E_2$ où E_1 et E_2 sont deux sous-modules libres de E, de rang strictement plus petit que n et invariants par ∇_{q+1}.

Ainsi, en recommençant un nombre fini de fois le processus décrit aux 1) et 2), on arrivera soit à augmenter s, soit à décomposer E en somme directe de deux sous-modules libres de rang strictement plus petit que n.

Remarque

Si $\bar{\nabla}_{q+1} = \lambda I_n$, $\lambda \in \mathbb{C}$, on pose $\nabla'_q = x^{-1} \nabla_{q+1} - \lambda x^{-1} I_n$. Ce qui nous ramène (en recommençant au besoin) soit à un des cas précédents, soit à un opérateur différentiel régulier.

Lemme 4

Soit $\nabla_{q+1} : E \to E$ un operateur différentiel sur le réseau E. Supposons qu'il existe deux sous σ-modules libres E_1 et E_2 de E, de rang respectif n_1 et n_2 $(1 \leq n_1 \leq n_2 \leq n)$ et qui possèdent les propriétés suivantes :

a) E est somme directe de E_1 et de E_2

b) E_1 et E_2 sont ∇_{q+1} - cycliques.

Il existe alors un réseau E' de V et un vecteur $e' \in E'$, tel que $(e', \nabla_{q+1} e', \ldots, \nabla_{q+1}^{n-1} e')$ soit une base de E'

Démonstration :

L'hypothèse b) signifie qu'il existe deux vecteurs $e_1 \in E_1$ et $e_2 \in E_2$ tels que $(e_1, \nabla_{q+1} e_1, \ldots, \nabla_{q+1}^{n_1-1} e_1)$ et $(e_2, \nabla_{q+1} e_2 \ldots, \nabla_{q+1}^{n_2-1} e_2)$ soient des bases de E_1 et E_2 respectivement. Soit alors e le vecteur défini par $e = x^k e_1 + e_2$.

Il est clair que $(e_1, \nabla_{q+1} e_1, \ldots, \nabla_{q+1}^{n_1-1} e_1, e, \nabla_{q+1} e, \ldots, \nabla_{q+1}^{n_2-1} e)$ est encore une base de E. De plus la matrice de ∇_{q+1} par rapport à cette base est de la forme :

$$A = \left[\begin{array}{ccc|ccc} 0 & & 0\ a_1 & 0 & \ldots & 0\ \alpha_1 \\ 1 & \ddots & 0\ a_2 & 0 & \ldots & 0\ \alpha_2 \\ 0 & & 1\ a_{n_1} & 0 & \ldots & 0\ \alpha_{n_1} \\ \hline & & & 0 & & 0\ b_1 \\ & 0 & & 1 & \ddots & 0\ b_2 \\ & & & 0 & & 1\ b_{n_2} \end{array}\right]$$

où l'un des α_i $(1 \leq i \leq n_1)$ au moins est différent de zéro (pour un choix convenable de k). Montrons par exemple qu'on peut choisir k de façon que α_1 soit différent de zéro. Un calcul direct donne :

$$\nabla^{n_2}e = k(k+p)\dots(k+(n_2-1)p)\,x^{k+n_2p}\,e_1 + n_2\,k(k+p)\dots(k+(n_2-2)p).$$

$$x^{k+(n_2-1)p}\,\nabla_{q+1}e_1 + \dots + x^k\,\nabla^{n_2}_{q+1}e_1 + \nabla^{n_2}_{q+1}e_2$$

$$(n_2-1)p = \alpha_1 e_1 + \dots + \alpha_{n_1}\nabla^{n_1-1}_{q+1}e_1 + b_1 e + \dots + b_{n_2}\nabla^{n_2-1}_{q+1}e$$

où α_1 est de la forme :

$$\alpha_1 = x^k\Big[k(k+p)\dots(k+(n_2-1)p)\,x^{n_2p} + k(k+p)\dots(k+(n_2-2)p).$$

$$x^{(n_2-1)p}\,C_1(x) + \dots + kx^p\,C_{n_2}(x) + C_{n_2}(x)\Big]$$

et où les $C_i(x) \in \sigma$ ($1 \leqslant i \leqslant n_2$) et ne dépendent pas de k. En regroupant dans cette expression les termes en x^{k+n_2p}, on obtient :

$$\alpha_1 = x^{k+n_2p}\quad k(k+p)\dots(k+(n_2-1)p) + \sum_{2\leqslant k\leqslant n_2} k(k+p)\dots(k+(n_2-j)p)\,\tilde{C}_j(o) \quad + \dots,$$

certains $\tilde{C}_j(o)$ pouvant être nuls.

La quantité entre crochets est un polynôme unitaire de degré n_2 en k. Elle ne peut donc être nulle que pour un nombre fini de valeurs de k. Ce qui démontre notre assertion.

On peut maintenant appliquer le processus décrit au 1° de la démonstration du lemme 3. Ce qui nous permettra de trouver un réseau E' de V et deux sous σ -modules libres E'_1 et E'_2 de E', de rang respectif n'_1 et n_2, et possédant les propriétés :

i) $E' = E'_1 \oplus E'_2$

ii) E'_1 et E'_2 sont ∇_{q+1} - cycliques

iii) $n'_1 < n_1$

En répétant la construction précédente (au besoin) un nombre fini de fois, on aboutira au résultat indiqué dans l'énoncé du lemme 4.

Remarque :

Le lemme 3 démontre le théorème 1 et les lemmes 3 et 4 entraînent le théorème 2.

B I B L I O G R A P H I E

1 N. BOURBAKI — Algèbre chap. 7 Hermann

2 P. DELIGNE — Equations différentielles à points singuliers réguliers, lecture Notes in Math., 163, Springer-Verlag 1970.

3 R. GERARD et A.H.M. LEVELT — Invariants mesurant l'irrégularité en un point singulier des systèmes d'équations différentielles linéaires. Ann. Inst. Fourier 23 (1973) pp 157-195.

4 A.H.M. LEVELT — Jordan decomposition for a class of singular differential operators(publication Mathematisch Instituut Katholieke NIJMEGEN)

5 B. MALGRANGE — Sur les points singuliers des équations différentielles. Séminaire GOULAOUIC - SCHWARTZ, 1971-1972, exposé n° XX (Ecole Polytechnique)

6 W. WASOW — Asymptotic expansions for ordinary differential equations. Interscience Publishers, 1965

THE MATRIX OF A CONNECTION HAVING REGULAR SINGULARITIES ON A VECTOR BUNDLE OF RANK 2 ON $\mathbb{P}^1(\mathbb{C})$

by

W. Dekkers

The theorem in section 4 is valid in the complex analytic situation as well as in the algebraic situation. For simplicity we shall restrict ourselves to the complex analytic situation, but in fact the proof is purely algebraic.

1. $X = \mathbb{P}^1(\mathbb{C})$, $\mathcal{O}$ is the sheaf of germs of holomorphic functions on X , $\mathcal{E}$ is a holomorphic vector bundle of rank 2 on X and Ω^1 is the sheaf of holomorphic differentials on X .

S is a finite non-void set of points of X and $\mathcal{O}(S)$ is the sheaf of germs of functions on X holomorphic on $X-S$ meromorphic in S .

Let 0 and ∞ be distinct points of X . Then on $U_o = X - \{\infty\}$ and on $U_\infty = X - \{0\}$ we have holomorphic co-ordinate functions z and x respectively, such that $z(0) = 0$, $x(\infty) = 0$ and $x = \frac{1}{z}$ on $U_o \cap U_\infty$.

2. Bases meromorphic in S .

Let $(e) = (e_1, e_2)$ be a basis of $\mathcal{E}/_{X-S}$.

(e) is called a basis of $\mathcal{E}$ meromorphic in S if for each $s \in S$ there exists a neighbourhood U of s , a basis (f) of $\mathcal{E}/_U$ and a $T \in GL(2, \Gamma(U, \mathcal{O}(S)))$ such that $(e) = (f)T$ on $U-S$.

For $n \in \mathbb{Z}$ let $\mathcal{O}(n)$ be the locally free sheaf of rank 1 in the sense of [2] no 54. There exist integers n and m such that $\mathcal{E}$ is isomorphic to $\mathcal{O}(n) \oplus \mathcal{O}(m)$ (cf. [3]). Now $S \neq \emptyset$, hence $X-S$ is different from X . Therefore there exists an isomorphism

$$\mathcal{O}(n) \oplus \mathcal{O}(m)/_{X-S} \to \mathcal{O}^2/_{X-S} \; .$$

Moreover this isomorphism can be chosen in such a way that the bases of $\mathcal{O}(n) \oplus \mathcal{O}(m)$ meromorphic in S correspond to the bases of $\mathcal{O}^2$ meromorphic in S . In particular $\mathcal{E}$ has a global basis meromorphic in S .

3. Connections.

Let ∇ be a (holomorphic) connection on $\mathcal{E}$.
∇ induces $\mathbb{C}$-linear morphisms

$$\nabla_{\frac{d}{dz}} \, , \, \nabla_{\frac{d}{dx}} : \mathcal{E} \to \mathcal{E}$$

(cf. [1], chap. I, 2.4 and 2.5).

Instead of $\nabla_{\frac{d}{dz}}$ and $\nabla_{\frac{d}{dx}}$ we shall write ${}_z\nabla$ and ${}_x\nabla$ respectively. One has

$${}_z\nabla = - \frac{1}{z^2} \, {}_x\nabla \; .$$

Let $(e) = (e_1, e_2)$ be a basis of $\mathcal{E}$ meromorphic in S . Then

$${}_z\nabla \, e_1 = \gamma_{11} \, e_1 + \gamma_{21} \, e_2$$

$${}_z\nabla \, e_2 = \gamma_{12} \, e_1 + \gamma_{22} \, e_2$$

$(\gamma_{ij} \in \Gamma(S, \mathcal{O}(S)))$.

$$\Gamma = \Gamma({}_z\nabla,(e)) = \begin{pmatrix} \gamma_{11} & \gamma_{12} \\ \gamma_{21} & \gamma_{22} \end{pmatrix}$$

is called the matrix of ${}_z\nabla$ with respect to the basis (e). If (e') is another basis of $\mathcal{E}$ meromorphic in S then $(e') = (e)T$ for some $T \in GL(2,\Gamma(X,\mathcal{O}(S)))$. We have

$$\Gamma' = T^{-1}\Gamma T + T^{-1}\frac{dT}{dz}\,.$$

Now let ∇ be a connection on $\mathcal{E}/_{X-S}$. ∇ is called a connection on $\mathcal{E}$ having regular singularities in S if for each $s \in U_o \cap S$ $(s \in U_\infty \cap S)$ there exist a neighbourhood U of s and a basis (e) of $\mathcal{E}/_U$ meromorphic in $\{s\}$ such that the coefficients of $\Gamma({}_z\nabla/_{U-S},(e))$ $(\Gamma({}_x\nabla/_{U-S},(e)))$ have poles of order at most 1 in s. This definition agrees with that of [1], page 52.

4. THEOREM. *Let* $S = \{s_1,\dots,s_n\}$ *be a finite collection of points of* $X = \mathbb{P}^1(\mathbb{C})$, $s_i \neq s_j$ *if* $i \neq j$, $n \geq 2$, $z(s_i) = a_i$. *Let* $\mathcal{E}$ *be a vector bundle of rank 2 on* X *and* ∇ *a connection on* $\mathcal{E}$ *having regular singularities in* S. *Then there exists a basis* (e) *of* $\mathcal{E}$ *meromorphic in* S *such that* :

i) *if one of the points, say* s_n, *is* ∞ *then*

$$\Gamma({}_z\nabla,(e)) = \frac{A_1}{z-a_1} + \dots + \frac{A_{n-1}}{z-a_{n-1}}$$

where $A_1,\dots,A_{n-1} \in M_2(\mathbb{C})$;

ii) *if* $S \subset U_o$ *then*

$$\Gamma({}_z\nabla,(e)) = \frac{A_1}{z-a_1} + \dots + \frac{A_n}{z-a_n}$$

where $A_1,\dots,A_n \in M_2(\mathbb{C})$, $A_1 + \dots + A_n = 0$.

($M_2(\mathbb{C})$ denotes the set of 2×2-matrices with complex coefficients.)

The proof of the theorem takes the rest of this article.

5. Reduction to the case where $\mathcal{E} = \mathcal{O}^2$.

Let

$$\varphi : \mathcal{E}/_{X-S} \to \mathcal{O}^2/_{X-S}$$

be an isomorphism such that the bases of $\mathcal{E}$ meromorphic in S correspond to the bases of $\mathcal{O}^2$ meromorphic in S . Let ∇' be the connection induced by φ on $\mathcal{O}^2/_{X-S}$. Then it's easy to prove that ∇' is a connection on $\mathcal{O}^2$ having regular singularities in S . Moreover if (g) is a basis of $\mathcal{O}^2$ meromorphic in S then $\varphi^{-1}(g)$ is a basis of $\mathcal{E}$ meromorphic in S and

$$\Gamma({}_z\nabla, \varphi^{-1}(g)) = \Gamma({}_z\nabla', (g)) .$$

This reduces the proof of the theorem to the case where $\mathcal{E} = \mathcal{O}^2$.

6. Case ii) in the theorem is an easy consequence of case i) (change of co-ordinate functions). Moreover in case i) we may assume $a_1 = 0$. Hence we only need to prove the theorem for the case

$$\underline{\mathcal{E} = \mathcal{O}^2 , \; a_1 = 0 , \; a_n = \infty} .$$

Remark : $\Gamma(X, \mathcal{O}(S)) = \mathbb{C}[z, \frac{1}{z}, \frac{1}{z-a_2}, \dots, \frac{1}{z-a_{n-1}}]$. Let (e) be a basis of $\mathcal{O}^2$ meromorphic in S and let $\Gamma = \Gamma({}_z\nabla, (e))$.
Then $\Gamma \in M_2(\Gamma(X, \mathcal{O}(S))) = M_2(\mathbb{C}[z, \frac{1}{z}, \frac{1}{z-a_2}, \dots, \frac{1}{z-a_{n-1}}])$ and we must prove the existence of $T \in GL(2, \mathbb{C}[z, \frac{1}{z}, \frac{1}{z-a_2}, \dots, \frac{1}{z-a_{n-1}}])$ such that

$$\Gamma' = T^{-1}\Gamma T + T^{-1}\frac{dT}{dz} = \frac{A_1}{z} + \frac{A_2}{z-a_2} + \dots + \frac{A_{n-1}}{z-a_{n-1}}$$

where $A_1, \dots, A_{n-1} \in M_2(\mathbb{C})$.

7. Réduction of the poles in $z = 0$ to simple poles.

Let f be a function meromorphic in 0, f not identically equal to zero. Then $f = z^n g$ where g is a function holomorphic in 0, $g(0) \neq 0$, $n \in \mathbb{Z}$. We define

$$v(f) = n \qquad (v(0) = \infty) .$$

Let $\Gamma = \Gamma({}_z\nabla,(e)) = (\gamma_{ij}) = \begin{pmatrix} \gamma_{11} & \gamma_{12} \\ \gamma_{21} & \gamma_{22} \end{pmatrix}$. ∇ has a regular singularity in $z = 0$. Now from lemma 1.9.6 in [1], one easily deduces :

LEMMA.

$$-v(\gamma_{11}) = n > 1 \Rightarrow -v(\gamma_{22}) = n \, , \; -v(\gamma_{12}\,\gamma_{21}) = 2n$$

$$-v(\gamma_{11}) \leq 1 \Rightarrow -v(\gamma_{22}) \leq 1 \, , \; -v(\gamma_{12}\,\gamma_{21}) \leq 2 .$$

Moreover if $-v(\gamma_{11}) = n > 1$ then

(*)
$$\gamma_{ij} = a_{ij}\, z^{-n_{ij}}(1 + z\, c_{ij})$$

where $a_{ij} \in \mathbb{C}$, $a_{ij} \neq 0$, c_{ij} holomorphic in $z = 0$

$$n = n_{11} = n_{22} = \frac{n_{12} + n_{21}}{2}$$

and

$$\begin{pmatrix} a_{11} & a_{12} \\ a_{21} & a_{22} \end{pmatrix} \text{ is nilpotent.}$$

Suppose that $-v(\gamma_{11}) \leq 1$.

Let

$$T = \begin{pmatrix} z^m & 0 \\ 0 & 1 \end{pmatrix}$$

where $m \in \mathbb{Z}$. Then

$$\Gamma' = T^{-1}\Gamma T + T^{-1}\frac{dT}{dz} = \begin{pmatrix} \gamma_{11} + \frac{m}{z} & z^{-m}\,\gamma_{12} \\ z^m\,\gamma_{21} & \gamma_{22} \end{pmatrix} .$$

From the lemma immediately follows that we can choose m in such a way that $-v(\gamma'_{ij}) \leq 1$ for all $i,j \in \{1,2\}$ and then we are ready.

So we may assume that $-v(\gamma_{11}) = n > 1$ and that (γ_{ij}) has the form (*) of the lemma. Let

$$T = \begin{pmatrix} 1 & \lambda z^{\ell} \\ 0 & 1 \end{pmatrix}$$

with $\lambda \in \mathbb{C}$ and $\ell \in \mathbb{Z}$.

Then

$$\Gamma' = \begin{pmatrix} \gamma_{11} - \lambda z^{\ell}\gamma_{21} & \gamma_{12} + \lambda z^{\ell}(\gamma_{11} - \gamma_{22}) - \lambda^2 z^{2\ell}\gamma_{21} + \lambda \ell z^{\ell-1} \\ \gamma_{21} & \gamma_{22} + \lambda z^{\ell}\gamma_{21} \end{pmatrix}.$$

Choose $\lambda = \frac{a_{11}}{a_{21}} = \frac{a_{12}}{a_{22}}$ and $\ell = n_{21} - n_{11} = n_{22} - n_{12}$. Look at the pole of $\gamma'_{11} = \gamma_{11} - \lambda z^{\ell}\gamma_{21}$ in $z = 0$. We have

$$a_{11} z^{-n_{11}} - \frac{a_{11}}{a_{21}} z^{n_{21}-n_{11}} \cdot a_{21} z^{-n_{21}} = 0 .$$

Hence $-v(\gamma'_{11}) < n$.

Proceeding in this way we finally get a matrix Γ' such that $-v(\gamma'_{11}) \leq 1$.

8. For the points s_i $(i = 2,\ldots,n-1)$ we proceed in a similar way, using T's $\in GL(2, \mathbb{C}[z, \frac{1}{z-a_i}])$ of the form

$$\begin{pmatrix} (z-a_i)^m & 0 \\ 0 & 1 \end{pmatrix} \quad \text{and} \quad \begin{pmatrix} 1 & \lambda (z-a_i)^{\ell} \\ 0 & 1 \end{pmatrix}.$$

Doing this we don't introduce new poles of order > 1 in s_j, $j = 1,\ldots,n-1$, $j \neq i$.

9. We now have

$$\Gamma({}_z\nabla,(e)) = \frac{A_1}{z} + \frac{A_2}{z-a_2} + \dots + \frac{A_{n-1}}{z-a_{n-1}} + C(z)$$

where (e) is a basis of $\mathcal{O}^2$ meromorphic in S , $A_i \in M_2(\mathbb{C})$, $C(z) \in M_2(\mathbb{C}[z])$.

Let $x(s_i) = b_i = \frac{1}{a_i}$. Then $b_n = 0$ and $b_1 = \infty$. Replacing z by x we may equally well suppose that we have reached

$$\Gamma({}_x\nabla,(e)) = \frac{B_1}{x} + \frac{B_2}{x-b_2} + \dots + \frac{B_{n-1}}{x-b_{n-1}} + D(x) .$$

Let $\Gamma = \Gamma({}_z\nabla,(e)) = -\frac{1}{z^2}\,\Gamma({}_x\nabla,(e))$ (cf. 3.). Then Γ has the form

(**) $$\frac{A_1}{z} + \frac{A_2}{z-a_2} + \dots + \frac{A_{n-1}}{z-a_{n-1}} + \frac{C_2}{z^2} + \dots + \frac{C_{m+1}}{z^{m+1}}$$

where A_i , $C_i \in M_2(\mathbb{C})$.

We try to reduce the poles in $z = 0$ to simple poles. We don't want to spoil the situation outside $z = 0$ during the reduction process, so after each step Γ should still have the form (**).

We distinguish two cases :

(I) $\underline{-v(\gamma_{11}) \le 1}$

(II) $\underline{-v(\gamma_{11}) > 1}$.

In case (I) again we distinguish two cases :

(Ia) $\underline{-v(\gamma_{11}) \le 1 , \gamma_{21} = 0 , -v(\gamma_{12}) \ge 2}$

(Ib) $\underline{-v(\gamma_{11}) \le 1 , \gamma_{21} \ne 0 , -v(\gamma_{21}) \le 0 , -v(\gamma_{12}) \ge 2}$.

10. Case (Ia) : $-v(\gamma_{11}) \le 1 , \gamma_{21} = 0 , -v(\gamma_{12}) \ge 2$.

Now $-v(\gamma_{22}) \le 1$ too. We may replace Γ by $\Gamma - \gamma_{22} I_2$ where I_2 denotes the identity element in $M_2(\mathbb{C})$. So we may assume $\gamma_{22} = 0$,

$$\Gamma = \begin{pmatrix} \frac{p_1}{z} + \frac{p_2}{z-a_2} + \dots + \frac{p_{n-1}}{z-a_{n-1}} & \frac{q_1}{z} + \frac{q_2}{z-a_2} + \dots + \frac{q_{n-1}}{z-a_{n-1}} + \frac{c_2}{z^2} + \dots + \frac{c_{m+1}}{z^{m+1}} \\ 0 & 0 \end{pmatrix}$$

where $m \geq 1$, $c_{m+1} \neq 0$.

We show that Γ can be transformed into a matrix Γ' with $-v(\gamma'_{11}) \leq 1$, $\gamma'_{21} = 0$, $-v(\gamma'_{12}) \leq m$. We have

1) $p_1 \neq m$

2) $p_i \neq 0$ for some $i \geq 2$

or

3) $p_1 + \dots + p_{n-1} \neq 0$.

Case 1) : $p_1 \neq m$.

$$T_1 = \begin{pmatrix} 1 & \alpha z^{-m} \\ 0 & 1 \end{pmatrix}$$

with $\alpha \in \mathbb{C}$ transforms Γ into

$$\Gamma' = \begin{pmatrix} \gamma_{11} & \gamma_{12} + \alpha z^{-m}\gamma_{11} - m\alpha z^{-m-1} \\ 0 & 0 \end{pmatrix}.$$

The coefficient of z^{-m-1} in γ'_{12} is

$$c_{m+1} + \alpha p_1 - m\alpha .$$

Take $\alpha = -\frac{c_{m+1}}{p_1 - m}$. Then $-v(\gamma'_{12}) \leq m$.

Case 2) : $p_i \neq 0$ for some $i \geq 2$.

Take

$$T_2 = \begin{pmatrix} z-a_i & \alpha \\ 0 & z \end{pmatrix}$$

with $\alpha \in \mathbb{C}$. Then

$$\Gamma' = \begin{pmatrix} \gamma_{11} + \frac{1}{z-a_i} & \frac{z}{z-a_i}\gamma_{12} + \frac{\alpha}{z-a_i}\gamma_{11} - \frac{\alpha}{z(z-a_i)} \\ 0 & \frac{1}{z} \end{pmatrix}$$

$$\gamma'_{12} = \frac{a_i q_i + \alpha p_i}{(z-a_i)^2} + \frac{q'_1}{z} + \frac{q'_2}{z-a_2} +\dots+ \frac{q'_{n-1}}{z-a_{n-1}} + \frac{c'_2}{z^2} +\dots+ \frac{c'_m}{z^m} .$$

Choose $\alpha = -\dfrac{a_i q_i}{p_i}$.

Case 3) : $p_1 +\dots+ p_{n-1} \neq 0$.

$$T_3 = \begin{pmatrix} 1 & \alpha z \\ 0 & z \end{pmatrix}$$

with $\alpha \in \mathbb{C}$ transforms Γ into

$$\Gamma' = \begin{pmatrix} \gamma_{11} & z(\gamma_{12} + \alpha\gamma_{11}) \\ 0 & \frac{1}{z} \end{pmatrix}$$

$$\gamma'_{12} = q_1 +\dots+ q_{n-1} + \alpha(p_1 +\dots+ p_{n-1}) + \frac{q'_1}{z} +\dots+ \frac{q'_{n-1}}{z-a_{n-1}} + \frac{c'_2}{z^2} +\dots+ \frac{c'_m}{z^m} .$$

Take $\alpha = -\dfrac{q_1 +\dots+ q_{n-1}}{p_1 +\dots+ p_{n-1}}$.

11. Case (Ib) : $-v(\gamma_{11}) \le 1$, $\gamma_{21} \neq 0$, $-v(\gamma_{21}) \le 0$, $-v(\gamma_{12}) \ge 2$.

As in case (Ia) here again we may assume $\gamma_{22} = 0$.

$$\Gamma = \begin{pmatrix} \frac{p_1}{z} + \frac{p_2}{z-a_2} +\dots+ \frac{p_{n-1}}{z-a_{n-1}} & \frac{q_1}{z} + \frac{q_2}{z-a_2} +\dots+ \frac{q_{n-1}}{z-a_{n-1}} + \frac{c_2}{z^2} +\dots+ \frac{c_{m+1}}{z^{m+1}} \\ \frac{r_2}{z-a_2} +\dots+ \frac{r_{n-1}}{z-a_{n-1}} & 0 \end{pmatrix}$$

$m \ge 1$, $c_{m+1} \neq 0$, $r_j \neq 0$ for at least one j .

Let $r_i \neq 0$. Then take

$$T_2 = \begin{pmatrix} z-a_i & \alpha \\ 0 & z \end{pmatrix} , \quad \alpha = \frac{a_i}{2r_i} \left(p_i + \sqrt{p_i^2 + 4r_i q_i}\right) .$$

Then Γ' again has the form (**) and $-v(\gamma'_{12}) \leq m$.

12. Case II : $-v(\gamma_{11}) = n > 1$.

Γ has the form (*) of the lemma in 7. We may suppose that $n_{21} - n_{11} \leq 0$ for if $n_{21} - n_{11} > 0$ then $n_{12} - n_{22} = n_{11} - n_{21} < 0$ and then we replace Γ by $T^{-1}\Gamma T$ where

$$T = \begin{pmatrix} 0 & 1 \\ 1 & 0 \end{pmatrix} .$$

Here we proceed in exactly the same way as at the end of 7. Taking

$$T = \begin{pmatrix} 1 & \lambda z^{\ell} \\ 0 & 1 \end{pmatrix}$$

with $\lambda = \dfrac{a_{11}}{a_{21}}$ and $\ell = n_{21} - n_{11}$ we get $-v(\gamma'_{11}) < n$. $\ell \leq 0$ hence Γ' has the form (**) (cf. the end of 7.). Proceeding in this way we finally get $-v(\gamma_{11}) \leq 1$ and then we have case (I) again.

This concludes the proof of the theorem.

13. Remark.

The theorem doesn't remain valid if one replaces $\mathbb{C}$ by an arbitrary field K of characteristic zero, K not closed.

If $S = \{0, 1, \infty\}$ and Γ is of type (Ib)

$$\Gamma = \begin{pmatrix} \dfrac{p_1}{z} \div \dfrac{p_2}{z-1} & \dfrac{q_1}{z} + \dfrac{q_2}{z-1} + \dfrac{c_2}{z^2} \\ \dfrac{r_2}{z-1} & 0 \end{pmatrix}$$

then Γ can be transformed into a matrix of the form $\dfrac{A_1}{z} + \dfrac{A_2}{z-1}$ if and only if at least one of the roots

$$\sqrt{(p_1-1)^2-4r_2c_2}\ ,\ \sqrt{p_2^2+4r_2q_2}\ ,\ \sqrt{(p_1+p_2)^2+4r_2(q_1+q_2)}$$

exists in K .

REFERENCES

[1] DELIGNE P. Equations différentielles à points singuliers réguliers. Lecture Notes in Math. 163 (1970).

[2] SERRE J.P. Faisceaux algébriques cohérents. Annals of Math. 61 (1955), pp. 197-278.

[3] GROTHENDIECK A. Sur la classification des fibrés holomorphes sur la sphère de Riemann. Amer. Jour. of Math. 79 (1957), pp. 121-138.

REDUCTION OF SINGULARITIES OF THE DIFFERENTIAL EQUATION $A\,dy = B\,dx$

Arno Van den Essen

INTRODUCTION.

In 1968 A. Seidenberg published a theorem on reduction of singularities of the differential equation $A\,dy = B\,dx$ (c.f.[4]). It's the aim of this paper to give an other (much simpler) proof of his main theorem (theorem 12) by using intersection-multiplicities (§ 2).

For completeness sake we describe the situation studed in Seidenbergs paper ([4]). (All results of § 1 can be found in [4]).

Let A and B are elements of the ring $k[[X,Y]]$ of formal power series in two letters. Seidenberg investigates the existence of algebraic solutions of the differential equation

$$\frac{dy}{dx} = \frac{B(x,y)}{A(x,y)} \,. \qquad (1)$$

This is done, by reducing this problem to the case where

$$r = \min\{\text{subd}\,A, \text{subd}\,B\} \leq 1$$

where $\text{subd}\,A = S$, if $0 \neq A = A_s + A_{s+1} + \ldots, A_k$ beiing homogenous of degree k .
We will now try to give an idea of the method we are going to use.

First, instead of (1) we consider the equation :

$$A(x,y)\,\frac{dy}{dt} = B(x,y)\,\frac{dx}{dt} \,. \qquad (2)$$

By a solution at the origin of (2) we mean an analytic branch (centered at the origin) which satisfies (2) ; such a branch is represented by a pair of power series

$$x = c_1 t + c_2 t^2 + \dots$$
$$y = d_1 t + d_2 t^2 + \dots$$

with not both x and y zero, and such that $A(x,y) \sum_i i c_i t^{i-1} = B(x,y) \sum_j j.d_j t^{j-1}$. We will then prove that the existence of an analytic branch of equation (2) is equivalent to the existence of an irreducible $F \in k[[X,Y]] \setminus \{0\}$ which satisfies :

$$\left(A \frac{\partial}{\partial X} + B \frac{\partial}{\partial Y}\right) F \equiv 0 \bmod F \ , \quad \text{in} \quad k[[X,Y]] \ . \qquad (3)$$

We will mainly use this (equivalent) form to attack our problem.

For the reduction we will use the so called blowing-up transformations (éclatements) and some well known facts about intersection multiplicities of analytic curves (we recall the main properties in § 3).

§ 1. - SOME TOOLS.

Let $k[[X,Y]]$ be the ring of formal power series in two letters over an algebraically closed base field k of characteristic zero.

DEFINITION 1.1.-

a) A branch representation is a pair of elements $x(t)$, $y(t)$ in $k[[t]]$, not both zero.

b) A branch representation $x(t)$, $y(t)$ is called in primitive or not primitive, if both are power series in a power series τ of order > 1, that is, there exist a power series $\tau(t) \in k[[t]]$ of order > 1, such that

$$x(t) = \tilde{x}(\tau(t))$$
$$y(t) = \tilde{y}(\tau(t))$$

for some power series $\tilde{x}(\tau)$ and $\tilde{y}(\tau)$ in $k[[\tau]]$.

In the contrary case the pair $x(t)$, $y(t)$ is called primitive.

c) Let (x,y) and (x',y') be branch representations in $k[[t]]$. We call (x,y) equivalent with (x',y') if there exist some power series $\tau = c_1 t + c_2 t^2 +$, $c_1 \neq 0$, in $k[[t]]$ such that $(x'(t), y'(t)) = (x(\tau(t)), y(\tau(t)))$. The following theorem can now be proved (we refer to [3] for a proof).

PROPOSITION 2.1.-

a) Let $F \in k[[X,Y]]$ be irreducible. Then there exist a branch representation $x(t)$, $y(t)$ in $k[[t]]$ with $F(x,y) = 0$. This branch representation is, up to equivalence, uniquely determined in the class of primitive branch representations.

b) Let $x(t)$, $y(t)$ be a primitive branch representation. Then there exist an irreducible F in $k[[X,Y]]$ (which is uniquely determined up to a unit in $k[[X,Y]]$) with the property $F(x,y) = 0$.

DEFINITION 3.1.- Let $A,B \in k[[X,Y]]$ and $D = A \frac{\partial}{\partial X} + B \frac{\partial}{\partial Y}$. By a solution of D

at (0,0) we mean an $F \in k[[X,Y]]\setminus 0$ with $F(0,0) = 0$ and such that

$$DF \equiv 0 \bmod F \quad \text{in} \quad k[[X,Y]]$$

(or, equivalently, there exist an $\lambda \in k[[X,Y]]$ with $DF = \lambda F$).
We now immediately see, that if F is a solution of D and u is a unit in $k[[X,Y]]$, then uF is also a solution of D. Furthermore we observe :

If FG is a solution of D at $(0,0)$ and F and G are non-units without common factor, then F and G (and hence their irreducible factors) are solutions of D at $(0,0)$, for there exist an $\lambda \in k[[X,Y]]$ with :

$$FDG + GDF = D(FG) = \lambda(FG)$$

and hence $G.DF \equiv 0 \bmod F$ and so $DF \equiv 0 \bmod F$ because F and G have no common factor.

As a consequence we see that we can restrict us to the study of irreducible solutions of D.

DEFINITION 4.1.- A solution of the equation $Ady = Bdx$ is a primitive branch representation $x(t), y(t)$ such that :

$$A(x,y)\frac{dy}{dt} = B(x,y)\frac{dx}{dt}.$$

We now prove :

PROPOSITION 5-1 :

a) Let $x(t), y(t)$ be a solution of $A\,dy = B\,dx$ and let $F \in k[[X,Y]]$ be irreducible and satisfy $F(x,y) = 0$.
Then F is a solution of $D = A\frac{\partial}{\partial X} + B\frac{\partial}{\partial Y}$.

b) Let F be an irreducible solution of $D = A\frac{\partial}{\partial X} + B\frac{\partial}{\partial Y}$ and let $x(t), y(t)$ be a primitive branch representation of F, then (x,y) is a solution of $A\,dy = B\,dx$.

Proof : a) We know $F(x(t), y(t)) = 0$, and hence by differentiation :

$$\left(\frac{\partial F}{\partial X}\right)_{(x,y)} \frac{dx}{dt} + \left(\frac{\partial F}{\partial Y}\right)_{(x,y)} \frac{dy}{dt} = 0$$

also
$$A(x,y)\,\frac{dy}{dt} - B(x,y)\,\frac{dx}{dt} = 0$$

hence
$$\det\begin{pmatrix} \frac{\partial F}{\partial X} & \frac{\partial F}{\partial Y} \\ -B & A \end{pmatrix}_{(x,y)} = 0$$

because
$$\left(\frac{dx}{dt}, \frac{dy}{dt}\right) \neq (0,0) .$$

But this implies $(DF)(x,y) = 0$ and hence $DF \equiv 0 \bmod F$ using Prop. 2-1. b).

b) Conversely, Let $F(x,y) = 0$ and $DF \equiv 0 \bmod F$, then we find

$$\left(\frac{\partial F}{\partial X}\right)_{(x,y)} \frac{dx}{dt} + \left(\frac{\partial F}{\partial Y}\right)_{(x,y)} \frac{dy}{dt} = 0$$

and by $(DF)(x,y) = 0$,

$$A(x,y)\left(\frac{\partial F}{\partial X}\right)_{x,y} + B(x,y)\left(\frac{\partial F}{\partial Y}\right)_{(x,y)} = 0$$

and hence
$$\det\begin{pmatrix} \frac{dx}{dt} & \frac{dy}{dt} \\ A(x,y) & B(x,y) \end{pmatrix} = 0$$

(this follows because $\left(\frac{\partial F}{\partial X}\right)_{(x,y)}$ and $\left(\frac{\partial F}{\partial Y}\right)_{(x,y)}$ are not both zero, because $\frac{\partial F}{\partial X}$ or $\frac{\partial F}{\partial Y}$ has a smaller subdegree then F and hence F cannot divide $\frac{\partial F}{\partial X}$ and $\frac{\partial F}{\partial Y}$ which would happen if both $\left(\frac{\partial F}{\partial X}\right)_{(x,y)} = \left(\frac{\partial F}{\partial Y}\right)_{(x,y)} = 0$, using prop. 2.1. b) again).

We are now going to study the solutions of the differential operator $D = A\frac{\partial}{\partial X} + B\frac{\partial}{\partial Y}$ by using three types of transformations, in fact we use :

1. Linear transformations
2. Translations.
3. Blowing-up transformations, that is transformations of the type

$X' = X \ , \ Y' = \frac{Y}{X}$.

1. In fact we only consider invertible linear transformations, that is

$$\begin{pmatrix} X' \\ Y' \end{pmatrix} = \begin{pmatrix} C_{11} & C_{12} \\ C_{21} & C_{22} \end{pmatrix} \begin{pmatrix} X \\ Y \end{pmatrix} \quad , \quad C_{11} C_{22} - C_{12} C_{21} \neq 0 \ ; \ C_{ij} \in k \ .$$

On the new coordinates we find

$$D = A_1 \frac{\partial}{\partial X'} + B_1 \frac{\partial}{\partial Y'}$$

with

$$A_1 = DX' = D(C_{11} X + C_{12} Y) = C_{11} A + C_{12} B$$

$$B_1 = DY' = D(C_{21} X + C_{22} Y) = C_{21} A + C_{22} B \ .$$

so :

$$\begin{pmatrix} A_1 \\ B_1 \end{pmatrix} = \begin{pmatrix} C_{ij} \end{pmatrix} \begin{pmatrix} A \\ B \end{pmatrix} \quad \text{and hence} \quad \begin{pmatrix} A_1 & X' \\ B_1 & Y' \end{pmatrix} = \begin{pmatrix} C_{ij} \end{pmatrix} \begin{pmatrix} A & X \\ B & Y \end{pmatrix} \ .$$

"Taking determinants" we find :

$$(B_1 X' - A_1 Y') = \det(C_{ij})(BX - AY) \ .$$

So we see that $BX - AY$ is a covariant under invertible linear transformations. As a consequence we see :

If $r = \min\{\text{subd}\, A, \text{subd}\, B\}$ then also :

$$I(D) \underset{\text{def}}{=} B_r X - A_r Y$$

is a covariant. We will also write $I(X,Y)$, when no confusion is possible. For the importance of the covariant $I(D)$ we refer to [4].

The solutions of D at $(0,0)$ transform in an obvious way to solutions of D in the new coordinates.

2. The translations need no further comment.

Before we consider the transformation $X' = X \ , \ Y' = \frac{Y}{X}$ we make some remarks. Let $F \in k[[X,Y]] \backslash 0$ be of subdegree r , that is F is of the form

$F = F_r + F_{r+1} + \dots$, where F_r is a form different from zero. The linear factors of F_r determine lines called the tangents to the cycle $F = 0$ at $(0,0)$.
If F is irreducible, it is known form Hensel's lemma that $F = 0$ has a only one tangent at $(0,0)$: $F_r = (aX + bY)^r$. Now consider again $F = F_r + F_{r+1} + \dots$ and make the transformation $X' = X$, $Y' = \frac{Y}{X}$. We then define the transformed function F' of F :

$$F'(X',Y') \underset{\text{def}}{=} \frac{1}{X'^r} F(X',X'Y) = F_r(1,Y') + XF_{r+1}(1,Y') + \dots$$

Remark : From the definition we see immediately that for every $C \in k$, F' can be viewed as an element of $k[[X',Y'-C]]$.

Let now F be an irreducible element in $k[[X,Y]]$, then as we remarked above, it follows that F has only one tangent, say a non-vertical tangent $Y - CX$. The following proposition can then be proved (see [3], for a proof).

PROPOSITION 6-1.- Let F be irreducible in $k[[X,Y]]$ with $Y-CX$ as tangent. Then $F'(X',Y')$ is irreducible in $k[[X',Y']]$.

We now consider the transformation $X' = X$, $Y' = \frac{Y}{X}$. Let $r = r(D) = \min\{\text{subd}\, A, \text{subd}\, B\}$ and suppose $r > 0$ (then $(0,0)$ is a singular point of the corresponding differential equation). When we investigate the question of existence of solutions with non vertical tangent (solutions always means irreducible solutions) we make the transformation $X' = X$, $Y' = \frac{Y}{X}$. We describe D in the new coordinates :

Let $D = A'\frac{\partial}{\partial X'} + B'\frac{\partial}{\partial Y'}$, then

$$A' = DX' = DX = A(X,XY')$$

$$B' = DY' = D\left(\frac{Y}{X}\right) = \frac{1}{X} B(X,XY') - \frac{Y'XA(X,XY')}{X^2} = \frac{B(X,XY') - Y'A(X,XY')}{X}.$$

Suppose $B_r(1,Y') - Y'A_r(1,Y')(= I(1,Y')) \neq 0$.

Then :

$$B'(X',Y') = \frac{1}{X}(X^r B_r(1,Y') - Y'X^r A_r(1,Y')) + X^r(\dots)$$

$$= X^{r-1}(I(1,Y') + X(\dots))$$

We then define :

$$D^T = \frac{D}{X^{r-1}} .$$

If $I(1,Y') = 0$, we define

$$D^T = \frac{D}{X^r} .$$

Finally we describe how the solutions of D correspond with the solutions of D^T :

PROPOSITION 7-1.- Let $F = (Y-CX)^m + F_{m+1} + ..$ be a solution of D at $(0,0)$ then $F'(X',Y') = (Y'-C)^m + XF_{m+1}(1,Y') + ..$ is a solution of D^T at $(0,C)$. Conversely, Let $F(X',Y')$ be a solution of D^T at $(0,C)$, $F' \neq X'$ then $X^r F(X, \frac{Y}{X})$ is a solution of D at $(0,0)$ (where r is defined by $F'(0,Y') = C_r Y'^r + C_{r+1} Y'^{r+1} + .. \; C_r \neq 0)$.

As an immediate consequence we have :

COROLLARY : Let $F(X,Y) = Y - \sum_{i=1}^{\infty} C_i X^i$ be a linear branch which is a solution of D (at $(0,0)$, then $F'(X',Y') = (Y'-C_1) - C_2 X - C_3 X^2 + ...$ is a linear branch at $(0,C_1)$ which is a solution of D^T at $(0,C_1)$.
Conversely, if $F(X',Y') = (Y'-C) - \sum_{i=1}^{\infty} C_i X^i$ is a linear branch at $(0,C)$ which satisfies D^T , then $Y - CX - \sum_{i=1}^{\infty} C_i X^{i+1}$ is a linear branch at $(0,0)$ with non-vertical tangent which satisfies D .

Summing up we see :

Analytic solution correspond with analytic solution.

§ 2. - THE MAIN THEOREM.

We can now formulate and prove the main theorem of this paper :

THEOREM 1-2.- Let $D = A \frac{\partial}{\partial X} + B \frac{\partial}{\partial Y}$, with $g.c.d(A,B) = 1$, and $r(D) > 1$. Then under a finite number of transformations of the type 1., 2., 3., the solutions of D at $(0,0)$ will go over into solutions of a differential operator D' (at $(0,C)$) with $r(D') \leq 1$.

<u>Proof.- Case $I(D) = 0$</u> . Then $XB_r = A_rY$ (so A_r and $B_r \neq 0$) . Let $F = (Y-CX)^m + F_{m+1} + ..$ be a solution at $(0,0)$ of D with non-vertical tangent (if F has X as tangent, make first the transformation $X' = Y$, $Y' = X$) . Then $F'(X',Y')$ is a solution at $(0,C)$ of

$$D^T = (A_r(1,Y') + X A_{r+1}(1,Y') + ..) \frac{\partial}{\partial X} + (..) \frac{\partial}{\partial Y'} .$$

If $A_r(1,C) \neq 0$, then $A_r(1,Y') + XA_{r+1}(1,Y') + ..$ is a unit in $k[[X',Y'-C]]$ and we see that when we divide by this unit we get a reduction to the case $r = 0$. So we suppose $A_r(1,C) = 0$, and hence A_r contains a factor $Y-CX$. But $A_r \neq (Y-CX)^r$ because $XB_r = YA_r$, and hence A_r contains a factor X . But this implies that $\deg A_r(1,Y') \leq r-1$, and therefore, because $A_r \neq 0$, $\deg(A_r(1,Y') + XA_r(1,Y') + ..) \leq r-1$. So again we have a reduction, now to the case $\leq r-1$.

<u>Case $I(D) \neq 0$</u> . Let $A_r \neq 0$. We may also suppose $B_r \neq 0$, for if $B_r = 0$ make the transformation $X' = X$, $X' = X+Y$, then $A' = A$, $B' = A+B$ and hence $B_r = A_r \neq 0$. By a similar argument we may suppose that A and B don't have X as a tangent. Let again F be a solution of D with non-vertical tangent $Y-CX$. By the transformation $X' = X$, $Y' = \frac{Y}{X}$ it will go over into a solution at $(0,C)$ of

$$D^T = X'A'(X',Y') \frac{\partial}{\partial X'} + (B'(X',Y') - Y'A(X',Y')) \frac{\partial}{\partial Y'} .$$

We now compare :

$$(*) = I(A \cap B ; (0,0)) \quad \text{with}$$

$$(**) = I(XA' \cap B' - Y'A' ; (0,C))$$

and we prove $(*) - (**) \geq 1$, if $r > 1$

($I(F \cap G : P)$ = the intersection multiplicity of F and G at P) .

$$\begin{aligned}(**) &= I(X \cap B' - Y'A' : (0,C)) + I(A' \cap B' ; (0,C)) \\ &= I(X \cap I(1,Y') : (0,C)) + I(A' \cap B' : (0,C))\end{aligned} \qquad (I)$$

(because $B' - Y'A' = B_r(1,Y') - Y'A_r(1,Y') + X(..) = I(1,Y') + X(..)$) .

We may assume that $A_r(1,C) = 0$, because otherwise $A'(X',Y')$ is a unit in $k[[X',Y'-C]]$ and then we have a reduction to the case $r \leq 1$. We may also assume $I(1,C) = 0$, for otherwise we have a reduction to $r = 0$. As a consequence we see :

$B_r(1,C) = B_r(1,C) - A_r(1,C) = I(1,C) = 0$, so we have

$(0,C)$ is a point of intersection of A' and B' on $X' = 0$ (II)

We now use (II) and the formula

$$I(A \cap B\,;(0,0)) = r.r + \sum_{i=1}^{t} I(A' \cap B'\,;(0,C_i))$$

where $C_i \in k$ is such that $(0,C_i)$ is a point of intersection of A' and B' on $X = 0$ (we refer to § 3). Hence by (II) we see :

$$(*) = r^2 + I(A' \cap B' : (0,C)) + \sum_{\substack{i=1 \\ C_i \neq C}}^{t} (..) .$$

From (I) and (II) we see

$$(*)-(**) = r^2 + I(A' \cap B'\,;(0,C)) + \Sigma(-) - I(A' \cap B'\,;(0,C)) - I(X \cap I(1,Y')\,;(0,C))$$

$$\geq r^2 - (r+1) \geq 1 \text{ , } \underline{\text{if } r > 1} \text{ ,}$$

where we have used that $\deg I(1,Y') \leq r+1$, and hence $I(X \cap I(1,Y')\,;(0,C)) \leq r+1$. Now because g.c.d $(A,B) = 1$ we have $I(A \cap B : (0,C) < \infty$ and hence by the above process we get a reduction by the simple arguments we met in the proof or we get a strict descending chain of natural numbers $I(A \cap B : (0,0)) > I(A_1 \cap B_1 : (0,0)) > \ldots$ which must therefore stop. So arrived at the operator where the chain stops, we must have $r \leq 1$, because otherwise we could again make an operator with a smaller naturel number as intersection multiplicity, a contradiction.

§ 3. - INTERSECTION MULTIPLICITY OF ANALYTIC BRANCHES.

For completeness sake we recall in this paragraph the main properties of the intersection number.

When F and G are (affine) plane curves the intersection number of F and G can be defined (we refer to [2]). Let $G = X$ and $P = (0,0)$, we then have for the number so defined

$$I(F \cap G,P) = I(F \cap X\,;\,0) = \mathrm{ord}_Y F(0,Y) = \mathrm{ord}_t F(x(t),(y(t))$$

where $x(t) = 0$ and $y(t) = t$, is the unique branch representation at $0,0)$ of the irreducible element $G = X$ in $k[[X,X]]$.

This property gives now rise to the following definition.

Let $F \in k[[X,Y]]$ and <u>$G \in k[[X,Y]]$ be irreducible</u> and such that $g\,c.d(F,G) = 1$ (so they don't have a common factor at $(0,0))$. We know, prop. 2.1. a), that there is a unique branch representation $\gamma = (x(t),y(t)$ of G in $k[[t]]$ with $G(x(t),y(t) = 0$. Then $F(x,y) = F(\gamma) \neq 0$, because otherwise G divides F , which is excluded by $g\,c.d(F,G) = 1$.

Hence $\mathrm{ord}_t\, F(\gamma) < \infty$.

We can therefore define, the intersection multiplicity of F and G (G irreducible) as :

$$\tilde{I}(F,G\,;\,0) \underset{def}{=} \mathrm{ord}_t\, F(\gamma)\,.$$

We now list up some simple properties of the so defined intersection number (which is till now only defined when G is irreducible).

1. If $F(0,0) \neq 0$, then $\tilde{I}(F,G;0) = 0$.

2. If F and G have a common factor at 0 , then $\mathrm{ord}_t\, F(\gamma) = \infty$, and the converse also holds, as we already remarked above, so :

$\tilde{I}(F,G\,;\,0) = \infty \Leftrightarrow F$ and G have a factor in common at $(0,0)$

in fact this means here G divides F) .

3. $\tilde{I}(F_1 \cdot F_2,G\,;\,0) = \tilde{I}(F_1,G\,;\,0) + \tilde{I}(F_2,G\,;\,0)$.

4. $\tilde{I}(F + AG,G\,;\,0) = \tilde{I}(F,G)\,;\,0)$.

<u>Proof</u> : Let γ be the unique branch representation of G, then $G(\gamma) = 0$ and hence $\mathrm{ord}_t(F + AG)(\gamma) = \mathrm{ord}_t\, F(\gamma) = \tilde{I}(F,G\,;\,0)$.

5. $\tilde{I}(F,X;0) = \mathrm{ord}_Y F(0,Y) \geq m_0(F)$ (= multiplicity of F at 0)

" = " if and only if F has not X as tangent.

<u>Proof</u>.- Using 1. and 3. and Weierstrass preparation theorem we may assume F irreducible and of the form

$$F(X,Y) = Y^r + B_{r-1}(X)Y^{r-1} + \ldots + B_0(X) \ , \text{ with } B_i(0) = 0 \quad (0 \leq i \leq r-1)$$

where r is defined by

$$F(0,Y) = C_r Y^r + C_{r+1} Y^{r+1} + \ldots \ ; \ C_r \neq 0 \ .$$

Hence using 4. we see

$$\tilde{I}(F,X;0) = \tilde{I}(Y^r,X;0) = r \quad (\text{using } x(t) = 0 \ , \ y(t) = t) \ .$$

Now suppose F has not X as tangent, then we know that

$$F = (Y + CX)^m + F_{m+1} + \ldots = Y^m + \ldots$$

hence $r = m$ and we are through.

6. $\tilde{I}(X,G:0) = m_0(G)$, if X is not a tangent of G .

<u>Proof</u>.- Because G is irreducible we have $G \not\equiv 0 \bmod X$. Hence using Weierstrass and 1. again we may assume that G is of the form

$$G = Y^r + B_{r-1}(X)\, Y^{r-1} + \ldots + B_0(X) \ .$$

Now using [3], theorem 21.16 (page 182) we know that the branch representation of G is of the forme $x(t)$, $y(t)$ with $x(t) = ct^r + \ldots$ $C \neq 0$. So we see $\tilde{I}(X,G;0) = \mathrm{ord}_t\, x(t) = r$. Again using the fact that X is not a tangent of G we see $r = m$ and we are done.

7. Somewhat more general we now define the following :

Let $F, G \in k[[X-a, Y-b]]$, $a,b \in k$, with G irreducible in $k[[X-a, Y-b]]$.

We then define :

$$\tilde{I}(F,G;(a,b)) \underset{\text{def}}{=} \mathrm{ord}_Y F \ .$$

Where γ is the unique branch representation of G at (a,b) (of the form :

$$x(t) = a + a_1 t + a_2 t^2 + \cdots \text{, hence } x(0) = a$$

$$y(t) = b + b_1 t + b_2 t^2 + \cdots \text{, hence } y(o) = b \text{) .}$$

Let now F and G in $k[[X,Y]]$, with G irreducible, and let's assume that F and G both don't have X as tangent, say,

$$G = (Y - CX)^m + G_{m+1} + \cdots$$

Then the branch representation of G is of the form :

$$x(t) = t^u + \cdots,\ y(t) = Ct^u + \cdots \qquad (*) \quad .$$

Further , $G'(X',Y') = (Y' - C)^m + XG_{m+1}(1,Y') + \cdots \in k[[X,Y' - C]]$.

As we remarked earlier, $F'(X',Y')$ can also be viewed as an element of $k[[X,Y' - C]]$. Now using the fact that G' is still irreducible in $k[[X,Y' - C]]$ (prop. 6.1) we see that the number $\tilde{I}(F',G';(0,C))$ is defined. Using (*) we find for the branch representation of G' at $(0,0)$; $\gamma' = (x',y')$ with :

$$x'(t) = x(t) = t^u + \cdots$$
$$y'(t) = \frac{y(t)}{x(t)} = C + a\ ,\ t + \cdots$$

Let $n = \text{subd } F$, then we see :

$$\text{ord}_\gamma F = \text{ord}_t F(x(t),y(t)) = \text{ord}_t F(x'(t),x'(t)y'(t)) =$$

$$= \text{ord}_t(x'^n \cdot F'(x',y')) = \text{ord}_{\gamma'}(X^n F'(X,Y')) .$$

Hence :

$$\text{ord}_\gamma F = \text{ord}_{\gamma'} (X^n F'(X,Y')) \qquad (**)$$

We now prove the important property :

8. Let $F,G \in k[[X,Y]]$ and F and G don't have X as a tangent. Furthermore suppose G irreducible (in $k[[X,Y]]$) and let $m_o(F) = n$ and $m_o(G) = m$. Then :

$$\tilde{I}(F,G;0) = m.n + \tilde{I}(F',G';(0,C)) ,$$

where $Y-CX$ is the tangent of G at $(0,C)$.

Proof : Using 3. and the equality (**) proved in 7. we find

$$\tilde{I}(F,G:0) = \mathrm{ord}_{\gamma} F = \mathrm{ord}_{\gamma'}(X^n F'(X,Y')) = \mathrm{ord}_{\gamma'} X^n + \mathrm{ord}_{\gamma'} F'(X,Y')$$

$$= \mathrm{ord}_{\gamma} X^n + \tilde{I}(F',G':(0,C)) .$$

Now using the same argument as in the proof of 6. we see $x(t) = dt^m+..$, $d \neq 0$, and hence $x'(t) = x(t) = dt^n+..$ and this gives, $\mathrm{ord}_{\gamma'} X^n = \mathrm{ord}_t (dt^m+..)^n = m.n$.

9. $\tilde{I}$ is invariant under affine transformations, that is :

a) If $F,G \in k[[X-a, Y-b]]$, with G irreducible in $k[[X-a, Y-b]]$ such that F and G can also be viewed as elements of $k[[X,Y]]$, denote these elements with $\tilde{F}$ and $\tilde{G}$, then

$$\tilde{I}(F,G,(a,b)) = \tilde{I}(\tilde{F},\tilde{G}:0) .$$

Then follows immediately from the definition.

b) Also we have invariance under invertible linear transformations

$$\begin{pmatrix} X' \\ Y' \end{pmatrix} = (c_{ij}) \begin{pmatrix} X \\ Y \end{pmatrix} , \quad \det(c_{ij}) \neq 0 .$$

We can now prove :

10. If F and G are both irreducible in $k[[X,Y]]$, then

$$\tilde{I}(F,G;0) = \tilde{I}(G,F;0) .$$

Proof : We may assume that $\mathrm{g.c.d}(F,G) = 1$, because otherwise we get the equality $\infty = \infty$. Furthermore, using 9. we may after a linear transformation assume that F and G don't have X as a tangent. Let $Y-CX$ be the tangent of G we make a transformation $X' = X$, $Y' = \frac{Y}{X}$. Using 8. we see :

$$\tilde{I}(F,G;0) = m.n + \tilde{I}(F',G';(0,C))$$

(where $n = \text{subd}\,F$, $m = \text{subd}\,G$) .

We now make an induction on $r = \max(\text{subd}\,F, \text{subd}\,G)$ and on the minimal number of steps we need to get a reduction of r , by using transformation of the type $X = X'$, $Y' = \frac{Y}{X}$. (In fact we use theorem 21.12 of [3], page 180).

We may then assume :

$$\tilde{I}(F',G':(0,C)) = \tilde{I}(G',F':(0,C)) .$$

Hence :

$$\tilde{I}(F,G) = mn + \tilde{I}(F',G';(0,C)) = \tilde{I}(G,F;0) .$$

In the induction we have tacitly used 9., to arrange that X is not a tangent of the new appearing branches, and also we made use of translations.

The only thing we have to do now is to prove the case $r = 1$, $\text{subd}\,F = \text{Subd}\,G$.

Using Weierstrass preparation theorem again we may assume :

$$F = Y - \sum_{i=1}^{\infty} C_i X^i , \quad G = Y - \sum_{i=1}^{\infty} d_i X^i .$$

Then using the branch representation ,

$$x_1(t) = t , \quad y_1(t) = \Sigma c_i t^i \quad , \text{for } F$$

$$x_2(t) = t , \quad y_2(t) = \Sigma d_i t^i \quad , \text{for } F$$

we then see immediately

$$\tilde{I}(F,G;0) = \text{ord}_t(\Sigma d_i t^i - \Sigma c_i t^i) = \text{ord}_t(\Sigma c_i t^i - \Sigma d_i t^i) = \tilde{I}(G,F,0).$$

Finally we define :

Let G be arbitrary $G = \prod_{i=1}^{r} G_i^{\ell_i}$, where all G_i are irreducible and different.

For every G_i we have one unique branch representation γ_i (prop.2-1), which are all different (theorem 21.18, page 179, [3]). Conversely, let γ be a primitive branch representation of G then there exist an i with $G_i(\gamma) = 0$ and hence $\gamma = \gamma_i$.

We can now define :

$$\tilde{I}(F,G;O) \underset{def}{=} \sum_{i=1}^{r} \ell_i \tilde{I}(F,G_i;O) .$$

The notion of intersection multiplicity so defined is now the same when we "restrict to above formula" to the case of affine plane curves as in [2], because our $\tilde{I}$ satisfies the properties (1) up to (7) in [2], and this implies the uniqueness of such an object.

Now using 8. it's not difficult to prove :

THEOREM 1.3. - Let $F,G \in k[[X,Y]]$, $gcd(F,G) = 1$, with $\text{subd}\, F = n$, $\text{subd}\, G = m$, and assume that neither F nor G has X as tangent. Let F' and G' be their transforms under $X' = X$, $Y' = \frac{Y}{X}$ and let $P', \ldots P'_t$ be the points of intersection of F' and G' on the Y' - axis. Then :

$$\tilde{I}(F,G;O) = n.m + \sum_{i=1}^{t} \tilde{I}(F',G';P'_i) .$$

REFERENCES

[1] L. BIEBERBACH — Theorie der gewöhnlichen differentialgleichungen. (Springer Verlag 1953).

[2] W. FULTON — Algebraic Curves (W.A. Benjamin, Inc. 1969).

[3] A. SEIDENBERG — Elements of the theory of Algebraic Curves (Addison-Wesley Publ. Comp. 1968).

[4] A. Seidenberg — Reduction of singularities of the differential equation $A\,dy = B\,dx$. (Am. Journal of Math. vol. 90, 1968).

UNIVERSITE DE NIJMEGEN

(Pays-Bas)

A POINCARE-BENDIXSON THEOREM FOR COMPACT KAHLER MANIFOLDS

David I. LIEBERMAN (*)

Brandeis University
Waltham, Massachusetts 02154

At the heart of the classical Poincare-Bendixson theory is the assertion that given a differentiable flow on a 2-manifold X and a minimal compact invariant subset Z then either Z is a point, or is a circle, or Z = X is a 2-torus, and in the latter case the flow is (up to reparametrization) skew translation on the torus (see for example [6]) . In higher dimensions there is no such simple description of the minimal invariant sets, even under rather stringent hypotheses, eg. X is required to be a compact complex manifold and the flow to be a one parameter group H of holomorphic self transformations. One does not even have a classification of those compact complex manifolds X admitting no proper closed invariant subsets for a suitable one parameter H . (The complex nilmanifolds all admit such actions [1].) If one imposes the further requirement that X be Kahlerian the situation becomes extremely simple. Letting X be Kahler and H a 1-(real) parameter group of holomorphic automorphisms :

THEOREM 1 : If H has a dense orbit then X is a complex torus, H is acting by skew translation and all orbits are dense.

COROLLARY : If $Z \subseteq X$ is minimal among the analytic subvarieties of X left invariant by H then Z is a complex torus.

(*) Partially supported by NSF GP MCS 76-11312 and a Sloan Foundation Fellowship.

The corollary follows by noting that if Z is invariant under H, so would be the singular locus $\mathrm{Sing}(Z)$ which is therefore empty by minimality. One may now apply Theorem 1 to Z.

More generally one has :

THEOREM 2: If G is ani connected group of holomorphic automorphisms of X and Z is minimal among the G invariant subvarieties then Z is a homogeneous Kahler manifold and hence [5] of the form $T \times F$ where T is a complex torus and F is a generalized flag manifold, (i.e. F is of the form S/P where S is a semi-simple complex Lie group and P is a parabolic subgroup). If G is solvable, $Z = T$.

THEOREM 3 : If $G \subseteq \mathrm{Aut}_o(X)$ acts with Zariski dense orbit on X, then X is a quasi-homogeneous Kahler manifold, and hence [3] a flat bundle over a complex torus with unirational fibre.

For 1-parameter H we have also the generalized Poincare Bendixson theorem :

THEOREM 4 : Let Z be a minimal closed subset invariant under H, then Z is a real torus (i.e. a product of a finite number of S^1's with the zero dimensional product corresponding to the case of a single point).

The validity of these results for Kahler manifolds is due to the fact that the automorphism group of a Kahler manifold is compactifiable in the following sense. There exists a compact complex manifold C such that $\mathrm{Aut}_o(X) = C - D$ where D is a divisor with normal corssings, and the natural map $\mathrm{Aut}_o(X) \times X \to X$, $(G,x) \to g.\,x$ extends to a meromorphic map of $C \times X \to X$. (The manifold C is obtained by taking the component of the Barlet Chow scheme of $X \times X$ containing the diagonal cycle $\Delta \subseteq X \times X$ and resolving its singularities. The fact that C is compact result by applying the work of Bishop [4] to Barlet's construction, [2], to conclude that all components of the Chow scheme of a compact Kahler manifold are themselves compact, [7].) The compactness is employed in the following manner.

One introduces a canonical Zariski topology on $Aut_o(X)$, in which the Zariski closed subsets are the intersection of $Aut_o(X)$ with the Zariski closed subsets of C . Given any subgroup of $Aut_o(X)$ one may form its Zariski closure, which will be again a subgroup and will be abelian (resp. nilpotent, solvable) if the original subgroup was abelian (resp. ...) . The key tool then

LEMMA 1 : If G is a Zariski closed subgroup of $Aut_o(X)$ and $Y \subset X$ is any closed subvariety then the topological closure of $G . Y \subseteq X$ is an analytic subvariety of X containing G . Y as a (Zariski) open dense subset. In particular the orbits of G are Zariski open subsets of their Zariski closure.

The lemma follows by considering the meromorphic map of compact spaces $\bar{G} \times Y \to X$ (where $\bar{G}$ denotes the closure of G in C) . The proper mapping theorem assures that G . Y must contain a Zariski open subset of is Zariski closure. Since we may employ G to move this subset about, we conclude G . Y is Zariski open in its closure.

Employing this lemma we turn to the proofs of the theorems. Let G be any connected group of holomorphic automorphisms of X and let K be the Zariski closure of G in $Aut_o(X)$. Clearly if G has a dense orbit, K has an open dense orbit whence Theorem 3 . We remark that the G invariant subvarieties of X are K-invariant [7] . Thus given Z a minimal G-invariant subvariety it is minimal K-invariant. Given $z \in Z$ we see that the orbit K . z is necessarily Zariski dense in Z (since its closure would be an invariant subvariety) . In view of the lemma K . z is therefore Zariski open in Z . Since Z - K . z is a K-invariant subvariety, it is necessarily empty, i.e. Z is homogeneous. The structure theorem for homogeneous compact Kahler manifolds, [5], (cf. [9] for a very direct proof) may then be employed to obtain the assertion of Theorem 2 .

When G is solvable (and hence K is) one may conclude that Z is necessarily a torus by analyzing the argument of [5] or [9] . When G is abelian one may see this quite direcly. In fact we turn to the more general situation of Theorem 1 .

LEMMA 2 : Let X be any complex Kahler manifold and $G \subseteq \mathrm{Aut}(X)$ a connected abelian subgroup such that for some $x \in X$ the orbit $G \cdot x$ is Zariski dense then there exists an abelian complex Lie group K , $G \subseteq K \subseteq \mathrm{Aut}(X)$ such that the map $K \to K \cdot x$ defines a biholomorphic equivalence of K with a Zariski open subset of K .

Proof : Let K be the Zariski closure of G . Note that $K \cdot x$ is Zariski open in $\overline{K \cdot x} = X$. Moreover the map $K \to K \cdot x$ is 1-1 since given $k \in K$ such that $k \cdot x = x$ then k fixes all points on $K \cdot x$ since K is abelian. But then k is the identify on $\overline{K \cdot x} = X$. Thus we see X is a compactification of a an abelian Lie group.

In the situation of Theorem 1 where X admits a 1-parameter group H with $H \cdot x$ dense - we see that K , the Zariski closure of H , is therefore a complex Lie group admitting a dense 1-(real)-parameter subgroup, in view of Lemma 2 .We claim that the only such K are the complex tori, whence K is compact and necessarily $K \cdot x$ is closed in X , i.e. $K \xrightarrow{\sim} X$. To obtain the claim, let V be the Lie algebra of K . The exponential homomorphism $V \to K$ identifies $K = V/\Gamma$ for Γ a discrete subgroup generated by $r \leq \dim_{\mathbb{R}} V$ real independent vectors. Let $W \subseteq V$ be Lie (H) . By hypothesis the subgroup $\{W,\Gamma\}$ is dense in V , which is clearly impossible if $r < \dim_{\mathbb{R}} V$. Thus Γ is necessarily a lattice and K is torus as asserted.

Finally turning to the proof of Theorem 4 , we assume again that $G \subseteq \mathrm{Aut}_o(X)$ is abelian, and denote by K its Zariski closure and by C a minimal G-invariant closed subset of X . We may assume G is closed subgroup of K , replacing G by its closure (not Zariski closure, which will not leave C invariant in general). We may further assume that for

$x \in C$ the orbit $G \cdot x$ is Zariski dense in X. (We replace X by $Z = \bigcap_{x \in C} \overline{G \cdot x}$ where $\overline{}$ denotes Zariski closure. This Z may be <u>singular</u>, although C will miss the singular locus of Z, since common points would not have Zariski dense orbits. One may desingularize Z by a sequence of monoidal transformations based at nonsingular, G-invariant subvarieties of $\mathrm{Sing}(Z)$, according to recent work of Hironaka. Thus one may obtain a new X without changing C. For our present purposes one could avoid this desingularization step by noting that the theorems and lemmas of this paper can be applied equally well to the case that X is a singular subvariety of an ambient compact Kahler manifold, or for that matter to a Kahler space X in the sense of Moisezon [8].

Fix $x \in C$ and let $E = X - K\,x$. Note that $C \cap E = \emptyset$ since E is clearly a G-invariant <u>closed</u> (by Lemma 2) subset of X. Identifying $K \xrightarrow{\sim} K \cdot x$ as in Lemma 2 we see that $G \cdot x$ is <u>closed</u> in $K \cdot x$ hence in fact $G \cdot x = C$ and G is therefore <u>compact</u>. Thus G is a compact connected subgroup of the abelian Lie group K, and G is therefore a real torus, as required.

BIBLIOGRAPHY

[1] AUSLANDER L. GREEN L. and HAHN F : Flows on homogeneous spaces, Ann. Math. Studies, n° 53, Princeton University Press. 1963, Page 157.

[2] BARLET D. Espace analytique reduit des cycles analytiques complexes compacts, in Fonctions de plusieurs variables complexes II, Springer Lecture Notes, vol. 482 (1975) Pages 1-158 .

[3] BARTH W. and OELJEKLAUS E. Uber die Albanesabbildung einer fast homogenen Kahler-Mannigfaltigkeit, Math. Ann. 211 (1974) Pages 47-62.

[4] BISHOP E. Conditions for the Analyticity of certain sets, Mich. Math. J. 11 (1964) Pages 289-304.

[5] BOREL A. and REMMERT R. Uber Kompakte homogene Kahlersche Mannigfaltigkeiten, Math. Ann. 145 (1961) Pages 429-439.

[6] HARTMAN P. Ordinary Differential Equations, Wiley, New York (1964).

[7] LIEBERMAN D. Compactness of the Chow scheme and automorphisms of Kahler manifolds, in Seminar Norguet 1975-76, Springer Lecture Notes, to appear.

[8] MOISEZON B. Singular Kahlerian spaces, in Proc. Internat. Conf. Manifolds, Tokyo 1973, University of Tokyo Press (1975).

[9] SOMMESE A. Holomorphic Vector Fields on Compact Kahler manifolds, Math. Ann. 2.0 (1974) Pages 74-82.

[10] SOMMESE A. Extension theorems for reductive group actions on Kahler manifolds, Math. Ann. 218 (1975) Pages 107-116.

BIRKHOFF INVARIANTS
AND MEROMORPHIC DIFFERENTIAL EQUATIONS

by

Donald A. LUTZ

Consider a system of n linear differential equations of the form

$$x' = A(z)x \, , \quad A(z) = z^{r-1} \sum_{\nu=0}^{\infty} A_\nu z^{-\nu} \, , \tag{1}$$

when r is a non-negative integer called the Poincaré rank and the power series converges for $|z| > R$. If $x = T(z)y$, where $T(z)$ is an $n \times n$ matrix of functions with determinant not identically zero, then

$$y' = B(z)y \, , \text{ where } B(z) = T^{-1}(z) A(z) T(z) - T^{-1}(z) T'(z) \, , \tag{2}$$

and we say that the differential systems (1) and (2) are <u>equivalent</u>. <u>Invariants</u> are defined to be quantities which remains unchanged with respect to equivalence, and we are interested in determining complete systems of invariants, which then characterize the differential system up to equivalence. This may be viewed as the extension of the theory of Jordan from matrices to systems of differential equations. Note that the equivalence is generated by a similarity transform $T^{-1}AT$ and the logarithmic derivative $T^{-1}T'$. At a regular point of the differential system the presence of the term $T^{-1}T'$ leads to the conclusion that nothing is invariant, while at a singular point this term distinguishes the problem from a purely algebraic one and is the source of interest.

These lectures are based upon joint work with W. Jurkat and A. Peyerimhoff.

The author's stay in the Federal Republic of Germany is supported in part by a grant from the Alexander von Humboldt Foundation.

In what follows we will discuss three groups of transformations which may act on the differential system $x' = A(z)x$. If the elements of $T(z)$ are meromorphic in a neighborhood of ∞ and such that $\det T(z) \not\equiv 0$ in this neighborhood, then $T(z)$ is called a meromorphic transformation and the group of meromorphic tranformations is denoted by $\mathcal{M}$. If the elements of $T(z)$ are analytic in a neighborhood of ∞ and $\det T(\infty) \neq 0$, then $T(z)$ is called an analytic transformation and the group of analytic transformations is denoted by $\mathcal{A}$. The subgroup of $\mathcal{A}$ which are normalized so that $T(\infty) = I$ are called strict transformations and is denoted by $\mathcal{A}_0$. Invariants corresponding to these groups are called meromorphic, analytic and Birkhoff invariants, respectively.

The Birkhoff invariants are named in honor of G.D. Birkhoff, who first investigated such problems as we discuss here and who actually calculated some invariants. Birkhoff [1] proved in 1913 that there exists $T(z) \in A$ such that $x = T(z)y$ transforms $x' = A(z)x$ into (2), where $B(z)$ has only two singularities, at 0 and at ∞, and 0 is a regular singular point of the solutions of (2). Thus such $B(z)$ may be considered as representatives for the differential system $x' = A(z)x$ in much the same way as Jordan matrices are representatives in that theory. In order to obtain true canonical forms, it is essential to be able to tell which representatives are themselves equivalent. This is a deeper question for differential systems than for matrices as we shall see.

Birkhoff claimed that it is even possible to make the singularity of $B(z)$ at 0 have at worst a simple pole, i.e., a singular point of the first kind. It was discovered that this is not generally correct by Gantmacher [2] and Masani [6] independently, who gave counter-examples when $n = 2$ and $r = 0$. In 1963 Turrittin [7] proved that if $r > 0$ and A_0, the leading coefficient matrix of $A(z)$, has all distinct eigenvalues, then there exists $T(z) \in \mathcal{M}$ such that $B(z)$ has the form

$$B(z) = z^{r-1} \sum_{\nu=0}^{r} B_\nu z^{-\nu} . \tag{3}$$

Several problems which remain open are :

i) Is this still true if A_o has some equal eigenvalues ? When $n = 2$, this is the case.

ii) If i) is not true, can we extend $T(z)$ to some more general class, for example, matrices which are meromorphic in some fractional power of z such that Birkhoff's claim would be true ?

iii) If A_o has distinct eigenvalues, characterize those situations for which $B(z)$ has the form (3) for some $T(z) \in \mathcal{G}$.

The results of Birkhoff and Turrittin were proven without reference to the invariants of the problem, yet we know that the invariants do control such questions in an essential way. For example, the problem i) can be reformulated by asking whether $y' = B(z)y$, where $B(z)$ has the form (3), gives rise to all possible sets of meromorphic invariants. Hence we can expect that such problems will be answered when we gain sufficient knowledge of the invariants.

Such information about the invariants would come about through the implementation of the following general program :

a) Give a complete and independent set of invariants for the differential system.

b) Give a list of representatives, or special systems, which give rise to all possible sets of invariants and tell which of the representatives are equivalent.

c) Construct a transformation between equivalent differential systems.

In the simplest interesting cases, namely when $n = 2$ and $r = 1$, all phases of this program have been completely discussed by W. Jurket, D. Lutz and A. Peyerimhoff, [3] and [4]. Moreover, in these cases it is possible to do more, namely, we can name in advance a representative to which a given differential system is equivalent. This comes about as a result of an explicit calculation of the invariants for the representatives.

These cases already contain many of the special differential equations of mathematical physics which have an irregular singular point. An outline of the results in these cases follows.

Let $n = 2$, $r = 1$ and consider $x' = A(z)x$, where

(4) $$A(z) = A_0 + A_1 z^{-1} + \sum_{\nu=2}^{\infty} A_\nu z^{-\nu} .$$

There are three naturally disjoint cases to consider, depending upon where A_o has distinct eigenvalues or not, and if A_o has equal eigenvalues, whether it is diagonal or not. If A_o has distinct eigenvalues, case I, it is important to make a fixed ordering for all pairs of complex numbers and consistent with that ordering label the eigenvalues as λ_1 , λ_2 . Then make a fixed choice of a non-singular matrix F_o such that $F_o^{-1}A_oF_o = \Lambda = \operatorname{diag}\{\lambda_1, \lambda_2\}$. If A_o has equal eigenvalues $\lambda_1 = \lambda_2$ and is not diagonal, case II, we choose a fixed non-singular matrix F_o such that $F_o^{-1}A_oF_o = \begin{bmatrix} \lambda & 0 \\ 1 & \lambda \end{bmatrix}$. We will not discuss the case $A_o = \lambda I$ here, but refer the reader to [4], Section 6.

One should point out here that in our discussion of the invariants, we calculate Birkhoff invariants first and because of the normalization of $T(z)$ they turn out to be numbers instead of equivalence classes. The analytic and meromorphic invariants are then equivalence classes based on the Birkhoff invariants. In the calculation of the Birkhoff invariants, the fixed ordering of the eigenvalues in case I and fixed choice of F_o is essential.

We will treat case I first and then apply a rather general transfer principle to reduce the discussion of case II to a special situation involving case I.

We first construct a formal fundamental situation matrix in case I of the form

(5) $$F(z)z^{\Lambda'} \exp(\Lambda z) ,$$

where $\Lambda' = \operatorname{diag}\{F_o^{-1}A_1F_o\}$ and $F(z) = F_o + \sum_{\nu=1}^{\infty} F_\nu z^{-\nu}$, and where the coefficients F_ν of the formal series are calculated recursively in a well-known manner. It is natural to expect that since the formal solution contains complete information about $A(z)$ and hence the differential system, the invariants can be calculated from this formal solution. This is indeed the case as we see in the following

THEOREM 1. Let $x' = A(z)x$ be given, where $A(z)$ has the form (4) and A_o has distinct eigenvalues $\lambda_1 \neq \lambda_2$. Let F_o be chosen so that $F_o^{-1}A_oF_o = \Lambda = \operatorname{diag}\{\lambda_1, \lambda_2\}$, let $\operatorname{diag}\{F_o^{-1}A_1F_o\} = \Lambda' = \operatorname{diag}\{\lambda_1', \lambda_2'\}$ and let (5) be the uniquely constructed fundamental solution matrix for $x' = A(z)x$. Define a sequence of diagonal matrices K_m as

$$K_m = \operatorname{diag}\{(-1)^m\, m^{\lambda_2'-\lambda_1'},\, m^{\lambda_1'-\lambda_2'}\}(\lambda_2-\lambda_1)^{-m}\,\Gamma(m)\ ,\quad m \geq 1\ .$$

Then A_o, Λ', and

$$C = \begin{pmatrix} 0 & \gamma_2 \\ \gamma_1 & 0 \end{pmatrix} = F_o^{-1} \lim_{m\to\infty} F_m K_m^{-1}\ , \tag{6}$$

form a complete set of Birkhoff invariants for the differential system $x' = A(z)x$. The invariants are independent, in fact even free, and the invariant $\gamma_i = 0$ iff the ith column of $F(z)$ converges for $|z|$ large, $i = 1,2$.

The quantities A_o and Λ' are easily seen to be a complete set of formal Birkhoff invariants, i.e., with respect to formal transformations $x = T(z)y$, where $T(z) = I + \sum_1^\infty T_i z^{-i}$ is just assumed to be a formal power series. The invariant C, on the other hand, is the one which controls the convergence of the transformation and depends in a transcendental manner on the coefficients of the formal series and the coefficient matrix A.

The proof of this theorem consists of two main parts, corresponding to the invariance and the completeness of the set $\{A_o, \Lambda', C\}$. Both parts are proven by reference to the representatives to which a given system is strictly equivalent by virtue of Birkhoff's result. In case I there are three types of representatives, the "standard" examples

$$y' = F_o\left(\begin{bmatrix} \lambda_1 & 0 \\ 0 & \lambda_2 \end{bmatrix} + \frac{1}{z}\begin{bmatrix} \lambda_1' & c_2 \\ c_1 & \lambda_2' \end{bmatrix}\right)F_o^{-1}y\ , \tag{7}$$

and the "exceptional" examples

(8) $$y' = F_o\left(\begin{bmatrix}\lambda_1 & 0\\ 0 & \lambda_2\end{bmatrix} + \frac{1}{z}\begin{bmatrix}\lambda_1' & 0\\ 0 & \lambda_2'\end{bmatrix} + \frac{1}{z^{1+k}}\begin{bmatrix}0 & 0\\ d_1 & 0\end{bmatrix}\right)F_o^{-1}y$$

$\lambda_1' - \lambda_2' = k$, a positive integer, $d_1 \neq 0$, and

(9) $$y' = F_o\left(\begin{bmatrix}\lambda_1 & 0\\ 0 & \lambda_2\end{bmatrix} + \frac{1}{z}\begin{bmatrix}\lambda_1' & 0\\ 0 & \lambda_2\end{bmatrix} + \frac{1}{z^{1+k}}\begin{bmatrix}0 & d_2\\ 0 & 0\end{bmatrix}\right)F_o^{-1}y$$

$\lambda_2' - \lambda_1' = k$, a positive integer, $d_2 \neq 0$.

To prove that the limit in (6) exists and the numbers γ_1 and γ_2 are invariants, we show that this is the case for the representatives (7), (8) and (9), and then show that under a strict transformation $x = T(z)y$ these properties are preserved. Moreover, the invariants γ_1 and γ_2 for the examples can be explicitly calculated as follows :

For (7) let $\{\alpha, \beta\}$ be defined by $\alpha + \beta = \lambda_2' - \lambda_1'$, $\alpha\beta = -c_1c_2$.

Then

(10) $$\gamma_1 = c_1/\Gamma(1+\alpha)\,\Gamma(1+\beta) \quad\text{and}\quad \gamma_2 = c_2/\Gamma(1-\alpha)\,\Gamma(1-\beta) .$$

Note that $\{\alpha, \beta\}$ is very closely related to the set of eigenvalues of the coefficient of z^{-1} .

For (8), $\gamma_1 = d_1$ and $\gamma_2 = 0$, while for (9), $\gamma_1 = 0$ and $\gamma_2 = d_2$.

All these results come about because the examples can be solved by explicit formal series for which we can make the calculation (6).

To prove the completeness, we list all examples having a given set of invariants and show that in all cases in which there is more than one example, then the examples are strictly equivalent by means of an explicitly constructed transformation. This is done in the following way :

Given A_o , λ_1' , λ_2' , γ_1 , and γ_2 , define an auxiliary invariant μ as the general solution of the equation

$$\cos 2\pi\mu = \cos \pi(\lambda_2' - \lambda_1') - 2\pi^2\,\gamma_1\,\gamma_2 .$$

This defines μ upto ($\pm$) sign and modulo one. Also define

$$\alpha_* = \tfrac{1}{2}(\lambda_2' - \lambda_1') + \mu \quad \text{and} \quad \beta_* = \tfrac{1}{2}(\lambda_2' - \lambda_1') - \mu$$

and note if μ changes sign this corresponds to an interchange of α_* and β_*, while if μ changes mod 1 then α_* and β_* both change modulo 1 but $\alpha_* + \beta_*$ remains fixed.

One can show using the identity $\Gamma(x)\,\Gamma(1-x) = \pi \operatorname{CSC} \pi x$ that for the example (7) with invariants given by (10), it follows that

$$\cos \pi(\alpha - \beta) = \cos \pi(\lambda_2' - \lambda_1') - 2\pi^2\, \gamma_1 \gamma_2 ,$$

so $(\alpha - \beta)/2$ must be a possible choice for μ, and $\alpha = \alpha_*$ and $\beta = \beta_*$. If neither α_* nor β_* is an integer, then we may take

(11) $$c_1 = \gamma_1\, \Gamma(1 + \alpha_*)\, \Gamma(1 + \beta_*) \quad \text{and} \quad c_2 = \gamma_2\, \Gamma(1 - \alpha_*)(1 - \beta_*)$$

and this gives all possible standard examples (7) having the prescribed invariants. This condition that neither α_* nor β_* is an integer means exactly that $\gamma_1\gamma_2 \neq 0$, i.e., both of the columns of the formal series diverge. Hence there are no exceptional examples in this case because for those $\gamma_1\gamma_2 = 0$.

Thus problems may occur when α_* or β_* is an integer, for then the formulas (11) are not defined. If $\gamma_1 \neq 0$ and $\gamma_2 = 0$, then instead of (11) we may write

(12) $$c_1 = \gamma_1\, \Gamma(1 + \alpha_*)\, \Gamma(1 + \beta_*) , \quad c_2 = -\alpha_*\beta_*/C_1$$

and the standard example with these values of c_1 and c_2 has the invariants $\gamma_1, \gamma_2 = 0$ provided that one of α_* or β_* is an integer, but neither is a negative integer. As long as $\lambda_2' - \lambda_1' = \alpha_* + \beta_*$ is not a negative integer there exists a standard example having γ_1 and $\gamma_2 = 0$ as its invariants, but when $\lambda_2' - \lambda_1' = -k$, a negative integer, then this is clearly no longer possible and we must take the exceptional example (8) with $d_1 = \gamma_1$. These exceptional examples are exactly the cases in which Birkhoff's claim is not correct. The case when $\gamma_1 = 0$ and $\gamma_2 \neq 0$ is treated analogously. If both $\gamma_1 = 0$ and $\gamma_2 = 0$, then both columns of the formal series converge and we may take the standard example (7) in this case with $c_1 = c_2 = 0$.

To prove completeness it remains to show that in all cases in which there are several examples with the same invariants, they are equivalent. This is done by explicitly constructing strict transformations between them, which turn out to be polynomials in z^{-1} and are generated by iteration of transformations of the form $T(z) = I + Nz^{-1}$, where N is nilpotent and such a $T(z)$ has the effect of moving the parameter set $\{\alpha, \beta\}$ either into $\{\alpha+1, \beta-1\}$ or $\{\alpha-1, \beta+1\}$.

The details for the proof of this theorem can be found in [3], Sections 2-4. To see what changes take place in these invariants under analytic or meromorphic equivalence, we state the following results :

THEOREM 2. <u>Two systems</u> $x' = A(z)x$ <u>and</u> $y' = B(z)y$ <u>are analytically equivalent iff</u> $\Lambda_A = \Lambda_B$, $\Lambda'_A = \Lambda'_B$, and $C_A = D_o^{-1} C_B D_o$, <u>where</u> D_o <u>is a non-singular diagonal matrix. In case of equivalence, all possible analytic transforms are given by</u> $x = F_A(z) D^{-1} F_B^{-1}(z)y$, where D satisfies $C_A = D^{-1} C_B D$.

THEOREM 3. <u>Two systems</u> $x' = A(z)x$ <u>and</u> $y' = B(z)y$ <u>are meromorphically equivalent iff</u> $\Lambda_A = \Lambda_B$, $\Lambda'_A = \Lambda'_B + K$, <u>and</u> (*) $C_A = D_o^{-1} C_B \operatorname{diag}\{(-1)^{k_1-k_2}, 1\} D_o$, <u>where</u> $K = \operatorname{diag}\{k_1, k_2\}$, k_1 , k_2 <u>are integers and</u> D_o <u>is a non-singular diagonal matrix. In case of equivalence, all possible meromorphic transformations are given by</u> $x = F_A(z) z^K \operatorname{diag}\{(\lambda_2 - \lambda_1)^{k_1-k_2}, 1\} D^{-1} F_B^{-1}(z)y$ <u>where</u> D <u>is any</u> D_o <u>satisfying</u> (*).

Theorem 2 is proven by applying Theorem 1 and Theorem 3 is proven by applying Theorem 2. From Theorem 3 we see that since Λ' can be changed modulo one arbitrarily, then the standard examples give rise to all meromorphic invariants since the exceptional examples only occur when $\pm(\lambda'_2 - \lambda'_1)$ is a positive integer. Of course, it can also be seen directly that (8) and (9) are meromorphically equivalent to a system of the form (7).

We now turn to case II, i.e.,

$$F_o^{-1} A(z) F_o = \begin{bmatrix} \lambda & 0 \\ 1 & \lambda \end{bmatrix} + \frac{1}{z} \begin{bmatrix} a_{11}^{(1)} & a_{12}^{(1)} \\ a_{21}^{(1)} & a_{22}^{(1)} \end{bmatrix} + \sum_{2}^{\infty} \hat{A}_k z^{-k} .$$

It is not difficult to see that in this situation the quantity $a_{12}^{(1)}$ is a formal meromorphic invariant of the differential system. If $a_{12}^{(1)} = 0$, then aside from the scalar factor $e^{\lambda z}$, the solutions of $x' = A(z)x$ have a regular singular point at ∞. This case is treated in [4],,Section 6 and we will not pursue it here. Of more interest is the case when $a_{12}^{(1)} \neq 0$, which we denote simply by a since in this case fractional powers appear in the formal solutions.

The key to the discussion of this case is the transformation

$$(13) \qquad x(z) = e^{\lambda z} \operatorname{diag}\{1,t\}\, C_a\, \tilde{x}(t) ,$$

where $z = t^2$ and $C_a = \begin{bmatrix} \sqrt{a} & \sqrt{a} \\ -1 & 1 \end{bmatrix}$, where the squareroot is selected so that in $\operatorname{diag}\{-2\sqrt{a}, 2\sqrt{a}\}$, the entries are consistent with the fixed ordering of all pairs of complex numbers. Then $\tilde{x}$ satisfies $\tilde{x}' = \tilde{A}(t)\tilde{x}$, where $\tilde{A}(t)$ is analytic at ∞ and $\tilde{A}(\infty)$ has the distinct eigenvalues $\pm 2\sqrt{a}$. We call $\tilde{x}' = \tilde{A}(t)\tilde{x}$ the associated system corresponding to $x' = A(z)x$. The following theorem contains the transfer principle for analytic equivalence.

THEOREM 4. Two systems $x' = A(z)x$ and $y' = B(z)y$ (in case II with $a \neq 0$) are analytically equivalent iff their associated systems are strictly equivalent.

As a consequence of this result and Theorem 1, we obtain :

THEOREM 5. Assume $x' = A(z)x$, where $A(z)$ has the form (4), $A_o \cong \begin{bmatrix} \lambda & 0 \\ 1 & \lambda \end{bmatrix}$, and $\operatorname{tr} A_o A_1 \neq \operatorname{tr} A_o \operatorname{tr} A_1$ (this implies that $a \neq 0$). Let the associated system $\tilde{x}' = \tilde{A}(t)\tilde{x}$ have the unique formal fundamental solution matrix $\tilde{F}(t)^{\tilde{\Lambda}'} \exp[-2\sqrt{a}t, 2\sqrt{a}t]$, where $\tilde{\Lambda} = (\operatorname{tr} A_1 - \frac{1}{2})I$, and $\tilde{F}(t) = I + \sum_{1}^{\infty} \tilde{F}_m t^{-m}$. Then a complete system of analytic invariants for the differential system $x' = A(z)x$ is given by

$$(14) \qquad \operatorname{tr} A_o ,\ \operatorname{tr} A_1 ,\ \operatorname{tr} A_o A_1 ,\ \text{and}\ \gamma ,$$

<u>where</u> $\lim_{m \to \infty} \tilde{F}_m \operatorname{diag}\{(-1)^m, 1\}(4\sqrt{a})^m/\Gamma(m) = \begin{bmatrix} 0 & \gamma \\ \gamma & 0 \end{bmatrix}$.

The first three quantities in (14) are a complete system of formal analytic invariants. In this case it can be shown (contrary to case I) that formal analytic transformations between equivalent systems are unique modulo a non-zero constant scalar factor. Hence there is a formal Birkhoff invariant in this case which has no analogue in case I. It is calculated from the first three coefficients of $A(z)$. There is a meromorphic analogue of the analytic transfer principle of Theorem 4 and from it and Theorem 3 one can obtain a complete system of meromorphic invariants in this case. For the proof of all these results, the reader is refered to [3] and [4]. For an application of the results to second order linear differential equations, the reader is refered to [5].

REFERENCES

[1] BIRKHOFF G.D. Equivalent singular points for ordinary linear differential equations. Math. Ann. 74 (1913), 134-139.

[2] GANTMACHER F.R. Theory of Matrices, vol. II. Chelsea, New York, 1959.

[3] JURKAT W., LUTZ D., PEYERIMHOFF A. Birkhoff invariants and effective calculations for meromorphic linear differential equations, I. J. Math. Anal. Appl. (1976).

[4] JURKAT W., LUTZ D., PEYERIMHOFF A. Birkhoff invariants and effective calculations for meromorphic linear differential equations, II. Houston, J. Math. (1976).

[5] JURKAT W., LUTZ D., PEYERIMHOFF A. Invariants and canonical forms for meromorphic second order differential equations. Proc. Second Scheveningen Conf. on Differential Equations, North. Holland Pub. Co. (1976).

[6] MASANI P. On a result of G.D. Birkhoff on linear differential equations. Proc. Amer. Math. Soc. 10 (1959), 696-698.

[7] TURRITTIN H.L. Reduction of ordinary differential equations to the Birkhoff canonical form. Trans. Amer. Math. Soc. 107 (1963), 485-507.

INSTITUT DE RECHERCHE MATHEMATIQUE AVANCEE
Laboratoire Associé au C.N.R.S.
7, rue René Descartes
67084 STRASBOURG Cédex

REMARQUES SUR LES EQUATIONS DIFFERENTIELLES A POINTS SINGULIERS IRREGULIERS

par B. MALGRANGE

§ 1. GENERALITES SUR LES DEVELOPPEMENTS ASYMPTOTIQUES

On se place au voisinage de 0 dans $\mathbb{C}$; on fait un "éclatement réel" de 0 ; i.e. on passe en coordonnées polaires $(\rho,\theta) \in \mathbb{R}_+ \times \mathbb{T}$; on note S l'image réciproque $\{0\} \times \mathbb{T}$ de 0, et on fabrique un faisceau $\mathcal{A}$ sur S de la manière suivante :

Soit U un ouvert de S, et $\tilde{U}$ le secteur angulaire de $\mathbb{C}$ associé i.e. $\{(\rho,\theta) | \rho > 0,\ \theta \in U\}$; soit $\bar{\mathcal{A}}(U)$ l'ensemble des germes en 0 de fonctions holomorphes dans U, admettant en 0 un "développement asymptotique de Taylor" ; de façon plus précise, pour $f \in \bar{\mathcal{A}}(U)$, il existe une série formelle $\Sigma a_n t^n \in \mathbb{C}[[t]]$ tel qu'on ait, pour tout p, et pour $t \to 0$

$$f(t) - \sum_{0}^{p} a_n t^n = O(t^{p+1}),$$

le "Oh" étant uniforme dans tout secteur $\tilde{V}$ tel que V soit relativement compact dans U (en abrégé : $V \subset\subset U$). On définit alors $\mathcal{A}$ comme le faisceau associé au préfaisceau $U \mapsto \bar{\mathcal{A}}(U)$.

Un théorème classique de Ritt nous assure que, si $U \neq S$, l'application "série de Taylor" : $\bar{\mathcal{A}}(U) \to \mathbb{C}[[t]]$ est surjective (voir par exemple une démonstration dans [5]). Dans la suite, cette application sera notée $f \mapsto \hat{f}$.

Soit $\mathcal{A}_0$ le sous-faisceau des $f \in \mathcal{A}$ vérifiant $\hat{f} = 0$. Considérons un recouvrement $\mathcal{U} = \{U_i\}$ de S par des ouverts connexes $\neq S$, et soit $g \in \mathbb{C}[[t]]$, donné ; pour tout i, soit $f_i \in \Gamma(U_i, \mathcal{A})$, qui représente g, i.e. qui vérifie $\hat{f}_i = g$; dans $U_i \cap U_j$, on a manifestement $f_i - f_j \in \Gamma(U_i \cap U_j, \mathcal{A}_0)$; la classe de cohomologie de $\{f_i - f_j\}$ dans $H^1(S, \mathcal{A}_0)$ ne dépend que de g (détails laissés au lecteur), d'où une application $\tilde{\gamma} : \mathbb{C}[[t]] \to H^1(S, \mathcal{A}_0)$ dont on voit aussitôt que le noyau est égal à $\mathbb{C}\{t\}$, ensemble des séries convergentes en 0.

<u>Proposition 1.1</u> : <u>L'application $\tilde{\gamma}$ définit un isomorphisme</u> $\gamma : \mathbb{C}[[t]]/\mathbb{C}\{t\} \to H^1(S, \mathcal{A}_0)$.

Il suffit de montrer que γ est surjective ; en fait, on va démontrer ce résultat en utilisant un calcul du H^2 à la Dolbeault; soit, pour cela $\mathcal{C}$ l'espace des germes en 0 de fonctions $\mathcal{C}^\infty$ sur $\mathbb{C}$ (identifié à $\mathbb{R}^2$), $\mathcal{P}$ le sous-espace de $\mathcal{C}$ des fonctions plates en 0, i.e. ayant un développement de Taylor (en t et $\bar{t}$) nul en 0. On définit une application $\alpha : \mathbb{C}[[t]]/\mathbb{C}\{t\} \to \mathcal{P}/\frac{\partial}{\partial \bar{t}}\mathcal{P}$ de la manière suivante :

Soit $g \in \mathbb{C}[[t]]$; on prend un $h \in \mathcal{C}$ dont la série de Taylor $\hat{g}$ en 0 soit égale à g ; on a $\frac{\partial h}{\partial \bar{t}} \in \mathcal{P}$, et la classe de $\frac{\partial h}{\partial \bar{t}}$ modulo $\frac{\partial}{\partial \bar{t}}\mathcal{P}$ ne dépend que de g ; on la note $\alpha(g)$;

<u>Lemme 1.2</u> : <u>L'application</u> α <u>est un isomorphisme</u>.

Ceci résulte immédiatement de la surjectivité de $\frac{\partial}{\partial \bar{t}} : \mathcal{C} \to \mathcal{C}$.

[Une manière "plus savante" de dire les choses est de considérer le morphisme de complexes suivant, où les flèches verticales sont les applications "série de Taylor" :

$$\begin{array}{ccccccccc}
0 & \to & \mathbb{C}\{t\} & \longrightarrow & \mathcal{C} & \xrightarrow{\frac{\partial}{\partial \bar{t}}} & \mathcal{C} & \longrightarrow & 0 \\
 & & \downarrow & & \downarrow & & \downarrow & & \\
0 & \to & \mathbb{C}[[t]] & \to & \mathbb{C}[[t,\bar{t}]] & \xrightarrow{\frac{\partial}{\partial \bar{t}}} & \mathbb{C}[[t,\bar{t}]] & \to & 0
\end{array}$$

Les lignes sont exactes, et il suffit alors d'appliquer la suite exacte de cohomologie pour avoir les résultats cherchés.]

Soit maintenant $\tilde{\mathcal{P}}$ la restriction à S du faisceau des fonctions $\mathcal{C}^\infty$ sur $\mathbb{R}_+ \times \mathbb{T}$, et plates sur S ; si π désigne la projection évidente (= celle définie par les coordonnées polaires) $\mathbb{R}_+ \times \mathbb{T} \to \mathbb{C}$, on a $\pi_*(\tilde{\mathcal{P}}) = \mathcal{P}$; de plus $\tilde{\mathcal{P}}$ est manifestement mou, donc $H^i(S,\tilde{\mathcal{P}}) = 0$, $i \geq 1$; enfin, l'application $\frac{\partial}{\partial \bar{t}}$ se relève en un morphisme de faisceaux $\tilde{\mathcal{P}} \to \tilde{\mathcal{P}}$, qu'on notera $\frac{\partial}{\partial \bar{t}}$, et dont le noyau est égal à $\mathcal{A}_0$.

<u>Lemme 1.3</u> : <u>La suite</u> $0 \to \mathcal{A}_0 \to \tilde{\mathcal{P}} \xrightarrow{\frac{\partial}{\partial \bar{t}}} \tilde{\mathcal{P}} \to 0$ <u>est exacte</u>.

Soit V un fermé de S, et $f \in \tilde{\mathcal{P}}(V)$; f prolonge en $f_1 \in \tilde{\mathcal{P}}(S)$ (immédiat), et il existe un $g \in \mathcal{P}$ unique tel qu'on ait $f_1 = \pi^* g$; soit $h \in \mathcal{E}$ tel qu'on ait $\frac{\partial h}{\partial \bar{t}} = g$; la série de Taylor $\hat{h}$ de h en 0 ne contient pas de termes en $\bar{t}$; donc, si $V \neq S$, on pourra corriger h par $h_1 \in \mathcal{A}(V)$, tel qu'on ait $\hat{h}_1 = \hat{h}$; si l'on pose $k = \pi^*(h - h_1) \in \tilde{\mathcal{P}}(V)$, il est clair que l'on a $\frac{\partial k}{\partial t} = f$.

Le lemme précédent, joint à la mollesse de $\widetilde{\mathcal{P}}$ donne un isomorphisme: $H^1(S, \mathcal{A}_o) \xrightarrow{\beta} \Gamma(S,\widetilde{\mathcal{P}})/\frac{\partial}{\partial t}\Gamma(S,\widetilde{\mathcal{P}})$; on a $\Gamma(S,\widetilde{\mathcal{P}}) = \mathcal{P}$ et d'autre part, l'on s'assure facilement que le diagramme

$$\begin{array}{ccc} \mathbb{C}[[t]]/\mathbb{C}\{t\} & \xrightarrow{\ \gamma\ } & H^1(S, \mathcal{A}_o) \\ & {\scriptstyle\alpha}\searrow \quad \swarrow{\scriptstyle\beta} & \\ & \mathcal{P}/\frac{\partial}{\partial t}\mathcal{P} & \end{array}$$

est commutatif ; cela démontre la proposition 1.1.

§ 2. UN THEOREME DE DUALITE

On va appliquer les considérations précédentes dans une situation "globale" : soient X une courbe analytique complexe compacte connexe, A un ensemble fini et non vide $\{a_1,\ldots,a_p\}$ de points de X, et V un fibré vectoriel holomorphe sur X, qu'on peut supposer sans inconvénients être le fibré trivial $X \times \mathbb{C}^n$. Désignons par $\mathcal{O}$ (resp.Ω) le faisceau des fonctions (resp. des 1 formes) holomorphes sur X, et par $\mathcal{O}_V$ (resp. M_V) le faisceau des sections holomorphes de V (resp. des sections méromorphes de V, avec pôles dans A). Soit D une connexion sur V, avec pôles dans A, i.e. une application

$$D : M_V \to M_V \underset{\mathcal{O}}{\otimes} \Omega$$

vérifiant, pour $f \in \mathcal{O}$, $\varphi \in M_V$: $D(f\varphi) = fD\varphi + \varphi \otimes df$.
[Le lecteur pourra vérifier que, en coordonnées locales, ceci n'est rien d'autre qu'une équation différentielle du 1er ordre : $\varphi \mapsto \frac{d\varphi}{dt} + M\varphi$, M une matrice à coefficients méromorphes avec pôles dans A].
En prenant les sections, on trouve un complexe

$$(K^{\cdot}) \quad \Gamma(X,M_V) \xrightarrow{D} \Gamma(X,M_V \underset{\mathcal{O}}{\otimes} \Omega)$$

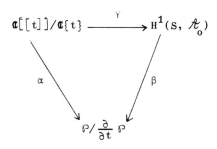

dont on se propose d'interpréter la cohomologie. Dans le cas où les pôles de D sont des points singuliers réguliers, il est bien connu [2] qu'on obtient ainsi la cohomologie de X - A, à valeurs dans le système local "(V,D) restreint à X - A", mais que ceci n'est plus vrai en général ; cela peut se voir ainsi : soit S_V le faisceau sur X des sections de V, holomorphes sur X - A, et admettant éventuellement des singularités essentielles sur A (en d'autres termes, $S_V = i_* i^* \mathcal{O}_V$, i désignant l'injection $X - A \to X$). Le faisceau S_V/M_V est concentré sur A ; soit $a \in A$; on sait que l'application

$$D : S_{V,a}/M_{V,a} \to (S_{V,a}/M_{V,a}) \underset{\mathcal{O}_a}{\otimes} \Omega_a$$

est surjective, et que son noyau N_a est de dimension finie, égale à $i_a(D)$, l'irrégularité de D en a (voir [3]).

D'autre part, il est connu que les faisceaux M_V et S_V sont acycliques , i.e. qu'on a, pour $i \geq 1$: $H^i(X,M_V) = 0$ et $H^i(X,S_V) = 0$ (le dernier résultat parce que toute "surface de Riemann" non compacte, en l'occurence X - A, est une variété de Stein ; le permier est, par exemple, un cas particulier du "vanishing theorem" de Kodaira-Serre) ; donc, de la suite exacte $0 \to M_V \to S_V \to S_V/M_V \to 0$, on déduit une suite exacte

$$0 \to \Gamma(X,M_V) \to \Gamma(X,S_V) \to \Gamma(X,S_V/M_V) \to 0 .$$

En désignant par $(S^\cdot)$ le complexe analogue à $K^\cdot$ avec M_V remplacé par S_V, on tire de là une suite exacte

$$0 \to H^0(K^\cdot) \to H^0(S^\cdot) \to \bigoplus_i N_{a_i} \to H^1(K^\cdot) \to H^1(S^\cdot) \to 0$$

enfin les groupes de cohomologie $H^i(S^\cdot)$ s'identifient aux groupes de cohomologie de X - A, à valeurs dans le système local défini par (V,D) (i.e. à valeurs dans le faisceau des $f \in \mathcal{O}_V|X - A$ qui vérifient $Df = 0$; ceci résulte, par un argument bien connu, du fait que X est un Stein]. Cela démontre le résultat annoncé plus haut, et, accessoirement, le résultat suivant dont nous aurons besoin.

<u>Lemme 2.1</u> : <u>Les $H^i(K^\cdot)$ sont de dimension finie sur</u> $\mathbb{C}$.

Soit maintenant $\tilde{X}$ l'espace obtenu en faisant un éclatement réel des points a_i, comme au paragraphe 1 ; on appelle π la projection $\tilde{X} \to X$, $S_i = \pi^{-1}(a_i)$, $S = \cup S_i$; on note $\mathcal{A}_o$ le faisceau suivant sur $\tilde{X}$: sur $\tilde{X} - S \sim X - A$, $\mathcal{A}_o$ est le faisceau structural $\mathcal{O}$; sur S_i, $\mathcal{A}_o$ est le faisceau défini précédemment qu'on recolle de la façon évidente avec $\mathcal{A}_o | \tilde{X} - S$.

Soient V^* le fibré dual de V, et $D^* : M_{V^*} \to M_{V^*} \otimes_{\mathcal{O}} \Omega$ connexion duale de D ; rappelons que cette dernière est définie par la formule $d\langle\varphi,\psi\rangle = \langle D\varphi,\psi\rangle + \langle\varphi, D^*\psi\rangle$, $\varphi \in M_V$, $\psi \in M_{V^*}$; désignons enfin par $\mathcal{A}_o(V^*)$ le faisceau des sections de $\mathcal{A}_o$ à valeurs dans V^*, et par $\mathcal{A}_o(V^*, D^*)$ le sous-faisceau du précédent formé des φ qui vérifient $D^*\varphi = 0$. Le résultat principal de ce paragraphe est le théorème suivant, qui m'a été proposé comme conjecture par P. Deligne sous une forme légèrement différente.

Théorème 2.2 : Le dual de $H^i(K^\cdot)$ est naturellement isomorphe à $H^{2-i}(\tilde{X}, \mathcal{A}_o(V^*, D^*))$.

La démonstration va se faire en trois étapes.

i) Désignons par $\mathcal{D}'$ le faisceau des distributions (= courants de degré 0) sur X, $\mathcal{D}'_A$ le sous-faisceau des sections de $\mathcal{D}'$ à support dans A, et posons $\mathcal{P}' = \mathcal{D}'/\mathcal{D}'_A$; c'est le faisceau des "distributions sur $X - A$, prolongeables à X" ; soient $\mathcal{P}'_V = \mathcal{P}' \otimes_{\mathcal{O}} \mathcal{O}_V$, et ${}^{(p,q)}\mathcal{P}'_V$ le faisceau des sections "de type (p,q)" de $\mathcal{P}'_V$; il est bien connu que $d'' : \mathcal{P}'_V \to {}^{(0,1)}\mathcal{P}'_V$ est surjective, et a pour noyau M_V ; en vertu de l'acyclicité de M_V, et de celle de $\mathcal{P}'_V$ (ce dernier faisceau est fin), on en déduit une suite exacte

$$0 \to \Gamma(X, M_V) \to \Gamma(X, \mathcal{P}'_V) \xrightarrow{d''} \Gamma(X, {}^{(0,1)}\mathcal{P}'_V) \to 0$$

on raisonne de même avec $M_V \otimes_{\mathcal{O}} \Omega$ au lieu de M_V, et l'on déduit une suite exacte

$$0 \to \Gamma(X, M_V \otimes \Omega) \to \Gamma(X, {}^{(1,0)}\mathcal{P}'_V) \xrightarrow{d''} \Gamma(X, {}^{(1,1)}\mathcal{P}'_V) \to 0$$

par suite la cohomologie de $(K^\cdot)$ est égale à la cohomologie du complexe simple associé au complexe double

$$
\begin{array}{ccc}
\Gamma(X,\mathcal{P}'_V) & \xrightarrow{d''} & \Gamma(X,{}^{(0,1)}\mathcal{P}'_V) \\
\Big\downarrow D & & \Big\downarrow D \\
\Gamma(X,{}^{(1,0)}\mathcal{P}'_V) & \xrightarrow{d''} & \Gamma(X,{}^{(1,1)}\mathcal{P}'_V)
\end{array}
$$

ii) Les espaces $\Gamma(X,{}^{(p,q)}\mathcal{P}'_V)$ sont du type "dual de Fréchet-Schwartz" (et même "dual de Fréchet nucléaire"). Le lemme 2.1, joint à un lemme de Schwartz montre alors que le dual des groupes de cohomologie du complexe précédent s'obtient en considérant le complexe "dual topologique", c'est-à-dire ici le complexe associé au complexe double :

$$
\begin{array}{ccc}
\Gamma(X,{}^{(1,1)}\mathcal{P}_{V*}) & \xleftarrow{d''} & \Gamma(X,{}^{(1,0)}\mathcal{P}_{V*}) \\
\Big\uparrow D^* & & \Big\uparrow D^* \\
\Gamma(X,\mathcal{P}^{(0,1)}{}_{V*}) & \xleftarrow{d''} & \Gamma(X,\mathcal{P}_{V*})
\end{array}
$$

où $\mathcal{P}_{V*}$ désigne le faisceau des sections $\mathcal{C}^\infty$ de V*, plates sur A (cf. paragraphe 1).

iii) Reste à interpréter les groupes de cohomologie de ce dernier complexe ; pour cela, on définit sur $\widetilde{X}$ le faisceau $\widetilde{\mathcal{P}}$ des fonctions de classe $\mathcal{C}^\infty$, et plates sur S. On a un isomorphisme évident $\pi^* : \Gamma(X,\mathcal{P}) \xrightarrow{\sim} \Gamma(\widetilde{X},\widetilde{\mathcal{P}})$; par suite, le complexe précédent est isomorphe au complexe analogue, avec X (resp. $\mathcal{P}_V$) remplacé par $\widetilde{X}$ (resp. $\widetilde{\mathcal{P}}_V$) ; le théorème résulte alors du lemme suivant, appliqué à V* et D* au lieu de V et D.

<u>Lemme 2.3</u> : <u>Considérons le complexe double de faisceaux</u>

$$
\begin{array}{ccc}
\widetilde{\mathcal{P}}_V & \xrightarrow{d''} & {}^{(0,1)}\widetilde{\mathcal{P}}_V \\
\Big\downarrow D & & \Big\downarrow \\
{}^{(1,0)}\widetilde{\mathcal{P}}_V & \xrightarrow{d''} & {}^{(1,1)}\widetilde{\mathcal{P}}_V
\end{array}
$$

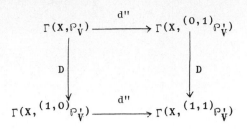

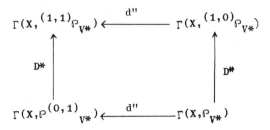

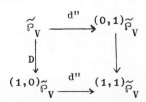

<u>Alors, la cohomologie du complexe simple associé vaut</u> $\mathcal{A}_0(V,D)$ <u>en degré</u> 0 <u>et</u> 0 <u>en degrés</u> $\neq 0$.

En appliquant le lemme (1.3), on voit qu'il revient au même de considérer le complexe (= l'application $\mathcal{A}_0(V) \xrightarrow{D} \mathcal{A}_0(V)$; par définition, son noyau est égal à $\mathcal{A}_0(V,D)$; d'autre part, le fait que cette application soit surjective résulte du théorème fondamental de la théorie des développements asymptotiques au voisinage d'un point singulier irrégulier (voir appendice). D'où le lemme et le théorème.

§ 3. UN PROBLEME DE MODULES

Nous revenons ici à la situation locale du paragraphe 1, et aux notations correspondantes. Nous allons montrer rapidement comment une "variante non commutative des considérations qui s'y trouvent permet de donner une systématisation de certains calculs de Balser-Jurkat-Lutz [1] relatives aux "invariants de Birkhoff". Des idées très voisines de celles exposées ici se trouvent dans Sibuya [4].

Soit n un entier fixé, et soit $G = G\ell(n,\mathbb{C}\{t\})$ l'ensemble des matrices carrées holomorphes inversibles d'ordre n en $0 \in \mathbb{C}$; posons de même $\hat{G} = G\ell(n,\mathbb{C}[[t]])$. Soit Λ le faisceau $G\ell(n,\mathcal{A})$, et soit Λ_0 le sous-faisceau des $A \in \Lambda$ qui vérifient $\hat{A}$ = identité. Une construction analogue à celle du paragraphe 1 permet de définir une application $\gamma : \hat{G}/G \to H^1(S,\Lambda_0)$; explicitons-la rapidement : soit $\mathcal{U} = \{U_i\}$ un recouvrement de S par des ouverts connexes, et $\neq S$; soit $A \in \hat{G}$; on choisit, pour chaque i, $B_i \in \Gamma(U_i,\Lambda)$ vérifiant $\hat{B}_i = A$; alors, on a $B_iB_j^{-1} \in \Gamma(U_i \cap U_j,\Lambda_0)$; d'où une classe de cohomologie dans $H^1(S,\Lambda_0)$, qui ne dépend manifestement que de la classe à droite AG, et définit ainsi un $\gamma : \hat{G}/G \to H^1(S,\Lambda_0)$.

<u>Théorème 3.1</u> : <u>L'application</u> γ <u>est bijective.</u>

Ce résultat est essentiellement équivalent à un théorème de Sibuya (voir [1], théorème B p.75, ou [4], théorème 1). Indiquons, sans entrer dans les détails, qu'on peut en donner une démonstration analogue à celle de la proposition 1.1, quoiqu'évidemment plus délicate.

Cela posé, soit r un entier ≥ 0, fixé une fois pour toutes et soit M une matrice carrée d'ordre n, à coefficients dans $\mathbb{C}\{t\}$ (on écrit cela $M \in \mathcal{G}$); on considère l'opérateur différentiel P défini par

$DF = t^{r+1}\frac{dF}{dt} + MF$, $F \in \mathbb{C}\{t\}^n$ [il reviendrait au même de considérer la connexion $F \mapsto dF + t^{-r-1}MF\,dt$]; Si $A \in G$, le changement de base $F = AG$ transforme l'opérateur donné en $A^{-1}DA = t^{r+1}\frac{d}{dr} + N$, avec N
$N = t^{r+1}A^{-1}\frac{dA}{dt} + A^{-1}MA$; on posera pour simplifier $N = M^A$.

Si D est à point singulier régulier, et si l'on a $N \in \mathfrak{g}$, et $A \in \hat{G}$ tels qu'on ait $N = M^A$, on sait que, nécessairement A converge; par contre, si D a un point singulier irrégulier, il se peut que A diverge et même qu'il n'existe aucun $B \in G$ vérifiant $N = M^B$; autrement dit, N peut être "formellement équivalente à M" sans lui être "analytiquement équivalente". Dans la suite, M étant donné une fois pour toutes, on se propose, en gros, de classer les N formellement équivalentes à M, modulo l'équivalence analytique. De façon précise, on considère l'ensemble (E) des couples $(N,A) \in \mathfrak{g}\times\hat{G}$ qui vérifient $M^A = N$; on munit E de la relation d'équivalence (R) suivante : $(N,A) \sim (N',A')$ s'il existe $B \in G$ tel qu'on ait $A' = AB$ (et par conséquent $N' = N^B$).

Désignons d'autre part $\Lambda_o(M)$ le sous-faisceau de Λ_o formé des A qui vérifient $M^A = M$; on a alors le théorème suivant

Théorème 3.2 : Il existe une bijection canonique $\delta : E/R \to H^1(S,\Lambda_o(M))$.
Cette bijection se définit ainsi ; prenons $(N,A) \in \mathfrak{g} \times \hat{G}$, avec $M^A = N$, et prenons un recouvrement $\mathcal{U} = \{U_i\}$ de S par des intervalles ouverts assez petits (par exemple, de longueur $< \frac{\pi}{r}$) ; la théorie des développements asymptotiques (cf. appendice) nous apprend qu'il existe des $B_i \in \Gamma(U_i,\Lambda)$ vérifiant $\hat{B}_i = A$, $M^{B_i} = N$; on a donc

$B_iB_j^{-1} \in \Gamma(U_i \cap U_j, \Lambda_o(M))$, d'où comme précédemment une application $E \to H^1(S,\Lambda_o(M))$, dont on vérifie immédiatement qu'elle passe au quotient par R ; l'injectivité de l'application $\delta : E/R \to H^1(S,\Lambda_o(M))$ ainsi définie est immédiate : si (A',N') définit la même classe que (A,N), et que A' est représentée par des B_i', on a (après avoir éventuellement remplacé $\mathcal{U}$ par un recouvrement plus fin) : $B_i'B_j'^{-1} = C_iB_iB_j^{-1}C_j^{-1}$, $C_i \in \Gamma(U_i,\Lambda_o(M))$, d'où $B_i^{-1}C_i^{-1}B_i' = B_j^{-1}C_j^{-1}B_j'$; par suite, il existe $D \in \Gamma(S,\Lambda) = G$ vérifiant, pour tout i : $B_i^{-1}C_i^{-1}B_i' = D$, ou encore $C_i^{-1}B_i' = B_iD$; en prenant les développements de Taylor en O, il vient $A' = AD$; d'où le résultat cherché.

Montrons enfin que δ est surjective ; soit $C \in H^1(S,\Lambda_o(M))$; en choisissant un recouvrement assez fin, γ peut être représenté par des $C_{ij} \in \Gamma(U_i \cap U_j,\Lambda_o(M))$; d'après le théorème 3.1, et quitte à raffiner le recouvrement considéré, il existe $A \in \hat{G}$ et des $B_i \in \Gamma(U_i,\Lambda_o)$ tels qu'on ait $\hat{B}_i = A$, $B_i B_j^{-1} = C_{ij}$; alors, dans $\tilde{U}_i \cap \tilde{U}_j$, on a $M^{B_i} = M^{B_j}$, donc il existe $N \in \mathcal{G}$ tel qu'on ait $M^{B_i} = N$ dans U_i ; il est clair qu'on a alors $\delta(N,A) = C$; d'où le théorème.

Pour terminer, remarquons que les théorèmes sur les développements asymptotiques nous montrent ceci : si $\mathcal{U}$ est un recouvrement fini de S par des intervalles U_i de longueur $< \frac{\pi}{r}$, alors les éléments de $\delta(E/R)$ [et par conséquent tous les éléments de $H^1(S,\Lambda_o(M)$] se laissent représenter par des cocycles de $\mathcal{U}$; il en résulte immédiatement que les éléments de E/R peuvent tous être "représentés" par les points d'un espace de dimension finie, à savoir par les cocycles de $\mathcal{U}$; en particulier, les N qui sont formellement équivalents à M peuvent être représentés, modulo l'équivalence analytique, par les points d'un espace de dimension finie. Naturellement, ces "représentations" seront en général surjectives, mais non bijectives, et les problèmes précis de modules qu'on est alors amené à se poser risquent de comporter des difficultés non triviales de passage au quotient. Dans le cas où les valeurs propres de la partie principale de M sont distinctes, ces questions étudiées dans [1] grâce à une analyse précise du "phénomène de Stokes". Dans le cas général une étude analogue s'imposerait ; nous ne l'aborderons pas ici.

§ 4. APPENDICE

Le théorème qui a été utilisé aux paragraphes 2 et 3 est le suivant :

Théorème 4.1 : Soit r un entier ≥ 0 ; et soit Φ une fonction holomorphe de $(t,Y) \in \mathbb{C} \times \mathbb{C}^n$ au voisinage de $(0, Y_o)$. Soit U un intervalle ouvert de S de mesure $< \frac{\pi}{r}$; supposons qu'il existe $Z \in \mathbb{C}[[t]]^n$, avec $Z(0) = Y_o$ qui vérifie $t^{r+1}\frac{dZ}{dt} = \Phi(t,Z)$; alors il existe $Y \in \bar{\mathcal{A}}(U)^n$ vérifiant $\hat{Y} = Z$, et $t^{r+1}\frac{dY}{dt} = \Phi(t,Y)$.

Quoique ce résultat soit "bien connu", je n'en ai pas de référence explicite. Il est essentiellement démontré dans [5]; voir à ce propos la remarque finale de [3], page 175.

BIBLIOGRAPHIE

[1] W. Balser, W. B. Jurkat, D. A. Lutz : Birkhoff invariants and Stokes multipliers for meromorphic linear differential equations, 1976 (à paraître).

[2] P. Deligne : Equations différentielles à points singuliers réguliers, Lect. Notes in Math., n° 163, Springer (1970).

[3] B. Malgrange : Sur les points singuliers des équations différentielle différentielles, l'Enseignement mathématique, t. XX, 1-2 (1974), p.147-176.

[4] Y. Sibuya : Stokes Phenomena, 1977 (à paraître au Bull. A. M. S.).

[5] W. Wasow : Asymptotic expansions for ordinary differential equations, Interscience Publ. (1965).

REGULAR SINGULARITIES ALONG NORMAL CROSSINGS

by

A.R.P. VAN DEN ESSEN

§0. Linear differential equations and modules over rings of differential operators.

Consider the linear differential equation

(0.1) $$y^{(n)} + a_{n-1}(z)y^{(n-1)} + \ldots + a_0(z)y = 0$$

where $a_0(z),\ldots,a_{n-1}(z)$ are meromorphic functions in a neighbourhood of $0 \in \mathbb{C}$. This is a particular case of

(0.2) $$\frac{dy}{dz} = A(z)y$$

where $A(z)$ is an $n\times n$ matrix, the elements of which being meromorphic functions in a neighbourhood of 0 in $\mathbb{C}$, and where y is a column vector of n such functions.

The problem is to solve equation (2).

If $A(z)$ is holomorphic in $z = 0$ it is well-known that this equation can be solved by Cauchys existence theorem. So from now on we can assume that A is of the form

$$A = z^{-p}\tilde{A}$$

where $p \in \mathbb{N}$ ($\mathbb{N}$ is the collection of positive integers, so $0 \notin \mathbb{N}$) and $\tilde{A}$ is a matrix of functions holomorphic in 0 and $\tilde{A}(0) \neq 0$. So we get

(0.3) $$z^p \frac{dy}{dz} = \tilde{A}.y.$$

In the investigation of (0.3) it appears that there is a great difference between the cases $p = 1$ and $p > 1$. More explicitely we have: If Φ is a so called fundamental matrix of (0.3) (for more details we refer to [1]) then Φ is of the form:

$$\Phi(z) = S(z)z^Q$$

for all $0 < |z| < a$, for suitable $a > 0$, where S is a single valued analytic matrix on $0 < |z| < a$ and Q is a constant matrix. When

$p = 1$, then S has at most a pole at $z = 0$. But if $p > 1$ then S can have an essential singularity at $z = 0$.

This leads to the (Fuchsian) classification of singular points of (0.3): $z = 0$ is called a regular singular point of (0.3) if S has a pole at $z = 0$ at most. $z = 0$ is called an irregular singular point of (0.3) otherwise. The above arguments give rise to the following question:

How can we see from $\tilde{A}$ (or A) if $z = 0$ is a regular singular point of (0.3) i.e. can we give necessary and sufficient conditions on $\tilde{A}$ (or A) to be sure that $z = 0$ is a regular singular point of (0.3)?

Let us return to the problem of solving equation (0.2). <u>Therefore transform this equation into a simpler equation</u>. We make use of linear transformations i.e.

(0.4) $\quad y = Tw$

where T is an $n\times n$ matrix of meromorphic functions in a neighbourhood of 0 and $\det T$ is not identically zero. Then the following fact can be proved:

$$(0.5)\quad \begin{cases} z = 0 \text{ is a regular singular point of (0.2) iff there} \\ \text{exists a transformation of the form (0.4) such that} \\ \dfrac{dw}{dz} = B.w \\ \text{where } zB \text{ is holomorphic in } z = 0. \end{cases}$$

If this is the case we can even choose T in such a way that $zB \in M_{n\times n}(\mathbb{C})$. So we see that if $z = 0$ is a regular singular point of (0.2), that we have reduced our problem of solving the equation (0.2) to a simpler one, namely

(0.6) $\quad z\dfrac{dy}{dz} = C.y,$

$C \in M_{n\times n}(\mathbb{C})$. (If R is a ring, we denote by $M_{n\times n}(R)$ the ring of $n\times n$

matrices with coefficients in R.) As is well-known a solution of this equation is given by the fundamental matrix z^C (see [1]). So we can solve the equation (0.2) if z = 0 is a regular singular point of (0.2). The moral of the preceeding discussion is, that it seems useful to study the behaviour of the equation (0.2) under linear transformations of the form (0.4) in more detail. To do this we want to develope a formalism suitable for studying this kind of problems.

The main idea is to interprete the transformation y = Tw as a coordinate transformation of some module. More precisely:

Let $C\langle z\rangle_z$ denote the field of germs of meromorphic functions in a neighbourhood of 0 and let $C\langle z\rangle_z^n$ denote the free $C\langle z\rangle_z$-module with standard basis $(e_1,\ldots,e_n)$, where $e_i = (0,\ldots,1,\ldots,0)$. We get a map

$$D = \frac{d}{dz} - A(z) \ : \ C\langle z\rangle_z^n \to C\langle z\rangle_z^n$$

defined by

$$D : \begin{pmatrix} \xi_1 \\ \vdots \\ \xi_n \end{pmatrix} \to \frac{d}{dz}\begin{pmatrix} \xi_1 \\ \vdots \\ \xi_n \end{pmatrix} - A(z)\begin{pmatrix} \xi_1 \\ \vdots \\ \xi_n \end{pmatrix}$$

Then D is an additive map satisfying the property

(0.7) $\quad D(av) = \frac{da}{dz}.v + aDv, \quad$ all $a \in C\langle z\rangle_z$, all $v \in C\langle z\rangle_z^n$

Such a map is called a differential operator on $C\langle z\rangle_z^n$ with respect to $\frac{d}{dz}$. Using property (0.7) it is not difficult to prove that D is completely determined by the elements De_i $(1 \leq i \leq n)$. Expressing this elements with respect to the $C\langle z\rangle_z$-basis $(e_1,\ldots,e_n)$ we find that D is completely determined by the matrix A, which has in his columns the images of the elements $De_1,\ldots,De_n$ (expressed in coordinates with respect to the $C\langle z\rangle_z$-basis $(e_1,\ldots,e_n)$). This matrix will denoted by Mat(D,(e)). Now let $(f) = (f_1,\ldots,f_n)$ be another $C\langle z\rangle_z$-basis of $C\langle z\rangle_z^n$ satisfying (f) = T(e). We then find:

(0.8) $\quad \mathrm{Mat}(D,(f)) = T^{-1}AT - T^{-1}\frac{d}{dz}T.$

Finally observe: If y satisfies (0.2), then w defined by $y = Tw$ satisfies:

(0.9) $\quad \frac{dw}{dz} = (T^{-1}AT - T^{-1}\frac{d}{dz}T)w.$

We are now able to formulate the question posed in the beginning of this section in the language of modules and differential operators. By (0.5), (0.8) and (0.9) we have:

(0.10) $\left\{ \begin{array}{l} z = 0 \text{ is a regular singular point of the equation } \frac{dy}{dz} = Ay \\ \text{iff there exists a } C\langle z\rangle_z\text{-basis } (f) = (f_1,\ldots,f_n) \text{ of } C\langle z\rangle_z^n \\ \text{such that the differential operator } D = \frac{d}{dz} - A : C\langle z\rangle_z^n \to C\langle z\rangle_z^n \\ \text{satisfies} \\ \qquad \mathrm{Mat}(zD,(f)) \in M_{n\times n}(C\langle z\rangle). \end{array} \right.$

(0.10) is a first step towards on <u>algebraic definition of the notion of regular singular point</u> of a linear system of differential equations in one complex variable.

Let k be a field and $k((t))$ denotes the field of formal Laurent series in one indeterminate with coefficients in the field k. $\frac{d}{dt}$ is the usual derivation. The next step is to consider finite dimensional $k((t))$-vector spaces equipped with a differential operator D with respect to $\frac{d}{dt}$. It is then possible to define the notion of regular singularity by a similar description as given in (0.10). This is done in [2] in a more general framework.

The important conclusion is: the notion of regular singularity in the case of one variable is a <u>formal</u> notion, i.e. can be expressed in terms of the completion of the ring (for more details we refer to [2]).

More generally, systems of linear partial differential equations can be studied, satisfying an integrability condition. Also in this case the notion of regular singularity (along a divisor) is defined. This can be done by saying that the solutions satisfy a so called moderate growth condition. We refer to [3] where also other equivalent descriptions of this notion are given.

Again we can ask for an algebraic definition of the notion of regular singularity in the style of [2]. As far as we know such an algebraic definition doesn't exist in the case of several variables.

It is the aim of this paper to give an algebraic description in the case that the singularities of the differential equation form a divisor with normal crossings.

§1. Preliminaries and the Main Theorem.

In this section we introduce some of the basic notions. Furthermore we state some well-known results.

Proposition 1.1: Let R be a regular local ring, then R is a unique factorization domain.

Proof: see [4], Appendix 7.

Corollary 1.2: Let R be a regular local ring, $0 \neq f \in R$. Then R_f is a unique factorization domain.

Proof: Immediately from prop.1.1.

Examples 1.3:

(1) If k is a field, we denote by $\mathcal{O}$ the ring $k[[x_1,\dots,x_m]]$ of formal power series in the indeterminates $x_1,\dots,x_m$ and coefficients in k. $\mathcal{O}$ is a regular local ring of dimension m.

(2) If k is a field with a non-trivial valuation and if k is complete with respect to the valuation, then $K_m \underset{D}{\equiv} k\langle x_1,\dots,x_m\rangle$ is defined in [5] (the ring of convergent power series). K_m is regular local ring of dimension m.

Definition 1.4: Let R be a commutative ring and S a multiplicative subset of R. Let M be an R_S-module of finite type. Then an R-submodule M_0 of M is called an R-lattice if

(1) M_0 is an R-module of finite type

(2) $S^{-1}(M_0) = M$.

Definition 1.5: Let A be a ring, $\vartheta : A \to A$ a derivation and M an

A-module. A <u>differential operator</u> D on M with respect to ϑ is:

(1) An additive map $D : M \to M$ satisfying

(2) $D(am) = (\vartheta a)m + aDm$, all $m \in M$, all $a \in A$.

1.6 <u>Connections</u>.

<u>Lemma 1.7</u>: Let $m \in \mathbb{N}$, R a ring; $x_1,\ldots,x_m \in R$. Then equivalent:

(1) There exist derivations $\frac{\partial}{\partial x_1},\ldots,\frac{\partial}{\partial x_m} : R \to R$ satisfying

(a) $\frac{\partial}{\partial x_i}(x_j) = \delta_{ij}$, all $1 \le i, j \le m$.

(b) $[\frac{\partial}{\partial x_i},\frac{\partial}{\partial x_j}] = 0$, all $1 \le i, j \le m$.

(2) There exist

A free R-module Ω^1 of rank m, a free R-module Ω^2 of rank $\binom{m}{2}$

a derivation $d : R \to \Omega^1$, an R-bilinear map $\wedge : \Omega^1 \times \Omega^1 \to \Omega^2$

satisfying: $\wedge(u,v) = -\wedge(v,u)$, all $u,v \in \Omega^1$.

(instead of $\wedge(u,v)$ we will write $u \wedge V$) an additive map

$d_1 : \Omega^1 \to \Omega^2$ satisfying

$$d_1(a\omega) = da \wedge \omega + ad_1\omega \quad , \text{ all } a \in R, \text{ all } \omega \in \Omega^1$$

satisfying:

(a) $dx_1,\ldots,dx_m$ generate Ω^1 as a free R-module.

(b) $dx_i \wedge dx_j$ generate Ω^2 as a free R-module (all $1 \le i < j \le m$).

(c) $d_1 \circ d = 0$.

<u>Proof</u>: (2) $\Rightarrow$ (1) follows immediately from the definitions.

(1) $\Rightarrow$ (2) Define Ω^1 as the free R-module on the symbols $[x_1],\ldots,[x_m]$.

Now define $d : R \to \Omega^1$ by the formula

$$dg = \frac{\partial g}{\partial x_1}[x_1] + \ldots + \frac{\partial g}{\partial x_m}[x_m], \quad \text{all } g \in R.$$

In particular we see:

$$dx_i = [x_i].$$

Define Ω^2 as the free R-module on $\binom{m}{2}$ symbols $[x_i \wedge x_j]$, all $1 \leq i < j \leq m$, and define the map $\wedge : \Omega^1 \times \Omega^1 \to \Omega^2$ by the formula

$$\wedge([x_i],[x_j]) = [x_i \wedge x_j] = -\wedge([x_i],[x_j]), \quad \text{all } 1 \leq i < j \leq m.$$

$$\wedge([x_i],[x_i]) = 0 \quad , \text{ all } 1 \leq i \leq m.$$

Extend $\wedge$ R-bilinearly to a map from $\Omega^1 \times \Omega^1 \to \Omega^2$.

If $u,v \in \Omega^1$ write $u \wedge v$ instead of $\wedge(u,v)$. Finally define $d_1 : \Omega^1 \to \Omega^2$ by the formula:

$$d_1(a_1[x_1]+\ldots+a_m[x_m]) = da_1 \wedge [x_1]+\ldots+da_m \wedge [x_m], \quad \text{all } a_i \in R.$$

Writing out all definitions completes the proof of this lemma.

Let A be a commutative integral domain and let B denote the ring $A[[x_1,\ldots,x_m]]$ of formal power series in the indeterminates $x_1,\ldots,x_m$ with coefficients in A. Let $0 \neq f \in B$. B has derivations $\frac{\partial}{\partial x_1},\ldots,\frac{\partial}{\partial x_m}$ and so we can apply lemma 1.7. We then have the free B-modules Ω^1 and Ω^2 and the maps d, d_1, $\wedge$ as in lemma 1.7. Let $\Omega^1_f = B_f \otimes_B \Omega^1$, then $\Omega^1_f = B_f dx_1 \oplus \ldots \oplus B_f dx_m$. We can extend d, d_1 and $\wedge$ in the obvious way ($d : B_f \to \Omega^1_f$ etc.) and denote this extension d, d_1, $\wedge$. Let now M be a free B_f-module of rank n.

<u>Definition 1.8</u>: A <u>connection</u> on M is an additive map

$$\nabla : M \to \Omega^1_f \otimes_{B_f} M$$

satisfying Leibniz rule i.e.

$$\nabla(gm) = dg \otimes m + g\,\nabla m, \quad \text{all } g \in B_f, \text{ all } m \in M.$$

Let now a connection $\nabla : M \to \Omega^1_f \otimes_{B_f} M$ be given. $\Omega^2_f = B_f \otimes_B \Omega^2$ is a free B_f-module of rank $\binom{m}{2}$. We define a map

$$\nabla_1 : \Omega^1_f \otimes_{B_f} M \to \Omega^2_f \otimes_{B_f} M$$

by the formula:

$$\nabla_1(\omega \otimes m) = d\omega \otimes m + \sum_{i=1}^{1} (\omega \wedge \omega_i) \otimes m_i$$

where

$$\nabla\omega = \sum_{i=1}^{1} \omega_i \otimes m_i .$$

<u>Definition 1.9</u>: The connection ∇ is called <u>integrable</u> if $\nabla_1 \circ \nabla = 0$.

We will now consider the notion of an integrable connection in more detail. Let $\eta \in M$, then $\nabla\eta \in \Omega_f^1 \otimes_{B_f} M$. Since Ω_f^1 is a free B_f-module there exist uniquely determined elements $v_i \in M$ satisfying:

(1.10) $\quad \nabla\eta = dx_1 \otimes v_1 + \ldots + dx_m \otimes v_m.$

From (1.10) we find m maps, $\nabla_{\frac{\partial}{\partial x_1}}, \ldots, \nabla_{\frac{\partial}{\partial x_m}} : M \to M$ defined by

$$\nabla\eta = dx_1 \otimes \nabla_{\frac{\partial}{\partial x_1}}(\eta) + \ldots + dx_m \otimes \nabla_{\frac{\partial}{\partial x_m}}(\eta).$$

It is not difficult to verify that for every $1 \leq i \leq m$ $\nabla_{\frac{\partial}{\partial x_i}}$ is a differential operator on M with respect to $\frac{\partial}{\partial x_i}$. If ∇ is an integrable connection, it follows from the definitions that

$$[\nabla_{\frac{\partial}{\partial x_i}}, \nabla_{\frac{\partial}{\partial x_j}}] = 0, \qquad \text{all } 1 \leq i, j \leq m.$$

More generally, for $a_1, \ldots, a_m \in B_f$ let $\tau = \sum_{i=1}^{m} a_i \frac{\partial}{\partial x_i}$ be a derivation from B_f to B_f then

$$\nabla_\tau \underset{D}{=} \sum_{i=1}^{m} a_i \nabla_{\frac{\partial}{\partial x_i}}$$

is a differential operator on M with respect to τ.

Conversely, for $i = 1, \ldots, m$ let D_i be a differential operator on M with respect to $\frac{\partial}{\partial x_i}$ and assume that

$$[D_i, D_j] = 0, \text{ all } 1 \leq i, j \leq m.$$

then define $\nabla : M \to M$ by

$$\nabla v = \sum_{i=1}^{m} dx_i \otimes D_i v, \qquad \text{all } v \in M.$$

It is left to the reader to verify that ∇ is an integrable connection on M. So using the notation introduced above we have:

$$D_i = \nabla_{\frac{\partial}{\partial x_i}}, \text{ all } 1 \leq i \leq m.$$

Summarizing we can say:

Proposition 1.11: Let M be a free B_f-module of rank n. Then equivalent:

(1) M is equipped with an integrable connection

(2) M is equipped with m pairwise commutating differential operators $D_1,\ldots,D_m$ (D_i is a differential operator with respect to $\frac{\partial}{\partial x_i}$).

1.12 The language of $\mathcal{D}$-modules.

Let again A and B be as above. For all $p,q \in B$ we then have

$$(1.13) \qquad \frac{\partial}{\partial x_i}(pq) = \frac{\partial p}{\partial x_i} q + p \frac{\partial q}{\partial x_i}.$$

Now define for $p \in B$ the operator sending each element $q \in B$ into the element $pq \in B$. We call this operator a differential operator of order zero. For each $1 \leq i \leq m$ we also have an operator $\frac{\partial}{\partial x_i} : B \to B$ sending each $q \in B$ into the element $\frac{\partial q}{\partial x_i} \in B$. This operator is called a differential operator of the first order.

Definition 1.14: The ring of A-linear differential operators of B is the associative A-algebra of all A-linear operators on B which is generated by the zero and first order differential operators.

We denote this ring by $\mathcal{D}$ and sometimes we write

$$\mathcal{D} = B[\frac{\partial}{\partial x_1},\ldots,\frac{\partial}{\partial x_m}]$$

From the definition of $\mathcal{D}$ we see that B appears as a subring of $\mathcal{D}$.

Using (1.13) we find the following relations:

$$[\frac{\partial}{\partial x_i},\frac{\partial}{\partial x_j}] = 0, \quad \text{all } 1 \leq i, j \leq m$$

$$[\frac{\partial}{\partial x_i},p] = \frac{\partial p}{\partial x_i}, \quad \text{all } 1 \leq i \leq m, \quad \text{all } p \in B.$$

We will now use the language of $\mathcal{D}$ - modules to give yet another description of a module equipped with an integrable connection.

Proposition 1.15: Let M be a free B_f-module of rank n. Then equivalent:

(1) M is equipped with an integrable connection ∇.

(2) M is a $\mathcal{D}$-module.

(3) M is equipped with m pairwise commutating differential operators $D_1,\ldots,D_m$ (D_i is a differential operator with respect to $\frac{\partial}{\partial x_i}$, all i).

Proof: The equivalence of (1) and (3) is proved in proposition 1.11.

(2) ⇒ (3): Define the differential operator $D_i : M \to M$ by the formula

$$D_i v = \frac{\partial}{\partial x_i}.v, \quad \text{all } 1 \leq i \leq m, \quad \text{all } v \in M.$$

(3) ⇒ (2): Define: $\frac{\partial}{\partial x_i}.v = D_i v$, all $1 \leq i \leq m$, all $v \in M$.

Then it follows immediately from the definitions that M is equipped with a $\mathcal{D}$-module structure.

Remark 1.16: When we take A = k is a field and $B = k[x_1,\ldots,x_m]$ the ring of polynomials in the indeterminates $x_1,\ldots,x_m$ with coefficients in k then we can also define a ring $\mathcal{D} = k[x_1,\ldots,x_m][\frac{\partial}{\partial x_1},\ldots,\frac{\partial}{\partial x_m}]$, the so called Weyl algebra in m variables with coefficients in k. This ring is often denoted $A_m(k)$. In [6] and [7] Bernstein studies this ring to solve the divison problem of distributions. We also refer to [8] and [9] for more details.

When we take A = k and $B = \mathcal{O}_m = k[[x_1,\ldots,x_m]]$ we get the ring $\mathcal{O}_m[\frac{\partial}{\partial x_1},\ldots,\frac{\partial}{\partial x_m}]$ which will be denoted by $\mathcal{D}_m$.

1.17 The algebraic definition of regular singularity in the one dimensional case.

We will now recall the algebraic definition of regular singularity in the one dimensional case. We refer to [2] and [3] for more details. Let A denote a discrete valuation ring of equicharacteristic zero, K the quotient field of A, t a uniformerising parameter of A, $\frac{d}{dt} : A \to A$ a derivation satisfying $\frac{d}{dt}(t) = 1$, V a K vector space of dimension n. Let $D : V \to V$ be a differential operator on V with respect to $t\frac{d}{dt}$. Then the following theorem can be proved:

Theorem 1.18: The following five conditions are equivalent:

(1) There exists a K-basis $(e) = (e_1,\ldots,e_n)$ of V such that

$$\mathrm{Mat}(D,(e)) \in M_{n\times n}(A).$$

(2) There exists an A-lattice Λ_0 of V such that $D\Lambda_0 \subset \Lambda_0$.

(3) If Λ_1 is any A-lattice in V, then the chain of A lattices

$$\Lambda_1 \subset \Lambda_1 + D\Lambda_1 \subset \Lambda_1 + D\Lambda_1 + D^2\Lambda_1 \subset \ldots \subset V$$

is stationary.

(4) For every $v \in V$ the chain of A modules

$$Av \subset Av + ADv \subset Av + ADv + AD^2v \subset \ldots \subset V$$

is stationary.

(5) There exists an $e \in V$, $e \neq 0$ such that $(e, De, \ldots, D^{n-1}e)$ is a K-basis of V satisfying

$$D^n e + a_{n-1}D^{n-1}e + \ldots + a_0 e = 0, \text{ with } a_0,\ldots,a_{n-1} \in A.$$

Proof: See [2], Th.3.1, Th.4.1 and Corollaire 4.1.

Definition 1.19: With the notations of 1.17 a differential operator $D : V \to V$ is called regular with respect to t, if it satisfies one of the conditions of Th.1.18. We then also say that D is regular with respect to A.

1.20 Statement of the main theorem.

In the rest of this paper we use the following notations:

k : a field of characteristic zero.

m : a positive integer.

$\mathcal{O} = k[[x_1,\ldots,x_m]]$ the ring of formal power series in m indeterminates $x_1,\ldots,x_m$ with coefficients in k.

$\mathfrak{m}$: the maximal ideal of $\mathcal{O}$.

$K_{(i)}$: $k((x_1,\ldots,\hat{x}_i,\ldots,x_m))$ the field of fractions of $k[[x_1,\ldots,x_{i-1},x_{i+1},\ldots,x_m]]$.

$\mathcal{O}_{(i)}$: $K_{(i)}[[x_i]]$ the ring of formal power series in x_i with coefficients in $K_{(i)}$.

$L_{(i)}$: the quotient field of $\mathcal{O}_{(i)}$.

d : a positive integer $\leq m$.

h : a positive integer satisfying $d \leq h \leq m$.

n : a positive integer.

$\mathcal{O}_{x_1\ldots x_d}$: the ring $\mathcal{O}$ localized in $x_1\ldots x_d$.

Λ : a free $\mathcal{O}_{x_1\ldots x_d}$-module of rank n.

$(e) = (e_1,\ldots,e_n)$ a fixed $\mathcal{O}_{x_1\ldots x_d}$-basis of Λ.

$N = \mathcal{O}e_1+\ldots+\mathcal{O}e_n$.

$N_{(i)} = \mathcal{O}_{(i)} \otimes_{\mathcal{O}} N$.

$V_{(i)} = L_{(i)} \otimes_{\mathcal{O}_{x_1\ldots x_d}} \Lambda$.

$\frac{\partial}{\partial x_i}$: The unique extension of $\frac{\partial}{\partial x_i}$ on $\mathcal{O}$ to the quotient field of $\mathcal{O}$.

$D_1,\ldots,D_h$: h differential operators on Λ where D_i corresponds to $x_i\frac{\partial}{\partial x_i}$ for all $1 \leq i \leq d$ and D_i corresponds to $\frac{\partial}{\partial x_i}$ for all $d+1 \leq i \leq h$ and $[D_i,D_j] = 0$, all $1 \leq i, j \leq h$.

Before stating the main theorem (Th. 1.22) we need one more definition.

Let M be an $\mathcal{O}_{x_1 \ldots x_d}$-module of finite type, $D : M \to M$ a differential operator with respect to $x_i \frac{\partial}{\partial x_i}$. Then consider

$$M_{(i)} = K_{(i)}((x_i)) \otimes_{\mathcal{O}_{x_1 \ldots x_d}} M = L_{(i)} \otimes_{\mathcal{O}_{x_1 \ldots x_d}} M.$$

We can extend $x_i \frac{\partial}{\partial x_i}$ to a derivation

$$\vartheta_i : K_{(i)}((x_i)) \to K_{(i)}((x_i))$$

by the formula

$$\vartheta_i\left(\sum_{s=-N}^{\infty} \mu_s x_i^s\right) = \sum_{s=-N}^{\infty} \mu_s . s . x_i^s \quad ; \qquad \mu_s \in K_{(i)}, \text{ all } s.$$

We denote this derivation again by $x_i \frac{\partial}{\partial x_i}$. Now we extend D to a differential operator $D_{L_{(i)}} : M_{(i)} \to M_{(i)}$, with respect to $x_i \frac{\partial}{\partial x_i}$ by:

$$D_{L_{(i)}}(a \otimes m) = (\vartheta_i a) \otimes m + a \otimes Dm, \text{ all } a \in L_{(i)}, \text{ all } m \in M.$$

(It is left to the reader to verify that $D_{L_{(i)}}$ is well-defined).

We shall write D instead of $D_{L_{(i)}}$.

<u>Definition 1.21</u>: The differential operator $D : M \to M$ is <u>called regular with respect to x_i</u> if the differential operator $D : M_{(i)} \to M_{(i)}$ is regular with respect to x_i in the sense of definition 1.19.

Theorem 1.22 (the "main theorem") which follows gives five equivalent conditions on a connection in the situation of a "singular divisor with normal crossings". This will lead to the notion of regular singularity in that case.

<u>In the remainder of section 1 we assume k is algebraically closed.</u>

Let $\Lambda, D_1, \ldots, D_h$ be as above. Using proposition 1.15 we can equivalently say that Λ is equipped with an integrable connection ($A = k[[x_{k+1}, \ldots, x_m]]$ and $B = \mathcal{O} = A[[x_1, \ldots, x_h]]$). The following Theorem will be proved:

Theorem 1.22: The following five conditions are equivalent:

(1) There exist an $\mathcal{O}_{x_1\ldots x_d}$-basis $(b) = (b_1,\ldots,b_n)$ of Λ such that

$$\mathrm{Mat}(D_i,(b)) \in M_{n\times n}(\mathcal{O}), \quad \text{all } 1 \leq i \leq h.$$

(2) There exists an $\mathcal{O}$-lattice Λ_0 in Λ such that for all $1 \leq i \leq h$:

$$D_i\Lambda_0 \subset \Lambda_0.$$

(3) For any $\mathcal{O}$-lattice Λ_1 in Λ and all $1 \leq i \leq h$, the chain of $\mathcal{O}$-modules

$$\Lambda_1 \subset \Lambda_1 + D_i\Lambda_1 \subset \Lambda_1 + D_i\Lambda_1 + D_i^2\Lambda_1 \subset \ldots \subset \Lambda$$

is stationary.

(4) For any $v \in \Lambda$ and all $1 \leq i \leq h$, the chain of $\mathcal{O}$-modules

$$\mathcal{O}v \subset \mathcal{O}v + \mathcal{O}D_iv \subset \mathcal{O}v + \mathcal{O}D_iv + \mathcal{O}D_i^2v \subset \ldots \subset \Lambda$$

is stationary.

(5) D_i is regular with respect to x_i, all $1 \leq i \leq d$.

Remark 1.23: Instead of (1) we shall even prove:

(1') There exists an $\mathcal{O}_{x_1\ldots x_d}$-basis $(f) = (f_1,\ldots,f_n)$ of Λ such that

$$\mathrm{Mat}(D_i,(f)) \in M_{n\times n}(k[[x_{h+1},\ldots,x_m]]), \qquad \text{all } 1 \leq i \leq d$$

$$\mathrm{Mat}(D_i,(f)) = 0, \qquad \text{all } d+1 \leq i \leq h$$

(if $h = m$, read k instead of $k[[x_{h+1},\ldots,x_m]]$).

1.24 Consequences of Th.1.22.

1°. First we reformulate the equivalence of (1) and (5) of Th.1.22 in terms of connections. Before we do this, we introduce some terminology. We adopt the same notations as in prop.1.15. From (1.10) we deduced

$$(1.25) \qquad \nabla\eta = dx_1 \otimes \nabla_{\frac{\partial}{\partial x_1}}(\eta) + \ldots + dx_m \otimes \nabla_{\frac{\partial}{\partial x_m}}(\eta), \quad \text{all } \eta \in M.$$

Hence ∇ is completely determined by the values ∇g_i, where $(g_1,\ldots,g_n)$ is a B_f-basis of M. Write:

$$(1.26) \qquad \nabla_{\frac{\partial}{\partial x_k}} g_j = \sum_{i=1}^{m} \alpha_{ij}^{(k)} g_i; \qquad \alpha_{ij}^{(k)} \in B_f$$

where the $\alpha_{ij}^{(k)}$ are uniquely determined.

From (1.25) and (1.26) we deduce

$$\nabla g_j = dx_1 \otimes \sum_{i=1}^{m} \alpha_{ij}^{(1)} g_i + \ldots + dx_m \otimes \sum_{i=1}^{k} \alpha_{ij}^{(m)} g_i$$
$$= \sum_{i=1}^{m} (\alpha_{ij}^{(1)} dx_1 + \ldots + \alpha_{ij}^{(m)} dx_m) \otimes g_i.$$

The matrix (with differential forms as matrix elements)

(1.27) $\qquad (\alpha_{ij}^{(1)} dx_1 + \ldots + \alpha_{ij}^{(m)} dx_m)_{i,j=1}^{m}$

is called the <u>matrix of the connection ∇ on the B_f-basis $(g_1,\ldots,g_n)$</u>.

Notation: $\mathrm{Mat}(\nabla,(g_1,\ldots,g_n))$.

<u>Definition 1.28</u>: Let $f = x_1\ldots x_d$. $\mathrm{Mat}(\nabla,(g_1,\ldots,g_n))$ is said to have at most a logarithmic pole along $x_1\ldots x_d$ if

(1) $\alpha_{ij}^{(k)} \in B$, all $d+1 \leq k \leq m$

(2) $x_k\alpha_{ij}^{(k)} \in B$, all $1 \leq k \leq d$.

We can now reformulate the equivalence (1) $\Longleftrightarrow$ (5) of Th.1.22 in terms of connections:

<u>Theorem 1.29</u>: The following conditions are equivalent:

(1) There exists an $\mathcal{O}_{x_1\ldots x_d}$-basis $(b) = (b_1,\ldots,b_n)$ of Λ such that $\mathrm{Mat}(\nabla,(b_1,\ldots,b_n))$ has at most a logarithmic pole along $x_1\ldots x_d$.

(2) $\nabla_{x_i\frac{\partial}{\partial x_i}}$ is regular with respect to x_i, all $1 \leq i \leq d$.

<u>Definition 1.30</u>: <u>The connection ∇ on Λ is called regular along $x_1\ldots x_d$</u> if the differential operators $D_1 = \nabla_{x_1\frac{\partial}{\partial x_1}}, \ldots, D_n = \nabla_{\frac{\partial}{\partial x_n}}$ satisfy the conditions of Th.1.22.

Now consider the special case $h = m$.

The equivalence (1) $\Longleftrightarrow$ (2) of Th.1.29 is a formal analogue of the equivalence (iv) $\Leftrightarrow$ (i) of Th.4.1 of [3].

2°. In [10] B. Malgrange raises the question of the definition of Fuchsian $\mathcal{D}_m$-modules. In the one dimensional case (i.e. m = 1) this question was solved by Y. Manin in [11].

We will now use Th.1.22 to give a definition of a Fuchsian $\mathcal{D}_m$-module along $x_1 \ldots x_d$. Therefore we reformulate Th.1.22 in the particular case h = m. We then find

Theorem 1.31: Let M be a free $\mathcal{O}_{x_1 \ldots x_d}$-module of rank n with integrable connection. The following conditions are equivalent:

(1) (M,∇) is regular along $x_1 \ldots x_d$.

(2) M is a $\mathcal{D}_m$-module satisfying

$$(F)\begin{cases} \Lambda_{1\leq i\leq d}\Lambda_{v\in M}[\mathcal{O}v+\mathcal{O}(x_i\frac{\partial}{\partial x_i}v)+\ldots \text{ is an } \mathcal{O}\text{-module of finite type}] \\ \Lambda_{d+1\leq i\leq m}\Lambda_{v\in M}[\mathcal{O}v+\mathcal{O}(\frac{\partial}{\partial x_i}v)+\ldots \text{ is an } \mathcal{O}\text{-module of finite type}]. \end{cases}$$

Now observe, looking in particular to the equivalent statements (1) and (1)' of Th.1.22, that every reasonable definition of a Fuchsian $\mathcal{D}_m$-module must imply that the modules studied in Th.1.22 (for the case h = m) are Fuchsian. So we deduce:

Every $\mathcal{D}_m$-module which is a free $\mathcal{O}_{x_1 \ldots x_d}$- module of rank n and which has the property (F) must be Fuchsian.

Bearing in mind Manins definition of a Fuchsian module in the one dimensional case, we are lead to the following definition:

Definition 1.32: Let M be a $\mathcal{D}_m$-module. Then M is called Fuchsian along $x_1 \ldots x_d$ if it has property (F).

This definition will be the starting point of the theory of Fuchsian -modules which will be developed in further papers on this subject. (see [13] and [14]).

§2. Some fundamental lemmas and the proof of 1⇒2⇒3⇒4⇒5 of Th.1.22.

The proof of 1⇒2⇒3⇒4⇒5 of Th.1.22 is based on the following five lemmas, which are of fundamental importance.

Lemma 2.1: Let R be a noetherian ring and $f \in R$. Let M be an R_f-module of finite type such that f is not a zero-divisor in M (i.e. for all $m \in M$, $fm = 0$ implies $m = 0$). Let

(2.2) $\quad N_0 \subset N_1 \subset N_2 \subset \ldots$

be a chain of R-modules of finite type contained in M such that $(N_0)_f = M$
Then the following conditions are equivalent:

(1) The chain (2.2) is stationary.

(2) $\bigvee_{q\in \mathbb{N}} \bigwedge_{h\in \mathbb{N}} [f^q N_h \subset N_0]$.

Proof: (1) ⇒ (2): There exists a $p \in \mathbb{N}$ such that

$$N_p = N_{p+1} = \ldots$$

Let $g_1,\ldots,g_t \in M = (N_0)_f$ be generators of N_p, then there exists a $q \in \mathbb{N}$:

$$f^q g_h \in N_0, \qquad \text{all } 1 \leq h \leq t,$$

hence

$$f^q N_p \subset N_0$$

from which (2) follows.

(2) ⇒ (1): The chain

$$f^q N_0 \subset f^q N_1 \subset f^q N_2 \subset \ldots$$

is stationary because this chain of R-modules is contained in the noetherian R-module N_0. Let $p \in \mathbb{N}$ be such that

$$f^q N_p = f^q N_{p+1} = \ldots$$

then using the fact that f is not a zero divisor in M it follows that the endomorphism $m \to f^q.m$ of M is injective. Hence $N_p = N_{p+1} = \ldots$ as desired.

Lemma 2.3: Let R be a ring, $\Theta : R \to R$ a derivation. M an R-module $D : M \to M$ a differential operator with respect to Θ.

If $\Theta f \in Rf$ then:

$$\Lambda_{q\in N} \Lambda_{v\in M} \Lambda_{h\in N} [f^q(Rv+R\,Dv+\ldots+RD^h v) \subset R(f^q v)+\ldots+RD^h(f^q v)].$$

Proof: By induction on h we prove:

$$(2.4) \quad \Lambda_{q\in N} \Lambda_{v\in M} \Lambda_{h\in N} V_{a_0,\ldots,a_{h-1}\in R} [f^q D^h v = D^h(f^q v)+a_{h-1}D^{h-1}(f^q v)+\ldots+a_0(f^q v)].$$

Using $\Theta f \in Rf$ the case $h = 1$ follows from $D(f^q v) = qf^{q-1}(\Theta f)v+f^q Ds$.

For arbitrary h we have

$$D(f^q D^h v) = qf^{q-1}.\Theta f.D^h v + f^q D^{h+1} v.$$

Since $\Theta f = gf$, for some $g \in R$ we find:

$$f^q D^{h+1} v = (-qg)f^q D^h v + D(f^q D^h v).$$

By the induction hypothesis we find:

$$f^q D^{h+1} v = (-qg)(D^h(f^q v)+\ldots+a_0(f^q v))+D(D^h(f^q v)+\ldots+a_0(f^q v))$$

for some $a_0,\ldots,a_{h-1} \in R$. By writing out this expression (2.4) follows, which proves our lemma.

Lemma 2.5: Let R be a noetherian ring, $0 \neq f \in R$ and M an R_f-module of finite type. Let $D : M \to M$ be a differential operator with respect to a derivation τ satisfying $\tau f \in Rf$.

Suppose there exists an R-lattice Λ_0 in M satisfying

$$D\Lambda_0 \subset \Lambda_0$$

Then for any R-lattice Λ_1 in M the chain

$$\Lambda_1 \subset \Lambda_1 + D(\Lambda_1) \subset \Lambda_1 + D(\Lambda_1) + D^2(\Lambda_1) \subset \ldots$$

is stationary.

Proof: Let Λ_1 be an R-lattice in M. Then there exists a $q \in \mathbb{N}$ such that

$$f^q\Lambda_1 \subset \Lambda_0.$$

Because $\tau f \in Rf$, we can apply lemma 2.3 and find (using the fact that $f^q\Lambda_1 + D(f^q\Lambda_1) +\ldots+ D^h(f^q\Lambda_1)$ is an R-module):

$$f^q(\Lambda_1+D\Lambda_1+\ldots+D^h\Lambda_1) \subset f^q\Lambda_1+D(f^q\Lambda_1)+\ldots+D^h(f^q\Lambda_1) \ .$$

Since $D(f^q\Lambda_1) \subset D\Lambda_0 \subset \Lambda_0$ we find:

$$D^h(f^q\Lambda_1) \subset \Lambda_0, \quad \text{all } h \in \mathbb{N} \ ;$$

hence

$$f^q(\Lambda_1+D\Lambda_1+\ldots+D^h\Lambda_1) \subset \Lambda_0, \qquad \text{all } h \subset \mathbb{N}.$$

The desired result follows now from lemma 2.1.

Lemma 2.6: Let R be a noetherian ring and

$$(2.7) \qquad N_0 \subset N_1 \subset N_2 \subset \ldots$$

a chain of R-modules of finite type contained in some R-module N. Let

$$N_0' \subset N_1' \subset N_2' \subset \ldots$$

be a subchain of (2.7) of R-modules, i.e. $N_i' \subset N_i$ for all i. Then: If the chain (2.7) is stationary, the same holds for $N_0' \subset N_1' \subset \ldots$.

Proof: There exists a $p \in \mathbb{N}$ such that

$$N_0 \subset N_1 \subset \ldots \subset N_p = N_{p+1} = \ldots$$

N_p is an R-module of finite type and hence a noetherian R-module which contains the chain $N_0' \subset N_1' \subset \ldots$, which therefore must be stationary.

Lemma 2.8: Let M be an R_f-module of finite type. $D : M \to M$ a differential operator with respect to the derivation τ. If for any R-lattice Λ_1 in M the chain of R-modules

$$\Lambda_1 \subset \Lambda_1 + D\Lambda_1 \subset \Lambda_1 + D\Lambda_1 + D^2\Lambda_1 \subset \ldots$$

is stationary, then for any $v \in M$ the chain of R-modules

$$Rv \subset Rv + R(Dv) \subset \ldots$$

is stationary.

Proof: Let Λ_0 be an R-lattice and $v \in M$. Then Λ_0+Rv is also an R-lattice of M and hence applying lemma 2.6 to the chains

$$\Lambda_0+Rv \subset \Lambda_0+Rv+D(\Lambda_0+Rv) \subset \dots$$

$$Rv \subset Rv+D(Rv) \subset \dots$$

we see that both chains are stationary. Using the equality of R-modules

$$Rv+D(Rv)+\dots+D^h(Rv) = Rv+RDv+\dots+RD^hv$$

lemma 2.8 follows.

Proof of (1) ⇒ (2) ⇒ (3) ⇒ (4) ⇒ (5) of Th.1.22.

Before we proof the implications (1) ⇒ ... ⇒ (5) we will make some remarks about them (i) The complete integrability condition is not used.

(ii) The implications are proved for every D_i seperately.

(1) ⇒ (2): Obvious, take $\Lambda_0 = \mathcal{O}b_1 + \dots + \mathcal{O}b_n$.

(2) ⇒ (3): Immediate from lemma 2.5.

(3) ⇒ (4): Immediate from lemma 2.8.

(4) ⇒ (5): Let i be fixed, $1 \le i \le d$. Because for every $1 \le j \le n$ the chain of $\mathcal{O}$-modules

$$\mathcal{O}e_j \subset \mathcal{O}e_j+\mathcal{O}D_ie_j \subset \mathcal{O}e_j+\mathcal{O}D_ie_j+\mathcal{O}D_i^2e_j \subset \dots \subset \Lambda$$

is stationary, it follows that the chain of $\mathcal{O}$-modules

$$N \subset N+D_iN \subset N+D_iN+D_i^2N \subset \dots \subset \Lambda \tag{2.9}$$

is stationary. Since $\mathcal{O} \subset \mathcal{O}_{(i)}$ is flat (the proof is left to the reader) tensoring of (2.9) with $\mathcal{O}_{(i)}$ yields: The chain of $\mathcal{O}_{(i)}$ modules

$$N_{(i)} \subset N_{(i)}+D_iN_{(i)} \subset \dots \subset L_{(i)} \otimes_{\mathcal{O}_{x_1\dots x_d}} \Lambda$$

is stationary, and hence in virtue of Th.1.18 and definition 1.21 D_i is regular with respect to x_i.

§3. The proof of (5) ⇒ (1) (started).

Introduction to the proof of (5) ⇒ (1).

We have to prove the existence of an $\mathcal{O}_{x_1\ldots x_d}$-basis $(b) = (b_1,\ldots,b_n)$ of Λ such that $\mathrm{Mat}(D_i,(b)) \in M_{n\times n}(\mathcal{O})$, all $1 \le i \le h$.

Obviously once we have found such a basis, we have found an $\mathcal{O}$-module, in fact a free $\mathcal{O}$-lattice of rank n, invariant under $D_1,\ldots,D_h$ namely $\Lambda_0 = \mathcal{O}b_1+\ldots+\mathcal{O}b_n$.

Conversely, if Λ_0 is a free $\mathcal{O}$-lattice invariant under $D_1,\ldots,D_h$, then $\mathrm{rank}_{\mathcal{O}}\Lambda_0 = n$ (because $\mathrm{rank}_{\mathcal{O}}\Lambda_0 = \mathrm{rank}_{\mathcal{O}_{x_1\ldots x_d}}(\Lambda_0)_{x_1\ldots x_d} = \mathrm{rank}_{\mathcal{O}_{x_1\ldots x_d}}\Lambda = n$).

Hence $\Lambda_0 = \mathcal{O}f_1+\ldots+\mathcal{O}f_n$, for certain elements $(f_1,\ldots,f_n)$ in Λ_0, and $(f_1,\ldots,f_n)$ is an $\mathcal{O}_{x_1\ldots x_d}$-basis of Λ satisfying

$$\mathrm{Mat}(D_i,(f)) \in M_{n\times n}(\mathcal{O}), \text{ all } 1 \le i \le h.$$

This argument leads to the proof of (5) ⇒ (1). In fact the proof will consist of two separate parts, say part A and part B.

In part A we prove the existence of an $\mathcal{O}$-lattice of Λ invariant under $D_1,\ldots,D_h$. In part B we deduce from the existence of an $\mathcal{O}$-lattice of Λ, invariant under $D_1,\ldots,D_h$, the existence of a <u>free</u> $\mathcal{O}$-lattice of Λ, invariant under $D_1,\ldots,D_h$.

In this section we will deal with the proof of part A. Part B is treated in section 4. So we have to construct an $\mathcal{O}$-lattice Λ_0 of Λ invariant under $D_1,\ldots,D_h$. This construction will be carried out as follows:

1°. We prove: For all $1 \le i \le h$ the chain

$$N \subset N+D_iN \subset \ldots \subset \Lambda$$

is stationary. From this we deduce

2°. $\Lambda_0 = \sum_{i_1\ldots i_h \ge 0} D_1^{i_1}\ldots D_h^{i_h} N$

is an $\mathcal{O}$-lattice of Λ invariant under $D_1,\dots,D_h$.

So our main aim in this section is to prove:

Theorem 3.1: $\Lambda_0 = \sum_{i_1,\dots,i_h\geq 0} D_1^{i_1}\dots D_h^{i_h}N$ is an $\mathcal{O}$-lattice of Λ invariant under $D_1,\dots,D_h$.

We will now treat the points 1° and 2° (described above) in more detail. Before we start the proof of 1°, we will show that 1° implies 2°.

Proposition 3.2: If for all $1 \leq i \leq h$ the chain $N \subset N+D_iN \subset \dots$ is stationary. Then:

(1) There exists a $g \in \mathbb{N}$ such that:

$$D_i^{\mu}N \subset N+D_iN+\dots+D_i^gN, \quad \text{all } 1 \leq i \leq h, \text{ all } \mu \in \mathbb{N}.$$

(2) $\Lambda_0 = \sum_{0\leq i_1\dots\leq i_h\leq g} D_1^{i_1}\dots D_h^{i_h}N$ is an $\mathcal{O}$-lattice of Λ with $D_i\Lambda_0 \subset \Lambda_0$, all i.

Proof: (1) Obvious.

(2) Let $0 \leq i_1,\dots,i_h \leq g$. Then:

$$\begin{aligned} D_j(D_1^{i_1}\dots D_j^{i_j}\dots D_h^{i_h}N) &= D_1^{i_1}\dots D_j^{i_j+1}\dots D_h^{i_h}N = D_1^{i_1}\dots D_{j-1}^{i_{j-1}}\dots D_h^{i_h}D_j^{i_j+1}N \\ &\subset D_1^{i_1}\dots D_{j-1}^{i_{j-1}}D_{j+1}^{i_{j+1}}\dots D_h^{i_h}(N+D_jN+\dots+D_j^gN) \\ &= \sum_{k=0}^{g} D_1^{i_1}\dots D_{j-1}^{i_{j-1}}D_j^kD_{j+1}^{i_{j+1}}\dots D_h^{i_h}N \quad (\text{because } [D_i,D_j]=0) \end{aligned}$$

So, $D_j(D_1^{i_1}\dots D_j^{i_j}\dots D_h^{i_h}N) \subset \Lambda_0$ for all $0 \leq i_1,\dots,i_h \leq g$.

From this the proposition easily follows.

The remainder of this section is devoted to the examination of point 1°. Our aim is to prove:

Proposition 3.3: If condition (5) of Th.1.22 is satisfied, then for all $1 \leq k \leq h$

$$N \subset N+D_k N \subset \ldots \subset \Lambda$$

is a stationary chain of $\mathcal{O}$-modules.

Proof of Th.3.1: Immediate from prop.3.2 and prop.3.3.

Before we can enter the proof of proposition 3.3 we shall develop some preliminaries.

Lemma 3.4: Let $K \subset L$ be a finite field extension, char $K = 0$. Let $\Theta : K[[t]] \to K[[t]]$ be a derivation on $K[[t]]$ (not necessarily a K-derivation). Then there exists one and only one extension to a derivation on $L[[t]]$ (and $L((t))$).

Proof: Let $(l_1,\ldots,l_\mu)$ be a K-basis of L. Then $(l_1,\ldots,l_\mu)$ is also a $K((t))$-basis of $L((t))$ and hence $K((t)) \subset L((t))$ is a finite separable field extension. So we can extend Θ uniquely to a derivation on $L((t))$.

We now prove:

$$\Theta(L[[t]]) \subset L[[t]].$$

Let $\lambda \in L[[t]]$, then it can be written uniquely in the form:

$$\lambda = a_1 l_1 + \ldots + a_\mu l_\mu, \quad \text{where } a_1,\ldots,a_\mu \in K[[t]].$$

So it is sufficient to prove that

$$\Theta(L) \subset L[[t]].$$

Let $l \in L$ and let $P(X) = X^m + a_{m-1}X^{m-1} + \ldots + a_0$ denote the minimum polynomial of l over K. Then, because $K \subset L$ is a separable extension $P'(l) \neq 0$. From $\Theta(P(l)) = 0$ we deduce:

$$P'(l)\Theta(l) + (\Theta(a_{m-1})l^{m-1} + \ldots + \Theta(a_1)l + \Theta(a_0)) = 0.$$

Hence

$\Theta(1) \in L[[t]]$

and so $\Theta(L) \subset L[[t]]$ as desired.

Let $K \subset L$ be a finite field extension with char $K = 0$ and let V be an n-dimensional $K((t))$-vector space. Denote

$$\overline{V} = L((t)) \otimes_{K((t))} V.$$

Suppose D is a differential operator on V with respect to Θ. The map $v \rightarrow 1 \otimes v$ identifies V with a $K((t))$-subspace of $\overline{V}$. Extending Θ to $L[[t]]$ (cf Lemma 3.4), D can be extended to a differential operator on $\overline{V}$. Let Δ be a $K[[t]]$-lattice in V and denote by $\overline{\Delta}$ the $L[[t]]$-lattice in $\overline{V}$:

$$\overline{\Delta} = L[[t]] \otimes_{K[[t]]} V.$$

<u>Lemma 3.5</u>: With the notation just introduced the following conditions are equivalent:

(1) The chain of $K[[t]]$-lattices

$$\Delta \subset \Delta + D\Delta \subset \ldots \subset V$$

is stationary.

(2) The chain of $L[[t]]$-lattices

$$\overline{\Delta} \subset \overline{\Delta} + D\overline{\Delta} \subset \ldots \subset \overline{V}$$

is stationary.

<u>Proof</u>: (1) $\Rightarrow$ (2) Follows immediately by tensoring of (1), using the fact that $\Theta(L[[t]] \subset L[[t]]$ and the flatness of $K[[t]] \subset L[[t]]$.

(2) $\Rightarrow$ (1) From (2) and lemma 2.1 we deduce

$$\vee_{q \in N} \wedge_{h \in N} [t^q D^h \overline{\Delta} \subset \overline{\Delta}].$$

Because $\Delta \subset \overline{\Delta}$, this in particular implies that there exists $q \in \mathbb{N}$ such that

(3.6) $\qquad \wedge_{h \in \mathbb{N}} [t^q D^h \Delta \subset \overline{\Delta}]$.

Obviously we have

$$D^h\Delta \subset \Delta_t = V, \quad \text{all } h \in \mathbb{N},$$

hence

(3.7) $\quad \Lambda_{h\in\mathbb{N}}[t^q D^h \Delta \subset \Delta_t].$

From (3.6) and (3.7) we deduce

(3.8) $\quad \Lambda_{h\in\mathbb{N}}[t^q D^h \Delta \subset \overline{\Delta} \cap \Delta_t]$.

In virtue of Corollary 3.10 (below) $\overline{\Delta} \cap \Delta_t = \Delta$, consequently

$$\Lambda_{h\in\mathbb{N}}[t^q D^h \Delta \subset \overline{\Delta}].$$

Now apply lemma 2.1 again and we are done.

Looking at the conditions (5) and (1) of Th.1.22 one may wonder how to get information about our connection with respect to the ring $\mathcal{O}_{x_1 \ldots x_d}$ from the "rough information" about the connections with respect to the "large" fields $L_{(i)}$. Put in a different way; how can we descend from the "large" fields $L_{(i)}$ to the ring $\mathcal{O}_{x_1 \ldots x_d}$?

The key-result is the following rather trivial lemma.

Lemma 3.9: (descent lemma)

(1) If $K \subset L$ is a field extension and $L[[t]]$ the ring of formal power series in t,

Then inside $L((t))$ we have:

$$K((t)) \cap L[[t]] = K[[t]] \ ,$$

(2) Inside $L_{(i)}$ we have:

$$\mathcal{O}_{(i)} \cap \mathcal{O}_{x_1 \ldots x_d} = \mathcal{O}_{x_1 \ldots \hat{x}_i \ldots x_d}.$$

(3) Inside $\mathcal{O}_{x_1 \ldots x_d}$ we have:

$$\bigcap_{i=1}^{d} \mathcal{O}_{x_1 \ldots \hat{x}_i \ldots x_d} = \mathcal{O}.$$

Proof: (1) Obvious.

(3) Follows easily from the fact that $\mathcal{O}$ is a unique factorization domain.

(2) Let v denote the valuation on $K_{(i)}((x_i))$ associated with the discrete valuation ring $K_{(i)}[[x_i]]$; $vx_i = 1$.

If $\eta = \frac{a}{b} \in \mathcal{O}_{x_1\ldots x_d} \cap \mathcal{O}_{(i)}$ $(a,b \in \mathcal{O}\setminus\{0\})$ with $g.c.d(a,b) = 1$ (in $\mathcal{O}$), then $g.c.d(b,x_i) = 1$ (in $\mathcal{O}$).

Proof: If $g.c.d(b,x_i) \neq 1$ (in $\mathcal{O}$), then $v(b) > 0$, so $v(a) = 0$ (because $g.c.d(a,b) = 1$ in $\mathcal{O}$). Hence $v(\frac{a}{b}) = -v(b) < 0$. But $\eta \in \mathcal{O}_{(i)}$, so $v(\eta) \geq 0$, a contradiction. Hence $g.c.d(b,x_i) = 1$. From $\frac{a}{b} \in \mathcal{O}_{x_1\ldots x_d}$, $\frac{a}{b} \in \mathcal{O}_{x_1\ldots\hat{x}_i\ldots x_d}$ follows.

Corollary 3.10: (1) Notations as in lemma 3.5. Then inside $\bar{V}$:

$$\Delta_t \cap \bar{\Delta} = \Delta .$$

(2) Inside $V_{(i)}$ we have:

$$N_{(i)} \cap N_{x_1\ldots x_d} = N_{x_1\ldots\hat{x}_i\ldots x_d}$$

(3) Inside Λ:

$$\bigcap_{i=1}^{d} N_{x_1\ldots\hat{x}_i\ldots x_d} = N ,$$

Proof: (1) If $(f_1,\ldots,f_n)$ is a $K[[t]]$-basis of Δ, then $(f_1,\ldots,f_n)$ is a $L((t))$-basis of $\bar{V}$. So, if $\eta \in \Delta_t \cap \bar{\Delta}$, then $\eta = \sum_{i=1}^{n} a_i f_i$ with $a_i \in K((t)) \cap L[[t]]$, all $1 \leq i \leq n$. From lemma 3.9 $\eta \in \Delta$ follows.

(2) resp. (3) follow from (2) resp. (3) of lemma 3.9 by exactly the same argument.

Proof of prop.3.3 (started): We claim:

If for all $1 \leq i \leq d$ and all $1 \leq k \leq h$ the chain of $\mathcal{O}_{(i)}$-modules

(3.11) $\quad N_{(i)} \subset N_{(i)}+D_k N_{(i)} \subset \ldots \subset V_{(i)}$

is stationary, then proposition 3.3 holds.

Proof: By lemma 2.1, there exist $q_1,\ldots,q_d \in \mathbb{N}$ with

(3.12) $x_i^{q_i} D_k^{\mu} N_{(i)} \subset N_{(i)}$, all $1 \leq i \leq d$, all $1 \leq k \leq h$, all $\mu \in \mathbb{N}$.

Because $N \subset N_{(i)}$ and obviously $D_k^{\mu} N \subset N_{x_1 \ldots x_d}$ $(= \Lambda)$ we deduce by Cor3.10(2)

(3.13) $x_i^{q_i} D_k^{\mu} N \subset N_{x_1 \ldots \hat{x}_i \ldots x_d}$, all $1 \leq i \leq d$, all $1 \leq k \leq h$, all $\mu \in \mathbb{N}$.

From (3.13) and Cor.3.10(3)

(3.14) $x_1^{q_1} \ldots x_d^{q_d} D_k^{\mu} N \subset N$, all $1 \leq k \leq h$, all $\mu \in \mathbb{N}$.

By lemma 2.1 (applied with $f = x_1 \ldots x_d$, $q = \max_i q_i$), our claim follows.

For $k = i$ the chain (3.11) is stationary; this follows from our hypothesis (5) and Th.1.18. So it remains to show that for $k \neq i$, $1 \leq k \leq h$ the chain of $\mathcal{O}_{(i)}$- modules

$$N_{(i)} \subset N_{(i)} + D_k N_{(i)} \subset \ldots$$

is also stationary. For this we use the commutation relations $D_i D_k = D_k D_i$. The reader should notice that these relations have not been used until now.

<u>Theorem 3.15</u>: Let K be a field, char K = 0, and V an n-dimensional K((t))-vector space. Let $D : V \to V$ be a differential operator with respect to $t\frac{d}{dt}$ and $H : V \to V$ a differential operator on V with respect to a derivation Θ which satisfies:

(1) $\Theta(K[[t]]) \subset K[[t]]$.

(2) $\Theta t = 0$.

(3) $DH = HD$.

Then: If Δ is a K[[t]]-lattice of V such that the chain

$$\Delta \subset \Delta + D\Delta \subset \ldots$$

is stationary, then the chain

$$\Delta \subset \Delta + H\Delta \subset \ldots$$

is also stationary.

Proof of prop (3.3):(concluded)

Apply Th.3.15 to $K = K_{(i)}$, $v = V_{(i)}$, $t = x_i$, $D = D_i$, $H = D_k$, $\Delta = N_{(i)}$.

Proof of Th.3.15: (started)

(1) We may assume $D\Delta \subset \Delta$. For since $\Delta \subset \Delta+D\Delta \subset \ldots$ is stationary, there exist a $g \in \mathbb{N}$ such that

$$E = \Delta+D\Delta+\ldots+D^g\Delta$$

is a $K[[t]]$-lattice invariant under D. If

$$E \subset E+HE \subset \ldots$$

is stationary, then using $\Delta \subset E$ and lemma 2.6 we find that

$$\Delta \subset \Delta+H\Delta \subset$$

is also stationary.

(2) So assume $D\Delta \subset \Delta$. Observe that Δ is a free $K[[t]]$-module of rank n (since it is a $K[[t]]$-lattice of V). The following lemma leads to the proof of Th.3.15 in a special case:

Lemma 3.16: Notations as in Th.3.15.

Let (f) be a $K((t))$-basis of V such that $A \underset{D}{=} \mathrm{Mat}(D,(f)) \in M_{n\times n}(K[[t]])$ has a constant term $A_0 \in M_{n\times n}(K)$ with the property that all eigenvalues of A_0 don't differ by a positive integer. Then:

$$\mathrm{Mat}(H,(f)) \in M_{n\times n}(K[[t]]).$$

Proof: Let $B = B_{-N}t^{-N}+B_{-N+1}t^{-N+1}+\ldots$, $B_i \in M_{n\times n}(K)$ be the power series development of the matrix $B \underset{D}{=} \mathrm{Mat}(H,(f))$. Suppose $B_{-N} \neq 0$ and $N > 0$. From DH = HD we deduce

$$(3.17) \qquad AB + t\frac{d}{dt}B = BA + \Theta A.$$

Using the hypothesis on Θ and A we have $\Theta A \in M_{n\times n}(K[[t]])$. Then equating the coefficients of t^{-N} in the expansion of equation (3.17) into powers of t gives:

$$(3.18) \qquad (A_0-NI)B_{-N} = B_{-N}A_0.$$

By a well-known result from linear algebra $B_{-N} = 0$ follows from (3.18) and the hypothesis on A_0, a contradiction.

Proof of Th.3.15: (concluded)

Let $(g_1,\dots,g_n)$ be a $K[[t]]$-basis of Δ and write $A = \mathrm{Mat}(D,(g))$. Since $D\Delta \subset \Delta$, $A \in M_{n\times n}(K[[t]])$. Let $K \subset L$ be a finite field extension containing all eigenvalues of the constant matrix A_0 (of A). By lemma 3.4 we can extend $t\frac{d}{dt}$ and Θ (uniquely) to $L[[t]]$. We extend D and H to $\overline{V} = L((t)) \otimes_{K((t))} V$. Denote this extensions again by D and H. Observe that the relation

$$DH = HD$$

still holds. $(g_1,\dots,g_n)$ is an $L[[t]]$-basis of $\overline{\Delta} = L[[t]] \otimes_{K[[t]]} \Delta$ and $\mathrm{Mat}(D,(g)) = A$. Because L contains all eigenvalues of A_0 it is well-known (see [1]) that there exists an $L[[t]]$-lattice

$$\Delta^* = L[[t]]g_1^* + \dots + L[[t]]g_n^*$$

such that

$$\mathrm{Mat}(D,(g^*)) = A_0^* + A_1^* t + \dots, \quad A_i^* \in M_{n\times n}(L)$$

where the eigenvalues of A_0^* don't differ by a positive integer. From lemma 3.16

$$\mathrm{Mat}(H,(g^*)) \in M_{n\times n}(L[[t]]) \quad .$$

Hence $H(\Delta^*) \subset \Delta^*$ and in particular the chain

$$\Delta^* \subset \Delta^* + H\Delta^* \subset \dots \tag{3.19}$$

is stationary. To finish the proof of Th.3.15 we need:

Lemma 3.20: Let A be a noetherian ring, $0 \neq f \in A$, M a free A_f-module of rank n, $D : M \to M$ a differential operator with respect to the derivation $\Theta : A \to A$ satisfying $\Theta f = af$, for some $a \in A$. Let W_1 and W_2 be A-submodules of M of finite type satisfying $(W_1)_f = (W_2)_f$. If the chain of A-modules

$$W_1 \subset W_1 + DW_1 \subset \dots$$

is stationary, so is the chain

$$W_2 \subset W_2+DW_2 \subset \dots .$$

<u>Proof</u>: Because $(W_1)_f = (W_2)_f$ and W_2 is an A-module of finite type there exists an element $p \in \mathbb{N}$ such that

$$f^p W_2 \subset W_1.$$

From lemma 2.3 we deduce

$$f^p D^h(W_2) \subset D^h(f^p W_2)+D^{h-1}(f^p W_2)+\dots+f^p W_2$$
$$\subset D^h W_1+D^{h-1}W_1+\dots+W_1 \quad , \qquad \text{all } h \in \mathbb{N}$$

Because $W_1 \subset W_1+DW_1 \subset \dots$ is stationary, there exists a $g \in \mathbb{N}$ such that $E = W_1+DW_1+\dots+D^g W_1$ is an A-module of finite type. This proves:

$$f^p D^h W_2 \subset E, \text{ all } h \in \mathbb{N}.$$

Since E is a noetherian A-module the chain $f^p W_2 \subset f^p W_2+f^p DW_2 \subset \dots$ is stationary. Because $m \to f^p m$ is an injective map from M to M, the chain $W_2 \subset W_2+DW_2 \subset \dots$ is also stationary.

<u>Proof of Th.3.15:</u> (concluded)

Apply lemma 3.20 to $A = L[[t]]$, $f = t$, $D = H$, $W_1 = \Delta^*$, $W_2 = \overline{\Delta}$. Then using (3.19) the chain

$$\overline{\Delta} \subset \overline{\Delta}+D(\overline{\Delta}) \subset \dots \subset \overline{V}$$

is stationary. Finally apply lemma 3.5 to H and we are done.

§4. A Theorem on free $\mathcal{O}$-modules and the proof of (5) ⇒ (1) (completed).

In this section we assume:

k is algebraically closed.

Our main aim in this section in to prove the following theorem (Th.4.2) which generalizes Th.3.4 of [12].

Definition 4.1: A matrix $A = \sum_{i_1,\dots,i_m \geq 0} A_{i_1,\dots,i_m} x_1^{i_1} \dots x_m^{i_m} \in M_{n\times n}(\mathcal{O})$ with $A_{i_1,\dots,i_m} \in M_{n\times n}(k)$ is said to have the (P)-property if not two eigenvalues of $A_{0\dots 0}$ differ by a positive integer.

Theorem 4.2: If there exists an $\mathcal{O}$-submodule M of finite type of Λ such that

(1) $N \subset M \subset N_{x_1\dots x_d} = \Lambda$.

(2) $D_i M \subset M$, all $1 \leq i \leq h$,

then there exists a free $\mathcal{O}$-lattice Λ_0 of Λ (hence free of rank n) satisfying:

(i) $D_i \Lambda_0 \subset \Lambda_0$, all $1 \leq i \leq h$.

(ii) there exists an $\mathcal{O}$-basis $(g) = (g_1,\dots,g_n)$ of Λ_0 such that

(a) $\mathrm{Mat}\,(D_i,(g)) \in M_{n\times n}(k[[x_{h+1},\dots,x_m]])$, all $1 \leq i \leq d$,

$\mathrm{Mat}\,(D_i,g)) = 0$, all $d+1 \leq i \leq h$.

(b) $\mathrm{Mat}\,(D_i,(g))$ has the (P)-property, for all $1 \leq i \leq d$.

(if $h = m$, read k instead of $k[[x_{h+1},\dots,x_m]]$).

Remark 4.3: In [12] the case $d = h = m$ is treated.

Proof of (5) ⇒ (1) of Th.1.22:

Apply Th.3.1 and Th.4.2 and we are done.

We now start to prove Th.4.2. This theorem follows immediately from the following two theorems.

<u>Theorem 4.4</u>: Let Λ_0 be an $\mathcal{O}$-lattice in Λ satisfying

(1) $N \subset \Lambda_0 \subset \Lambda$

(2) $D_i\Lambda_0 \subset \Lambda_0$, all $1 \leq i \leq h$.

Let δ_i denote the k-linear endomorphism of $\Lambda_0/\mathfrak{m}\Lambda_0$ induced by D_i (all $1 \leq i \leq d$) and let $\alpha_{1i},\ldots,\alpha_{qi}$ ($q = \dim \Lambda_0/\mathfrak{m}\Lambda_0$) denote the eigenvalues of δ_i. Suppose

(4.5) $\alpha_{ki}-\alpha_{li} \notin \mathbb{N}$, all $1 \leq i \leq d$, all $1 \leq k$, $l \leq q$.

Then Λ_0 is a free $\mathcal{O}$-module.

<u>Theorem 4.6</u>: Let M be an $\mathcal{O}$-module of finite type satisfying the conditions (1) and (2) of Th.4.4. Then there exists an $\mathcal{O}$-lattice Λ_0 of Λ satisfying:

(i) $D_i\Lambda_0 \subset \Lambda_0$, all $1 \leq i \leq h$.

(ii) The eigenvalues of the k-linear endomorphisms $\delta_i : \Lambda_0/\mathfrak{m}\Lambda_0 \to \Lambda_0/\mathfrak{m}\Lambda_0$ induced by $D_i : \Lambda_0 \to \Lambda_0$ (all $1 \leq i \leq d$) satisfy the condition (4.5).

(iii) There exists an $\mathcal{O}$-basis $(f) = (f_1,\ldots,f_n)$ of Λ_0 such that

$\text{Mat}\,(D_i,(f)) \in M_{n\times n}(k[[x_{h+1},\ldots,x_m]])$, all $1 \leq i \leq d$

$\text{Mat}\,(D_i,(f)) = 0$, all $d+1 \leq i \leq h$

(if $h = m$ read k instead of $k[[x_{h+1},\ldots,x_m]]$).

<u>Proof of Th.4.2</u>: Immediate from Th.4.4 and Th.4.6.

<u>Proof of Th.4.4</u>: Let K denote the quotient field of $\mathcal{O}$. Because

$$K \otimes_{\mathcal{O}} \Lambda_0 = K \otimes_{\mathcal{O}_{x_1\ldots x_d}} \Lambda$$

is an n-dimensional K-vector space it is necessary and sufficient to prove $q = n$. It is clear that $q \geq n$. We therefore suppose $q > n$ and deduce a contradiction. Consider the h differential operators $E_1,\ldots,E_h$ on Λ defined by

$E_i = D_i$, for all $1 \leq i \leq d$

$E_i = x_iD_i$, for all $d+1 \leq i \leq h$.

Let $\mathcal{E}_i$ denote the k-linear endomorphism from $\Lambda_0/\mathfrak{m}\Lambda_0$ to $\Lambda_0/\mathfrak{m}\Lambda_0$ induced by $E_i : \Lambda_0 \to \Lambda_0$ (all $1 \leq i \leq h$). For $d+1 \leq i \leq h$ we have $D_i\Lambda_0 \subset \Lambda_0$ and so $E_i\Lambda_0 \subset \mathfrak{m}\Lambda_0$, hence the k-linear endomorphism $\mathcal{E}_i$ is the zero map. So the eigenvalues of $\mathcal{E}_i$ denoted by $\alpha_{1i},\ldots,\alpha_{qi}$ are equal to zero. In particular we see: For all $1 \leq i \leq h$ the eigenvalues of $\mathcal{E}_i$ satisfy (4.5).

We now apply some results developed in [12], in particular we follow the proof of Th.3.4.

There exist endomorphisms S_i, N_i of Λ_0 satisfying:

(a) S_i is semisimple and N_i is topologically nilpotent.

(b) $E_i = S_i+N_i$.

(c) $[S_i,N_i] = 0$.

Furthermore, S_i and N_i are uniquely determined by the properties (a), (b), (c). It is then proved in [12] that S_i is even a differential operator with respect to $x_i \frac{\partial}{\partial x_i}$. Moreover, since $\mathfrak{m}\Lambda_0$ is stable under all E_i and all E_i commute, there exists a q-dimensional k-vector space $W \subset \Lambda_0$ satisfying

(i) $\Lambda_0 = W \oplus \mathfrak{m}\Lambda_0$.

(ii) $S_iW \subset W$, all $1 \leq i \leq h$.

Take in W a k-basis $(f_1,\ldots,f_q)$ of simultaneous eigenvectors of the S_i $(1 \leq i \leq h)$. Then

(4.7) $\qquad S_jf_i = \alpha_{ij}f_i, \qquad$ all $1 \leq i \leq h$, all $1 \leq i \leq q$.

Using Nakayama's lemma it follows from (i) that

(4.8) $\qquad \Lambda_0 = \mathcal{O}f_1 +\ldots+\mathcal{O}f_q.$

Because $K \otimes_{\mathcal{O}} \Lambda_0 = K \otimes_{\mathcal{O}_{x_1\ldots x_d}} \Lambda$ we see that $(f_1,\ldots,f_q)$ is a system of generators of the K-vector space $K \otimes \Lambda$ and hence contains a K-basis, say $(f_1,\ldots,f_n)$. Then there exist $\lambda_1,\ldots,\lambda_n \in K$ (not all zero) such that

(4.9) $f_{n+1} = \lambda_1 f_1 + \ldots + \lambda_n f_n$.

We now prove that $\lambda_1, \ldots, \lambda_n \in k((x_{h+1}, \ldots, x_m))$.

This goes as follows:

$$\begin{aligned} S_j(f_{n+1}) &= \alpha_{n+1j} f_{n+1} \\ &= \alpha_{n+1j}(\lambda_1 f_1 + \ldots + \lambda_n f_n) \\ &= (\alpha_{n+1j}\lambda_1) f_1 + \ldots + (\alpha_{n+1j}\lambda_n) f_n \end{aligned}$$

also:

$$\begin{aligned} S_j f_{n+1} &= S_j(\lambda_1 f_1 + \ldots + \lambda_n f_n) \\ &= (\Theta_j \lambda_1 + \lambda_1 \alpha_{1j}) f_1 + \ldots + (\Theta_j \lambda_n + \lambda_n \alpha_{nj}) f_n \end{aligned}$$

(where $\Theta_j = x_j \frac{\partial}{\partial x_j}$).

From these two equations, using the fact that $(f_1, \ldots, f_n)$ are linearly independent over K we deduce:

(4.10) $\Theta_j \lambda_i + \lambda_i(\alpha_{ij} - \alpha_{n+1,j}) = 0$, all $1 \leq i \leq n$, all $1 \leq j \leq h$.

We now make use of the following simple fact:

Let $\alpha \in k$ and $\mu \in K$ satisfy

$$\Theta_j \mu = \alpha\mu, \quad \text{all } 1 \leq j \leq h.$$

Then:

$$\mu = 0 \quad \text{if} \quad \alpha \in k \setminus \mathbf{Z}$$

$$\mu \in k((x_{h+1}, \ldots, x_m)) \quad \text{if} \quad \alpha = 0.$$

Now using condition (4.5) in Th.4.4, it follows by our previous remark and relation (4.10) that

(4.11) $\lambda_1, \ldots, \lambda_n \in k((x_{h+1}, \ldots, x_m))$.

So we see that if $h = m$ (4.11) contradicts

(4.12) $\Lambda_0 = kf_1 \oplus \ldots \oplus kf_n \oplus \mathfrak{m}\Lambda_0$

which is just a reformulation of (i) and the fact that $(f_1, \ldots, f_q)$ is a k-basis of W. From now on we assume $h < m$.

We proceed to study the relation $f_{n+1} = \lambda_1 f_1 + \ldots + \lambda_n f_n$.

We can multiply this relation by a suitable element of $k[[x_{h+1}, \ldots, x_m]]$ in such a way that we get:

There exist $\lambda'_1,\ldots,\lambda'_{n+1} \in k[[x_{h+1},\ldots,x_m]]$, not all zero with

$$(4.13) \quad \begin{cases} \lambda'_1 f_1 + \ldots + \lambda'_{n+1} f_{n+1} = 0 \\ \text{g.c.d.}(\lambda'_1,\ldots,\lambda'_{n+1}) = 1 \quad (\text{in } k[[x_{h+1},\ldots,x_m]]) , \end{cases}$$

From (4.12) we get a contradiction if one of the elements λ'_i is a unit in $k[[x_{h+1},\ldots,x_m]]$ (because $\lambda'_1(0)f_1 + \ldots + \lambda'_{n+1}(0)f_{n+1} = 0$ is then a non-trivial relation between the k-basis elements $(f_1,\ldots,f_q)$ of W; here $\lambda'_i(0)$ stands for the constant term of the power series λ'_i).

More generally we will consider all (n+1)-tuples $(i_1,\ldots,i_{n+1})$ $(1 \leq i_1 <\ldots< i_{n+1} \leq q)$ such that $\dim(Kf_{i_1} + \ldots + Kf_{i_n}) = n$.
In the same way as above we then find:
there exist $\lambda_1^{(i_1\ldots i_{n+1})},\ldots,\lambda_{n+1}^{(i_1\ldots i_{n+1})}$ satisfying

$$(4.14) \quad \begin{cases} \lambda_1^{(i_1\ldots i_{n+1})} f_{i_1} + \ldots + \lambda_{n+1}^{(i_1\ldots i_{n+1})} f_{i_{n+1}} = 0 \\ \lambda_1^{(i_1\ldots i_{n+1})},\ldots, \lambda_{n+1}^{(i_1\ldots i_{n+1})} \in k[[x_{h+1},\ldots,x_m]] \\ \text{g.c.d.}(\lambda_1^{(i_1\ldots i_{n+1})},\ldots, \lambda_{n+1}^{(i_1\ldots i_{n+1})}) = 1 \ (\text{in } k[[x_{h+1},\ldots,x_m]]) , \end{cases}$$

We will now prove the existence of such an (n+1)-tuple with the property that at least one of the $\lambda_j^{(i_1\ldots i_{n+1})}$ is a unit in $k[[x_{h+1},\ldots,x_m]]$) (as remarked above this gives a contradiction). So we may assume:

$$(4.15) \quad \lambda_1^{(i_1\ldots i_{n+1})},\ldots, \lambda_{n+1}^{(i_1,\ldots,i_{n+1})} \in (x_{h+1},\ldots,x_m)$$

for all (n+1)-tuples satisfying (4.14). We derive a contradiction (here $(x_{h+1},\ldots,x_m)$ denotes the maximal ideal of $k[[x_{h+1},\ldots,x_m]]$.)

We have now reduced our problem to a situation where no more differential operators are involved. In fact the following proposition describes the situation and serves to solve our problem.

<u>Proposition 4.16</u>: There does not exists an $\mathcal{O}$-module Λ_0 of Λ satisfying:

(1) $N \subset \Lambda_0 \subset N_{x_1 \dots x_d}$.

(2) $\Lambda_0 = \mathcal{O}f_1 + \dots + \mathcal{O}f_q$, $q = \dim \Lambda_0/m\Lambda_0$ with $\underline{q > n}$.

(3) If $(i_1,\dots,i_n,i_{n+1})$ is an (n+1)-tuple such that $\dim(Kf_{i_1} + \dots + Kf_{i_n}) = n$

then there exist $\lambda_1^{(i_1\dots i_{n+1})},\dots,\lambda_{n+1}^{(i_1\dots i_{n+1})} \in k[[x_{h+1},\dots,x_m]]$,

not all zero satisfying

(i) g.c.d $(\lambda_1^{(i_1\dots i_{n+1})},\dots,\lambda_{n+1}^{(i_1\dots i_{n+1})}) = 1$ (in $k[[x_{h+1},\dots,x_m]]$)

(ii) $\lambda_1^{(i_1\dots i_{n+1})} f_{i_1} + \dots + \lambda_{n+1}^{(i_1\dots i_{n+1})} f_{i_{n+1}} = 0$.

Proof of Th.4.4 (concluded):

We have proved that our $\mathcal{O}$-module Λ_0 satisfies the conditions (1), (2), (3) of proposition 4.16 assuming $q > n$. Applying prop.4.16 we get a contradiction. Hence $q = n$ as desired.

4.17 Examination of the case $q = 2$, $n = 1$ of proposition 4.16.

In order to understand the proof of prop.4.16 we will analyse the simplest case $q = 2$, $n = 1$ as an example. Before we start this examination we observe the following:

From conditions (2) and (3) it follows that

$$\lambda_1^{(i_1\dots i_{n+1})},\dots,\lambda_{n+1}^{(i_1\dots i_{n+1})} \in \mathcal{O}x_{h+1} + \dots + \mathcal{O}x_m \tag{4.18}$$

for all (n+1)-tuples $(i_1,\dots,i_{n+1})$.

Now to the proof in the case $n = 1$, $q = 2$.

(a) First we express the fact that $N \subset \Lambda_0$. Using (1) and (2) this gives: $N = \mathcal{O}e_1$, $\Lambda_0 = \mathcal{O}f_1 + \mathcal{O}f_2$. Let $f_1 = \alpha_1 e_1$, $f_2 = \alpha_2 e_2$ (using $\Lambda_0 \subset N_{x_1\dots x_d}$) with $\alpha_1,\alpha_2 \in \mathcal{O}_{x_1\dots x_d}$. Then $N \subset \Lambda_0$ can be expressed by $e_1 \in \Lambda_0$ i.e.

$$e_1 = \tau_1 f_1 + \tau_2 f_2 = (\tau_1\alpha_1 + \tau_2\alpha_2)e_1; \qquad \tau_1,\tau_2 \in \mathcal{O}.$$

So we have the equation:

$$1 = \tau_1\alpha_1 + \tau_2\alpha_2. \tag{4.19}$$

(b) From condition (3) we deduce:

There exist $\lambda_1, \lambda_2 \in k[[x_{h+1}, \dots, x_m]]$ not both zero $(\lambda_1, \lambda_2) = 1$ satisfying $\lambda_1 f_1 + \lambda_2 f_2 = 0$. Writing this equation with respect to the $\mathcal{O}_{x_1 \dots x_d}$- basis (e_1) of Λ we find:

$$\lambda_1 \alpha_1 + \lambda_2 \alpha_2 = 0.$$

Now using $(\lambda_1, \lambda_2) = 1$ we find

(4.20) λ_1 divides α_2, λ_2 divides α_1 (in $\mathcal{O}_{x_1 \dots x_d}$) .

Let now $\rho \in \mathbb{N}$ satisfy $(x_1 \dots x_d)^\rho \alpha_i \in \mathcal{O}$ $(i = 1,2)$. From (4.18) and 4.20 we see:

(4.21) $(x_1 \dots x_d)^\rho \alpha_i \in \mathcal{O} x_{h+1} + \dots + \mathcal{O} x_m$.

(c) From (4.21) and (4.19) we find

$$(x_1 \dots x_d)^\rho \in \mathcal{O} x_{h+1} + \dots + \mathcal{O} x_m.$$

Substitute $x_{h+1} = \dots = x_m = 0$ and we find a contradiction.

<u>Proof of proposition 4.16:</u>

We suppose that there exists an $\mathcal{O}$-module Λ_0 satisfying the conditions of prop.4.16. We derive a contradiction. Therefore we generalize the proof given in the case $n = 1$, $q = 2$ above.

(a) We express $N \subset \Lambda_0$ by $e_i \in \Lambda_0 = \mathcal{O} f_1 + \dots + \mathcal{O} f_q$, all $1 \leq i \leq n$. Writing f_i on the $\mathcal{O}_{x_1 \dots x_d}$- basis $(e_1, \dots, e_n)$ of Λ we find:

$$f_i = \sum_{j=1}^{n} \alpha_{ji} e_j ; \qquad \alpha_{ji} \in \mathcal{O}_{x_1 \dots x_d}.$$

Now writing out the relations $e_i \in \mathcal{O} f_1 + \dots + \mathcal{O} f_q$ on the $\mathcal{O}_{x_1 \dots x_d}$- -basis $(e_1, \dots, e_n)$ we find in matrix notation: There exist $\tau_{ij} \in \mathcal{O}$ (all $1 \leq i \leq q$, all $1 \leq j \leq n$) such that:

$$I_n = \begin{pmatrix} 1 & & \\ & \ddots & \\ & & 1 \end{pmatrix} = \begin{pmatrix} \alpha_{11} & \dots & \alpha_{1q} \\ \vdots & & \vdots \\ \alpha_{n1} & \dots & \alpha_{nq} \end{pmatrix} \begin{pmatrix} \tau_{11} & \dots & \tau_{1n} \\ & & \\ \tau_{q1} & \dots & \tau_{qn} \end{pmatrix}.$$

Now we take the determinant on both sides of this matrix equation.

Let $1\leq i_1<\ldots<i_n\leq q$ and define $\Delta_{i_1\ldots i_q}$ as the determinant of the submatrix of (α_{ij}) formed by the columns numbered $i_1,\ldots,i_n$. Similarly, define $\Delta^*_{i_1\ldots i_n}$ as the determinant of the submatrix of (τ_{ij}) formed by the rows numbered $i_1,\ldots,i_n$. Using [15], Chap. III, §8, n°.2, Cor. we find:

$$\det(\alpha_{ij})(\tau_{ij}) = \sum_{1\leq i_1<\ldots<i_n\leq q} \Delta_{i_1\ldots i_n} \Delta^*_{i_1\ldots i_n} .$$

So we find the relation:

$$1 = \sum_{1\leq i_1<\ldots<i_n\leq q} \Delta_{i_1\ldots i_n} \Delta^*_{i_1\ldots i_n} . \tag{4.22}$$

Because every $\Delta_{i_1\ldots i_n} \in \mathcal{O}_{x_i\ldots x_d}$, there exists an $N \in \mathbb{N}$ such that

$(x_1\ldots x_d)^N \Delta_{i_1\ldots i_n} \in \mathcal{O}$, for all n-tuples $1 \leq i_1< \ldots < i_n \leq q$.

We deduce

$$(x_1\ldots x_d)^N = \sum_{1\leq i_1<\ldots<i_n\leq q} (x_1\ldots x_d)^N \Delta_{i_1\ldots i_n} \Delta^*_{i_1\ldots i_n} . \tag{4.23}$$

This is now an equation in $\mathcal{O}$.

(b) We will now prove, using the observation (4.18) that

$$(x_1\ldots x_d)^N \Delta_{i_1\ldots i_n} \in \mathcal{O}x_{h+1} +\ldots+\mathcal{O}x_m \quad (\text{all } 1 \leq i_1 <\ldots< i_n \leq q). \tag{4.24}$$

From (4.23) and (4.24) we get a contradiction by substituting $x_{h+1} =\ldots= x_m = 0$.

Proof of (4.24): We distinguish two cases:

Case 1: $\Delta_{i_1\ldots i_n} = 0$, then we are done.

Case 2: $\Delta_{i_1\ldots i_n} \neq 0$. It then follows that $(f_{i_1},\ldots,f_{i_n})$ are linearly independent over K. Let now $i_{n+1} \in \{1,2,\ldots,q\}\setminus\{i_1,\ldots,i_n\}$ (this is possible because $q > n!$), Then by condition (3) there exists $\lambda_1^{(i_1\ldots i_{n+1})},\ldots,\lambda_{n+1}^{(i_1\ldots i_{n+1})} \in k[[x_{h+1},\ldots,x_m]]$ not all zero such that

$$\text{g.c.d}\,(\lambda_1^{(i_1\ldots i_{n+1})},\ldots,\lambda_{n+1}^{(i_1\ldots i_{n+1})}) = 1 \quad \text{and}$$

$$\lambda_1^{(i_1\ldots i_{n+1})} f_{i_1} +\ldots+ \lambda_{n+1}^{(i_1\ldots i_{n+1})} f_{i_{n+1}} = 0 .$$

Expressing this equation in coordinates with respect to $(e_1,\ldots,e_n)$ we find that $(\lambda_1^{(i_1\ldots i_{n+1})},\ldots,\lambda_{n+1}^{(i_1\ldots i_{n+1})})$ is a non-trivial solution of the following system of (n+1) linear equations in n unknowns:

$$X_1\begin{pmatrix}\alpha_{1i_1}\\ \vdots\\ \alpha_{ni_n}\end{pmatrix} + \ldots + X_{n+1}\begin{pmatrix}\alpha_{1i_{n+1}}\\ \vdots\\ \alpha_{ni_{n+1}}\end{pmatrix} = \begin{pmatrix}0\\ \vdots\\ 0\end{pmatrix}$$

Because the matrix of coefficients has rank n (for $\Delta_{i_1\ldots i_n} \neq 0$) we deduce by Cramers rule that the one dimensional solution space is spanned by the vectors:

$$(\Delta_{i_2\ldots i_{n+1}}, -\Delta_{i_1 i_3\ldots i_{n+1}},\ldots,(-1)^n\Delta_{i_1\ldots i_n}) = (\Delta^{(1)}, -\Delta^{(2)},\ldots,(-1)^n\Delta^{(n+1)})$$

Hence there exists an element $\mu \in K$, $\mu \neq 0$ satisfying

$$(\lambda_1^{(i_1\ldots i_{n+1})},\ldots,\lambda_{n+1}^{(i_1\ldots i_{n+1})}) = \mu(\Delta^{(1)},-\Delta^{(2)},\ldots,(-1)^n\Delta^{(n+1)})$$

Write $\mu = \mu_1/\mu_2$, with $\mu_1,\mu_2 \neq 0$ in $\mathcal{O}$ and g.c.d $(\mu_1,\mu_2) = 1$.

We then find the equations:

$$\text{(4.25)} \qquad \mu_2\lambda_j^{(i_1\ldots i_{n+1})} = \mu_1(-1)^{j+1}\,\Delta^{(j)} \quad , \qquad \text{all } 1 \leq j \leq n+1.$$

From (4.25) we deduce:

$$\text{(4.26)} \qquad \lambda_j^{(i_1\ldots i_{n+1})} \text{ divides } \Delta^{(j)} \ (\text{in } \mathcal{O}_{x_1\ldots x_d}), \quad \text{all } 1 \leq j \leq n+1$$

(namely, fix j_0: by 4.25 it is sufficient to prove that every prime factor p of $\lambda_{j_0}^{(i_1\ldots i_{n+1})}$ divides $\Delta^{(j_0)}$. So suppose p is a prime factor of $\lambda_{j_0}^{(i_1\ldots i_{n+1})}$ and p doesn't divide $\Delta^{(j_0)}$, then p divides μ_1. But then, because $(\mu_1,\mu_2) = 1$, p divides $\lambda_j^{(i_1\ldots i_{n+1})}$ all $1 \leq j \leq n+1$, a contradiction with g.c.d $(\lambda_1^{(i_1\ldots i_{n+1})},\ldots,\lambda_{n+1}^{(i_1\ldots i_{n+1})}) = 1$).

From (4.18) and (4.26) we deduce

$$\text{(4.27)} \qquad (x_1\ldots x_d)^N\,\Delta^{(j)} \in \mathcal{O}x_{n+1}+\ldots+\mathcal{O}x_m \,, \qquad \text{all } 1 \leq j \leq n+1 \,.$$

Because $\Delta^{(n+1)} = \Delta_{i_1\ldots i_n}$, (4.24) follows from (4.17) by putting $j = n+1$ which proves our proposition.

Proof of Th.4.6: We first follow the proof of Th.4.4 and define E_i again for all $1 \leq i \leq h$. Because $E_i(M) \subset M$ we have the Jordan decomposition:

$$E_i = S_i + N_i \qquad (\text{all } 1 \leq i \leq h)$$

and furthermore $M = W \oplus \mathfrak{m} M$

with $\qquad W = kf_1 \oplus \ldots \oplus kf_q \quad ,$

where $(f_1, \ldots, f_q)$ is a basis of simultaneous eigenvectors of $S_1, \ldots, S_h$; more precisely

$$S_i f_j = \alpha_{ji} f_j; \qquad \alpha_{ji} \in k, \quad \text{all } i,j.$$

The proof of this theorem consists of two parts.

1°. We make an $\mathcal{O}$-module Λ_0 of finite type satisfying

(1) $S_i \Lambda_0 \subset \Lambda_0$, all $1 \leq i \leq h$

(2) $(\Lambda_0)_{x_1 \ldots x_d} = M_{x_1 \ldots x_d} = \Lambda$

(3) The k-linear endomorphism $\delta_{S_i} : \Lambda_0/\mathfrak{m}\Lambda_0 \to \Lambda_0/\mathfrak{m}\Lambda_0$

induced by S_i has no eigenvalues which differ by a positive integer.

2°. We then prove that for this $\mathcal{O}$-module Λ_0 we have $D_i \Lambda_0 \subset \Lambda_0$, all $1 \leq i \leq h$ and furthermore assertion (ii) of the theorem.

Because the semisimple part of the k-linear endomorphism $\delta_i : \Lambda_0/\mathfrak{m}\Lambda_0 \to \Lambda_0/\mathfrak{m}\Lambda_0$ induced by $D_i : \Lambda_0 \to \Lambda_0$ equals δ_{S_i} (remember $D_i = E_i$ for all $1 \leq i \leq d$) theorem 4.2 follows.

Proof of 1°: If we have for example

$$S_{i_0} f_j = \alpha_{ji_0} f_j \quad \text{and} \quad S_{i_0} f_\mu = (\alpha_{ji_0} + \bar{m}) f_\mu$$

with $\bar{m} \in \mathbb{Z} \setminus \{0\}$, then replace f_μ by $x_{i_0}^{-\bar{m}} f_\mu$ and define $g_k = f_k$ for $k \neq \mu$, $g_\mu = x_{i_0}^{-\bar{m}} f_\mu$.

Then consider

$$\Lambda_0' = \mathcal{O} g_1 + \ldots + \mathcal{O} g_q$$

This is again an $\mathcal{O}$-module of finite type satisfying $(\Lambda_0')_{x_1 \ldots x_d} = M_{x_1 \ldots x_d} = \Lambda$

(because $1 \leq i_0 \leq d$, namely $\alpha_{ji} = 0$ for all $d+1 \leq i \leq h$, all $1 \leq j \leq h$ as we deduced in the proof of Th.4.4).

We also have: $S_i\Lambda_0' \subset \Lambda_0'$ (all $1 \leq i \leq h$), namely:

$$S_{i_0}g_k = S_{i_0}f_k = \alpha_{ki_0}f_k = \alpha_{ki_0}g_k, \qquad k \neq \mu$$

$$S_{i_0}g_\mu = -\bar{m}\, x_{i_0}^{-\bar{m}}f_\mu + x_{i_0}^{-\bar{m}}\alpha_{\mu i_0}f_\mu = (\alpha_{\mu i_0}-\bar{m})f_\mu = \alpha_{ji_0}f_\mu.$$

For $i \neq i_0$ it is also easy to verify $S_i\Lambda_0' \subset \Lambda_0'$.

So it is clear that when we continue this process we finally arrive at an $\mathcal{O}$-module Λ_0 of finite type satisfying (1), (2) and (3).

Proof of 2°: Apply theorem 4.4 (to $S_1,\ldots,S_h$). We then see that Λ_0 is a free $\mathcal{O}$-module of rank n. Let $(g) = (g_1,\ldots,g_n)$ be the $\mathcal{O}$-basis of the free $\mathcal{O}$-module Λ_0 satisfying $S_ig_j = \alpha_{ji}g_j$ and $\alpha_{ji}-\alpha_{ki} \notin \mathbb{N}$, all i,j,k as constructed above in 1°. Let T be a K-linear endomorphism of $V = K \otimes_{\mathcal{O}_{x_1\ldots x_d}} \Lambda$ (K= the quotient field of $\mathcal{O}$) satisfying $[S_i,T] = 0$ for all $1 \leq i \leq h$. Then it follows immediately by writing out the equations $S_iT = TS_i$ on the K-basis (f) of V that we have

$$\theta_i t_{j\mu} + (\alpha_{ji}-\alpha_{\mu i})t_{j\mu} = 0, \quad \text{all } i,j,\mu \qquad (t_{ij}) = \mathrm{Mat}(T,(g)).$$

Now using $\alpha_{ji}-\alpha_{\mu i} \notin \mathbb{N}$, all i,j,μ we find

(4.28) $\quad t_{j\mu} \in k((x_{h+1},\ldots,x_m)), \quad$ all j,μ .

Now apply this argument to $T = N_i$. This then gives:

(4.29) $\quad \mathrm{Mat}(N_i,(g)) \in M_{n\times n}(k((x_{h+1},\ldots,x_m)))$.

We also know

(4.30) $\quad \mathrm{Mat}(S_i,(g)) \in M_{n\times n}(k)$.

From (4.29) and (4.30) we deduce, using $E_i = S_i+N_i$

(4.31) $\quad \mathrm{Mat}(E_i,(g)) \in M_{n\times n}(k((x_{h+1},\ldots,x_m))), \quad$ all $1 \leq i \leq h$.

Since obviously $\mathrm{Mat}(D_i,(g)) \in M_{n\times n}(\mathcal{O}_{x_1\ldots x_d})$, all $1 \leq i \leq h$

(4.32) $\quad \mathrm{Mat}(D_i,(g)) \in M_{n\times n}(\mathcal{O}_{x_1\ldots x_d} \cap k((x_{h+1},\ldots,x_m))) = M_{n\times n}(k[[x_{h+1},\ldots,x_m]]),$

all $1 \leq i \leq d$

(from the fact that $\mathcal{O}$ is a U.F.D. $\mathcal{O}_{x_1 \ldots x_d} \cap k((x_{h+1},\ldots,x_m)) = k[[x_{h+1},\ldots,x_m]]$ follows).

Similarly, if $d+1 \leq i \leq h$ it follows from 4.31 and $E_i = x_i D$ that

$$\mathrm{Mat}(D_i(g)) \in M_{n\times n}(\mathcal{O}_{x_1\ldots x_d} \cap \frac{1}{x_i} k((x_{h+1},\ldots,x_m))).$$

It is readily verified that $\mathcal{O}_{x_1\ldots x_d} \cap \frac{1}{x_i} k((x_{h+1},\ldots,x_m)) = \{0\}$, which concludes the proof of the theorem.

References.

[1] Coddington,E.A. and N.Levinson, Theory of ordinary differential equations. Mc Graw-Hill Book Company, Inc., 1955.

[2] Gérard,R. - Levelt,A., Invariants mesurants l'irrégularité en un point singulier des systèmes d'equation différentielles linéaires. Ann.Inst.Fourier 23,1 (1973), 157-195.

[3] Deligne,P., Equations Différentielles à Points Singuliers Réguliers. Lecture notes in Math. 163 (1970),Springer-Verlag.

[4] Zariski,O. - Samuel,P., Commutative Algebra, II. Van Nostrand Cy., 1960.

[5] Grauert,H. - Remmert,R., Analytische Stellenalgebren: Die Grundlehren der math.Wiss. in Einzeldarstellungen. Bd.176, Springer-Verlag, Berlin/Heidelberg/New York 1971.

[6] Bernstein,I.N., Modules over a ring of differential operators. Study of fundamental solutions of equations with constant coefficients. Functional Analysis and its Applications, Vol. 5, 1971.

[7] Bernstein,I.N., The Analytic continuation of generalized functions with respect to a parameter. Functional Analysis and its Applications, Vol.6, 1972.

[8] Björk,J.-E., The Weyl Algebra $A_n(\mathbb{C})$. Lectures from the Summer School at Grebbestad, June 1975. Department of Mathematics, University of Stockholm, Sweden.

[9] Björk,J.-E., The Weyl Algebra $A_n(\mathbb{C})$. September 1976. Mathematiska Institutionen Stockholms Universitet.

[10] Malgrange,B., Le polynôme de Bernstein d'une singularité isolée. Lectures notes in Math. 459 pp. 98-119. Berlin/ Heidelberg/New York, Springer (1975).

[11] Manin.Y., Moduli Fuchsiani. Annali Scuola Normale Sup. di Pisa Ser. III 19 (1965), pp.113-126.

[12] Gérard,R. - Levelt,A., Sur les Connexions a Singularités Régulières dans le cas de Plusieurs Variables. Funkcialaj Ekvacioj, 19 (1976), 149-173.

[13] van den Essen,A., On the definition of Fuchsian modules (to appear).

[14] van den Essen,A., Dimensions of Fuchsian modules (to appear).

[15] Bourbaki,N., Eléments de Mathématique. Fasc.VII. Algèbre.Chap.3. Algèbre multilinéaire. Hermann Paris 1958.

MATHEMATISCH INSTITUUT
KATHOLIEKE UNIVERSITEIT
Toernooiveld
Nijmegen
The Netherlands

ETUDE DE CERTAINS SYSTEMES DE PFAFF
AVEC SINGULARITES

par

R. GERARD
Institut de Recherche Mathématique Avancée
7, rue René Descartes
67084 STRASBOURG FRANCE

et

Y. SIBUYA
School of Mathematics
University of Minnesota
Minneapolis
Minnesota 55455

Durant l'élaboration de ce travail, le second auteur était d'avril à juin 1976 Professeur associé au département de Mathématique de Strasbourg.

A.M.S. : 34 - 35 C 45 E

Mots clefs : Systèmes de Pfaff. Singularités. Solutions formelles. Solutions convergentes. Développements asymptotiques. Systèmes de Pfaff linéaires avec singularités.

INTRODUCTION.

Pour des raisons de simplicité de l'exposition une bonne partie de ce mémoire est consacrée au cas de deux variables, le chapitre IV donnant les résultats dans le cas général. On se consacre à l'étude des systèmes de Pfaff complètement intégrable de la forme

$$(1) \qquad dy = \frac{f_1(x_1,x_2,y)}{x_1^{p_1}} dx_1 + \frac{f_2(x_1,x_2,y)}{x_2^{p_2}} dx_2$$

où f_1 et f_2 sont des applications à valeurs dans $\mathbb{C}^n$ et p_1, p_2 des entiers positifs.

Notre étude peut être considérée comme comportant deux parties :

(I) f_1 et f_2 sont holomorphes au voisinage de l'origine.

(II) f_1 et f_2 admettent des développements asymptotiques d'un certain type au voisinage de l'origine.

Parmi les résultats obtenus sous les hypothèses (I) signalons les suivants $(f_i(0,0) = 0)$

A) Si $p_1 = p_2 = 1$. Toute solution formelle de (1) est convergente.

B) Si par exemple $p_1 = 1$ et $p_2 > 1$ et si $A_1(0,0) = \frac{\partial f_1}{\partial y}(0,0)$ n'a pas de valeurs propres entières alors le système (1) admet une solution φ holomorphe et une seule qui vérifie $\varphi(0,0) = 0$.

C) Si $p_1 > 1$ et $p_2 > 1$ et si pour $i = 1,2$; $A_i(0,0) = \left(\frac{\partial f_i}{\partial y}(0,0)\right)$ est inversible, alors le système (1) admet une solution φ holomorphe et une seule qui vérifie $\varphi(0,0) = 0$.

Le résultat C) est un peu surprenant et nous a valu de recevoir des contre exemples qui heureusement n'en étaient pas. Ces résultats A), B) et C) ont des applications importantes aux connexions linéaires et en particulier à la réduction analytique de certains systèmes de Pfaff linéaires complètement intégrable. Par exemple considérons le système de Pfaff complètement intégrable.

(2) $$dy = \left(\frac{A(x_1,x_2)}{x_1^{p_1}} dx_1 + \frac{B(x_1,x_2)}{x_2^{p_2}} dx_2 \right) y$$

avec par exemple ,

$$p_1 > 1 \quad \text{et} \quad p_2 > 1 .$$

Si $A(0,0)$ et $B(0,0)$ ont des valeurs propres distinctes le système (2) est analytiquement équivalent à un système diagonal qu'il est alors facile d'intégrer. On a des résultats analogues lorsque $p_1 = 1$, $p_2 = 1$ ou lorsque $p_1 = 1$ et $p_2 > 1$.

Au cours des démonstrations on utilise des lemmes qui en eux-mêmes sont fort intéressants quant à leurs applications, citons le suivant :

Soit le système différentiel

(3) $$x \frac{dz}{dx} = f(x,y,z)$$

$y = (y_1, y_2 .. y_p)$ paramètre.

Alors si ce système admet une solution formelle (série formelle) de la forme

$$\sum_{n=0}^{+\infty} a_n(y) x^n$$

où $a_o(0) = 0$ et les $a_i(y)$ sont des séries formelles alors le système (3) admet une solution formelle de la même forme où les $a_i(y)$ sont des séries convergentes et un autre lemme nous permet alors de montrer que cette dernière série est en fait convergente.

Dans ce que nous avons appelé la deuxième partie ci-dessus on reprend l'étude des systèmes (1) avec les hypothèses (II) et on démontre des résultats du type suivant.

Soient $S = S_1 \times S_2$ un secteur de C^2 , U un polydisque centré à l'origine de C^n , $f_i (i = 1,2)$ deux fonctions holomorphes dans $S \times U$ telles que

$$f_i \underset{u.U}{\overset{S}{\sim}} \sum_{|r|=o}^{\infty} f^i_{r_1,r_2}(y) x_1^{r_1} x_2^{r_2}$$

$$\frac{\partial f_i}{\partial x_1} \underset{u.U}{\overset{S}{\sim}} \sum_{|r|=o}^{+\infty} f^i_{r_1,r_2}(y) r_1 x_1^{r_1-1} x_2^{r_2}$$

$$\frac{\partial f_i}{\partial x_2} \underset{u.U}{\overset{S}{\sim}} \sum_{|r|=o}^{+\infty} f^i_{r_1,r_2}(y) r_2 x_1^{r_1} x_2^{r_2-1} .$$

Nous avons de plus

$$f_i(x_1,x_2,y) = \sum_{|p|=o}^{+\infty} \hat{f}^i_p(x_1,x_2) y^p$$

dans $S \times U$.

On suppose $\hat{f}^i_o(0,0) = 0 \quad i = 1,2$.

Alors pour un système de Pfaff (1) complètement intégrable ou par exemple $p_1 > 1$ et $p_2 > 1$ on a le résultat suivant :

Si les deux matrices $A_i(0,0)$ sont régulières (ce n'est pas absolument nécessaire) alors si φ est une solution formelle du système formel associé à (1), il existe une vraie solution Φ de (1) holomorphe dans un secteur $S^1 \subset S$ et telle que

$$\Phi \overset{S^1}{\sim} \varphi .$$

On étudie également les cas où par exemple

$$f_i(x_1,x_2,y) \underset{u.S_2 \times U}{\overset{S_1}{\sim}} \sum_{|m|=o} f^i_{1,m}(x_2,y) x_1^m$$

$$f_i(x_1,x_2,y) \underset{u.S_1 \times U}{\overset{S_2}{\sim}} \sum_{m \geq o} f^i_{2,m}(x_1,y) x_2^m$$

où pour tout m

$$f^i_{1,m}(x_2,y) \underset{u.U}{\overset{S_2}{\sim}} \Sigma\, f^i_{1,m,\ell}(y)x_2^\ell$$

$$f^i_{2,m}(x,y) \underset{u.U}{\overset{S_1}{\sim}} \sum_{\ell \geq o} f^i_{2,m}(y)x_1^\ell$$

et on cherche dans ce cadre des solutions holomorphes de (1) admettant des développements asymptotiques d'un certain type dans des secteurs. L'utilisation dans cet article de plusieurs notions de développement asymptotique dans le cas de plusieurs variables nous a conduit à faire précéder l'étude des systèmes de Pfaff par un chapitre consacré aux développements asymptotiques et aux préliminaires nécessaires à la simplification des calculs que nous sommes amenés à faire par la suite.

CHAPITRE I

NOTIONS FONDAMENTALES.

1ère partie : Développements asymptotiques.

§ 1. Définitions

§ 2. Propriétés élémentaires des développements asymptotiques.

§ 3. Développements asymptotiques de fonctions dépendant de parametres.

2ème partie : Inégalités fondamentales.

§ 4. Inégalités fondamentales

§ 5. Secteurs propres

§ 6. Choix des chemins d'intégration.

Dans le cas d'une seule variable, la notion de développement asymptotique est très ancienne et bien connue, voir par exemple la bibliographie de l'ouvrage de W. WASOW [14]. Elle est un outil presque indispensable pour l'étude des équations différentielles au voisinage d'une singularité [2,3,7,8,9,12,13]. Dans le cas de plusieurs variables, cette notion est implicitement connue, mais à notre connaissance, on ne trouve pas une exposition facilement utilisable et donc pour aider à la compréhension des problèmes abordés dans cet article, il est utile de consacrer un chapitre aux développements asymptotiques pour avoir un catalogue de leurs propriétés qui parfois diffèrent de celles des développements asymptotiques dans le cas d'une variable, par exemple on perd la possibilité de deviner les développements asymptotiques mais heureusement on peut encore les intégrer !

Notations.

Nous désignerons par : $\mathbf{C}$, $\mathbf{R}$, $\mathbf{Q}$, $\mathbf{Z}$ respectivement le corps des nombres réels, le corps des nombres complexes, le corps des nombres rationnels et l'anneau des entiers ; $\mathbf{R}^+$, $\mathbf{Q}^+$, $\mathbf{Z}^+$ l'ensemble des éléments non négatifs de $\mathbf{R}$, $\mathbf{Q}$, $\mathbf{Z}$; $\mathbf{R}^n$, $\mathbf{C}^n$, $\mathbf{Q}^n$, $\mathbf{Z}^n$, ... le produit de n exemplaires de $\mathbf{R}$, $\mathbf{C}$, $\mathbf{Q}$, $\mathbf{Z}$ ...

Pour tout $p \in (\mathbf{Z}^+)^n$, $r \in \mathbf{R}^n$, $s \in \mathbf{R}^n$ $e \in (\mathbf{R}^+)^n$ et $x \in \mathbf{C}^n$, on écrira

$p!$ pour $p_1!\, p_2! \ldots p_n!$

$|p|$ pour $p_1 + p_2 + \ldots + p_n$

$r \leq s$ si pour tout $i = 1,2,\ldots n$ $\quad r_i \leq s_i$

$r < s$ si pour tout $i = 1,2,\ldots n$ $\quad r_i < s_i$

$r \leq \arg x \leq s$ si pour tout $i = 1,2,\ldots n$ $\quad r_i \leq \arg x_i \leq s_i$

$r < \arg x < s$ si pour tout $i = 1,2,\ldots n$ $\quad r_i < \arg x < s_i$

$|x| \leq e$ si pour tout $i = 1,2,\ldots n$ $\quad |x_i| \leq e_i$

$$\|x\|_m = \left[\sum_{i=1}^{n} |x_i|^m\right]^{\frac{1}{m}}$$

$$x^p = x_1^{p_1} x_2^{p_2} \dots x_n^{p_n}$$

Une série formelle ou convergente centrée à l'origine s'écrira donc

$$\sum_{|p|=0}^{+\infty} c_p x^p$$

à la place de

$$\sum_{p_i \geq 0} c_{p_1 \dots p_n} x_1^{p_1} \dots x_n^{p_n}$$

§ 1. - DEFINITIONS.

Un secteur (resp. secteur ouvert) de $\mathbb{C}^n$ de sommet l'origine est par définition une partie S de $\mathbb{C}^n$ définie par

$$S = \{x \in \mathbb{C}^n \mid \theta_1 \leq \arg x \leq \theta_2 \qquad 0 < |x| \leq r\}$$

$$(\text{resp. } S = \{x \in \mathbb{C}^n \mid \theta_1 < \arg x < \theta_2 \qquad 0 < |x| < r\})$$

$r = (r_1, r_2, \dots r_n)$ est le rayon du secteur $\theta_2 - \theta_1 = (\theta_2^1 - \theta_1^1, \dots \theta_2^n - \theta_1^n)$ est l'ouverture du secteur. Un secteur S est dit strict si son ouverture est inférieure strictement à 2π.

On peut se représenter un secteur non strict comme étant un secteur du revêtement universel d'un polydisque épointé à l'origine.

DEFINITION 1.1. - *On dit qu'une série formelle* $\sum_{|p|=0}^{m} a_p x^p$ *représente asymptotiquement dans un secteur* S *une fonction* f *à valeurs complexes définie dans* S *si*

$$\forall\, m \in \mathbb{Z}^+ \quad \left|f(x) - \sum_{|p|=0}^{m} a_p x^p\right| \leq C_m \|x\|_{m+1}^{m+1} \quad \text{dans } S$$

où C_m *est une constante.*

Notation.

$$f \overset{S}{\sim} \sum_{|p|=0}^{+\infty} a_p \, x^p$$

Remarques.

1.1. - Si $f \overset{S}{\sim} \Sigma\, a_p\, x^p$ alors pour tout secteur $S' \subset S$ on a $f \overset{S'}{\sim} \Sigma\, a_p\, x^p$

1.2. - Si $f \overset{S}{\sim} \Sigma\, a_p\, x^p$ alors $\lim\limits_{\substack{x \to 0 \\ x \in S}} f(x) = a_o$.

1.3. - La définition 1.1. s'étend sans difficulté aux fonctions à valeurs vectorielles et nous utiliserons cette notion dans les chapitres suivants sans autre précision.

1.4. - Dans la définition 1.1., on peut remplacer $\| \ \|_{m+1}$ par toute autre norme sur $\mathbb{C}^n$.

1.5. - Dans la définition 1.1., on peut remplacer le secteur S par une partie A quelconque de $\mathbb{C}^n$ ayant l'origine dans son adhérence. Cette notion un peu plus générale sera parfois utilisée dans la suite.

Nous dirons qu'une série formelle $\Sigma\, a_p\, x^p$ représente asymptotiquement une fonction f dans un secteur ouvert S si elle représente f dans tout sous-secteur S' de S .

Exemples.

1.1. - Tous les exemples rencontrés pour le cas d'une variable.

1.2. - Considérons, la fonction

$$f(x,y) = \exp - \frac{b}{x^{\alpha}\, y^{\beta}}$$

où b, α et β sont des constantes réelles positives et le secteur

$$S = \left\{ \begin{array}{ll} -u \le \arg x \le u & 0 < |x| \le r_1 \\ -v \le \arg y \le v & 0 < |y| \le r_2 \end{array} \right\} .$$

les nombres u et v sont positifs et vérifient

$$\alpha u + \beta v < \frac{\pi}{2} .$$

Si on pose $x = \rho e^{i\theta}$ $y = r e^{i\varphi}$, on voit que

$$\mathrm{Re}(-\frac{b}{x^{\alpha} y^{\beta}}) = -\frac{b}{\rho^{\alpha} r^{\beta}} \cos(\alpha\theta + \beta\varphi)$$

donc

$$\mathrm{Re}(-\frac{b}{x^{\alpha} y^{\beta}}) < 0 \quad \text{dans } S \text{ car}$$

$$-\frac{\pi}{2} < \alpha\theta + \beta\varphi < +\frac{\pi}{2} .$$

De plus, $\cos(\alpha\theta + \beta\varphi) > k_o > 0$ et donc

$$\mathrm{Re}(-\frac{b}{x^{\alpha} y^{\beta}}) < -\frac{b\,k_o}{\rho^{\alpha} r^{\beta}} .$$

Alors pour tout couple (p,q) d'éléments de $\mathbb{Z}^+$, on a

$$\left| \frac{\exp -\frac{b}{x^{\alpha} y^{\beta}}}{x^p\, y^q} \right| \leq \frac{\exp -\frac{b\,k_o}{\rho^{\alpha} r^{\beta}}}{\rho^p\, r^q} = Q .$$

et $\log Q = -\frac{1}{\rho^{\alpha} r^{\beta}} (b\,k_o + p\,\rho^{\alpha} r^{\beta} \log\rho + q\,\rho^{\alpha} r^{\beta} \log r)$.

ce qui montre que Q tend vers zéro lorsque

(ρ,r) tend vers zéro, donc il existe (r'_1, r'_2) tel que si $\rho \leq r'_1$ et $r \leq r'_2$

on ait

$$Q \leq 1 .$$

Comme Q est une fonction continue de (ρ,r) dans $r'_1 \leq \rho \leq r_1$ $r'_2 \leq r \leq r_2$.

Nous avons

$$Q \leq C \quad \text{dans} \quad 0 < \rho \leq r_1 \quad 0 < r \leq r_2$$

où C est une constante. Donc

$$\forall\, p \in \mathbb{Z}^+ \quad q \in \mathbb{Z}^+ \qquad \left|\exp -\frac{b}{x^{\alpha} y^{\beta}}\right| \leq C\, |x|^p\, |y|^q .$$

Or, pour tout $p \in \mathbb{Z}^+$, $q \in \mathbb{Z}^+$

$$(|x|^p - |y|^p)(|x|^q - |y|^q) \geq 0$$

c'est-à-dire que

$$|x|^p |y|^q + |x|^q |y|^p \leq |x|^{p+q} + |y|^{p+q}$$

et

$$\forall\, p \in \mathbb{Z}^+ ,\ q \in \mathbb{Z}^+ \qquad |x|^p |y|^q \leq |x|^{p+q} + |y|^{p+q} .$$

Ceci implique :

$$\forall\, p \in \mathbb{Z}^+\ \forall\, q \in \mathbb{Z}^+ \qquad \left|\exp - \frac{b}{x^\alpha y^\beta}\right| \leq C\left[|x|^{p+q} + |y|^{p+q}\right]$$

Donc, pour tout $m \in \mathbb{Z}^+$

$$\left|\exp - \frac{b}{x^\alpha y^\beta}\right| \leq C\left[|x|^{m+1} + |y|^{m+1}\right] .$$

Mais ceci prouve que la fonction $\exp - \frac{b}{x^\alpha y^\beta}$ est asymptotique à zéro dans le secteur S . Comme la fonction nulle est aussi asymptotique à zéro dans S , on voit que deux fonctions différentes peuvent avoir le même <u>développement asymptotique</u> dans un même secteur S .

1.3. - De la même manière que dans 1.2., on montre que la fonction

$$f(x) = \exp - \frac{b}{\prod_{i=1}^{n} x_i^{\alpha_i}} \qquad \text{où} \quad b > 0$$

et pour tout $i = 1,2,\ldots n$ $\quad \alpha_i > 0$ $\quad$ est asymptotique à zéro dans tout secteur S de la forme

$$-u \leq \arg x \leq u \qquad 0 < |x| \leq r$$

où $u = (u_1,\ldots u_n)$ est tel que

$$\Sigma\, \alpha_i\, u_i < \frac{\pi}{2} .$$

§ 2. - PROPRIETES ELEMENTAIRES DES DEVELOPPEMENTS ASYMPTOTIQUES.

2.1. - Propriétés algébriques.

PROPOSITION 2.1.1. - *Toute fonction* f *définie dans un secteur* S *a au plus un développement asymptotique dans* S.

En d'autres termes, si $f \overset{S}{\sim} \sum_p a_p x^p$ et $f \overset{S}{\sim} \sum_p b_p x^p$ alors pour tout p, $a_p = b_p$. Ceci permet donc de dire que $\sum_{|p|=0}^{+\infty} a_p x^p$ *est le développement asymptotique de* f *dans* S à la place de $\sum_{|p|=0}^{+\infty} a_p x^p$ représente asymptotiquement f dans S.

Preuve. - Supposons que $f \overset{S}{\sim} \sum_{|p|=0}^{+\infty} a_p x^p$ et $f \overset{S}{\sim} \sum_{|p|=0}^{+\infty} b_p x^p$. On a donc :

$$\forall m \in \mathbf{Z}^+ \qquad \left| \sum_{|p|=0}^{m} a_p x^p - \sum_{|p|=0}^{m} b_p x^p \right| \leq C_m \|x\|_{m+1}^{m+1}$$

si $m = 0$, on a :

$$|a_o - b_o| \leq C_o \|x\|_1$$

donc

$$a_o = b_o .$$

On va donc démontrer la proposition par récurrence sur m. Pour cela, il suffit de prouver le

LEMME 2.1.1. - *Si* P *est un polynôme homogène de degré* m *vérifiant*

$$|P(x)| \leq C \|x\|_{m+1}^{m+1} \quad \text{\underline{dans}} \; S$$

alors $P = 0$.

$$S = \left\{ x \in \mathbf{C}^n \mid \theta_1 \leq \arg x \leq \theta_2 \qquad 0 < |x| \leq r \right\} .$$

Posons

$$x_i = t_i x_1 \qquad i = 2,3,\dots n$$

avec

$$\theta_1^i - \theta_2^1 < \arg t_i < \theta_2^i - \theta_1^1 \qquad i = 2,3, \dots n$$

$$0 < |t_i| < \frac{r_i}{r_1} .$$

Notons U l'ouvert de $\mathbb{C}^{n-1}$ ainsi défini. Nous avons

$$|P(x_1, t_2\, x_2, \ldots, t_n\, x_n)| \leq \sum_{i=2}^{n} |t_i\, x_1|^{m+1} + |x_1|^{m+1}$$

$$\leq |x_1|^{m+1} \left[\sum_{i=2}^{n} |t_i|^{m+1} + 1\right]$$

Comme

$$P(x_1, t_2\, x_1, \ldots, t_n\, x_1) = x_1^m\, P(1, t_2, \ldots, t_n) .$$

On en déduit que

$$P(1, t_2, \ldots, t_n) = 0 \quad \text{dans } U .$$

c'est-à-dire que $P = 0$. Ce qui prouve le lemme, donc également la Proposition 2.1.1.

PROPOSITION 2.1.2. - <u>Si</u> $f \overset{S}{\sim} \sum_{|p|=0}^{+\infty} a_p\, x^p$ <u>et</u> $g \overset{S}{\sim} \sum_{|p|=0}^{+\infty} b_p\, x^p$ <u>alors pour tout</u> $\alpha \in \mathbb{C}$ <u>et</u> $\beta \in \mathbb{C}$

$$\alpha f + \beta g \overset{S}{\sim} \sum_{|p|=0}^{+\infty} (\alpha a_p + \beta b_p)\, x^p .$$

La preuve de cette proposition est immédiate.

PROPOSITION 2.1.3. - <u>Si</u> $f \overset{S}{\sim} \sum_{|p|=0}^{+\infty} a_p\, x^p$ <u>et</u> $g \overset{S}{\sim} \sum_{|p|=0}^{+\infty} b_p\, x^p$ <u>et si</u> $\sum_{|p|=0}^{+\infty} c_p\, x^p$ <u>est la série formelle produit des deux séries précédentes, alors</u>

$$f g \overset{S}{\sim} \sum_{|p|=0}^{+\infty} c_p\, x^p .$$

<u>Preuve</u>. - Ecrivons

$$f(x) = \sum_{|p|=0}^{m} a_p\, x^p + E_m^1(x) \quad , \quad g(x) = \sum_{|p|=0}^{m} b_p\, x^p + E_m^2(x) \quad ;$$

avec

$$|E_m^1(x)| \leq C_m^1\, \|x\|_{m-1}^{m+1} \quad \text{dans } S$$

$$|E_m^2(x)| \leq C_m^2\, \|x\|_{m-1}^{m+1} \quad \text{dans } S .$$

Alors

$$f(x)\,g(x) = \sum_{|p|=0}^{m} c_p\, x^p + H_m(x) + E_m^1(x)\Big(\sum_{|p|=0}^{m} b_p\, x^p\Big)$$

$$+ E_m^2(x)\Big(\sum_{|p|=0}^{m} a_p\, x^p\Big) + E_m^1(x)\,.\,E_m^2(x)$$

où $H_m(x)$ est la somme des termes de degré total supérieur à m figurant dans le produit

$$\Big(\sum_{|p|=0}^{m} a_p\, x^p\Big)\Big(\sum_{|p|=0}^{m} b_p\, x^p\Big)\ .$$

Du fait que $|x| \le r$ dans S , on déduit :

$$|E_m^1(x)\,.\,E_m^2(x)| \le K_m^1\, \|x\|_{m+1}^{m+1} \qquad \text{dans } S$$

$$|E_m^1(x)\,.\sum_{|p|=0}^{m} b_p\, x^p| \le K_m^2\, \|x\|_{m+1}^{m+1} \qquad \text{dans } S$$

$$|E_m^2(x)\,.\sum_{|p|=0}^{m} a_p\, x^p| \le K_m^3\, \|x\|_{m+1}^{m+1} \qquad \text{dans } S\ .$$

Une majoration analogue pour $H_m(x)$ va nous être donnée par le

LEMME 2.1.2. - <u>Si</u> $p = (p_1, p_2, \dots, p_n) \in (\mathbb{Z}^+)^n$, <u>alors</u>

$$|x|^p = \prod_{i=1}^{n} |x_i|^{p_i} \le \|x\|_{|p|}^{|p|}$$

Si $n = 2$, on a vu (exemple 1.2.) que

$$|x_1|^{p_1}\,|x_2|^{p_2} \le |x_1|^{p_1+p_2} + |x_2|^{p_1+p_2}$$

pour tout $(p_1, p_2) \in (\mathbb{Z}^+)^2$.

On a de manière générale

$$|x|^p \le \{\max_i |x_i|\}^p \le \|x\|_p^p$$

Ce résultat est le fait que $|x| \leq r$ dans S entraîne

$$|H_m(x,y)| \leq K_m^4 \, \|x\|_{m+1}^{m+1}$$

et donc

$$\left|f(x) - \sum_{|p|=0}^{m} c_p \, x^p\right| \leq C_m \, \|x\|_{m+1}^{m+1}$$

ce qui prouve la Proposition 2.1.3.

PROPOSITION 2.1.4. - <u>Soient</u> f_i $(i = 1,2,\dots q)$, q <u>fonctions définies dans un secteur</u> S <u>de</u> $\mathbb{C}^n$ <u>telles que</u>

1) $\lim_{\substack{x \to 0 \\ x \in S}} f_i(x) = 0 \qquad i = 1,2,\dots q$

2) $f_i(x) \overset{S}{\sim} \sum_{|p|=0}^{m} a_p^i \, x^p$

3) $f_i(S) \subset \Sigma_i \qquad$ (<u>secteur de</u> $\mathbb{C}$) .

<u>Alors si</u> g <u>est une fonction définie dans</u> $\Sigma = \Sigma_1 \times \Sigma_2 \dots \Sigma_q \subset \mathbb{C}^q$ <u>telle que</u>

$$g(u) \overset{\Sigma}{\sim} \sum_{|p|=0}^{+\infty} b_p \, u^p$$

<u>Alors</u>

$$g \circ f(x) \overset{S}{\sim} \sum_{|p|=0}^{+\infty} c_p \, x^p$$

<u>où</u> $\sum_{|p|=0}^{+\infty} c_p x^p$ <u>est la série formelle obtenue en substituant les séries</u>

$\sum_{|p|=0}^{+\infty} a_p^i x^p$ <u>dans la série formelle</u> $\sum_{|p|=0}^{+\infty} b_p u^p$.

<u>Preuve</u>.- Remarquons que la démonstration est très facile lorsque

$g(u) = \sum_{|p|=0}^{N} b_p u^p$ c'est-à-dire lorsque g est un polynôme.

Dans le cas général écrivons

$$f_i(x) = \sum_{|p|=0}^{m} a_p^i x^p + E_m^i(x)$$

avec

$$|E_m^i(x)| \leq C_m^i \|x\|_{m+1}^{m+1} \quad \text{dans} \quad S$$

et

$$g(u) = \sum_{|p|=0}^{m} b_p u^p + G_m(u)$$

avec

$$|G_m(u)| \leq D_m \|u\|_{m+1}^{m+1} \quad \text{dans} \quad \Sigma .$$

Vu la remarque ci-dessus, il suffit de prouver que pour tout m

$$\left|G_m\left(\sum_{|p|=0}^{m} a_p x^p + E_m|x)\right)\right| \leq D_m^1 \|x\|_{m+1}^{m+1} \quad \text{dans} \quad S .$$

On a $$|G_m(u)| \leq D_m \|u\|_{m+1}^{m+1} \quad \text{dans } \Sigma$$

donc

$$\left|G_m\left(\sum_{|p|=0}^{m} a_p x^p + E_m(x)\right)\right| \leq D_m \left\| \sum_{|p|=0}^{m} a_p x^p + E_m(x) \right\|_{m+1}^{m+1}$$

$$\left\| \sum_{|p|=0}^{m} a_p x^p + E_m(x) \right\|_{m+1}^{m+1} = \sum_{i=1}^{q} \left| \sum_{|p|=0}^{m} a_p^i x^p + E_m^i(x) \right|^{m+1}$$

Or

$$\left| \sum_{|p|=0}^{m} a_p^i x^p + E_m^i(x) \right|^{m+1} \leq K_m^i \|x\|_{m+1}^{m+1}$$

Car

1°) $a_o^i = \lim_{\substack{x \to 0 \\ x \in S}} g^i(x) = 0$

2°) Lemme 2.1.2.

3°) $|x| \leq r$ dans S

4°) $|E_m^i(x)| \leq C_m^i \|x\|_{m+1}^{m+1}$ dans S .

Il en résulte que

$$\left|G_m\left(\sum_{|p|=0}^{m} a_p x^p + E_m(x)\right)\right| \leq D_m^3 \|x\|_{m+1}^{m+1}$$

et en définitive, on a pour tout $m \in \mathbb{Z}^+$

$$\left|g(f_1(x), f_2(x), \ldots f_q(x)) - \sum_{|p|=0}^{m} c_p x^p\right| \leq C_m \|x\|_{m+1}^{m+1} \quad \text{dans } S$$

ce qui prouve notre proposition.

PROPOSITION 2.1.5. - Soit $f \overset{S}{\sim} \sum_{|p|=0}^{+\infty} a_p x^p$ alors si $a_o \neq 0$, $\frac{1}{f}$ existe dans un sous-secteur S' de S et de plus

$$\frac{1}{f} \overset{S'}{\sim} \sum_{|p|=0}^{+\infty} b_p x^p$$

où $\sum_{|p|=0}^{+\infty} b_p x^p$ est la série formelle inverse de la série $\sum_{|p|=0}^{+\infty} b_p x^p$.

Preuve. - Considérons la fonction d'une variable u , $g(u) = \frac{1}{a_o + u}$.

Nous savons que cette fonction est développable en série entière de u dans tout disque D fermé centré en 0 et de rayon strictement inférieur à $|a_o|$, désignons par $\sum_{|p|=0}^{+\infty} c_p u^p$ cette série ; on a évidemment :

$$g \overset{D}{\sim} \sum_{p=0}^{+\infty} c_p u^p .$$

Il existe un secteur $S' \subset S$ tel que la fonction $h = f - a_o$ soit à valeurs dans D sur S'. Comme $h(o) = 0$, toutes les hypothèses nécessaires pour faire la composition de g et de h sont satisfaites. Or $g(h(x)) = \frac{1}{f(x)}$ dans S' ce qui nous donne le résultat par la Proposition 2.1.4.

2.2. Propriétés analytiques.

PROPOSITION 2.2.1. - Si f est une fonction holomorphe dans

$$S = \{x \in \mathbb{C}^n \mid 0 \leq |x| \leq r\}$$

alors, on sait que

$$f(x) = \sum_{|p|=0}^{+\infty} a_p x^p$$

et on a

$$f \overset{S}{\sim} \sum_{|p|=0}^{+\infty} a_p x^p .$$

Preuve. - Pour tout $m \in \mathbb{Z}^+$, on peut écrire

$$f(x) = \sum_{|p|=0}^{m} a_p x^p + \sum_{|p|=m+1} \varphi_p(x) x^p$$

où pour tout p $\varphi_p(x)$ est une fonction holomorphe dans S donc bornée dans S.

Comme

$$|x^p| \leq \|x\|_{|p|}^{|p|} .$$

On a

$$|f(x) - \sum_{|p|=0}^{m} a_p x^p| \leq C_m \|x\|_{m+1}^{m+1} \quad \text{dans } S$$

ce qui prouve la proposition.

PROPOSITION 2.2.2. - Soit f une fonction holomorphe dans

$$S = \left\{x \in \mathbb{C}^n \quad 0 < |x| \leq r\right\}$$

telle que

$$f \overset{S}{\sim} \sum_{|p|=0}^{+\infty} a_p x^p .$$

Alors

1°) f se prolonge holomorphiquement à $\bar{S}$.

2°) la série $\sum_{|p|=0}^{+\infty} a_p x^p$ converge dans $\bar{S}$.

3°) $f(x) = \sum_{|p|=0}^{+\infty} a_p x^p$ dans $\bar{S}$.

Preuve. - Nous avons pour tout $m \in \mathbb{Z}^+$

$$|f(x) - \sum_{|p|=0}^{+\infty} a_p x^p| \leq C_m \|x\|_{m+1}^{m+1} \quad \text{dans } S .$$

$$S = S_1 \times S_2 \times \ldots \times S_n \qquad S_i = \left\{x_i \in \mathbb{C} \mid 0 < |x_i| \leq r_i\right\} .$$

Fixons $x_2 = x_2^o, \ldots, x_n = x_n^o$ dans $S_2 \times S_3 \times \ldots \times S_n$, nous avons

$$|f(x_1, x_2^o, \ldots, x_n^o)| \leq \sum_{|p|=0}^{m} |a_p| |x_1|^{p_1} |x_2^o|^{p_2} \ldots |x_n^o|^{p_n}$$
$$+ C_m\left[|x_1|^{m+1} + \sum_{i=2}^{m+1} |x^o|^{m+1}\right] \quad \text{dans } S .$$

Il en résulte que la fonction $f(x_1, x_2^o, \ldots x_n^o)$ de la seule variable x_1 est bornée dans S_1 et donc se prolonge holomorphiquement à l'origine. Ceci est également vrai pour toutes les autres variables, c'est-à-dire que $f(x_1, x_2, \ldots x_n)$ se prolonge à $\bar{S}$ en une fonction holomorphe par rapport à chacune des variables et d'après le théorème d'Hartog f est holomorphe dans $\bar{S}$.

On a donc dans $\bar{S}$

$$f(x) = \sum_{|p|=0}^{+\infty} b_p x^p$$

mais, d'après l'unicité des développements asymptotiques, nous avons, pour tout p , $a_p = b_p$ ce qui donne la Proposition 2.2.2.

Soit S un secteur et f une fonction holomorphe dans S , on notera :

$$D^{\alpha}f = \left(\frac{\partial}{\partial x_1}\right)^{\alpha_1} \left(\frac{\partial}{\partial x_2}\right)^{\alpha_2} \cdots \left(\frac{\partial}{\partial x_n}\right)^{\alpha_n} f .$$

PROPOSITION 2.2.3. - Si pour tout α , $D^{\alpha}f(x)$ admet une limite f_{α} lorsque x tend vers zéro dans un secteur S , alors

$$f(x) \overset{S}{\sim} \sum_{|\alpha|=0}^{+\infty} \frac{f_{\alpha} x^{\alpha}}{\alpha!} .$$

Preuve. - Soit x un point de S , considérons la fonction de la seule variable t

$$\varphi(t) = f(tx) \qquad 0 < |t| \leq 1 .$$

Pour tout a tel que $0 < |a| \leq 1$, on peut écrire pour tout m entier :

$$\varphi(t) = \varphi(a) + (t-a) \frac{\varphi'(a)}{1!} + \ldots + \frac{(t-a)^m}{m!} \varphi^{(m)}(a) + \frac{1}{m!} \int_a^t (t-u)^m \varphi^{(m+1)}(u) \quad du$$

et en particulier

$$\varphi(1) = \varphi(a) + \frac{1-a}{1!} \varphi'(a) + \ldots + \frac{(1-a)^m}{m!} \varphi^{(m)}(a) + \frac{1}{m!} \int_a^1 (1-u)^m \varphi^{(m+1)}(u) \, du$$

Or

$$\begin{aligned} \varphi(t) &= f(tx) \\ \varphi'(t) &= \sum_{|\alpha|=1} x^{\alpha} D^{\alpha}f(tx) \\ &\vdots \\ \varphi^{m}(t) &= \sum_{|\alpha|=m} x^{\alpha} D^{\alpha}f(tx) \end{aligned}$$

Il en résulte que lorsque t tend vers zéro toute dérivée $\varphi^{(p)}(t)$ de φ a une limite φ_p et on a :

$$\varphi(1) = \varphi_o + \frac{1}{1!} \varphi_1 + \ldots + \frac{1}{m!} \varphi_m + \frac{1}{m!} \int_0^1 (1-u)^m \varphi^{(m+1)}(u) \quad du .$$

Comme

$$\varphi(1) = f(x)$$

et

$$\varphi_p = \sum_{|\alpha|=p} x^\alpha f_\alpha$$

nous avons :

$$f(x) = \sum_{|\alpha|=0}^{m} \frac{x^\alpha}{\alpha!} f_\alpha + \frac{1}{m!} \int_0^1 (1-u)^m \sum_{|\alpha|=m+1} x^\alpha D^\alpha f(ux)\, du \quad .$$

Or, pour tout α, $D^\alpha f$ est bornée dans $S \times \{0 \leq |u| \leq 1\}$. Donc :

$$\left|f(x) - \sum_{|\alpha|=0}^{m} \frac{x^\alpha}{\alpha!} f_\alpha\right| \leq \frac{1}{m!} \sum_{|\alpha|=m+1} |x|^\alpha C_\alpha$$

ce qui entraîne que pour tout m

$$\left|f(x) - \sum_{|\alpha|=0}^{m} x^\alpha \frac{f_\alpha}{\alpha!}\right| \leq C_m \|x\|_{m+1}^{m+1} \quad \text{dans } S \ .$$

et la proposition est démontrée. On en déduit également la proposition 2.2.1 :

COROLLAIRE 2.2.1. - <u>Si</u> f <u>est une fonction holomorphe dans</u>

$$S = \{x \in \mathbb{C}^n \mid 0 \leq |x| \leq r\}$$

<u>alors dans</u> S

$$f(x) = \sum_{|p|=0}^{+\infty} a_p x^p$$

<u>et</u>

$$f(x) \underset{S}{\sim} \sum_{|p|=0}^{+\infty} a_p x^p \ .$$

PROPOSITION 2.2.4. - <u>Si</u> f <u>est une fonction holomorphe dans le secteur</u> $S = S_1 \times S_2 \times \ldots \times S_n$ <u>de</u> $\mathbb{C}^n$ <u>et si</u>

$$f \underset{S}{\sim} \sum_{|p|=0}^{+\infty} a_p x^p \ .$$

Alors pour tout $i = 1,2,\ldots n$

$$\int_0^{x_i} f(x_1,x_2,\ldots x_{i-1},t,x_{i+1},\ldots x_n)dt \overset{S}{\sim} \sum_{|p|=0}^{+\infty} \frac{a_p}{p_i+1} x_1^{p_1}\ldots x_i^{p_{i+1}} x_{i+1}^{p_{i+1}}\ldots x_n^{p_n}$$

si le chemin d'intégration est contenu dans S^i à l'exception de l'origine.

Preuve. - Pour tout entier m , nous avons

$$f(x) = \sum_{|p|=0}^{m} a_p x^p + E_m(x) \quad \text{dans } S$$

où

$$|E_m(x)| \leq C_m \|x\|_{m+1}^{m+1} .$$

Nous démontrons le résultat lorsque $i=1$.

Fixons maintenant $(x_2,x_3,\ldots x_n) = (x_2^o,x_3^o,\ldots x_n^o)$ dans $S_2 \times S_3 \times \ldots \times S_n$. Nous avons

$$|f(x_1,x^o)| \leq \sum_{|p|=0}^{m} |a_p| \, |x_1|^{p_1} |x_2^o|^{p_2} \ldots |x_n^o|^{p_n} + C_m\Big[|x_1|^{m+1} + \sum_{i=2}^{n} |x_i^o|^{m+1}\Big]$$

Il en résulte que lorsque x_1 tend vers zéro, la fonction $f(x_1,x^o)$ reste bornée et donc l'intégrale $\int_0^{x_1} f(t,x_2 \ldots x_n)dt$ a un sens et on peut prendre pour chemin d'intégration le segment joignant 0 à x_1 dans S_1 . Nous avons donc :

$$\int_0^{x_1} f(t,x_2,\ldots x_n)dt = \sum_{|p|=0}^{m} \frac{a_{p_1,p_2,\ldots p_n}}{p_1+1} x_1^{p_1+1} x_2^{p_2}\ldots x_n^{p_n} + \int_0^{x_1} E_m(t,x_2,\ldots x_n)dt$$

Et

$$\int_0^{x_1} E_m(t,x_2,\ldots x_n)dt = \int_0^1 E_m(\tau x_1,x_2,\ldots x_n)x_1 \, d\tau$$

$$\begin{aligned}\Big|\int_0^{x_1} E_m(t,x_2,\ldots x_n)dt\Big| &\leq \int_0^1 |E_m(\tau x_1,x_2,\ldots x_n)| \, |x_i| \, d\tau \\ &\leq C_m |x_1| \int_0^1 \Big(|\tau x_1|^{m+1} + \sum_{i=2}^{n} |x_i|^{m+1}\Big) d\tau \\ &\leq C_m |x_1| \Big[\frac{|x_1|^{m+1}}{m+2} + \sum_{i=2}^{n} |x_i|^{m+1}\Big] \\ &\leq K_m \|x\|_{m+2}^{m+2}\end{aligned}$$

ce qui prouve le résultat.

COROLLAIRE 2.2.2. - Supposons que f holomorphe dans un secteur S de $\mathbb{C}^n$ vérifie :

1) $f \overset{S}{\sim} \sum_{|p|=0}^{+\infty} a_p\, x^p$

2) $f(x)$ a une limite $\varphi(x_2, x_3, \ldots x_n)$ lorsque x_1 tend vers zéro

3) $\dfrac{\partial f}{\partial x_1}(x) \overset{S}{\sim} \sum_{|p|=0}^{+\infty} b_p\, x^p$

alors

$$\sum_{|p|=0}^{+\infty} b_p\, x^p = \sum_{|p|=0}^{+\infty} \frac{\partial}{\partial x_1}(a_p\, x^p) .$$

Preuve. - Nous avons pour tout entier m

$$\left|f(x) - \sum_{|p|=0}^{m} a_p\, x^p\right| \leq C_m \|x\|_{m+1}^{m+1} \quad \text{dans } S$$

et si on fait tendre x_1 vers zéro dans S_1, il vient

$$\left|\varphi(x_2, \ldots x_n) - \left(\sum_{|p|=0}^{m} a_p\, x^p\right)_{x_1=0}\right| \leq C_m \left[\sum_{i=2}^{n} |x_i|^{m+1}\right]$$

Donc

$$\varphi(x_2, \ldots x_n) \overset{S}{\sim} \sum_{|p|=0}^{+\infty} (a_p\, x^p)_{x_1=0} .$$

La Proposition 2.2.4. montre que

$$\int_0^{x_1} \frac{\partial f}{\partial x_1}(t, x_2, \ldots, x_n)\,dt \overset{S}{\sim} \sum b_p \int_0^{x_1} x^p\, dx_1 .$$

Donc

$$f(x) - \varphi(x_2, x_3, \ldots x_n) \overset{S}{\sim} \sum_{|p|=0} b_p \int_0^{x_1} x^p\, dx_1$$

et donc

$$f(x) \overset{S}{\sim} \sum_{|p|=0}^{+\infty} \frac{b_p}{p_1+1}\, x_1^{p_1+1} x_2^{p_2} \ldots x_n^{p_n} + \sum_{|p|=0}^{+\infty} a_{0,p_2,\ldots p_n}\, x_2^{p_2} \ldots x_n^{p_n} .$$

et l'unicité du développement asymptotique implique le corollaire.

THEOREME 2.2.1. - Soient $\sum_{|p|=0}^{+\infty} a_p x^p$ une série formelle et $S = S_1 \times S_2 \times \dots \times S_n$ un secteur strict de $\mathbb{C}^n$. Alors il existe une fonction f holomorphe dans S telle que

$$f \overset{S}{\sim} \sum_{|p|=0}^{+\infty} a_p x^p .$$

Remarques.

1. - Si $f \overset{S}{\sim} \sum_{|p|=0}^{+\infty} a_p x^p$ alors

$$f(x e^{i\theta}) \overset{S'}{\sim} \sum_{|p|=0}^{+\infty} a_p e^{ip\theta} x^p \quad \text{où}$$

$$S' = e^{i\theta} S .$$

Rappelons qu'avec nos notations $x e^{i\theta} = x_1 e^{i\theta_1} . x_2 e^{i\theta_2} \dots x_n e^{i\theta_n}$

$$S' = e^{i\theta_1} S_1 \times e^{i\theta_2} S_2 \times \dots \times e^{i\theta_n} S_n .$$

De plus, si f est holomorphe dans S, la fonction $f^* = f(x e^{i\theta})$ est holomorphe dans S'.

2. - On peut supposer que $a_o = 0$, quitte à remplacer f par $f - a_o$, c'est ce que nous ferons dans la suite.

La remarque 1 permet sans nuire à la généralité du résultat de supposer que

$$S = S_1 \times S_2 \times \dots \times S_n$$

où

$$S_i = \{ - u_i < \arg x_i < u_i \qquad 0 < |x_i| \leq r_i \} .$$

Idée de la démonstration.

Nous allons introduire une suite de fonctions $\varphi_p(x)$ holomorphes dans S et telles que la série $\sum_{|p|=0}^{+\infty} a_p \varphi_p(x) x^p$ converge uniformément dans S

Ensuite on montrera que la somme $\Phi(x) = \sum_{|p|=0}^{+\infty} a_p \varphi_p(x) x^p$ qui est holomorphe dans S admet $\sum_{|p|=0}^{+\infty} a_p x^p$ comme développement asymptotique dans S .

1ère étape. - Choix des φ_p .

Posons

$$\varphi_p(x) = 1 - \exp\left(- \frac{b_p}{x^{\alpha_p}}\right)$$

où

1) pour tout p $\quad b_p > 0$

2) $\alpha^i_{p_i} = 0$ si $p_i = 0$

$\alpha^i_{p_i} = \alpha^i_{q_i} = \alpha^i$ si $p_i \neq 0$ et $q_i \neq 0$.

De plus, pour tout i $\quad 0 < \alpha^i < 1$ et

$$0 < \sum_{i=1}^{n} \alpha^i u_i < \frac{\pi}{2} .$$

Si on écrit $x_j = \rho_j \exp(i\theta_j)$, comme $-u_j < \theta_j < u_j$, on a

$$h - \frac{\pi}{2} < \sum_{i=1}^{n} \alpha^i \theta_i < \frac{\pi}{2} - h \qquad h > 0$$

qui implique que

$$\cos\left(\sum_{i=1}^{n} \alpha^i \theta_i\right) \geq k_o > 0 .$$

Comme $\beta = \sum_{i=1}^{n} \alpha^i_{p_i} u_i$ vérifie

$$0 < \beta < \sum_{i=1}^{n} \alpha^i u_i < \frac{\pi}{2}$$

on a

$$h - \frac{\pi}{2} < \sum_{i=1}^{n} \alpha^i_{p_i} \theta_i < \frac{\pi}{2} - h$$

et

$$\cos\left(\sum_{i=1}^{n} \alpha^i_{p_i} \theta_i\right) \geq k_o > 0 .$$

De ce qui précède, on déduit que :

$$\mathrm{Re}\left(-\frac{b_p}{x^{\alpha_p}}\right) = -\frac{b_p}{\rho^{\alpha_p}} \cos\left(\sum_{i=1}^{n} \alpha^i_{p_i} \theta_i\right) < 0$$

<u>2ème étape</u>. - <u>Choix des</u> b_p .

Si $r_i < 1$ pour tout i , on pose

$$b_p = |a_p|^{-1} \qquad \text{si} \qquad a_p \neq 0$$

$$\text{et} \qquad b_p = 0 \qquad \text{si} \qquad a_p = 0 \ .$$

Si $r_i \geq 1$ pour un certain i , on pose

$$b_p = |a_p\, r^p|^{-1} \qquad \text{si} \qquad a_p \neq 0$$

$$b_p = 0 \qquad \text{si} \qquad a_p = 0 \ .$$

Nous allons poursuivre la démonstration dans le cas où pour tout i , $r_i < 1$ dans l'autre cas elle est tout à fait analogue.

<u>3ème étape</u>. - <u>Convergence de la série</u> $\sum_{|p|=0}^{+\infty} a_p\, \varphi_p(x)\, x^p$

Nous avons

$$|a_p\, \varphi_p(x)\, x^p| = |a_p(1 - \exp\left(-\frac{b_p}{x^{\alpha}}\right))\, x^p|$$

et en utilisant le fait que

$$|1 - e^z| \leq |z| \qquad \text{si} \qquad \mathrm{Re}(z) < 0$$

on a

$$|a_p\, \varphi_p(x)\, x^p| \leq |a_p|\, |b_p|\, |x|^{p-\alpha_p}$$

$$\leq |x_1|^{p_1 - \alpha^1_{p_1}}\, |x_2|^{p_2 - \alpha^2_{p_2}} \cdots |x_n|^{p_n - \alpha^n_{p_n}}$$

Comme

$$\alpha^i_{p_i} = 0 \qquad \text{si} \qquad p_i = 0$$

$$\alpha^i_{p_i} = \alpha^i_{q_i} = \alpha_i \qquad \text{si} \qquad p_i \neq 0 \text{ et } q_i \neq 0$$

et $$0 < \alpha^i < 1 \quad ,$$

on voit que la série

$$\sum_{|p|=0}^{+\infty} |x|^{p-\alpha_p}$$

converge uniformément dans

$$|x| \leq r < 1 \quad .$$

Dans la série $\sum_{|p|=0}^{+\infty} a_p \, \varphi_p(x) \, x^p$ représente une fonction $f(x)$ holomorphe dans S .

4ème étape.

Pour tout m $\left|\exp - \frac{b_p}{x^{\alpha_p}}\right| \leq K_{m,p} \|x\|_{m+1}^{m+1}$.

La démonstration est analogue à celle qui a été donnée pour l'exemple 1.2. .

Ceci entraîne que pour tout entier m

$$\left| \sum_{|p|=0}^{m} a_p (1 - \varphi_p(x)) x^p \right| \leq K_m^1 \, \|x\|_{m+1}^{m+1}$$

5ème étape. - Nous avons

$$\left| \sum_{|p|=m+1}^{+\infty} a_p \, \varphi_p(x) x^p \right| \leq K_m^2 \, \|x\|_m^m$$

La démonstration se fait par récurrence sur le nombre des variables. Pour une variable

$$\left| \sum_{p=m+1}^{+\infty} a_p \, \varphi_p(x) \, x^p \right| \leq \sum_{p=m+1}^{+\infty} |x|^{p-\alpha} = \frac{1}{|x|^{\alpha}} \quad \frac{|x|^{m+1}}{1-|x|}$$

$$\leq |x|^{m+1-\alpha} \leq r^{1-\alpha} \, |x|^m$$

Supposons le résultat vrai pour un nombre de variables strictement inférieur à n . Nous avons

$$\Big|\sum_{|p|=m+1}^{+\infty} a_p\, \varphi_p(x)\, x^p\Big| \le \sum_{|p|=m+1}^{+\infty} |x|^{p-\alpha_p}$$

$$\le \sum_{\substack{|p|=m+1\\ p_i>0,\, i=1,2\ldots n}}^{+\infty} |x|^{p-\alpha_p} + H$$

où

$$H = \sum_{i=1}^{n} \Big(\sum_{\substack{|p|=m+1\\ p_i=0}}^{+\infty} |x|^{p-\alpha_p} \Big)$$

Or, si $p_i = 0$, $\alpha^i_{p_i} = 0$, donc $\sum_{\substack{|p|=m+1\\ p_i=0}}^{+\infty} |x|^{p-\alpha_p}$ ne contient que les n-1 variables $x_1, x_2, \ldots x_{i-1}, x_{i+1} \ldots x_n$. Alors, d'après l'hypothèse de récurrence

$$\sum_{\substack{|p|=m+1\\ p_i=0}}^{+\infty} |x|^{p-\alpha_p} \le D^i_m\, \|x\|^m_m$$

et par suite

$$|H| \le D_m\, \|x\|^m_m \quad .$$

Considérons donc

$$\sum_{\substack{|p|=m+1\\ p_i>0}} |x|^{p-\alpha_p} = \frac{1}{|x|^\alpha} \sum_{\substack{|p|=m+1\\ p_i>0}} |x|^p$$

$$= \frac{1}{|x|^\alpha} \Big[|x_1| \sum_{\substack{p_2+p_3+\ldots+p_m=m\\ p_i>0}}^{+\infty} |x_2|^{p_2} \ldots |x_n|^{p_n} + |x_1|^2 \sum_{\substack{p_2+\ldots+p_n=m+1\\ p_i>0}}^{+\infty} |x_2|^{p_2} \ldots |x_n|^{p_n}$$

$$+ \ldots + |x_1|^{m+1-n} \sum_{\substack{p_2+\ldots+p_n=n\\ p_i>0}}^{+\infty} |x_2|^{p_2} \ldots |x_n|^{p_n} + |x_1|^{m+1-n} \sum_{\substack{p_2+\ldots+p_n=n+1\\ p_i>0}}^{+\infty} |x_2|^{p_2} \ldots |x_n|^{p_n}$$

$$+ |x_1|^{m+1-n+1} \sum_{\substack{p_2+\ldots+p_n=n+1\\ p_i>0}}^{+\infty} |x_2|^{p_2} \ldots |x_n|^{p_n} + \ldots \Big]$$

Alors, d'après l'hypothèse de récurrence, on a :

$$\sum_{\substack{|p|=m+1\\ p_i>0}}^{+\infty} |x|^{p-\alpha_p} \leq \frac{1}{|x|^{\alpha}} \Big[|x_1| \, E_m\Big(\sum_{i=2}^{n} |x_i|^m\Big) + |x_1|^2 \, E_{m-1}\Big(\sum_{i=2}^{n} |x_i|^{m-1}\Big)$$

$$+ \dots + |x_1|^{m+1-n} \, E_n\Big(\sum_{i=2}^{n} |x_i|^n\Big) + |x_1|^{m+1-n} \, E_{n+1}\Big[\sum_{i=2}^{n} |x_i|^{n+1}\Big] \frac{1}{1-|x_1|} \Big].$$

Comme pour tout entier q , on a $|x_1|^{q-\alpha} \leq |x_1|^{q-1}$ si $0<\alpha<1$ nous en déduisons que :

$$\sum_{\substack{|p|=m+1\\ p_i>0}}^{+\infty} |x|^{p-\alpha_p} \leq K_m \, \|x\|_m^m$$

ce qui implique :

$$\Big| \sum_{|p|=m+1}^{+\infty} a_p \, \varphi_p(x) \, x^p \Big| \leq K_m^2 \, \|x\|_m^m$$

<u>6ème étape</u>. - $f \overset{S}{\sim} \sum_{|p|=0} a_p \, x^p$

En effet :

$$\Big|f(x) - \sum_{|p|=0}^{m} a_p \, x^p\Big| \leq \Big|f(x) - \sum_{|p|=0}^{m+1} a_p \, x^p\Big| + \Big|\sum_{|p|=m+1} a_p \, x^p\Big|$$

$$\leq \Big|\sum_{|p|=0}^{+\infty} a_p \, \varphi_p(x) \, x^p - \sum_{|p|=0}^{m+1} a_p \, x^p\Big| + \Big|\sum_{|p|=m+1} a_p \, x^p\Big|$$

$$\leq \Big|\sum_{|p|=0}^{m+1} a_p(\varphi_p(x)-1)x^p\Big| + \Big|\sum_{|p|=m+1} a_p \, x^p\Big|$$

$$+ \Big|\sum_{|p|>m+1} a_p \, \varphi_p(x) \, x^p\Big|$$

Or

$$\Big|\sum_{|p|>m+1} a_p \, \varphi_p(x) x^p\Big| \leq K_{m+1}^2 \, \|x\|_{m+1}^{m+1} \qquad \text{(5ème étape)}$$

$$\Big|\sum_{|p|=m+1} a_p \, x^p \Big| \leq K_{m+1}^3 \, \|x\|_{m+1}^{m+1} \qquad \text{(évident)}$$

$$\Big|\sum_{|p|=1}^{m+1} a_p(\varphi_p(x)-1)x^p\Big| \leq K_m^4 \, \|x\|_m^m \qquad \text{(4ème étape)}$$

et

$$\varphi_p(x) - 1 = -\exp\Big(-\frac{b_p}{x^{\alpha_p}}\Big)$$

Il résulte finalement que

$$|f(x) - \sum_{|p|=0}^{m} a_p x^p| \le C_m \|x\|_m^m .$$

THEOREME 2.2.2. - Soient $\sum_{|p|=0}^{+\infty} a_p x^p$ une série formelle et S un secteur alors il existe une fonction Φ holomorphe dans S telle que :

1) $\Phi(x) \overset{S}{\sim} \sum_{|p|=0}^{+\infty} a_p x^p$

2) pour tout $i = 1,2,\dots n$

$$\frac{\partial \Phi}{\partial x_i} \overset{S}{\sim} \sum_{|p|=0}^{+\infty} a_p \frac{\partial}{\partial x_i} (x^p) .$$

La démonstration se fait par récurrence sur le nombre des variables. Dans le cas d'une variable, on sait [14] que si

$$f \overset{S}{\sim} \sum_{p=0}^{+\infty} a_p x^p$$

alors

$$\frac{\partial f}{\partial x} \overset{S}{\sim} \sum_{p=0}^{+\infty} p\, a_p\, x^{p-1} \quad .$$

Supposons donc que le résultat est vrai pour tout nombre de variables strictement inférieur à n .

Notons par φ la série formelle donnée, et considérons la série formelle $\frac{\partial^n \varphi}{\partial x_1 \partial x_2 \dots \partial x_n}$. Il existe une fonction Φ holomorphe dans le secteur S telle que

$$\Phi(x) \sim \frac{\partial^n \varphi}{\partial x_1 \partial x_2 \dots \partial x_n} \quad .$$

Alors par intégration successive dans le secteur de chacune des variables x_i le long d'un chemin contenu dans S_i à l'exception de l'origine qui est en 0 , nous obtenons

$$\int_0^{x_1} dt_1 \int_0^{x_2} dt_2 \dots \int_0^{x_n} \Phi(t_1, t_2, \dots t_n) dt_n \overset{S}{\sim} \varphi(x_1, x_2, \dots x_n) -$$

$$- \sum_{i=1}^{n} \varphi_i(x_1, \dots x_{i-1}, \tilde{x}_i, x_{i+1}, \dots n) + \sum_{i,j} \varphi_{ij}(x_1, \dots \tilde{x}_i, \dots \tilde{x}_j, \dots x_n)$$

$$- \sum_{i,j,k} \varphi_{ijk}(x_1, \dots \tilde{x}_i, \dots \tilde{x}_j, \dots \tilde{x}_k, \dots x_n) + \dots$$

$$+ (-1)^{n-1} \sum_{i, i_2 \dots i_n} \varphi_{i_1 \dots i_{n-1}}(\dots \tilde{x}_{i_1} \tilde{x}_{i_2} \dots \tilde{x}_{i_n}) + (-1)^n \varphi(0,0,\dots,0)$$

où

$$\varphi_{i_1 i_2, \dots, i_k} = \varphi(\dots \tilde{x}_{i_1}, \dots \tilde{x}_{i_2}, \dots \tilde{x}_{i_k}, \dots) \quad ,$$

x_i signifiant que l'on a remplacé x_i par 0 . Mais, alors, d'après l'hypothèse de récurrence, il existe des fonctions holomorphes dans S telles que

$$\begin{cases} \Phi_i \overset{S}{\sim} \varphi_i(x_1,\dots \tilde{x}_i,\dots x_n) \\ \text{avec} \\ \dfrac{\partial\varphi_i}{\partial x_k} \overset{S}{\sim} \dfrac{\partial\varphi_i}{\partial x_k}(x_1,\dots \tilde{x}_i,\dots x_n) \qquad \text{pour tout} \quad k\neq i \end{cases}$$

$$\begin{cases} \Phi_{ij} \overset{S}{\sim} \varphi_{ij}(x_1,\dots \tilde{x}_i,\dots \tilde{x}_j,\dots x_n) \\ \text{avec} \\ \dfrac{\partial\Phi_{ij}}{\partial x_k} \overset{S}{\sim} \dfrac{\partial\varphi_{ij}}{\partial x_k}(x_1,\dots \tilde{x}_j,\dots \tilde{x}_k,\dots x_n) \qquad \text{pour tout} \quad k\neq i\ ,\ k\neq j \end{cases}$$

$$\vdots \qquad\qquad \vdots$$

$$\begin{cases} \Phi_{i_1\dots i_{n-1}} \overset{S}{\sim} \varphi_{i_1,\dots i_{n-1}}(.\tilde{x}_{i_1},\dots \tilde{x}_{i_{n-1}}) \\ \text{avec} \\ \dfrac{\partial\Phi_{i_1\dots i_{n-1}}}{\partial x_k} \overset{S}{\sim} \dfrac{\partial\varphi_{i_1\dots i_{n-1}}}{\partial x_k}(..\tilde{x}_{i_1},\dots \tilde{x}_{i_{n-1}},\dots) \qquad \text{pour tout} \quad k\neq i_\ell \end{cases}$$

Considérons alors la fonction

$$f(x) = \int_0^{x_1} dt_1 \int_0^{x_2} dt_2 \dots \int_0^{x_n} \Phi(t_1,t_2,\dots t_n)dt_n + \sum_i \Phi_i - \sum_{i,j} \Phi_{ij}$$
$$+ \dots -(-1)^{n-1} \sum_{i=1}^{n} \Phi_{i_1,\dots i_{n-1}} -(-1)^n \varphi(0)\ .$$

Cette fonction est holomorphe dans S et satisfait aux conditions demandées.

En effet, pour tout $k = 1,2,\dots n$

$$\frac{\partial f}{\partial x_k} = \int_0^{x_1} dt_1 \int_0^{x_2} dt_2 \dots \int_0^{x_{k-1}} dt_{k-1} \int_0^{x_{k+1}} dt_{k+1} \dots \int_0^{x_n} \Phi(t_1,\dots$$
$$\dots,t_{k-1},x_k,t_{k+1},\dots t_n)dt_n$$
$$+ \sum_{i\neq k} \frac{\partial\Phi_i}{\partial x_k} - \sum_{\substack{i\neq k \\ j\neq k}} \frac{\partial\Phi_{ij}}{\partial x_k} +\dots+ (-1)^{n-1} \sum_{\substack{i_\ell\neq k \\ \ell=1,2,\dots n-1}} \frac{\partial\Phi_{i_1\dots i_{n-1}}}{\partial x_k}$$

et

$$\frac{\partial f}{\partial x_k} \overset{S''}{\sim} \int_0^{x_1} dt_1 \ldots \int_0^{x_{k-1}} dt_{k-1} \int_0^{x_{k+1}} dt_{k+1} \ldots \int_0^{x_n} \frac{\partial^n \varphi}{\partial x_1 \ldots \partial x_n} (t_1, \ldots$$

$$\ldots, t_{k-1}, x_k, t_{k+1}, \ldots t_n) dt_n$$

$$+ \sum_{i \neq k} \frac{\partial \varphi_i}{\partial x_k} (x_1 \ldots \tilde{x}_i \ldots x_n) - \sum_{\substack{i \neq k \\ j \neq k}} \frac{\partial \varphi_{ij}}{\partial x_k} (x_1 \ldots \tilde{x}_i \ldots \tilde{x}_j \ldots x_n)$$

$$+ \ldots + -(-1)^{n-1} \sum_{\substack{i_\ell \neq k \\ \ell = 1, 2, \ldots n-1}} \frac{\partial \varphi_{i_1 \ldots i_{n-1}}}{\partial x_k}$$

ce qui donne par intégration successive

$$\frac{\partial f}{\partial x_k} \overset{S}{\sim} \frac{\partial \varphi}{\partial x_k}$$

et ceci pour tout k .

COROLLAIRE 2.2.3. - <u>Soient</u> $\varphi = \sum_{|p|=0}^{+\infty} a_p x^p$ <u>une série formelle et</u> S <u>un secteur alors pour tout ordre de dérivation</u> q <u>donné, il existe une fonction</u> Φ <u>holomorphe dans</u> S <u>telle que</u> :

1) $\Phi(x) \overset{S}{\sim} \sum_{|p|=0}^{+\infty} a_p x^p$

2) <u>toutes les dérivées jusqu'à l'ordre</u> q <u>inclus de</u> Φ <u>sont asymptotiques dans</u> S <u>à la série dérivée de</u> φ <u>du même ordre.</u>

La démonstration de ce résultat est analogue à celle du théorème ci-dessus et le principe en est le même. On procède par récurrence sur le nombre des variables et par intégration.

§ 3. - DEVELOPPEMENTS ASYMPTOTIQUES DE FONCTIONS DEPENDANT DE PARAMETRES.

Dans la suite, sauf mention contraire, S dénotera toujours un secteur de $\mathbb{C}^n$.

Soit T une partie quelconque de l'espace $\mathbb{C}^q$ de la variable $y = (y_1, y_2, \ldots, y_q)$.

DEFINITION 3.1. - Soit $\sum_{|p|=0}^{+\infty} a_p(y)\, x^p$ une série formelle en x dont les coefficients sont des fonctions définies sur T. Nous dirons qu'une fonction f définie sur $S \times T$ admet la série ci-dessus comme développement asymptotique dans S si :

$$\forall m \qquad \left|f(x,y) - \sum_{|p|=0}^{m} a_p(y)\, x^p\right| \le K_m(y)\, \|x\|_{m+1}^{m+1} \qquad \text{sur} \quad S \times T .$$

On écrira

$$f(x,y) \underset{T}{\overset{S}{\sim}} \sum_{|p|=0}^{+\infty} a_p(y)\, x^p$$

Le développement asymptotique est dit uniforme sur T si pour tout m $K_m(y) \le K_m$ sur T où K_m est une constante indépendante de y. Dans ce cas, on écrira :

$$f \underset{u.T}{\overset{S}{\sim}} \sum_{|p|=0}^{+\infty} a_p(y)\, x^p .$$

Remarques.

1. Si

$$f \underset{u.T}{\overset{S}{\sim}} \sum_{|p|=0}^{+\infty} a_p(y)\, x^p$$

alors pour tout entier m $\left|f(x,y) - \sum_{|p|=0}^{m} a_p(y)\, x^p\right| \le K_m\, \|x\|_{m+1}^{m+1}$ où K_m est une constante.

2. Si

$$f \underset{u.T}{\overset{S}{\sim}} \sum_{|p|=0}^{+\infty} a_p(y)\, x^p$$

alors $\lim_{\substack{x \to 0 \\ x \in S}} f(x,y) = a_o(y)$ uniformément sur T.

3. Les définitions ci-dessus s'étendent aisément aux fonctions à valeurs vectorielles et nous les utiliserons sans donner d'autres précisions.

4. Beaucoup de propriétés et de remarques données dans les paragraphe 1 et 2 s'étendent trivialement au paragraphe 3 et il est donc inutile d'en donner une nouvelle énumération.

PROPOSITION 3.1. - Si $f(x,y)$ est holomorphe dans $S\times T$ et si

$$f \underset{u.T}{\overset{S}{\sim}} \sum_{|p|=0}^{+\infty} a_p(y)\, x^p$$

Alors

1) pour tout p , $a_p(y)$ est holomorphe dans T ;

2) pour tout $i = 1,2,\dots,q$

$$\frac{\partial f}{\partial y_i} \underset{u.T_1}{\overset{S}{\sim}} \sum_{|p|=0}^{+\infty} \frac{\partial a_p(y)}{\partial y_i}\, x^p$$

sur tout compact T_1 strictement contenu dans T .

Démonstration lorsque $n = 1$.

Alors

$$f \underset{u.T}{\overset{S}{\sim}} \sum_{p=0}^{+\infty} a_p(y)\, x^p$$

implique

$$\forall m \qquad \left|f(x,y) - \sum_{p=0}^{m} a_p(y)\, x^p\right| \leq K_m |x|^m \quad \text{sur } S\times T$$

et

$$a_m(y)\, x^m = \sum_{p=0}^{m} a_p(y)\, x^p - f(x,y) + f(x,y) - \sum_{p=0}^{m-1} a_p(y)\, x^p$$

$$a_m(y) = x^{-m}\left[\sum_{p=0}^{m} a_p(y)\, x^p - f(x,y)\right] + x^{-m}\left[f(x,y) - \sum_{p=0}^{m-1} a_p(y)\, x^p\right]$$

et donc

$$\left|a_m(y) - x^{-m}\left[f(x,y) - \sum_{p=0}^{m-1} a_p(y)\, x^p\right]\right| \leq |x|^{-m} K_m |x|^{m+1}$$

c'est-à-dire que

$$a_m(y) = \lim_{\substack{x\to 0\\ x\in S}} x^{-m}\left[f(x,y) - \sum_{p=0}^{m-1} a_p(y)\, x^p\right]$$

uniformément sur T , ce qui entraîne que pour tout m , $a_m(y)$ est holomorphe sur T .

Ecrivons maintenant

$$f(x,y) = \sum_{p=0}^{m} a_p(y)\, x^p + x^{m+1}\, E_m(x,y)$$

où pour tout m $|E_m(x,y)| \leq K_m$ dans $S \times T$.

Soit maintenant T_1 un compact strictement inclus dans T et r un nombre réel plus petit que la distance de T_1 à la frontière de T pour la distance associée à la norme $\sup_{i=1,2,\dots q} |y_i|$ sur $\mathbb{C}^q$.

Alors pour tout $y \in T_1$, la boule $\|y-z\| \leq r$ est contenue dans T .

La fonction $E_m(x,y)$ est holomorphe dans $S \times T$ donc en particulier holomorphe en y dans T et la formule intégrale de Cauchy nous donne

$$\left|\frac{\partial E_m(x,y)}{\partial y_i}\right| \leq \frac{K_m}{r} \quad \text{dans } S \times T_1 .$$

Mais alors

$$\frac{\partial f}{\partial y_i} = \sum_{p=0}^{m} \frac{\partial a_p}{\partial y_i}\, x^p + \frac{\partial E_m}{\partial y_i}\, x^{m+1}$$

donne

$$\forall\, m \qquad \left| \frac{\partial f}{\partial y_i} - \sum_{p=0}^{m} \frac{\partial a_p(y)}{\partial y_i}\, x^p \right| \leq \frac{K_m}{r}\, |x|^{m+1}$$

ce qui prouve la proposition dans le cas $n = 1$.

<u>Démonstration dans le cas général.</u>

Pour tout m

$$\left|f(x,y) - \sum_{p=0}^{m} a_p(y)\, x^p\right| \leq C_m\, \|x\|_{m+1}^{m+1} \quad \text{dans } S \times T .$$

Posons pour tout $i = 2,3,\dots,n$

$$x_i = t_i\, x_1$$

où

$$0 \leq |t_i| \leq \frac{r_i}{r_1}$$

$$\theta_1^i - \theta_2^1 \leq \arg t_i \leq \theta_2^i - \theta_1^1 ,$$

on notera U la partie de C^{n-1} définie par ces inégalités. Alors

$$|f(x_1, t_2 x_1, \dots, t_n x_1, y) - \sum_{|p|=0}^{m} a_p(y)\, t_2^{p_2} \dots t_n^{p_n}\, x_1^{|p|}|$$

$$\leq C_m |x_1|^{m+1} \left[1 + t_2^{m+1} + \dots + t_n^{m+1}\right]$$

$$\leq \tilde{C}_m |x_1|^{m+1} .$$

La fonction $\varphi(x_1, t_2, t_3, \dots, t_n, y) = f(x_1, t_2 x_1, \dots, t_n x_1, y)$ est donc une fonction holomorphe dans $T \times U \times S_1$ qui est asymptotique sur S_1 uniformément sur $T \times U$ à la série

$$\sum_{|p|=0}^{+\infty} b_p(y,t)\, x_1^{|p|}$$

où

$$b_p(y,t) = \sum_{p_1+p_2+\dots+p_n=|p|} a_p(y)\, t_2^{p_2} \dots t_n^{p_n} .$$

D'après la première partie de notre démonstration $(n=1)$, les fonctions b_p sont holomorphes dans $T \times U$, mais comme pour tout p, b_p est un polynôme en $t_2, t_3, \dots t_n$ sont les coefficients sont les $a_p(y)$. Ces dernières fonctions sont holomorphes dans T.

Il reste à démontrer la propriété de dérivation. Pour cela, comme dans le cas $n = 1$, on prend un compact T_1 strictement inclus dans T et on introduit également le nombre r comme ci-dessus.

Nous avons pour tout m

$$f(x,y) = \sum_{|p|=0}^{m} a_p(y)\, x^p + E_m(x,y)$$

avec

$$|E_m(x,y)| \leq C_m \|x\|_{m+1}^{m+1} \quad \text{sur } S \times T$$

et

$$\frac{\partial f}{\partial y_i} = \sum_{|p|=0}^{m} \frac{\partial a_p}{\partial y_i}(y)\, x^p + \frac{\partial E_m}{\partial y_i}$$

c'est-à-dire, que par la formule intégrale de Cauchy

$$\left|\frac{\partial f}{\partial y_i} - \sum_{|p|=0}^{m} \frac{\partial a_p}{\partial y} x^p\right| \leq \frac{C_m \|x\|_{m+1}^{m+1}}{r}$$

ce qui prouve complètement la Proposition 3.1.

Exemples.

1. $f(x,y) = e^{-\frac{y}{x}}$ $\qquad S = \left\{ \begin{array}{l} x \in \mathbb{C} \mid \ 0 < |x| \leq 1 \\ |\arg x| \leq \frac{\pi}{8} \end{array} \right\}$

$T = \left\{ y \in \mathbb{C} \mid \ |y| \leq 1 \ , \ |\arg y| \leq \frac{\pi}{8} \right\}$.

La fonction f admet un développement asymptotique en x dans S, mais qui n'est pas uniforme sur T, et les fonctions $a_p(y)$ ne sont pas holomorphes sur T.

2. S un secteur de $\mathbb{C}$, situé dans le quart de plan $\mathrm{Re}\, x > 0$ et $\mathrm{Im}\, x > 0$ avec une ouverture inférieure à $\pi/2$. T un compact du plan de la variable y. Considérons la fonction $f(x,y) = e^{-\frac{1}{x}|y|}$ n'est pas holomorphe dans $S \times T$ et en

$$f \underset{u.T}{\overset{S}{\sim}} 0$$

et le développement asymptotique à des coefficients holomorphes en y.

Soient S un secteur de $\mathbb{C}^n$, T un compact de $\mathbb{C}^p$ et f une fonction holomorphe dans $S \times T$. On suppose que T contient un polydisque $D = D_1 \times D_2 \times \ldots \times D_q$ où $D_i = \left\{ y_i \in \mathbb{C} \mid \ |y_i| \leq r_i \right\}$ (c'est toujours le cas si T est un domaine).

Ces hypothèses entraînent que l'on peut écrire

$$f(x,y) = \sum_{s=0}^{+\infty} c_s(x)\, y^s$$

où la série est convergente sur D pour tout $x \in S$.

Supposons de plus que

$$f(x,y) \underset{u.T}{\overset{S}{\sim}} \sum_{|p|=0}^{+\infty} a_p(y)\, x^p$$

où les a_p sont holomorphes dans T, donc aussi dans D, c'est-à-dire que pour tout p, on peut écrire

$$a_p(y) = \sum_{|p|=0}^{+\infty} a_{p,t}\, y^t$$

où la série est convergente sur D .

Par substitution formelle et en réordonnant, on obtient une série

$$\sum_{|t|=0}^{+\infty} \left(\sum_{|p|=0}^{+\infty} a_{p,t}\, x^p \right) y^t \quad .$$

THEOREME 3.1. - Pour tout s

$$c_s(x) \overset{S}{\sim} \sum_{|p|=0}^{+\infty} a_{p,s}\, x^p \quad .$$

Démonstration. - Nous avons pour tout m

$$f(x,y) = \sum_{|p|=0}^{m} a_p(y)\, x^p + E_m(x,y)$$

avec

$$|E_m(x,y)| \leq C_m \, \|x\|_{m+1}^{m+1} \qquad \text{sur} \quad S \times D$$

Remplaçons pour tout p , a_p par

$$\sum_{|t|=0}^{+\infty} a_{p,t}\, y^t$$

il vient

$$f(x,y) = \sum_{|p|=0}^{m} \left(\sum_{|t|=0}^{+\infty} a_{p,t}\, y^t \right) x^p + E_m(x,y)$$

$$= \sum_{|t|=0}^{+\infty} \left(\sum_{|p|=0}^{m} a_{p,t}\, x^p \right) y^t + E_m(x,y) \quad \text{sur} \quad S \times D \quad .$$

Donc

$$\sum_{|s|=0}^{+\infty} c_s(x)\, y^s - \sum_{|t|=0}^{+\infty} \left(\sum_{|p|=0}^{m} a_{p,t}\, x^p \right) y^t = E_m(x,y)$$

c'est-à-dire que pour tout m :

$$\sum_{|s|=0}^{+\infty} \left(c_s(x) - \sum_{|p|}^{m} a_{p,s}\, x^p \right) y^s = E_m(x,y) \quad .$$

On sait que

$$g(x,y) = \sum_{|s|=0}^{+\infty} g_s^m(x)\, y^s$$

où

$$g_s^m(x) = c_s(x) - \sum_{|p|=0}^{m} a_{p,s}\, x^p$$

converge dans D .

Pour obtenir le résultat annoncé, il suffit de montrer que pour tout

m

$$|g_s^m(x)| \leq K_m \, \|x\|_{m+1}^{m+1} \quad \text{sur } S .$$

Notons pour tout i , γ_i le cercle frontière de $D_i = \{y_i \mid |y_i| \leq r_i\}$.

Alors si $s = (s_1, s_2, \ldots s_q)$

$$g_s^m(x) = s\,! \; \frac{\partial^{|s|} g}{\partial^s y} = s_1! \ldots s_q! \; \frac{\partial^{s_1+s_2+\ldots+s_q} g}{\partial y_1^{s_1}, \ldots \partial y_q^{s_q}}$$

$$= \frac{1}{(2\pi_i)^{|s|}} \int_{\gamma_1} \ldots \int_{\gamma_q} \frac{g(x,z)\,d\eta_1\, d\eta_2 \ldots d\eta_q}{\eta_1^{s_1+1} \ldots \eta_q^{s_q+1}}$$

Mais

$$|g(x,y)| \leq C_m \, \|x\|_{m+1}^{m+1} \quad \text{sur } S \times D$$

entraîne

$$|g_s^m(x)| \leq \frac{C_m}{(2\pi)^{|s|}} \|x\|_{m+1}^{m+1} \int_{\gamma_1} \ldots \int_{\gamma_q} \frac{|d\eta_1| \ldots |d\eta_q|}{|\eta_1|^{s_1+1} \ldots |\eta_q|^{s_q+1}}$$

$$\leq \frac{C_m}{(2\pi)^{|s|}} \|x\|_{m+1}^{m+1} \; \frac{(2\pi)^{|q|}}{r_1^{s_1} \ldots r_q^{s_q}}$$

ce qui prouve le résultat.

Nous avons également :

THEOREME 3.2. - <u>Soient</u> $a_p(y)$ <u>des fonctions holomorphes dans un polydisque</u> D <u>et</u> S <u>un secteur de</u> $\mathbb{C}^n$.

<u>Alors il existe une fonction</u> f <u>holomorphe dans</u> $S \times D$ <u>telle que</u>

$$f(x,y) \underset{u.D}{\overset{S}{\sim}} \sum_{|p|=0}^{+\infty} a_p(y)\, x^p \; .$$

La démonstration est analogue à celle de la démonstration du théorème 2.2.1 . Il suffit de prendre

$$b_p = \frac{1}{\sup\limits_{y \in D} |a_p(y)|} \qquad \text{si} \quad a_p \neq 0$$

et

$$b_p = 0 \qquad\qquad \text{si} \quad a_p = 0 \; .$$

Les propriétés suivantes qui sont faciles à établir seront également utilisées dans la suite.

Soient S_1 un secteur de $\mathbb{C}^n(x_1,x_2 \ldots x_n)$ et S_2 un secteur de $\mathbb{C}^p(y_1,y_2 \ldots y_p)$.

1. Si

$$f(x,y) \underset{u.S_2}{\overset{S_1}{\sim}} \sum_{|m|=0}^{+\infty} a_m(y)\, x^m$$

et pour tout m

$$a_m(y) \overset{S_2}{\sim} \sum_{|\ell|=0}^{+\infty} a_{m\ell}\, y^\ell$$

alors

$$f(x,y) \overset{S_1 \times S_2}{\sim} \sum_{m,\ell} a_{m\ell}\, x^m\, y^\ell$$

2. Si

$$f(x,y) \underset{u.S_2}{\overset{S_1}{\sim}} \sum_{|m|=0}^{+\infty} a_m(y)\, x^m$$

$$a_m(y) \overset{S_2}{\sim} \sum_{|\ell|=0}^{+\infty} a_{m\ell}\, y^\ell$$

et

$$f(x,y) \underset{u.S_1}{\overset{S_2}{\sim}} \sum_{|\ell|=0}^{+\infty} b_\ell(x)\, y^\ell$$

$$b_\ell(x) \overset{S_1}{\sim} \sum_{|m|=0}^{+\infty} b_{\ell m}\, x^m$$

alors

pour tout (ℓ,m) $\quad a_{m\ell} = b_{\ell m}$.

3. Si pour tout $N = 1,2\ldots$

$$f(x,y) = \sum_{|m|=0}^{N} a_m(y)\, x^m + x^{N+1} f_N(x,y)$$

$$a_m(y) \overset{S_2}{\sim} \sum_{|\ell|=0}^{+\infty} a_{m\ell}\, y^\ell$$

$$f_N(x,y) \underset{u.S_1}{\overset{S_2}{\sim}} \sum_{|\ell|=0}^{+\infty} b_{N\ell}(x)\, y^\ell .$$

Alors les fonctions

$$b_\ell(x) = \sum^{N} a_{m\ell}\, x^m + x^{N+1}\, b_{N\ell}(x)$$

sont indépendantes de N et de plus

$$f_N(x,y) \underset{u.S_2}{\overset{S_1}{\sim}} \sum_{|m|=N+1}^{+\infty} a_m(y)\, x^{m-N-1}$$

$$f(x,y) \underset{u.S_1}{\overset{S_2}{\sim}} \sum_{|\ell|=0}^{+\infty} b_\ell(x)\, y^\ell$$

$$b_\ell(x) \overset{S_1}{\sim} \sum_{|m|=0}^{+\infty} a_{m\ell}\, x^m .$$

§ 4. - LES INEGALITES FONDAMENTALES.

Nous allons dans ce paragraphe établir un certain nombre d'inégalités qui seront utilisées dans les chapitres suivants. Ces inégalités se trouvent dans [9] et [10].

4.1. - Considérons dans le plan de la variable ζ la demi-droite ℓ représentée par

$$\zeta = z + te^{i\theta} \qquad 0 \leq t < +\infty$$

où $$|\theta| < \frac{\pi}{2}$$

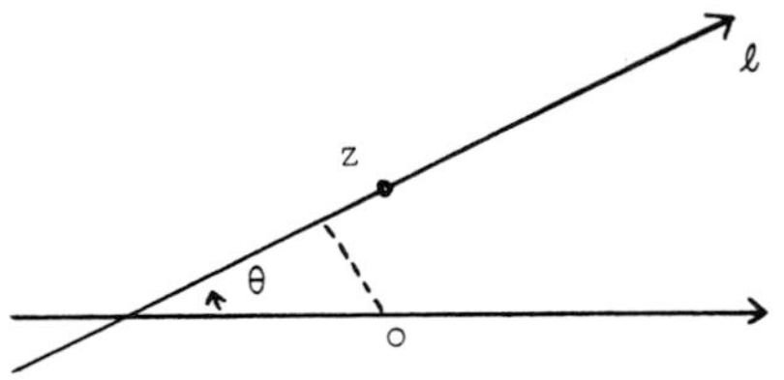

on suppose que $|z| \leq |\zeta|$ pour tout $\zeta \in \ell$.

Pour tout nombre $\rho > 0$, on cherche une majoration pour les intégrales.

$$I = \int_{\ell} |\zeta|^{-\rho} |e^{-\zeta}| |d\zeta| \quad \text{et} \quad J = \int_{\ell} |\zeta|^{-\rho} |e^{-\lambda\zeta}| |d\zeta|$$

$(\lambda > 0)$.

Nous avons sur ℓ $\quad |z| \leq |\zeta|$

donc $$|\zeta|^{-\rho} \leq |z|^{-\rho} .$$

D'autre part

$$|e^{-\zeta}| = |e^{-z}| |e^{-te^{i\theta}}| = |e^{-z}| e^{-t\cos\theta}$$

Donc

$$\int_{\ell} |\zeta|^{-\rho} |e^{-\zeta}| |d\zeta| \leq |z|^{-\rho} |e^{-z}| \int_{0}^{+\infty} e^{-t\cos\theta}\, dt \leq |z|^{-\rho} |e^{-z}| \frac{1}{\cos\theta}$$

Donc

$$\int_{\ell} |\zeta|^{-\rho} |e^{-\zeta}| |d\zeta| \leq \frac{|z|^{-\rho} |e^{-z}|}{\cos\theta}$$

De la même manière on a

$$\int_{\ell} |\zeta|^{-\rho} |e^{-\lambda\zeta}| |d\zeta| \leq \frac{|z|^{-\rho} |e^{-\lambda z}|}{\lambda\cos\theta}$$

4.2. - On considère maintenant la demi-droite ℓ définie par

$$\zeta = z_o + te^{i\theta} \qquad -t_o \leq t \leq +\infty$$

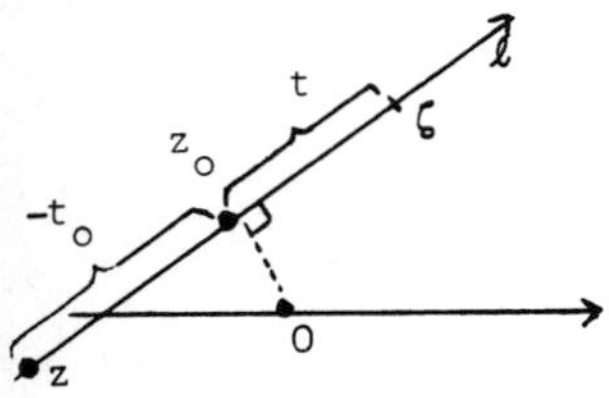

$$|\theta| < \frac{\pi}{2} \text{ avec } |z_o| = a > 0 .$$

On cherche encore à majorer

$I = \int_{\ell} |\zeta|^{-\rho} |e^{-\zeta}| |d\zeta|$ et ceci de manière à encore avoir en facteur

dans la borne $|z|^{-\rho} |e^{-z}|$.

Comme
$$|\zeta| = (a^2 + t^2)^{\frac{1}{2}}$$

$$e^{-\zeta} = e^{-z_o} e^{-te^{i\theta}}$$

$$|e^{-\zeta}| = |e^{-z_o}| e^{-t\cos\theta}$$

et
$$I = \int_{-t_o}^{+\infty} \frac{|e^{-z_o}| e^{-t\cos\theta} dt}{(a^2 + t^2)^{\rho/2}}$$

Considérons

$$|z|^{\rho} |e^{z}| I = (a^2 + (-t_o)^2)^{\rho/2} |e^{z_o}| e^{-t_o\cos\theta} I .$$

Nous avons

$$|z|^{\rho}|e^{z}|I = Y(-t_o)$$

où

$$Y(s) = (a^2+s^2)^{\rho/2} e^{s\cos\theta} \int_s^{+\infty} \frac{e^{-t\cos\theta}}{(a^2+t^2)^{\rho/2}}\, dt \ .$$

Il est facile de voir que

$$Y'(s) = \{\cos\theta + \frac{\rho s}{a^2+s^2}\} Y(s) - 1 \ .$$

Prenons $$a \geq \frac{\rho}{2}(\cos\theta - \delta_o)^{-1}$$

où $$0 < \delta_o < \cos\theta \ .$$

Alors

$$\frac{\cos\theta - \delta_o}{\rho} \geq \frac{1}{2a} \geq \frac{|s|}{a^2+s^2} \ .$$

Comme $$\frac{\cos\theta - \delta_o}{\rho} > 0$$

nous avons

$$\frac{\cos\theta - \delta_o}{\rho} > \frac{-s}{a^2+s^2}$$

c'est-à-dire

$$\cos\theta + \frac{\rho s}{a^2+s^2} \geq \delta_o \ .$$

On se propose de majorer $Y(-t_o)$, pour cela utilisons

$$Y'(s) \geq \delta_o Y(s) - 1$$

qui donne

$$(Y(s)e^{-\delta_o s})' \geq -e^{-\delta_o s}$$

et

$$\int_{-t_o}^{o} (Y(s)e^{-\delta_o s})' ds \geq \int_{-t_o}^{o} (-e^{-\delta_o s}) ds$$

c'est-à-dire

$$Y(0) - Y(-t_o)e^{\delta_o t_o} \geq \frac{1}{\delta_o}(1-e^{\delta_o t_o}) .$$

D'où

$$Y(-t_o) \leq Y(0)e^{-\delta_o t_o} - \frac{1}{\delta_o}(e^{-\delta_o t_o} - 1) \leq Y(0)e^{-\delta_o t_o} + \frac{1}{\delta_o} .$$

D'après 4.1. $Y(0) \leq \frac{1}{\cos\theta} \leq \frac{1}{\delta_o}$.

On a donc

$$Y(-t_o) \leq \frac{2}{\delta_o}$$

c'est-à-dire que

$$\boxed{\int_{\ell} |\zeta|^{-\rho} |e^{-\zeta}| |d\zeta| \leq |z|^{-\rho} |e^{-z}| \frac{2}{\delta_o}}$$

lorsque $a \geq \frac{\rho}{2(\cos\theta - \delta_o)}$.

4.3. - On considère maintenant le segment ℓ défini par

$$\zeta = z_o + te^{i\theta} \qquad 0 \leq t \leq t_o = |z - z_o|$$

$$|\theta| < \frac{\pi}{2}$$

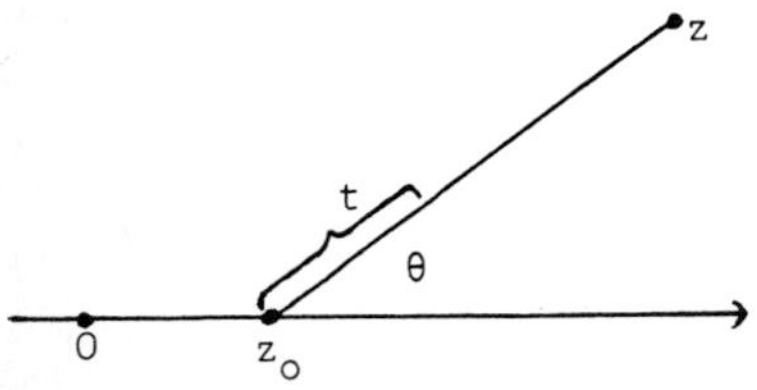

Et on cherche une majoration pour

$$I = \int_{\ell} |\zeta|^{-\rho} |e^{\zeta}| |d\zeta| \qquad \rho > 0$$

telle que $|z|^{-\rho}|e^{z}|$ soit un facteur dans la borne

$$I = \int_0^{t_0} \frac{1}{(z_0^2+t^2+2z_0 t\cos\theta)^{\rho/2}} |e^{z_0}| e^{t\cos\theta} dt$$

$$|z|^{\ell}|e^{-z}| I = (z_0^2+t_0^2+2z_0 t_0)\cos\theta)^{\frac{\rho}{2}} e^{-t_0\cos\theta} \int_0^{t_0} \frac{e^{t\cos\theta} dt}{(z_0^2+t^2+2z_0 t\cos\theta)^{\ell/2}}$$

$$= Y(t_0)$$

avec

$$Y(s) = (z_0^2+s^2 2sz_0 \cos\theta)^{\rho/2} e^{-s\cos\theta} \int_0^{s} \frac{e^{t\cos\theta} dt}{(z_0^2+t^2+2z_0 t\cos\theta)^{\rho/2}} .$$

On cherche à majorer $Y(t_0)$ pour cela on va utiliser la même méthode que dans 4.2.

Nous avons

$$\frac{s+z_0\cos\theta}{z_0^2+s^2+2s\,z_0\cos\theta} \le \frac{s+z_0\cos\theta}{(s+z_0\cos\theta)^2} \le \frac{1}{s+z_0\cos\theta} \le \frac{1}{z_0\cos\theta} .$$

Prenons z_0 assez grand pour que

$$z_0 \ge \frac{2\rho}{\cos^2\theta} .$$

Alors

$$\frac{\rho(s+z_0\cos\theta)}{z_0^2+s^2+2s\,z_0\cos\theta} - \cos\theta \le \frac{\rho}{z_0\cos\theta} - \cos\theta$$

$$\le -\tfrac{1}{2}\cos\theta \left(\frac{-2\rho}{z_0\cos^2\theta} + 2\right)$$

$$\le -\tfrac{1}{2}\cos\theta \left[\left(\frac{-2\rho}{z_0\cos^2\theta} + 1\right) + 1\right]$$

$$\le -\tfrac{1}{2}\cos\theta .$$

Alors

$$Y'(s) \leq -\tfrac{1}{2}\cos\theta\, Y(s)+1 ,$$

et

$$(Y(s)e^{\frac{1}{2}\cos\theta\, s})' \leq e^{\frac{\cos\theta}{2}s} .$$

Par intégration entre 0 et t_o nous obtenons

$$Y(t_o)\, e^{\frac{1}{2}\cos\theta\, t_o} - Y(0) \leq \frac{2}{\cos\theta}\left[e^{\frac{\cos\theta}{2}t_o} - 1\right] .$$

Comme $Y(0) = 0$ nous avons

$$Y(t_o) \leq \frac{2}{\cos\theta}\left[1 - e^{-\frac{\cos\theta}{2}t_o}\right]$$

$$\leq \frac{2}{\cos\theta}$$

et finalement

$$\boxed{\int_{\ell} |\zeta|^{-\rho}|e^{\zeta}|\,|0|\zeta| \leq |z|^{-\rho}|e^{z}|\,\frac{2}{\cos\theta}}$$

pour

$$z_o \geq \frac{2\rho}{\cos^2\theta} .$$

§ 5. - SECTEURS PROPRES.

Dans les chapitres suivants nous aurons à étudier certaines équations intégrales portant sur des fonctions qui ne sont définies que dans certains secteurs de $\mathbb{C}^2$ ou de $\mathbb{C}^n$. Dans cette étude on est amené à chercher des domaines dans lesquels on peut trouver des "bons" chemins d'intégration pour avoir des équations intégrales facilement utilisables.

Un domaine $\mathcal{D}$ de $\mathbb{C}$ est dit admissible pour une fonction f si

1. $\mathcal{D}$ est simplement connexe
2. f est holomorphe dans $\mathcal{D}$

3. il existe un point x_0 sur la frontière de $\mathcal{D}$ tel que pour tout point $x \in \mathcal{D}$ il existe un chemin $\Gamma(x)$ contenu dans $\mathcal{D}$ joignant x_0 à x et tel que

$$\operatorname{Re}\left(\int_{\xi}^{x} (f(\tau))d\tau\right) \leq 0 \quad \text{le long de } \Gamma(x) .$$

<u>Exemples</u>.

1. Prenons $f(x) = \lambda \qquad \lambda \in \mathbb{C} \qquad \lambda \neq 0$,

alors $\mathcal{D} = \{x \in \mathbb{C} \mid |x| < 1\}$ est un domaine admissible pour f .

En effet

$$\int_{\xi}^{x} f(\tau)d\tau = \lambda(x-\xi) \qquad \lambda = |\lambda| e^{i\varphi}$$

si $x - \xi = |x-\xi| e^{i\theta}$ alors

$$\operatorname{Re}\left(\int_{\xi}^{x} f(\tau)d\tau\right) = (|\lambda| \; |x-\xi| \cos(\varphi+\theta) .$$

On doit avoir $\qquad \cos(\varphi+\theta) < 0$ dans $\mathcal{D}$

c'est-à-dire

$$\frac{\pi}{2} < \varphi + \theta < \frac{3\pi}{2}$$

ou encore $\qquad |\theta - (\pi - \varphi)| < \frac{\pi}{2}$.

La figure suivante montre alors que $\mathcal{D}$ est admissible pour $f = \lambda$.

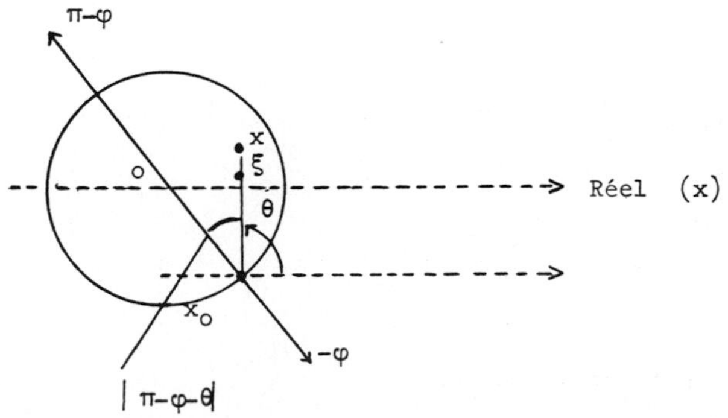

2. Tout domaine borné ou non mais convexe est admissible pour $f(x) = \lambda \neq 0$.

3. Donnons nous φ_o et considérons

$$\lambda = |\lambda| e^{i\varphi} \quad \text{avec} \quad |\varphi - \varphi_o| \leq \frac{\pi}{2} - \delta \qquad \delta > 0$$

c'est-à-dire

$$-\varphi_o - \frac{\pi}{2} + \delta \leq -\varphi \leq -\varphi_o + \frac{\pi}{2} - \delta$$

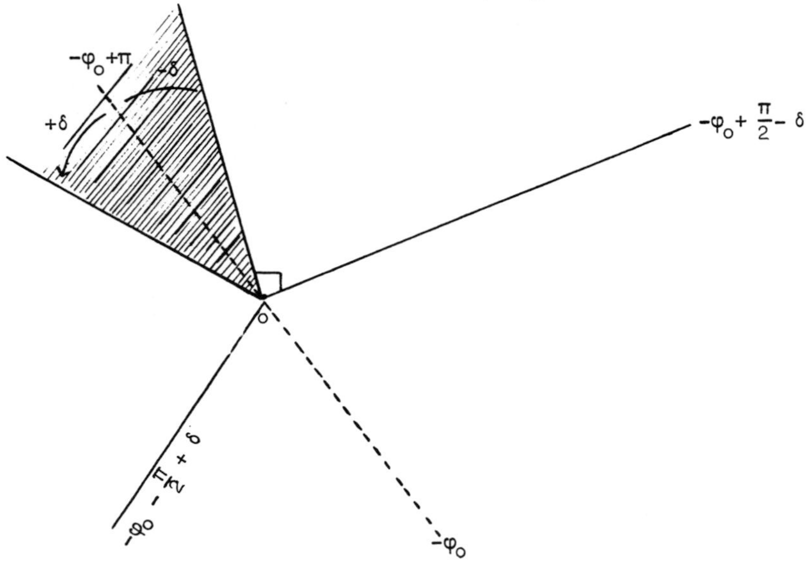

Le domaine hachuré est admissible pour tous les λ vérifiant

$$|\varphi - \varphi_o| \leq \frac{\pi}{2} - \delta .$$

4.

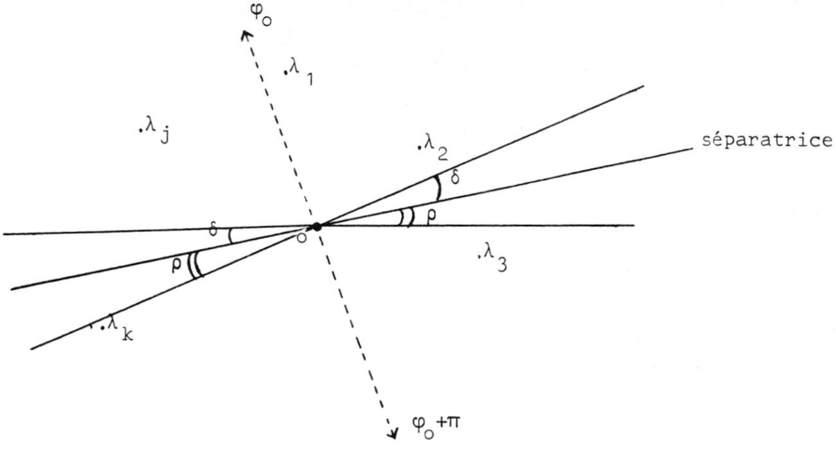

Alors le domaine représenté ci-dessous est admissible où ρ et δ sont assez petits.

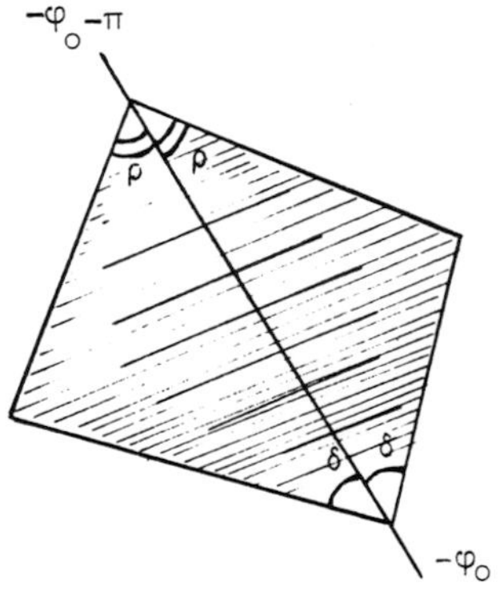

Les secteurs propres. Cette notion a été introduite par Hukuhara et Iwano [4].

Nous allons considérer une fonction F de la forme suivante

$$F(x) = \int_{x_o}^{x} f(\tau)d\tau \qquad \text{qui est un polynôme}$$

en ξ où $\xi^p = x$ $\quad$ p entier positif .

Un secteur fermé $\mathcal{D}$ du plan de la variable x est dit propre pour F s'il existe une constante positive γ telle que l'on puisse déterminer $\arg F(x)$ comme fonction continue de x vérifiant

$$|\arg F(x)| \leq \frac{3\pi}{2} - \gamma \text{ dans } \mathcal{D}$$

pour $|x|$ assez grand.

Soit
$$F(x) = a_o x^{\sigma}\{1 + O(\tfrac{1}{\xi})\}$$

avec $\sigma > 0$ $\quad a_o = |a_o| e^{i\omega}$ $\quad x = |x| e^{i\theta}$

alors

$$\mathrm{Re}(F(x)) = |a_o| \, |x|^{\sigma}\{\cos(\sigma\theta + \omega) + O(\tfrac{1}{\xi})\} .$$

Une <u>direction singulière</u> pour $F(x)$ est par définition une direction θ telle que

$$\cos(\sigma\theta + \omega) = 0 .$$

Ces directions sont donc données par

$$\theta_m = \frac{1}{\sigma}(\frac{\pi}{2} - \omega + m\pi) \qquad m \in \mathbb{Z} .$$

On appelle <u>secteur élémentaire</u> tout secteur compris entre deux directions singulières consécutives.

Les secteurs élémentaires pour $F(x)$ sont donc

$$\mathcal{D}_m = \{x \,|\, \theta_{m-1} < \arg x < \theta_m\} .$$

Si $m = 2p$ on a

$$\frac{\pi}{2} + (2p-1)\pi < \sigma\theta + \omega < \frac{\pi}{2} + 2p\pi$$

$$\cos(\sigma\theta + \omega) > 0$$

et
$$\mathrm{Re}\, F(x) > 0$$

si $m = 2p+1$ on a $\qquad \mathrm{Re}(F(x)) < 0 .$

Pour m pair on dit que $\mathcal{D}_m$ est un secteur élémentaire positif et si m est impair on dit que $\mathcal{D}_m$ est un secteur élémentaire négatif.

Par l'application $x \mapsto z = F(x)$ un secteur $\mathcal{D}_{2p}$ (resp $\mathcal{D}_{2p+1}$) s'envoit sur le demi-plan positif (resp. négatif).

Alors : Un secteur $\mathcal{D}$ est propre pour $F(x)$ si et seulement si il ne contient aucun secteur élémentaire négatif dans son intérieur.

Exemples de secteurs propres.

1. Tout secteur d'ouverture inférieur à π/σ est propre pour $F(x)$.

2. Soit S un secteur d'ouverture π/σ dont les bords ne sont pas des lignes singulières.

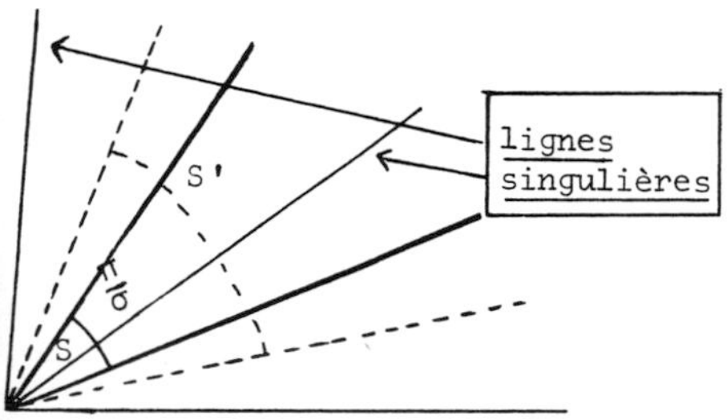

Ce secteur S est propre et même il existe un secteur $S' \supset S$ d'ouverture plus grande que π/σ qui est encore propre pour $F(x)$.

3. $S = \mathcal{D}_{m-1} \cup \mathcal{D}_m \cup \mathcal{D}_{m+1}$

avec $m = 2p$ est un secteur propre.

4. Considérons les fonctions

$$F_i(x) = \lambda_i x \qquad i = 1,2..n .$$

$$\lambda_i \neq 0 \text{ pour tout } i .$$

Alors

$$\mathcal{D} = \bigcap_{j=1}^{n} \{x \mid |\arg F_j(x)| \leq \frac{3\pi}{2} - \delta\}$$

est un secteur propre pour toutes les fonctions F_i $(i = 1,2..n)$.

§ 6. - CHOIX DES CHEMINS D'INTEGRATION.

6.1. - Dans certains des chapitres qui suivent nous aurons à étudier des intégrales de la forme

$$H(x_1,x) = \int_{\gamma(x_1)} \exp(-\frac{\lambda}{p}(\frac{1}{x_1^p}-\frac{1}{t^p}))\varphi(t,x)t^{-p-1}dt$$

où

$x = (x_2, x_3, \ldots x_n)$

$\varphi(x_1,x)$ est une fonction holomorphe dans un secteur $S = S_1 \times S_2 \times .. \times S_n$ ayant son sommet à l'origine de $\mathbb{C}^n$. De plus φ aura certaines propriétés d'asymptoticité qu'il est inutile de préciser ici.

λ est un nombre complexe non nul.

$\gamma(x_1)$ un chemin d'extrémité x_1 situé dans S_1 et à choisir convenablement.

C'est le choix de $\gamma(x_1)$ que nous allons expliquer ici, il est basé sur le souci d'avoir $\exp(-\frac{\lambda}{p}(-\frac{1}{x_1^p}-\frac{1}{t^p}))$ borné sur $\gamma(x_1)$.

Pour éclairer ce choix posons

$$\tau = -\frac{1}{pt^p} \qquad \xi = -\frac{1}{px_1^p}.$$

Par cette transformation nous sommes conduit à étudier une intégrale de la forme

$$H^*(\xi,x) = \int_{\gamma^*(\xi)} \exp\lambda(\xi-\tau)\varphi^*(\tau,x)d\tau$$

dans $\Sigma = \Sigma_1^* \times S_2 \times \ldots \times S_n$.

Le chemin $\gamma^*(\xi)$ étant à choisir convenablement dans Σ_1^* qui est maintenant un secteur ayant son sommet à l'infini.

Si $$S_1 = \{x_1 \in \mathbb{C} \mid 0 < |x_1| \le r_1 \quad \theta_1 \le \arg x_1 \le \theta_2\}$$

alors

$$\Sigma_1^* = \{\xi \in \mathbb{C} \mid |\xi| \geq R_1 \quad \theta_1^* \leq \arg \xi \leq \theta_2^*\}$$

avec $\qquad R_1 = \dfrac{1}{p\,r_1^p} \qquad \theta_1^* = \pi - p\theta_2 \qquad \theta_2^* = \pi - p\theta_1$.

Nous allons considérer plusieurs cas :

I. <u>Il existe un secteur</u> $S_1' \subset S_1$ <u>propre pour la fonction</u> $-\dfrac{\lambda}{p x_1^p}$ <u>et tel que</u>

$$\frac{2\pi}{p} < \text{ouv } S_1' < \frac{3\pi}{p} .$$

Un calcul élémentaire montre que le secteur Σ_1' associé à S_1' dans le plan de la variable ξ vérifie

$$2\pi. < \text{ouv}(\Sigma_1') < 3\pi .$$

Dans ce cas pour tout $\xi \in \Sigma_1'$ nous prendrons pour chemin $\gamma^*(\xi)$ une demi-droite venant de l'infini dans la région $\mathrm{Re}\,\xi > 0$ pour aboutir à ξ et situé de plus à une distance assez grande de l'origine.

Avec ce choix l'exponentielle figurant dans $H(x_1,x)$ est majorée par une expression de la forme

$$\left(\exp - \frac{|\lambda|}{p}\left|\frac{1}{x_1^p} - \frac{1}{t^p}\right|\right)\mu$$

où μ est une constante positive.

La figure ci-dessous concrétise dans le plan de la variable ξ le choix des chemins $\gamma^*(\xi)$ et c'est un exercice facile de transporter cette figure dans le plan de la variable x_1 .

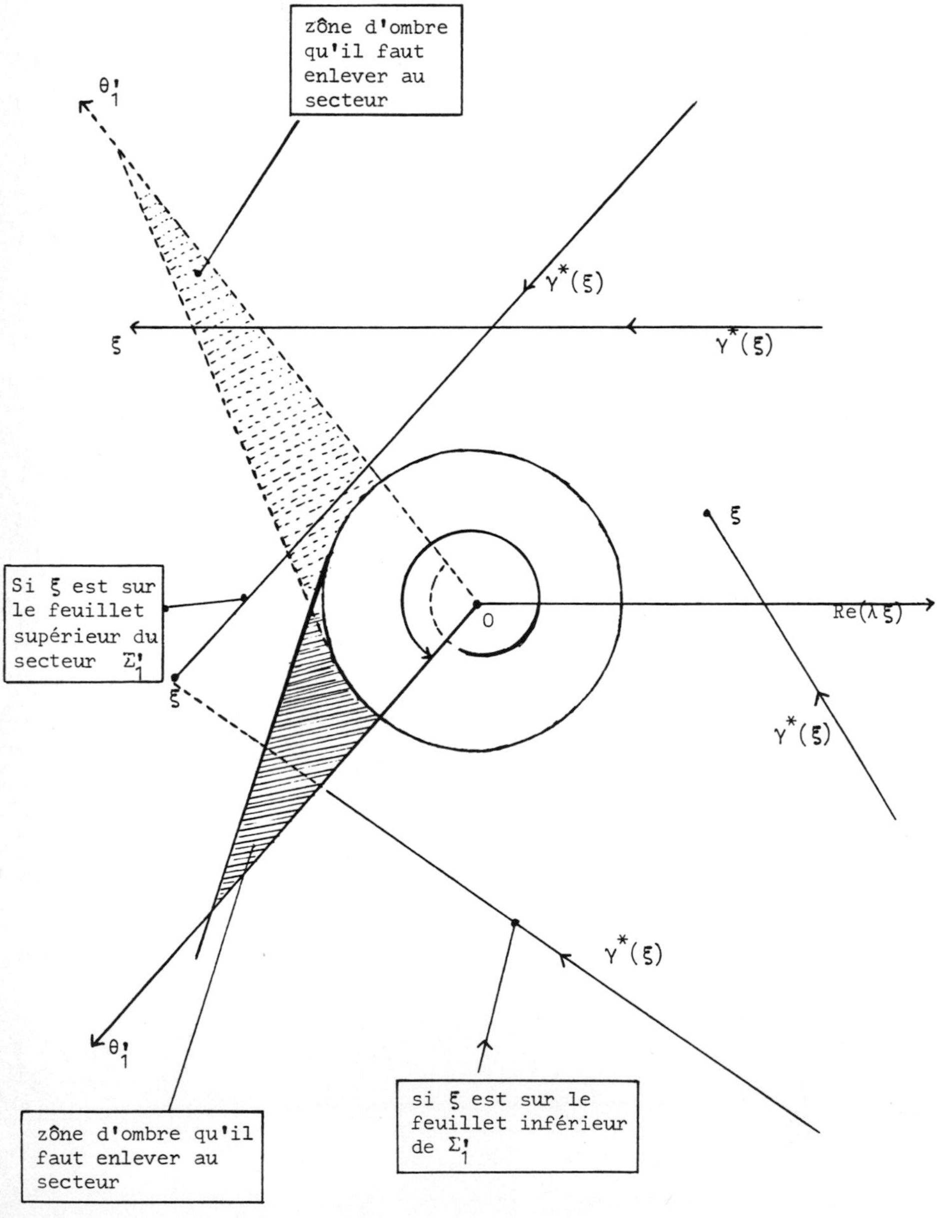

II. Il existe un secteur $S_1' \subset S_1$ propre pour la fonction $-\frac{\lambda}{px_1^p}$ tel que

$$\frac{\pi}{p} < \text{ouv}(S_1') < \frac{2\pi}{p}$$

alors

$$\pi < \text{ouv}\ \Sigma_1' < 2\pi\ .$$

Nous allons simplement indiquer le choix des chemins $\gamma^*(\xi)$ sur des figures. Les majorations cherchées pour l'exponentielle ayant été indiquées ci-dessus.

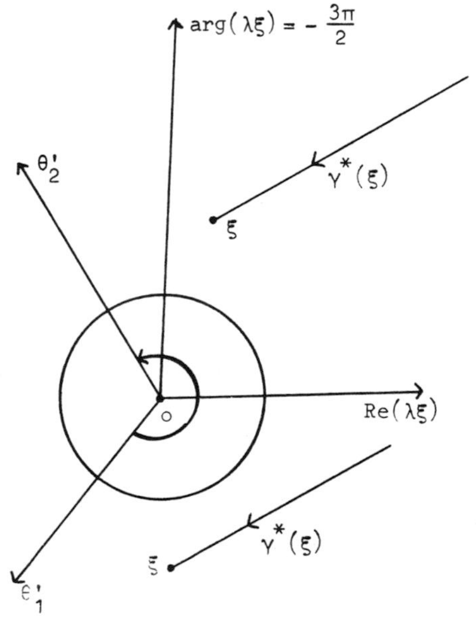

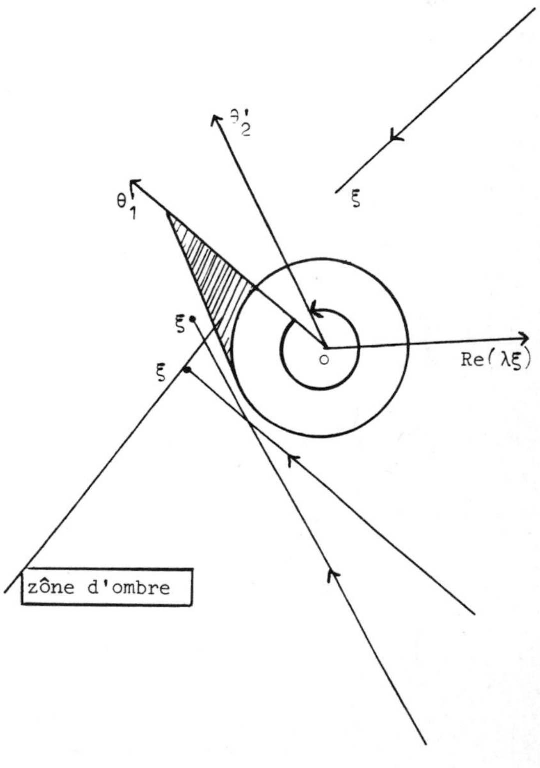

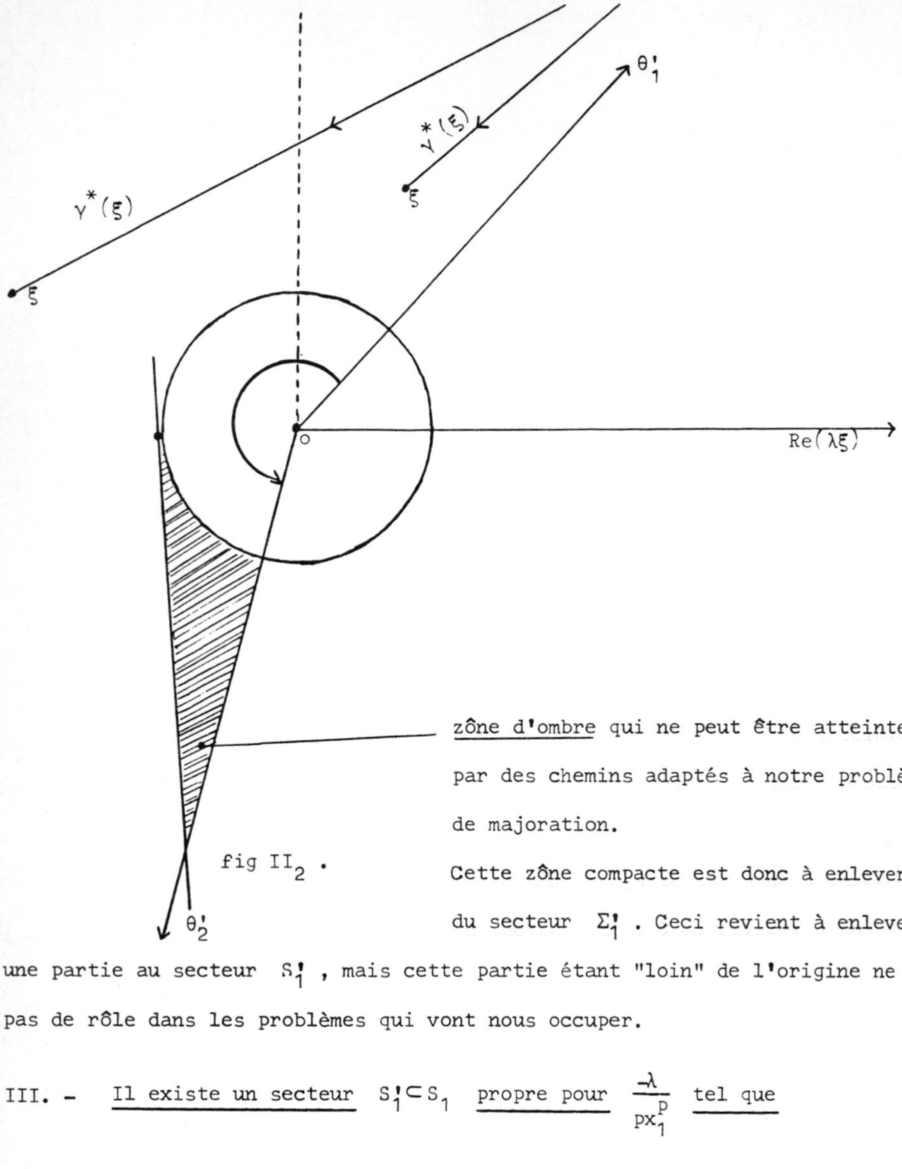

zône d'ombre qui ne peut être atteinte par des chemins adaptés à notre problème de majoration.

fig II_2 .

Cette zône compacte est donc à enlever du secteur Σ'_1 . Ceci revient à enlever une partie au secteur S'_1 , mais cette partie étant "loin" de l'origine ne joue pas de rôle dans les problèmes qui vont nous occuper.

III. - Il existe un secteur $S'_1 \subset S_1$ propre pour $\frac{-\lambda}{px_1^p}$ tel que

$$0 < \text{ouv } S'_1 < \pi/p .$$

Donc

$$0 < \text{ouv } \Sigma'_1 < \pi .$$

Les figures qui suivent explicitent le choix des chemins $\gamma^*(\xi)$ dans ce cas.

Plan de la variable ξ

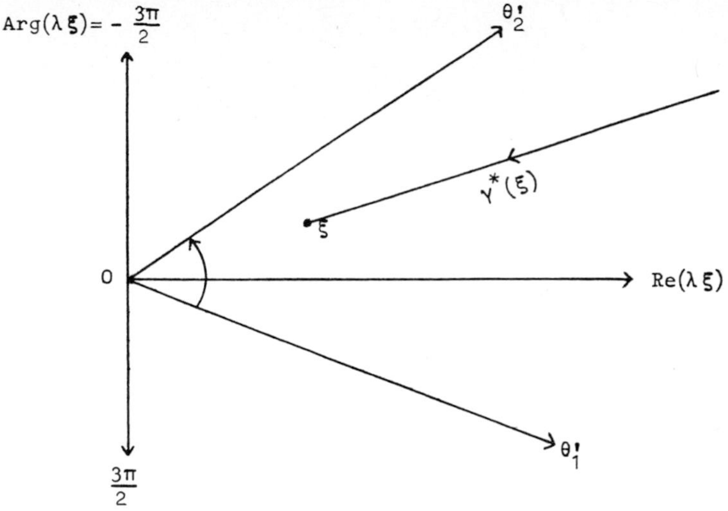

fig. III_1

Plan de la variable ξ

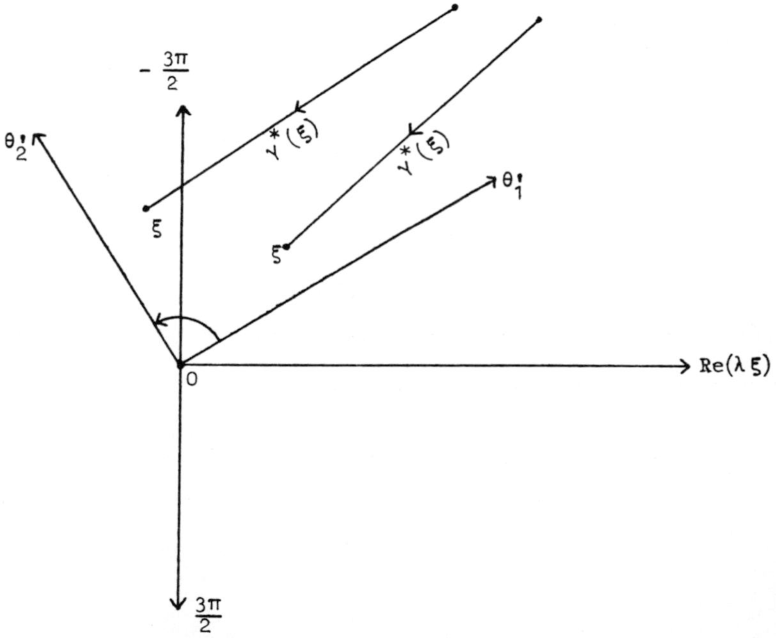

fig. III_2

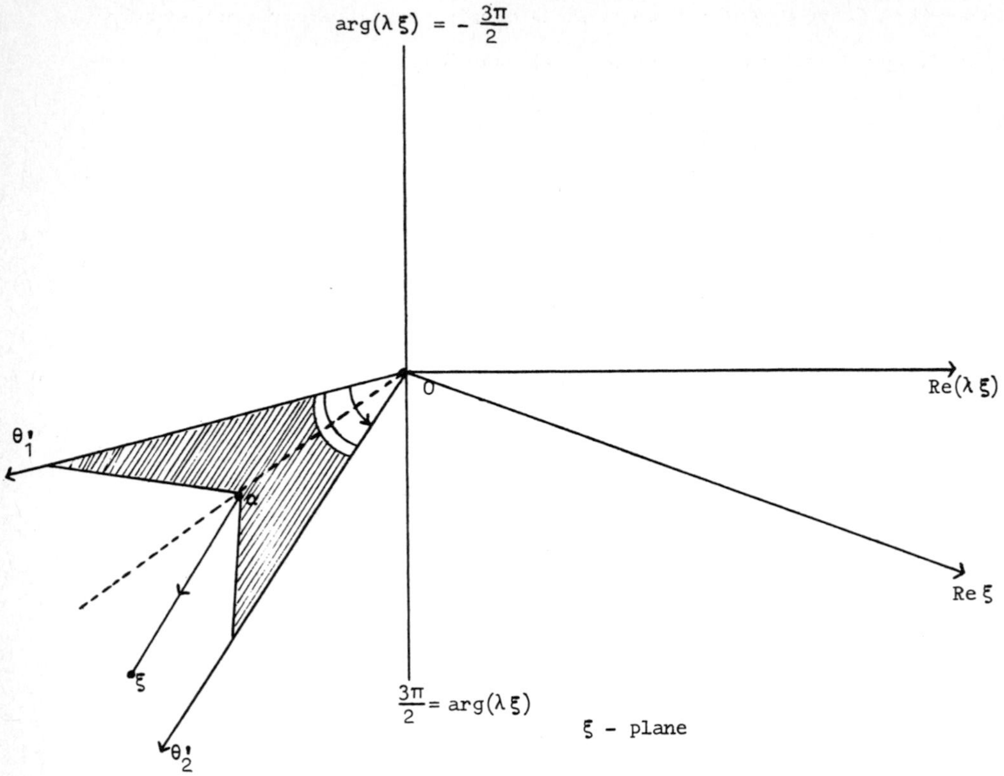

fig. III_3

Dans ce cas on prend pour chemin d'intégration un segment de droite allant d'un point α situé sur la bissectrice du secteur et assez loin de l'origine. Pour avoir le type d'inégalité indiqué dans le cas I il est encore nécessaire d'enlever une zône compacte de notre secteur.

6.2. - Considérons maintenant une intégrale de la forme

$$H(x_1,x) = \int_{\gamma(x_1)} \left(\frac{x_1}{t}\right)^{\lambda} \varphi(t,x)\, \frac{dt}{t}$$

où x,φ,λ sont comme dans § 6.1.

On cherche à faire un choix convenable du chemin $\gamma(x_1)$ en suivant des principes analogues à ceux qui ont été indiqués dans § 6.1.

Posons

$$t = e^x \qquad x_1 = e^\xi .$$

Alors nous avons à considérer

$$H^*(\xi,x) = \int_{\gamma^*(\xi)} e^{\lambda(\xi-\tau)}\varphi^*(\tau,x)d\tau .$$

Le secteur

$$S_1 = \{x_1 \in \mathbb{C} \mid 0 < |x_1| \le r_1, \theta_1 \le \arg x_1 \le \theta_2\}$$

et transformé en la demi-bande

$$\Sigma_1 = \{\xi \in \mathbb{C} \mid -\infty < \mathrm{Re}\,\xi \le \log r_1 \ \ \theta_1 \le \mathrm{Im}\,\xi \le \theta_2\} .$$

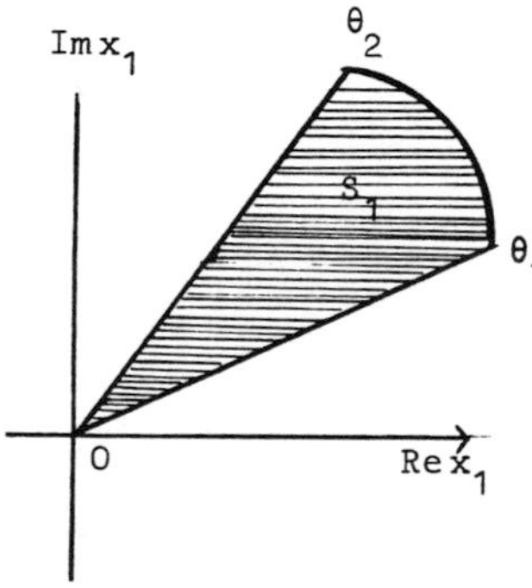

plan x_1

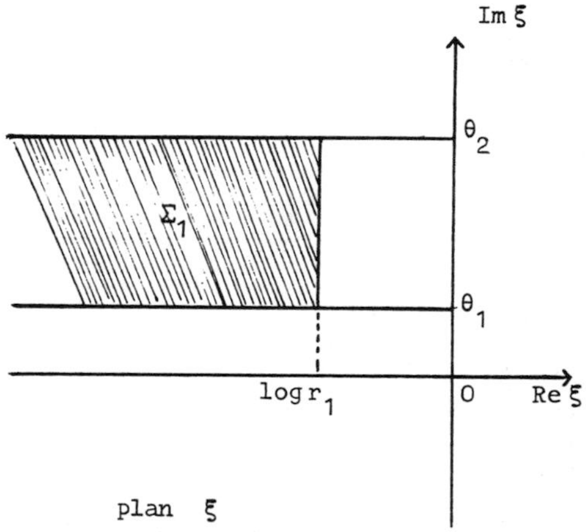

plan ξ

Considérons maintenant la demi-bande Σ_1 dans le plan de la variable $\lambda\xi$.

Nous avons trois cas :

(I) $\frac{\pi}{2} < |\arg \lambda| \le \pi$ (fig I)

(II) $|\arg \lambda| < \frac{\pi}{2}$ (fig II)

(III) $|\arg \lambda| = \frac{\pi}{2}$ (fig III) .

Les figures suivantes concrétisent le choix des chemins $\gamma^*(\xi)$ suivant chacun de ces cas.

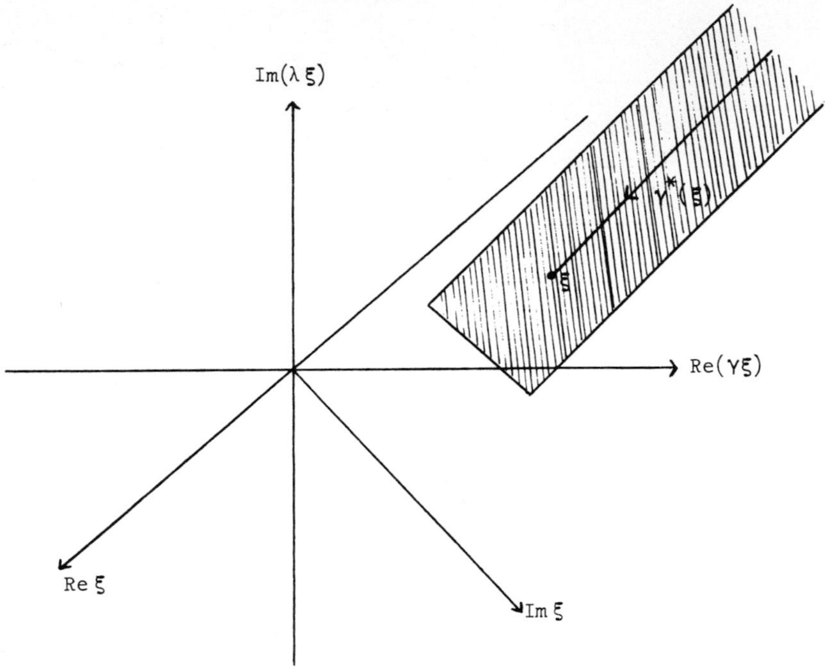

fig. I

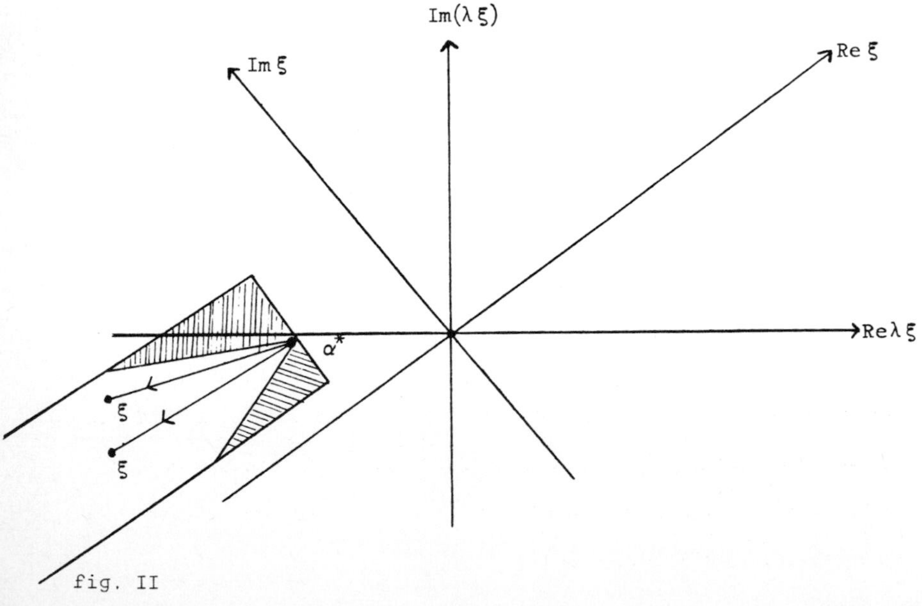

fig. II

Dans le plan de la variable x_1 on obtient les figures suivantes :

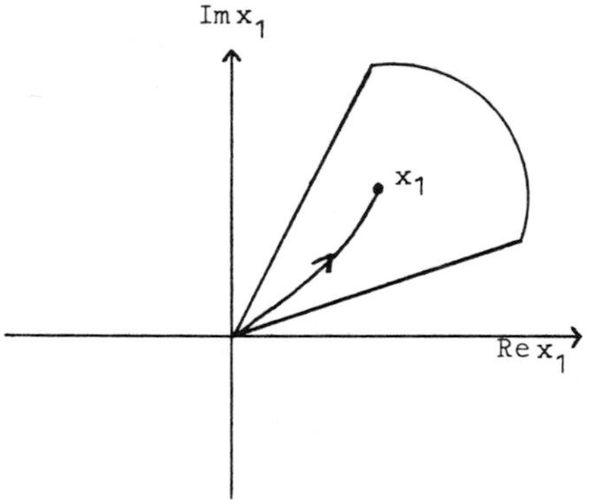

fig. I'

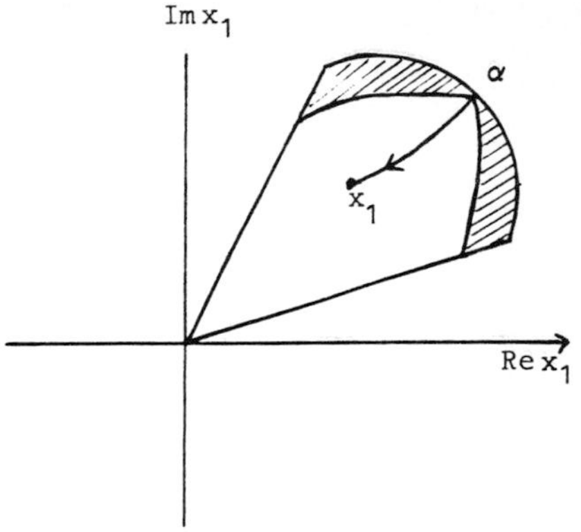

fig. II'

Pour un choix convenable de $\gamma^*(\xi)$ (ou $\gamma(x_1)$) il faut supposer que $\text{Re}\,\lambda \neq 0$ $(\arg \lambda \neq \frac{\pi}{2})$. Le cas III est précisément le cas $\arg \lambda = \frac{\pi}{2}$ c'est-à-dire :

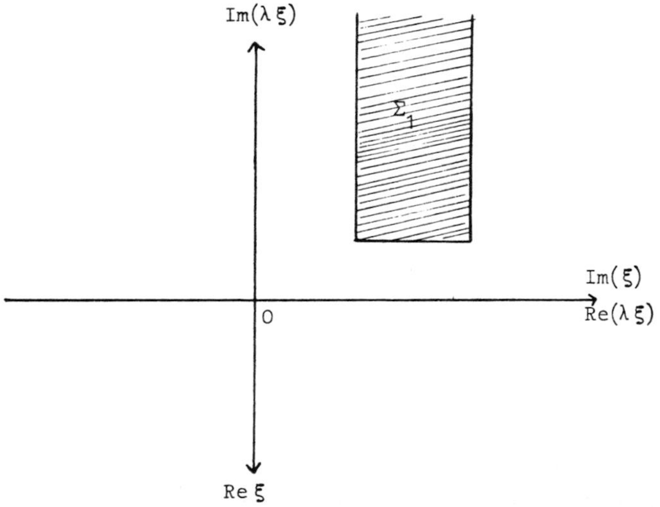

fig. III

Dans ce cas on ne peut pas en général choisir des chemins convenables. Toutefois si φ vérifie certaines conditions il est possible de réduire ce cas III au cas I . Par exemple si $\varphi(x_1,x) = O(x_1^N)$ uniformément en x , où N est un entier positif, on écrit

$$H(x_1,x) = x_1^N \int_{\gamma(x_1)} \left(\frac{x_1}{t}\right)^{\lambda-N} \psi(t,x) \frac{dt}{t}$$

où

$$\psi(x_1,x_2) = \frac{\varphi(x_1,x_2)}{x_1^N} .$$

La constante λ est remplacée par $\lambda-N$ et si $\operatorname{Re}\lambda = 0$ on a $\operatorname{Re}(\lambda-N) = -N<0$ (ce qui est le cas I).

CHAPITRE II

ETUDE DES SYSTEMES DE PFAFF COMPLETEMENT INTEGRABLES DE LA FORME

(1) $$dy = \frac{f^1(x_1,x_2,y)}{x_1^{p_1+1}}\,dx_1 + \frac{f^2(x_1,x_2,y)}{x_2^{p_2+1}}\,dx_2$$

avec $p_1 > 0$ et $p_2 > 0$.

§ 1. Rappels de résultats sur les équations différentielles ordinaires, Unicité des solutions asymptotiques.

§ 2. Cas où les fonctions f^1 et f^2 sont holomorphes au voisinage de l'origine de $\mathbf{C}^2 \times \mathbf{C}^m$.

§ 3. Cas où les fonctions f^1 , f^2 admettent des développements asymptotiques en (x_1,x_2) .

§ 4. Cas où les fonctions f^1 , f^2 admettent des développements asymptotiques en x_1 uniforme en (x_2,y) .

§ 5. Applications aux systèmes de Pfaff linéaires.

§ 1. RAPPELS DE RESULTATS SUR LES EQUATIONS DIFFERENTIELLES ORDINAIRES. UNICITE DES SOLUTIONS ASYMPTOTIQUES.

NOTATIONS.

$$\mathcal{D}(R_o, \rho_1, \rho_2) = \{x \in \mathbf{C} \ | 0 < |x| < R_o \ \rho_1 < \arg x < \rho_2\}$$

$$\Delta(r_o, \rho_o) = \{\varepsilon \in \mathbf{C} \ | 0 < |\varepsilon| < r_o \quad | \arg \varepsilon | < \rho_o\}$$

$$U = \{y \in \mathbf{C}^m | \ \|y\| < \delta_o\}$$

Considérons un système différentiel ordinaire de la forme .

$$\varepsilon^\sigma x^{p+1} \frac{dy}{dx} = f(x,y,\varepsilon) \tag{1}$$

satisfaisant aux hypothèses suivantes :

1) σ et p sont des entiers positifs ou nuls

2) f est une application à valeurs dans $\mathbf{C}^m$ holomorphe dans

$$\mathcal{D}(R_o, \rho_1, \rho_2) \times \Delta(r_o, \rho_o) \times U$$

3) $f(x,y,\varepsilon) \underset{u.\Delta \times U}{\overset{\mathcal{D}(R_o,\rho_1,\rho_2)}{\frown}} \sum_{m \geq o} \hat{f}_m(y,\varepsilon) x^m$

avec pour tout m , $\hat{f}_m(y,\varepsilon)$ holomorphe dans $\Delta(r_o, \rho_o) \times U$ et

$$\hat{f}_m(y,\varepsilon) \underset{u.\,U}{\overset{\Delta(r_o,\rho_o)}{\frown}} \sum_{\ell \geq o} \hat{f}_{m,\ell}(y) \varepsilon^\ell .$$

où pour tout m et ℓ , $\hat{f}_{m,\ell}$ est une fonction holomorphe dans U .

4) $f(x,y,\varepsilon) \underset{u.\mathcal{D} \times U}{\overset{\Delta(r_o,\rho_o)}{\frown}} \sum_{\ell \geq o} \tilde{f}_\ell(x,y) \varepsilon^\ell$

où pour tout ℓ , $\tilde{f}_\ell$ est holomorphe dans $\mathcal{D}(R_o, \rho_1, \rho_2) \times U$ et

$$\tilde{f}_{\ell}(x,y) \underset{u.\,U}{\overset{\mathcal{D}(R_o,\rho_1,\rho_2)}{\frown}} \sum_{m\geq o} \tilde{f}_{\ell,m}(y)x^m$$

Remarques.

α) pour tout ℓ et tout m, $\tilde{f}_{\ell,m}(y) = \hat{f}_{m,\ell}(y)$

β) Nous avons

$$f(x,y,\varepsilon) = f_o(x,\varepsilon) + A(x,\varepsilon)y + \sum_{|p|\geq 2} f_p(x,\varepsilon)y^p$$

dans $\mathcal{D}(R_o,\rho_1,\rho_2) \times \Delta(r_o,\rho_o) \times U$.

On en déduit que :

$$f_o(x,\varepsilon) \underset{u.\Delta}{\overset{\mathcal{D}(R_o,\rho_1,\rho_2)}{\frown}} \sum_{m\geq o} \hat{f}_m(0,\varepsilon)x^m$$

$$A(x,\varepsilon) \underset{u.\Delta}{\overset{\mathcal{D}(R_o,\rho_1,\rho_2)}{\frown}} \sum_{m\geq o} A_m(\varepsilon)\, x^m$$

avec $A_m(\varepsilon) \overset{\Delta(r_o,\rho_o)}{\frown} \sum_{\ell\geq o} A_{m,\ell}\, \varepsilon^{\ell}$

donc $A_o(\varepsilon) = A_{oo} + O(\varepsilon)$.

5) $\hat{f}_o(0,\varepsilon) = O(\varepsilon)$

6) A_{oo} est inversible.

7) Si $\lambda_1,\lambda_2,\dots \lambda_n$ sont les valeurs propres de A_{oo} on suppose que

$$|\arg(-\lambda_j) - p\arg x| \leq \frac{3\pi}{2} - \sigma\rho_o$$

dans $\mathcal{D}(R_o,\rho_1,\rho_2)$ pour un choix convenable des $\arg(-\lambda_j)$ et ceci pour tout $j = 1,2,\dots n$.

Soient $\tilde{\rho}_1$ et $\tilde{\rho}_2$ deux nombres réels positifs quelconques vérifiant

$$\rho_1 < \tilde{\rho}_1 < \tilde{\rho}_2 < \rho_2$$

Nous avons alors :

THEOREME 1.1. Il existe R_1 et r_1 et une solution φ de (1) holomorphe dans $\mathcal{D}(R_1,\tilde{\rho}_1,\tilde{\rho}_2) \times \Delta(r_1,\rho_o)$ telle que :

$$\varphi(x,\varepsilon) \underset{u.\Delta(r_1,\rho_o)}{\overset{\mathcal{D}(R_1,\tilde{\rho}_1,\tilde{\rho}_2)}{\frown}} \sum_{m\geq o} \varphi_m(\varepsilon)x^m$$

où pour tout $m \geq 0$, φ_m est holomorphe dans $\Delta(r_1,\rho_o)$ et

$$\varphi_m(\varepsilon) \overset{\Delta(r_1,\rho_o)}{\frown} \sum_{\ell\geq o} \varphi_{m,\ell}\varepsilon^\ell$$

de plus $\varphi_o(\varepsilon) = O(\varepsilon)$.

Signalons pour être complet le résultat suivant :

THEOREME 1.2. Il existe R_1 et r_1 et une solution ψ de (1) holomorphe dans $\mathcal{D}(R_1,\tilde{\rho}_1,\tilde{\rho}_2) \times \Delta(r_1,\rho_o)$ telle que :

$$\psi(x,\varepsilon) \underset{u.\mathcal{D}(R_1,\tilde{\rho}_1,\tilde{\rho}_2)}{\overset{\Delta(r_1,\rho_o)}{\frown}} \sum_{\ell\geq o} \psi_\ell(x)\varepsilon^\ell$$

où pour tout ρ , ψ_ρ est holomorphe dans $\mathcal{D}(R_1,\tilde{\rho}_1,\tilde{\rho}_2)$ et

$$\psi_\ell(x) \overset{\mathcal{D}(R_1,\tilde{\rho}_1,\tilde{\rho}_2)}{\frown} \sum_{m\geq o} \psi_{\ell,m}x^m$$

de plus $\psi_o(x) = O(x)$.

Les démonstrations de ces résultats se trouvent dans [10] et [11] .

Nous avons également

THEOREME 1.3. Toujours sous les mêmes hypothèses, soient φ une solution donnée par le théorème 1.1 et ψ une solution donnée par le théorème 1.2 toutes les deux d'ordre $O(|x| + |\varepsilon|)$ alors on a

1) pour tout $N = 1,2,\ldots$

$$\|\varphi(x,\varepsilon) - \psi(x,\varepsilon)\| \leq K_N|\varepsilon^\sigma x^p|^N \quad \text{sur} \quad \mathcal{D}(R_1,\tilde{\rho}_1,\tilde{\rho}_2) \times \Delta(r_1,\rho_o)$$

2) <u>si</u> $\sigma = 0$ <u>et</u> $\tilde{\rho}_2 - \tilde{\rho}_1 > \frac{\pi}{p}$

$$\psi = \varphi .$$

<u>Démonstration de 2°</u> .

Posons $$y = u + \varphi(x,\varepsilon)$$

alors $$\varepsilon^\sigma x^{p+1} \frac{du}{dx} = \varepsilon^\sigma x^{p+1} \frac{dy}{dx} - \varepsilon^\sigma x^{p+1} \frac{d\varphi}{dx}$$

$$= f(x,u+\varphi(x,\varepsilon),\varepsilon) - f(x,\varphi(x,\varepsilon),\varepsilon)$$

Considérons la fonction

$$G(t) = f(x,tu+\varphi(x,\varepsilon),\varepsilon)$$

alors

$$\varepsilon^\sigma x^{p+1} \frac{du}{dx} = G(1) - G(0) = \int_0^1 G'(t)dt$$

or

$$G'(t) = \frac{\partial f}{\partial y}(x,tu+\varphi(x,\varepsilon),\varepsilon)u$$

Et

$$(E) \qquad \varepsilon^\sigma x^{p+1} \frac{du}{dx} = E(x,u,\varepsilon)u$$

avec $$E(x,u,\varepsilon) = \int_0^1 \frac{\partial f}{\partial y}(x,tu+\varphi(x,\varepsilon),\varepsilon)dt$$

Vu les hypothèses.

$$\frac{\partial f}{\partial y}(x,y,\varepsilon) = A(x,\varepsilon) + O(y) .$$

donc $$E(x,u,\varepsilon) = A(x,\varepsilon) + O(|u| + |\varphi|)$$

$$= A(x,\varepsilon) + O(|u|+|x|+|\varepsilon|)$$

La fonction

$$u_o(x,\varepsilon) = \psi(x,\varepsilon) - \varphi(x,\varepsilon)$$

est une solution de l'équation (E) . Donc $u_o(x,\varepsilon)$ est également une solution du système linéaire

$$(E') \qquad \varepsilon^\sigma x^{p+1} \frac{dv}{dx} = E(x,u_o(x,\varepsilon),\varepsilon)v$$

ou $$E(x,u_o(x,\varepsilon),\varepsilon) = A(x,\varepsilon) + O(|u_o|+|x|+|\varepsilon|)$$

Comme $\varphi(x,\varepsilon)$ et $\psi(x,\varepsilon)$ sont d'ordre $O(|x|+|\varepsilon|)$ il en est de même de u_o et

$$E(x,u_o,\varepsilon) = A(x,\varepsilon) + O(|x|+|\varepsilon|)$$
$$= A_{oo} + O(|x|+|\varepsilon|)$$

On peut supposer quitte à faire éventuellement une transformation linéaire à coefficients constants que

$$A_{oo} = \begin{pmatrix} A_1^0 & & 0 \dots\dots\dots & 0 \\ 0 & A_2^0 & 0 \dots\dots & 0 \\ \vdots & & & \\ 0 & \dots\dots\dots & & A_s^0 \end{pmatrix}$$

avec $$A_j^0 = \lambda_j I_j + N_j$$

où I_j est la matrice identité d'ordre n_j qui est la multiplicité de la valeur propre λ_j, N_j est une matrice nilpotente de même ordre.
De plus $\lambda_j \neq \lambda_u$ si $j \neq h$.
Soit S un secteur inclus dans $\mathcal{D}(R_1,\tilde{\rho}_1,\tilde{\rho}_2)$ tel que

$$|\arg(\lambda_j - \lambda_h) - p \arg x| < \frac{3\pi}{2} - \sigma\rho_o$$

pour tout couple (j,h) avec $j \neq h$. Alors il existe une $n \times n$-matrice $Q(x,\varepsilon)$ holomorphe dans $S \times \Delta(r_1,\rho_o)$ vérifiant

$$Q(x,\varepsilon) = I + O(|x|+|\varepsilon|)$$

et telle que la transformation

$$v = Q(x,\varepsilon)w$$

transforme le système (E') en

$$\varepsilon^\sigma x^{p+1} \frac{dw}{dx} = G(x,\varepsilon)w$$

avec

$$G(x,\varepsilon) = \begin{pmatrix} G_1 & 0\dots & 0 \\ 0 & \ddots & \vdots \\ \vdots & & 0 \\ 0\dots & 0 & G_s \end{pmatrix}$$

et $$G_j(x,\varepsilon) = A_j^o + O(|x| + |\varepsilon|) .$$

Supposons maintenant que $\tilde{\rho}_2 - \tilde{\rho}_1 > \frac{\pi}{p}$ et que $\sigma = 0$, sous cette hypothèse on peut supposer que le secteur S a une ouverture supérieure à $\frac{\pi}{p}$.

La fonction $w_o(x,\varepsilon) = Q(x,\varepsilon)^{-1} u_o(x,\varepsilon)$ est solution du système

$$x^{P+1} \frac{dw}{dx} = G(x,\varepsilon)w$$

et $$w_o(x,\varepsilon) = \sum_{j=1}^{s} w_o^j(x,\varepsilon)$$

ou pour tout j , w_o^j est solution du système

$$x^{p+1} \frac{dw}{dx} = G_j(x,\varepsilon)w$$

Mais pour tout j , il existe un chemin allant à l'origine telle que toute solution $w^j(x)$ <u>non nulle</u> de ce système soit non bornée le long de ce chemin. Comme la solution

$u_o = \psi - \varphi$ de E' est bornée

au voisinage de l'origine, nous avons

$u_o = 0$ c'est-à-dire $\psi = \varphi$

ce qui démontre la deuxième partie de notre théorème.

§ 2. Cas où les fonctions f^1 et f^2 sont holomorphes au voisinage de l'origine de $\mathbb{C}^2 \times \mathbb{C}^m$.

Dans ce paragraphe, nous considérons les systèmes de Pfaff complètement intégrables de la forme

$$(1) \qquad dy = \frac{f^1(x_1,x_2,y)}{x_1^{p_1+1}}\, dx_1 + \frac{f^2(x_1,x_2,y)}{x_2^{p_2+1}}\, dx_2$$

avec $p_1 > 0$ et $p_2 > 0$

et où pour $i = 1,2$, f^i est holomorphe dans $U^1 \times U^2 \times V$.

$$U^i = \{x_i \mid 0 \leq |x_i| < r_i\} \qquad i = 1,2$$

$$V = \{y \in \mathbb{C}^m \mid 0 \leq |y_i| < \rho_i\}$$

On supposera que $f^1(0,0,0) = f^2(0,0,0) = 0$ et on se propose de démontrer

THEOREME 2.1. Si les deux matrices $A^i(0,0) = (\frac{\partial f^i}{\partial y})(0,0)$ sont inversibles alors le système de Pfaff (1) admet une solution et une seule φ holomorphe à l'origine et telle que $\varphi(0,0) = 0$.

Notons, $\lambda_1^i,\lambda_2^i,\ldots \lambda_m^i$, les valeurs propres non nécessairement distinctes de $A^i(0)$.

Soient pour $i = 1,2$:

$$S_1^i,S_2^i,\ldots S_{N_i}^i$$

un recouvrement de $U^i - \{0\}$ par des secteurs propres pour la famille de fonctions $\{-\lambda_j^i(\frac{1}{x_i})^{p_i}\}$ $j = 1,2,\ldots m$ et d'ouverture plus grande que $\frac{\pi}{p_i}$.

Regardons l'équation différentielle (1.1) $x_1^{p_1+1} \frac{dy}{dx_1} = f^1(x_1,x_2,y)$ x_2 étant considérée paramètre.

D'après les résultats rappelés dans le § 1, pour tout $h = 1,2,\ldots N_1$ il existe une solution

$$y = \varphi_h(x_1,x_2)$$

de (1.2) holomorphe dans $S_h^1 \times U^2$ telle que

$$\varphi_h(x_1,x_2) \underset{u.U^2}{\overset{S_h^1}{\sim}} \sum_{k=o}^{+\infty} \varphi_{hk}(x_2)x_1^k$$

et

$$\varphi_{h,o}(0) = 0$$

LEMME 2.2. <u>Pour tout</u> $h = 1,2,\ldots N_1$ <u>nous avons</u>

$$x_2^{p_2+1} \frac{\partial \varphi_h}{\partial x_2} = f^2(x_1,x_2,\varphi_h(x_1,x_2))$$

<u>sur</u> $S_h^1 \times U^2$.

<u>Démonstration</u> : Pour simplifier l'écriture, oublions l'indice h .

Nous avons sur $S^1 \times U^2$:

$$x_1^{p_1+1} \frac{\partial}{\partial x_1}(x_2^{p_2+1} \frac{\partial \varphi}{\partial x_2}) = x_2^{p_2+1} \frac{\partial}{\partial x_2}(x_1^{p_1+1} \frac{\partial \varphi}{\partial x_1})$$

$$= x_2^{p_2+1} \frac{\partial}{\partial x_2}(f^1(x_1,x_2,\varphi))$$

$$= x_2^{p_2+1} \frac{\partial f^1}{\partial x_2}(x_1,x_2,\varphi) + \frac{\partial f^1}{\partial y}(x_1,x_2,\varphi)x_2^{p_2+1} \frac{\partial \varphi}{\partial x_2}$$

La condition de complète intégrabilité du système (1) est

$$x_2^{p_2+1} \frac{\partial f^1}{\partial x_2}(x_1,x_2,y) + (\frac{\partial f^1}{\partial y}) f^2(x_1,x_2,y)$$

$$= x_1^{p_1+1} \frac{\partial f^2}{\partial x_1}(x_1,x_2,y)+(\frac{\partial f^2}{\partial y}(x_1,x_2,y))f^1(x_1,x_2,y)$$

et ceci identiquement sur $U^1 \times U^2 \times V$. Donc en particulier

$$x_2^{p_2+1} \frac{\partial f^1}{\partial x_2}(x_1,x_2,\varphi) + \frac{\partial f^1}{\partial y}(x_1,x_2,\varphi)f^2(x_1,x_2,\varphi)$$

$$= x_1^{p_1+1} \frac{\partial f^2}{\partial x_1}(x_1,x_2,\varphi) + \frac{\partial f^2}{\partial y}(x_1,x_2,\varphi)x_1^{p_1+1} \frac{\partial \varphi}{\partial x_1}$$

ceci nous donne

$$x_1^{p_1+1} \frac{\partial}{\partial x_1}(x_2^{p_2+1} \frac{\partial\varphi}{\partial x_2}) = x_1^{p_1+1} \frac{\partial f^2}{\partial x_1}(x_1,x_2,\varphi) + \frac{\partial f^2}{\partial y}(x_1,x_2,\varphi) \cdot x_1^{p_1+1} \frac{\partial\varphi}{\partial x_2}$$

$$- \frac{\partial f^1}{\partial y}(x_1,x_2,\varphi) f^2(x_1,x_2,\varphi) + \frac{\partial f^1}{\partial y}(x_1,x_2,\varphi) x_2^{p_2+1} \frac{\partial\varphi}{\partial x_2}$$

c'est-à-dire

$$x_1^{p_1+1} \frac{\partial}{\partial x_1}\left[x_2^{p_2+1} \frac{\partial\varphi}{\partial x_2} - f^2(x_1,x_2,\varphi)\right] = \left(\frac{\partial f^1}{\partial y}(x_1,x_2,\varphi)\right)\left[x_2^{p_2+1} \frac{\partial\varphi}{\partial x_2} - f^2(x_1,x_2,\varphi)\right]$$

Donc la fonction

$$v(x_1,x_2) = x_2^{p_2+1} \frac{\partial\varphi}{\partial x_2} - f^2(x_1,x_2,\varphi(x_1,x_2))$$

est une solution bornée sur $S^1 \times U^2$ du système linéaire

$$(2) \qquad x_1^{p_1+1} \frac{du}{dx_1} = \left(\frac{\partial f^1}{\partial y}(x_1,x_2,\varphi(x_1,x_2))\right)u$$

Mais $\frac{\partial f^1}{\partial y}(x_1,x_2,\varphi) = A^1(x_1,x_2) + O(\varphi)$ où $A^1(0)$ est inversible.

Comme le secteur S^1 a une ouverture plus grande que $\frac{\pi}{p_1}$ le système (2) n'a pas d'autre solution bornée que la solution 0 (voir § 1) .

Donc

$$x_2^{p_2+1} \frac{\partial\varphi}{\partial x_2} = f^2(x_1,x_2,\varphi(x_1,x_2))$$

c'est-à-dire que pour tout $h = 1,2,\ldots N_1$, φ_h est une solution du système (1) sur $S_h^1 \times U^2$ qui est holomorphe sur ce produit.

De la même manière, on montre qu'il existe pour tout $k = 1,2,\ldots N_2$ une solution ψ_k du système (1) sur $U^1 \times S_k^2$ qui est holomorphe sur ce produit.

D'après le théorème 1.3 , nous avons

$$\varphi_h(x_1,x_2) = \psi_k(x_1,x_2) \quad \text{sur} \quad S_h^1 \times S_k^2$$

La fonction φ_1 est définie dans $S_1^1 \times U^2$ et $\varphi_1(x_1,x_2) = \psi_k(x_1,x_2)$ dans $S_1^1 \times S_k^2$ pour tout $k = 1,2,\dots N_2$, donc comme $\psi_k(x_1,x_2)$ est définie et holomorphe dans $U^1 \times S_k^2$, cette fonction est le prolongement analytique de φ_1 à $U^1 \times S_k^2$.

Donc comme pour tout $h \neq k$, $\psi_h(x_1,x_2)$ est aussi le prolongement analytique de φ_1 à $U^1 \times S_h^2$ nous avons pour tout h et k prenant les valeurs $1,2,\dots N_2$

$$\varphi_h(x_1,x_2) = \psi_k(x_1,x_2) \quad \text{sur} \quad U^1 \times S_h^2 \cap S_k^2$$

c'est-à-dire qu'il existe une fonction ψ définie et holomorphe sur $U^1 \times \{U^2 - \{0\}\}$ telle que pour tout k

$$\psi | U^1 \times S_k^2 = \psi_k$$

Comme pour tout k, ψ_k admet un développement asymptotique dans $U^1 \times S_k^2$ la fonction ψ est bornée au voisinage de l'origine de $\mathbf{C}^2$ c'est-à-dire qu'elle se prolonge en une fonction notée encore ψ holomorphe dans $U^1 \times U^2$.

La construction qui a été faite de ψ à partir de φ_1 permet de la même manière de construire une fonction φ holomorphe dans $U^1 \times U^2$ à partir de ψ_1 et nous avons

$$\varphi = \psi \quad \text{sur} \quad U^1 \times U^2$$

ce qui prouve le théorème énoncé au début de ce paragraphe.

COROLLAIRE 2.3. <u>Le système</u> (1) <u>sous les hypothèses indiquées admet une solution formelle et une seule et cette solution formelle est convergente</u>.

§ 3. <u>Les fonctions</u> $f_i(i = 1,2)$ <u>admettent des développements asymptotiques en</u> (x_1,x_2) <u>uniformes en</u> y .

Soient :

$S = S_1 \times S_2$ un secteur de $\mathbb{C}^2$

U un polydisque centré à l'origine de $\mathbb{C}^m$.

$f_i(i = 1,2)$ deux fonctions holomorphes dans $S \times U$ telles que

$$f_i \underset{u.\ U}{\overset{S}{\sim}} \sum_{|r|=o}^{+\infty} f^i_{r_1,r_2}(y)x_1^{r_1}x_2^{r_2}$$

$$\frac{\partial f_i}{\partial x_1} \underset{u.\ U}{\overset{S}{\sim}} \sum_{|r|=o}^{+\infty} f^i_{r_1,r_2}(y)r_1x_1^{r_1-1}x_2^{r_2}$$

$$\frac{\partial f_i}{\partial x_2} \underset{u.\ U}{\overset{S}{\sim}} \sum_{|r|=o}^{+\infty} f^i_{r_1,r_2}(y)r_2x_1^{r_1}x_2^{r_2-1}$$

Nous avons de plus

$$f_1(x_1,x_2,y) = \sum_{|p|=o}^{+\infty} \hat{f}^i_p(x_1,x_2)\ y^p \quad \text{dans } S \times U$$

On supposera dans la suite que

$$\hat{f}^i_o(0,0) = 0 \quad \text{pour } i = 1,2 .$$

On se propose d'étudier le système de Pfaff que l'on supposera complètement intégrable

$$(1) \qquad dy = \frac{f_1(x_1,x_2,y)}{x_1^{p_1+1}}\,dx_2 + \frac{f_2(x_1,x_2,y)}{x_2^{p_2+1}}\,dx_2$$

dans le cas $p_1 > 0$ et $p_2 > 0$.

Ce système peut également s'écrire sous la forme

$$(1') \qquad \begin{cases} x_1^{p_1+1}\dfrac{\partial y}{\partial x_1} = f_1(x_1,x_2,y) & p_1 > 0 \\[2ex] x_2^{p_2+1}\dfrac{\partial y}{\partial x_2} = f_2(x_1,x_2,y) & p_2 > 0 \end{cases}$$

3.1. Complète intégrabilité et existence de solution formelle.

Ecrivons

$$f_i(x_1,x_2,y) = f_o^i(x_1,x_2) + A^i(x_1,x_2)y + R^i(x_1,x_2,y) .$$

avec

$$R^i(x_1,x_2,y) = O(y^2)$$

La condition de complète intégrabilité du système (1) est

$$x_1^{p_1+1} \frac{\partial f_2}{\partial x_1} = x_2^{p_2+1} \frac{\partial f_1}{\partial x_2}$$

c'est-à-dire

$$D_{12} = D_{21}$$

où

$$D_{12}(x_1,x_2,y) = x_2^{p_2+1} \left(\frac{\partial f_1}{\partial x_2} + \frac{\partial f_1}{\partial y} \cdot \frac{\partial y}{\partial x_2}\right)$$

$$= x_2^{p_2+1} \left(\frac{\partial f_o^1}{\partial x_2} + \frac{\partial A^1}{\partial x_2} y + \frac{\partial R^1}{\partial x_2}\right) + \frac{\partial f_1}{\partial y} f_2$$

LEMME 3.1. Nous avons $[A^1(0,0),\ A^2(0,0)] = 0$

En effet

$$D_{12}(0,0,y) = \left[\frac{\partial}{\partial y}(A^1 y + R^1) \right]_{\substack{x_1=0\\ x_2=0}} f_2(0,0,y)$$

Or $\frac{\partial}{\partial y}(A^1 y + R^1) = A^1 + \frac{\partial R^1}{\partial y}$ et $f_2(0,0,y) = A^2(0,0)y + O(y^2)$

Si $\tilde{D}_{12}(0,0,y)$ désigne le terme linéaire en y dans $D_{12}(0,0,y)$ nous voyons que

$$\tilde{D}_{12}(0,0,y) = A^1(0,0)\ A^2(0,0)$$

ce qui donne le lemme ci-dessus.

COROLLAIRE 3.2. Par une similitude $T \in Gl(p,C)$ il est possible de mettre $A^i(0,0)$ $(i = 1,2)$ sous la forme

$$\tilde{A}^i = \begin{pmatrix} (A^i)_1 & 0 & \dots & 0 \\ 0 & (A^i)_2 & & \vdots \\ \vdots & & \ddots & 0 \\ 0 & \dots & 0 & (A^i)_r \end{pmatrix}$$

avec pour tout $s = 1,2,\dots r$

$$(A^i)_s = \lambda_s^i I_s + (N^i)_s$$

où I_s est la matrice identité de même ordre que $(A^i)_s$, $(N^i)_s$ une matrice nilpotente sous forme triangulaire supérieure. De plus on peut supposer que pour tout $s = 1,2\dots r$ il existe $i \in \{1,2\}$ tel que $\lambda_s^i \neq \lambda_{s+1}^i$. On a également

$$[(A^1)_s,(A^2)_s] = [(N^1)_s(N^2)_s] = 0$$

Considérons maintenant le système formel (1^*) associé au système $(1')$ de la manière suivante :

On remplace $\qquad f^i(x_1,x_2,y) = \sum_{|p|=0}^{+\infty} \hat{f}_p^i(x_1,x_2)y^p$

par la série formelle que nous noterons encore $f^i(x_1,x_2,y)$ obtenue en remplaçant les coefficients $\hat{f}_p^i(x_1,x_2)$ par leurs développements asymptotiques dans S (ceux-ci existent voir par exemple chap. I § 3).

LEMME 3.3. Si une des matrices $A^i(0,0)$ est non singulière, le système formel (1^*) admet une solution formelle de la forme

$$\varphi = \sum_{|r|=1}^{+\infty} \varphi_{r_1 r_2} x_1^{r_1} x_2^{r_2}$$

Preuve : Supposons que $A^1(0,0)$ est non singulière et considérons la première équation du système (1^*)

$$(1_1)^* \qquad x_1^{p_1+1}\frac{\partial y}{\partial x_1} = f_o^1(x_1,x_2) + A^1(x_1,x_2)y + R^1(x_1,x_2,y)$$

où $R^1(x_1,x_2,y)$ est d'ordre supérieur ou égal à 2 en y .

Par identification on trouve facilement que les coefficients de la série formelle φ sont donnés par

$$A^1(0,0)\varphi_{10}+(f_o^1)_{10} = 0$$

$$A^1(0,0)\varphi_{01}+(f_o^1)_{01} = 0$$

et plus généralement

$$(r_1,r_2) \qquad A^1(0,0)\varphi_{r_1,r_2} = \mathcal{L}_{r_1,r_2}$$

Si toutes ces équations sont ordonnées convenablement, on constate que $\mathcal{L}_{r_1,r_2}$ est une quantité qui ne contient que des coefficients connus par les données ainsi que des solutions des équations qui la précèdent. Donc ce système infini est résoluble.

Montrons que la solution formelle φ_* de $(1_1)^*$ est aussi solution de $(1_2)^*$.

Nous avons

$$x_1^{p_1+1}\frac{\partial}{\partial x_1}(x_2^{p_2+1}\frac{\partial\varphi}{\partial x_2}) = x_2^{p_2+1}\frac{\partial}{\partial x_2}(x_1^{p_1+1}\frac{\partial\varphi}{\partial x_1})$$

$$= \quad x_2^{p_2+1}\frac{\partial}{\partial x_2}(f_1(x_1,x_2,\varphi))$$

$$= \quad x_2^{p_2+1}\frac{\partial f_1}{\partial x_2}(x_1,x_2,\varphi)+\frac{\partial f_1}{\partial y}(x_1,x_2,\varphi)x_2^{p_2+1}\frac{\partial\varphi}{\partial x_2}$$

Le système (1) étant complètement intégrable, nous avons

$$x_2^{p_2+1}\frac{\partial f_1}{\partial x_2}(x_1,x_2,y)+\frac{\partial f_1}{\partial y}(x_1,x_2,y)f_2(x_1,x_2,y) =$$

$$= x_1^{p_1+1}\frac{\partial f_2}{\partial x_1}(x_1,x_2,y)+\frac{\partial f_2}{\partial y}(x_1,x_2,y)f_1(x_1,x_2,y)$$

Nous avons ceci identiquement en y. Et vu l'hypothèse sur la dérivabilité de nos développements asymptotiques, cette dernière condition est encore valable formellement, c'est-à-dire que le système formel (1^*) est complètement intégrable.

Nous avons donc :

$$x_2^{p_2+1}\frac{\partial f_1}{\partial x_2}(x_1,x_2,\varphi)+\frac{\partial f_1}{\partial y}(x_1,x_2,\varphi)f_2(x_1,x_2,\varphi)$$

$$=x_1^{p_1+1}\frac{\partial f_2}{\partial x_1}(x_1,x_2,\varphi)+\frac{\partial f_2}{\partial y}(x_1,x_2,\varphi)f_1(x_1,x_2,\varphi)$$

en tenant compte de cette égalité et du fait que

$$f_1(x_1,x_2,\varphi)=x_1^{p_1+1}\frac{\partial\varphi}{\partial x_1}$$

nous obtenons

$$x_1^{p_1+1}\frac{\partial}{\partial x_1}(x_2^{p_2+1}\frac{\partial\varphi}{\partial x_2})$$

$$=x_1^{p_1+1}\frac{\partial f_2}{\partial x_1}(x_1,x_2,\varphi)+\frac{\partial f_2}{\partial y}(x_1,x_2,\varphi)x_1^{p_1+1}\frac{\partial\varphi}{\partial x_1}$$

$$-\frac{\partial f_1}{\partial y}(x_1,x_2,\varphi)f_2(x_1,x_2,\varphi)+\frac{\partial f_1}{\partial y}x_2^{p_2+1}\frac{\partial\varphi}{\partial x_2}$$

c'est-à-dire

$$x_1^{p_1+1}\frac{\partial}{\partial x_1}(x_2^{p_2+1}\frac{\partial\varphi}{\partial x_2}-f_2(x_1,x_2,\varphi))=\frac{\partial f_1}{\partial y}(x_1,x_2,\varphi)(x_2^{p_2+1}\frac{\partial\varphi}{\partial x_2}-f_2(x_1,x_2,\varphi))$$

La série formelle $v=x_2^{p_2+1}\frac{\partial\varphi}{\partial x_2}-f_2(x_1,x_2,\varphi)$ est donc solution du système linéaire

$$x_1^{p_1+1}\frac{\partial u}{\partial x_1}=\frac{\partial f_1}{\partial y}(x_1,x_2,\varphi(x_1,x_2))u$$

où

$$\frac{\partial f_1}{\partial y}=A^1(x_1,x_2)+O(|\varphi|)\ .$$

Mais vu l'hypothèse sur $A^1(0,0)$ la seule solution formelle de ce système est la solution zéro. Il en résulte que formellement

$$x_2^{p_2+1} \frac{\partial \varphi}{\partial x_2} = f_2(x_1,x_2,\varphi) .$$

Donc φ est également solution de la deuxième équation.

Remarque 3.4. La solution formelle donnée par le lemme 3.3 est unique.

Remarque 3.5. Si aucune des matrices $A^i(0,0)$ est régulière, le système formel peut quand même avoir des solutions formelles.

3.2. Equation intégrale associée au système (1).

Nous supposons que le système formel (1^*) admet une solution formelle de la forme

$$\varphi = \sum_{|r|=1}^{+\infty} \varphi_{r_1,r_2} x_1^{r_1} x_2^{r_2}$$

D'après le théorème de Ritt, il existe une fonction $\Phi : S \to \mathbb{C}^m$ holomorphe dans S et telle que

1) $\Phi \overset{S}{\sim} \varphi$

2) $\frac{\partial \Phi}{\partial x_i} \overset{S}{\sim} \frac{\partial \varphi}{\partial x_i} \quad i = 1,2$

Notons $x = (x_1,x_2)$, comme φ est solution du système formel (1^*) nous avons pour $i = 1,2$

$$x_1^{p_i+1} \frac{\partial \Phi}{\partial x_i} - f_o^i(x) - A^i(x)\Phi - R^i(x,\Phi) = - U^i(x)$$

où U^i est holomorphe dans S et asymptotique à zéro dans S.

La transformation $y = z + \Phi$ nous donne

$$x_i^{p_i+1} \frac{\partial z}{\partial x_i} = A^i(x)z + R^i(x,z+\Phi) - R^i(x,\Phi) + U^i(x)$$

Mais vu les hypothèses sur les f^i nous avons

$$R^i(x,z+\Phi)-R^i(x,\Phi) = B^i(x)z+H^i(x,z)$$

avec

$$\lim_{\substack{x\to o\\ x\in S}} B^i(x) = 0$$

c'est-à-dire que

$$dz = \left(\frac{A^1(0)z+P^1(x,z)}{x_1^{p_1+1}}\right)dx_1+\left(\frac{A^2(0)z+P^2(x,z)}{x_2^{p_2+1}}\right)dx_2$$

avec

$$P^i(x,z) = U^i(x)+H^i(x,z)+(A^i+B^i-A^i(0))\,z$$

Le système de Pfaff

$$dz = \left(\frac{A^1(0)}{x_1^{p_1+1}}\,dx_1+\frac{A^2(0)}{x_2^{p_2+1}}\,dx_2\right)z$$

est complètement intégrable car $[A^1(0),A^2(0)] = 0$.

Soit $V(x)$ une matrice fondamentale de ce système linéaire ; comme $p_1 > 0$ et $p_2 > 0$ on peut prendre

$$V(x) = \exp\left(-\frac{A^1(0)}{p_1x_1^{p_1}}\right)\exp\left(-\frac{A^2(0)}{p_2x_2^{p_2}}\right)$$

Remarque 3.6. Tant que nous n'utiliserons pas la forme explicite de $V(x)$ nos résultats resteront valables pour le cas $p_1 \geq 0$ et $p_2 \geq 0$.

En posant $z = V(x)U$ nous obtenons

$$du = V^{-1}(x)\left(\frac{P^1(x,V(x)u)}{x_1^{p_1+1}}\,dx_1+\frac{P^2(x,V(x)u)}{x_2^{p_2+1}}\,dx_2\right)$$

ou encore

$$(2)\qquad\left\{\begin{aligned} x_1^{p_1+1}\frac{\partial u}{\partial x_1} &= V^{-1}(x)\,P^1(x,V(x)u)\\ x_2^{p_2+1}\frac{\partial u}{\partial x_2} &= V^{-1}(x)P^2(x,V(x)u)\ . \end{aligned}\right.$$

et par intégration de la première de ces équations le long d'un chemin

$\gamma_1(x_1)$ situé dans le secteur S_1

d'origine a_1 et d'extrémité x_1 .

$$u = \int_{\gamma_1} V^{-1}(t_1,x_2)t_1^{-p_1-1} P^1(t_1,x_2,V(t_1,x_2)u(t_1,x_2))dt_1+h(x_2)$$

où h est une fonction arbitraire de x_2 .

Mais vu les hypothèses initiales faites sur les f^i

$$x_2^{p_2+1} \frac{\partial u}{\partial x_2} = \int_{\gamma_1} x_2^{p_2+1} \frac{\partial}{\partial x_2}(V^{-1}t_1^{-p_1-1} P^1)dt_1+x_2^{p_2+1} \frac{\partial h}{\partial x_2}$$

La complète intégrabilité du système (1) implique celle du système (2) qui s'écrit

$$x_2^{p_2+1} \frac{\partial}{\partial x_2}(V^{-1}(x) P^1(x,V(x)u)) = x_1^{p_1+1} \frac{\partial}{\partial x_1}(V^{-1}(x)P^2(x,V(x)u) .$$

par suite

$$x_2^{p_2+1} \frac{\partial u}{\partial x_2} = \int_{\gamma_1} \frac{\partial}{\partial t_1}(V^{-1}(t_1,x_2)P^2(t_1,x_2,V(t_1,x_2)u(t_1,x_2)))dt_1+x_2^{p_2+1} \frac{\partial h}{\partial x_2}$$

c'est-à-dire que

$$x_2^{p_2+1} \frac{\partial h}{\partial x_2} = V^{-1}(a_1,x_2)P^2(a_1,x_2,V(a_1,x_2)u(a_1,x_2))$$

et
$$h = \int_{\gamma_2(x_2)} V^{-1}(a_1,t_2)P^2(a_1,t_2,V(a_1,t_2)u(a_1,t_2))t_2^{-p_2-1} dt_2+ k$$

où $\gamma_2(x_2)$ est un chemin d'origine a_2 et d'extrémité x_2 dans S_2 et k une constante qui sera à choisir convenablement plus loin et que nous supposerons nulle pour le moment.

En revenant à z nous avons

$$z = \mathcal{P}_{12}(z)$$

avec

$$\mathcal{P}_{12}(z) = \int_{\gamma_1} V(x)V^{-1}(t_1,x_2)t_1^{-p_1-1} P^1(t_1,x_2,z)dt_1 + \int_{\gamma_2} V(x)V^{-1}(a_1,t_2)P^2(a_1,t_2,z)t_2^{-p_2-1} dt_2$$

Remarquons que l'on a également

$$z = \mathcal{P}_{21}(z)$$

et plus généralement

$$z = \widetilde{\mathcal{P}}_{12}(z)$$

avec

$$\widetilde{\mathcal{P}}_{12}(z) = \int_{\widetilde{\Gamma}_1} V(x)V^{-1}(t_1,x_2)t_1^{-p_1-1} P^1(t_1,x_2,z)dt_1$$

$$+ \int_{\widetilde{\Gamma}_2} V(x)V^{-1}(a_1,t_2)P^2(a_1,t_2,z)t_2^{-p_2-1} dt_2$$

où cette fois $\widetilde{\Gamma}_i$ est une matrice $(\gamma_i)_{k\ell}$ de chemin et $\widetilde{\mathcal{P}}_{12}(z)$ donné par

$$(\widetilde{\mathcal{P}}_{12}(z))_{k\ell} = \int_{(\gamma_i)_{k\ell}} (V(x)V^{-1}(t_1,x_2)t_1^{-p_1-1} P_1)_{k\ell}dt_1$$

$$+ \int_{(\gamma_2)_{k\ell}} (V(x)V^{-1}(a_1,t_2)P^2 t_2^{-p_2-1})_{k\ell}dt_2$$

THEOREME 3.7. <u>Si une des équations intégrales</u> $z = \widetilde{\mathcal{P}}_{12}(z)$ où $z = \widetilde{\mathcal{P}}_{21}(z)$ <u>admet une solution</u> $Z(x)$ <u>holomorphe dans un secteur</u> $S' \subset S$ <u>et asymptotique à zéro dans ce secteur, alors le système de Pfaff</u> (1) <u>a pour solution</u> $Y = Z + \Phi$ <u>et de plus cette solution est asymptotique à</u> φ <u>dans</u> S' .

La preuve de ce résultat est une simple vérification laissée au lecteur.

Remarquons que l'on a de plus

$$\frac{\partial Y}{\partial x_1} \overset{S'}{\sim} \frac{\partial \varphi}{\partial x_1} \qquad \text{et} \qquad \frac{\partial Y}{\partial x_2} \overset{S'}{\sim} \frac{\partial \varphi}{\varphi x_2}$$

Si aux hypothèses du début de ce paragraphe on ajoute

$$\frac{\partial^{|r|} f_i}{\partial x_1^{r_1} \partial x_2^{r_2}} \underset{u.\ U}{\overset{S}{\sim}} \sum_{|r|=0}^{+\infty} f^i_{r_1,r_2}(y) \frac{\partial^r}{\partial x_1^{r_1} \partial x_2^{r_2}} (x_1^{r_1} x_2^{r_2})$$

pour tout $|r| \leq q$, alors nous avons également

THEOREME 3.8. Si une des équations intégrales

$$z = \widetilde{\mathcal{P}}_{12}(z) \quad \text{ou} \quad z = \widetilde{\mathcal{P}}_{21}(z) .$$

admet une solution holomorphe dans $S' \subset S$ qui est asymptotique à zéro dans S' ainsi que toutes ses dérivées jusqu'à l'ordre q alors l'équation de Pfaff (1) admet une solution Y holomorphe dans S' telle que

$$\frac{\partial^{|r|} Y}{\partial x_1^{r_1} \partial x_2^{r_2}} \underset{\sim}{S'} \frac{\partial^{|r|} \varphi}{\partial x_1^{r_1} \partial x_2^{r_2}}$$

pour tout $|r|$ variant de 0 à q.

3.3. Etude des équations intégrales.

Supposons maintenant $p_1 > 0$ et $p_2 > 0$ alors

$$V(x) = \exp\left(-\frac{A^1(0)}{p_1 x_1^{p_1}}\right)\exp\left(-\frac{A^2(0)}{p_2 x_2^{p_2}}\right)$$

et par exemple

$$\mathcal{P}_{12}(z) = \int_{\gamma_1(x_1)} \exp\left(-\frac{A^1(0)}{p_1}\left(\frac{1}{x_1^{p_1}} - \frac{1}{t_1^{p_1}}\right)\right) t_1^{-p_1-1} P^1(t_1, x_2, z)\, dt_1$$

$$+ \exp\left(-\frac{A^1(0)}{p_1}\left(\frac{1}{x_1^{p_1}} - \frac{1}{a_1^{p_1}}\right)\right) \int_{\gamma_2(x_2)} \exp\left(-\frac{A^2(0)}{p_2}\left(\frac{1}{x_2^{p_2}} - \frac{1}{t_2^{p_2}}\right)\right) t_2^{-p_2-1} P^2(a_1, t_2, z)\, dt_2$$

3.3.1. Les matrices $A^1(0)$ et $A^2(0)$ sont simultanément diagonalisables.

Cette hypothèse est en particulier vérifiée si une des matrices $A^i(0)$ a toutes ses valeurs propres distinctes.

A l'aide éventuellement d'un changement linéaire de coordonnées dans $C^m(y)$ on peut supposer que

$$A^i(0) = \Lambda^i = \begin{pmatrix} \lambda_1^i & & 0 \\ & \ddots & \\ 0 & & \lambda_m^i \end{pmatrix}$$

Dans ce cas, on a par exemple

$$\tilde{\rho}_{12}(z) = \begin{pmatrix} \rho_{12}^1(z) \\ \vdots \\ \rho_{12}^m(z) \end{pmatrix}$$

avec

$$\rho_{12}^k(z) = \int_{\gamma_1^k(x_1)} \exp\left(-\frac{\lambda_k^1}{p_1}\left(\frac{1}{x_1^{p_1}} - \frac{1}{t_1^{p_1}}\right)\right) t_1^{-p_1-1} P_k^1(t_1,x_2,z)\,dt_1$$

$$+ \exp\left(-\frac{\lambda_k^1}{p_1}\left(\frac{1}{x_1^{p_1}} - \frac{1}{(a_1^k)^{p_1}}\right)\right) \int_{\gamma_2^k(x_2)} \exp\left(-\frac{\lambda_k^2}{p_2}\left(\frac{1}{x_2^{p_2}} - \frac{1}{t_2^{p_2}}\right)\right) t_2^{-p_2-1} P_k^2(a_1^k,x_2,z)\,dt_2$$

Par les changements de variables

$$\tau_1 = \frac{1}{t_1^{p_1}} \qquad \tau_2 = \frac{1}{t_2^{p_2}}$$

$$\xi_1 = \frac{1}{x_1^{p_1}} \qquad \xi_2 = \frac{1}{x_2^{p_2}}$$

$$\alpha_1^k = \frac{1}{(a_1^k)^{p_1}} \qquad \alpha_2^k = \frac{1}{(a_2^k)^{p_2}}$$

Nous obtenons :

$$\rho_{1,2}^{k*}(z) = -\frac{1}{p^1} \int_{\gamma_1^{k*}(\xi_1)} \exp\left(-\frac{\lambda_k^1}{p_1}(\xi_1-\tau_1)\right) P_k^{1*}(\tau_1,\xi_2,z)\,d\tau$$

$$-\frac{1}{p^2} \exp\left(-\frac{\lambda_k^1}{p^1}(\xi_1-\alpha_1^k)\right) \int_{\gamma_2^{*k}} \exp\left(-\frac{\lambda_k^2}{p_2}(\xi_2-\tau_2)\right) P_k^{2*}(\alpha_1^k,\tau_2,z)\,d\tau$$

Le secteur S donné au départ est défini par

$$S = \{S_1 = \{x_1 \mid 0 < |x_1| \leq r_1,\ \theta_1^1 \leq \arg x_1 \leq \theta_1^2\} \times$$

$$\{S_2 = \{x_2 \mid 0 < |x_2| \leq r_2,\ \theta_2^1 \leq \arg x_2 \leq \theta_2^2\}$$

Notons $\text{ouv}(S_i) = \theta_i^2 - \theta_i^1$ et soit

$$S_i' = \{x_i \mid 0 < |x_i| \leq r'_i, \tilde{\theta}_i^1 \leq \arg x_i \leq \tilde{\theta}_i^2\}$$

un sous-secteur de S_i propre pour les fonctions $\left(-\dfrac{\lambda_k^i}{p_i x_i^{p_i}}\right)_{k=1,2\ldots m}$

Choix des chemins d'intégration.

Cas I . Il existe $i \in \{1,2\}$ par exemple $i = 1$ tel qu'il existe $S_1' \subset S_1$ avec

$$\frac{2\pi}{p_1} < \text{ouv}(S_1') < \frac{3\pi}{p_1}$$

On prendra alors pour chemin $\gamma_1^{*k}(\xi_1)$ dans le plan de la variable τ_1 une demi-droite venant de l'infini pour aboutir à ξ_1 comme indiqué dans le § 6 du chapitre I .

Dans ce cas

$$\tilde{\rho}^k_{12}(z) = \int_{\gamma_1^k(x_1)} \exp\left(-\frac{\lambda_k^1}{p_1}\left(\frac{1}{x_1^{p_1}} - \frac{1}{t_1^{p_1}}\right)\right) t_1^{-p_1-1} P_k^1(t_1, x_2, z)\, dt_1$$

car " $a_1^k = 0$ " ce qui fait disparaître le second terme.

Cas II. Il existe $i \in \{1,2\}$ par exemple $i = 2$ tel que l'on puisse choisir $S_2' \subset S_2$ vérifiant

$$\frac{\pi}{p_2} < \text{ouv}(S_2') < \frac{2\pi}{p_2}$$

On prendra alors pour chemin $\gamma_2^{*k}(\xi_2)$ dans le plan de la variable τ_2 une demi-droite venant de l'infini comme indiqué au chapitre I , et dans ce cas

$$\tilde{\rho}^k_{21}(z) = \int_{\gamma_2^k(x_2)} \exp\left(-\frac{\lambda_k^2}{p_2}\left(\frac{1}{x_2^{p_2}} - \frac{1}{t_2^{p_2}}\right)\right) t_2^{-p_2-1} P_k^2(x_1, t_2, z)\, dt_2$$

Cas III. Pour $i = 1,2$

$$0 < \text{ouv } S'_i < \frac{\pi}{p_i}$$

On a encore une simplification de l'équation intégrale lorsqu'on peut pour l'un des secteurs S_i choisir une demi-droite comme chemin d'intégration et ceci de la manière indiquée au chapitre I .

Par contre si aucun des secteurs n'a la propriété ci-dessus, les chemins d'intégration seront des segments comme indiqué au § 6 du chapitre I et il faudra considérer l'équation intégrale complète.

Conformément à ce qui a été dit au chapitre I, les secteurs pour lesquels il est possible de choisir une demi-droite comme chemin d'intégration seront appelés des "grands" secteurs et les autres des "petits" secteurs.

LEMME 3.9. Si $\lambda \neq 0$ et si $\varphi : S'_1 \times S'_2 \to \mathbb{C}$ est une fonction holomorphe dans $S' = S'_1 \times S'_2 \subset \mathbb{C}^2$ et si de plus

1) S'_1 est un "grand" secteur

2) $|\varphi(x_1,x_2)| \leq C_m[\,|x_1|^m + |x_2|^m]$ dans $S'_1 \times S'_2$

alors

$$H(x_1,x_2) = \int_{\gamma_1(x_1)} \exp\left(-\frac{\lambda}{p_1}\left(\frac{1}{x_1^{p_1}} - \frac{1}{t_1^{p_1}}\right)\right) t_1^{-p_1-1}\varphi(t_1,x_2)\,dt_1$$

est holomorphe dans S' et vérifie

$$|H(x)| \leq K_m C_m[\,|x_1|^m + |x_2|^m] \quad \text{dans } S'$$

où K_m est une constante indépendante de φ .

Preuve : Posons $\tau_1 = \dfrac{1}{t_1^{p_1}}$ $\xi_1 = \dfrac{1}{x_1^{p_1}}$ il vient

$$H^*(\xi_1,x_2) = \int_{\gamma_1^*(\xi_1)} \exp\left(-\frac{\lambda}{p_1}(\xi_1-\tau_1)\right)\varphi^*(\tau_1,x_2)d\tau_1$$

$$|H^*(\xi_1,x_2)| \le C_m \int_{\gamma_1^*(\xi_1)} \left|e^{-\frac{\lambda}{p_i}(\xi_1-\tau_1)}\right| \left[|\tau|^{-\frac{m}{p_i}} + |x_2|^m\right] |d\tau_1|$$

$$\le K_m C_m \left[|\xi|^{-\frac{m}{p_i}} + |x_2|^m\right]$$

Cette dernière inégalité ayant été obtenue en utilisant une des inégalités du § 4 du chapitre I .

Donc

$$|H(x_1,x_2)| \le K_m C_m [\,|x_1|^m + |x_2|^m] .$$

En utilisant une autre inégalité du chapitre I, on montre aisément le

LEMME 3.10. <u>Si</u> $\lambda \neq 0$ <u>et</u> $\mu \neq 0$ <u>et si</u> φ_1 <u>et</u> φ_2 <u>sont deux fonctions holomorphes dans le produit</u> $S' = S_1' \times S_2'$ <u>de deux "petits" secteurs et si de plus pour</u> $i = 1,2$

$$|\varphi_i| \le C_m[\,|x_1|^m + |x_2|^m] \quad \text{dans } S'$$

<u>alors la fonction</u>

$$H(x_1,x_2) = \int_{\gamma_1} \exp\left(-\frac{\lambda}{p_1}\left(\frac{1}{x_1^{p_1}} - \frac{1}{t_1^{p_1}}\right)\right) t_1^{-p_1-1} \varphi_1(t_1,x_2)dt_1$$

$$+ \exp\left(-\frac{\lambda}{p_1}\left(\frac{1}{x_1^{p_1}} - \frac{1}{a_1^{p_1}}\right)\right) \int_{\gamma_2} \exp\left(-\frac{\mu}{p_2}\left(\frac{1}{x_2^{p_2}} - \frac{1}{t^{p_2}}\right)\right) t_2^{-p_2-1} \varphi_2(a_1,t_2)dt_2$$

<u>est holomorphe dans</u> S' <u>et vérifie</u>

$$|H(x_1,x_2)| \le K_m C_m[\,|x_1|^m + |x_2|^m] \quad \text{dans } S'$$

<u>où</u> K_m <u>est une constante indépendante de</u> φ_1 <u>et</u> φ_2

THEOREME 3.11. Si les deux matrices $A^1(0)$, $A^2(0)$ sont régulières, alors une des équations intégrales

$$z = \widetilde{\mathcal{P}}_{12}(z) \quad \text{ou} \quad z = \widetilde{\mathcal{P}}_{21}(z)$$

admet une solution holomorphe dans S' qui est asymptotique à zéro dans S'. Si S est un grand secteur, il suffit de supposer que l'une des matrices $A^i(0)$ est régulière.

Notons $\mathcal{a}_o$ l'ensemble des fonctions holomorphes dans S' à valeurs dans $\mathbb{C}^m$ et asymptotiques à zéro dans S'.

Les lemmes 3.9 et 3.10 entraînent immédiatement que pour tout $u \in \mathcal{a}_o$ on a $\widetilde{\mathcal{P}}_{12}(u) \in \mathcal{a}_o$. Montrons que l'application

$$\widetilde{\mathcal{P}}_{12} : \mathcal{a}_o \to \mathcal{a}_o$$

a un point fixe dans $\mathcal{a}_o$; pour cela, nous allons utiliser le procédé classique d'itération.

Considérons la suite $\{u_1\}$ définie par

$$u_o = 0 \qquad u_r = \widetilde{\mathcal{P}}_{12}(u_{r-1})$$

C'est une suite dans $\mathcal{a}_o$.

Calcul de u_1 .

$$P^i(x,0) = U^i(x) + H^i(x,0) = U^i(x)$$

alors

$$(u_1)_k = \int_{\gamma_1^k} \exp\left(-\frac{\lambda_k^1}{p_1}\left(\frac{1}{x_1^{p_1}} - \frac{1}{t_1^{p_1}}\right)\right) t_1^{-p_1-1} U_k^1(t_1,x_2)dt_1$$

$$+ \exp\left(-\frac{\lambda_k^1}{p_1}\left(\frac{1}{x_1^{p_1}} - \frac{1}{(a_1^k)^{p_1}}\right)\right)\int_{\gamma_2^k} \exp\left(-\frac{\lambda_k^2}{p_2}\left(\frac{1}{x_2^{p_2}} - \frac{1}{t_2^{p_2}}\right)\right) t_2^{-p_2-1} U_k^2(a_1^k,t_2)dt_2$$

Or $u^i(x) \overset{S}{\sim} 0$ donc pour tout m on a

$$\|U^i\| \leq C_m[\,|x_1|^m + |x_2|^m] \quad \text{dans } S'$$

alors d'après les lemmes ci-dessus on a :

1) u_1 est holomorphe dans S'

2) $\|u_1\| \leq \hat{K}_m C_m [\,|x_1|^m + |x_2|^m]$ dans S' .

<u>Majoration de</u> $\|u_{r+1} - u_r\|$

$$u_{r+1} - u_r = \int_{\tilde{\Gamma}_1} \exp\Big(-\frac{\Lambda^1}{p_1}\Big(\frac{1}{x_1^{p_1}} - \frac{1}{t_1^{p_1}}\Big)\Big) t_1^{-p_1-1} (P^1(t_1,x_2,u_r) - P^1(t_1,x_2,u_{r-1}))dt_1$$

$$+ \exp\Big(-\frac{\Lambda^1}{p_1}\Big(\frac{1}{x_1^{p_1}} - \frac{1}{a_1^{p_1}}\Big)\Big) \int_{\tilde{\Gamma}_2} \exp\Big(-\frac{\Lambda^2}{p_2}\Big(\frac{1}{x_2^{p_2}} - \frac{1}{t_2^{p_2}}\Big)\Big) t_2^{-p_2-1} (P^2(a_1,t_2,u_r) - P^2(a_1,t_2,u_{r-1}))dt_2$$

Comme pour $i = 1,2$, $P^i(x,z)$ admet une matrice jacobienne par rapport à z qui est nulle à l'origine de $\mathbb{C}^2$, il existe une constante α telle que dans un polydisque V assez petit centré à l'origine de $\mathbb{C}^m(z_1,\ldots z_m)$, on ait uniformément sur S

$$\|P^i(x,z_2) - P^i(x,z_1)\| \leq \alpha \|z_2 - z_1\| .$$

La constante α pouvant être prise aussi petite que l'on veut à condition de réduire si nécessaire le polydisque V et a_1 assez près de l'origine (choix de la constante k que nous avons prise égale à zéro plus haut) .

Fixons $m = m_o$ et choisissons $\alpha = \alpha_{m_o}$ tel que

$$\alpha_{m_o} \hat{K}_{m_o} < 1 .$$

Alors

$$\|P^i(x,u_1) - P^i(x,u_o)\| \leq \alpha_{m_o} \|u_1 - u_o\| \leq \alpha_{m_o} \hat{K}_{m_o} C_{m_o} [\,|x_1|^{m_o} + |x_2|^{m_o}]$$

et les lemmes ci-dessus nous donnent

$$\|u_2 - u_1\| \leq \alpha_{m_o} (\hat{K}_{m_o})^2 C_{m_o} [\,|x_1|^{m_o} + |x_2|^{m_o}]$$

et par récurrence

$$\|u_{r+1}-u_r\| \leq (\alpha_{m_o})^r(\hat{K}_{m_o})^{r+1}C_{m_o}[|x_1|^{m_o}+|x_2|^{m_o}]$$

Donc

$$\|u_{r+1}\| = \|\sum_{k=o}^{r}(u_{k+1}-u_k)\|$$

$$\leq \sum_{k=o}^{r}\|u_{k+1}-u_k\|$$

$$\leq \frac{C_{m_o}K_{m_o}}{1-\alpha_{m_o}\hat{K}_{m_o}}[|x_1|^{m_o}+|x_2|^{m_o}]$$

De ceci résulte que

1) la série $\sum_{o}^{+\infty}(u_{k+1}-u_k)$ est uniformément convergente sur S'

2) la somme $u = \lim_{r\to+\infty} u_{r+1} = \sum_{o}^{+\infty}(u_{k+1}-u_k)$ est holomorphe dans S'

3) $u = \tilde{P}_{12}(u)$ ceci résultant de la convergence uniforme des intégrales figurant dans $\tilde{P}_{12}$ ainsi que de 1) et 2) .

4) pour tout m entier on a

$$\|u\| \leq \frac{C_m\hat{K}_m}{1-\alpha_m\hat{K}_m}[|x_1|^m+|x_2|^m]$$

ce qui prouve le théorème 3.11.

Pour conclure le paragraphe 3.3.1., énonçons le résultat obtenu

THEOREME 3.12. <u>Si les fonctions</u> $f^i(x_1,x_2,y)$ <u>vérifient les conditions énoncées au début de ce paragraphe, et si de plus les deux matrices</u> $A^i(0)$ $i = 1,2$ <u>sont simultanément diagonalisables et toutes les deux régulières, alors si</u> φ <u>est une solution formelle du système de Pfaff</u>

$$(1) \qquad dy = \frac{f_1(x_1,x_2,y)}{x_1^{p_1+1}}dx_1+\frac{f_2(x_1,x_2,y)}{x_2^{p_2+1}}dx_2$$

<u>qui vérifie</u> $\varphi(0,0) = 0$, <u>il existe une solution</u> Φ de (1) <u>holomorphe dans</u>

un secteur $S' \subset S$ telle que

$$\Phi \overset{S'}{\sim} \varphi .$$

Ce théorème est une conséquence immédiate des développements des § 3.2 et 3.3 .

Remarque 3.13. Si le secteur S est assez grand, ce résultat reste valable si on suppose seulement que

$$A^1(0) = \begin{pmatrix} \lambda_1^1 & & & 0 \\ & \cdot & & \\ & & \cdot & \\ 0 & & & \lambda_m^1 \end{pmatrix} \qquad A^2(0) = \begin{pmatrix} \lambda_1^2 & & & 0 \\ & \lambda_2^2 & & \\ & & \ddots & \\ 0 & & & \lambda_m^2 \end{pmatrix}$$

avec $|\lambda_k^1| + |\lambda_k^2| \neq 0$ pour tout $k = 1,2 \ldots m$, car pour chaque composante de z on peut prendre une équation intégrale différente.

Remarque 3.14. La méthode utilisée s'adapte très bien à d'autres systèmes de Pfaff . En particuliers, le résultat ci-dessus et le résultat plus général indiqué dans la remarque 3.13 reste encore vrai sous les mêmes hypothèses pour un système de Pfaff, complètement intégrable de la forme

$$dy = \left(x_1^{P_1+1}\right)^{-1} f^1(x_1,x_2,y)dx_1 + \left(x_2^{P_2+1}\right)^{-1} f^2(x_1,x_2,y)dx_2$$

où

$$(x_1^{P_1+1}) = \begin{pmatrix} x_1^{p_1^1+1} & & & 0 \\ & x_1^{p_1^2+1} & & \\ & & \ddots & \\ 0 & & & x_1^{p_1^m+1} \end{pmatrix}$$

$$(x_2^{P_2+1}) = \begin{pmatrix} x_2^{p_2^1+1} & & & 0 \\ & x_2^{p_2^2+1} & & \\ & & \ddots & \\ 0 & & & x_2^{p_2^m+1} \end{pmatrix}$$

avec $p_i^j > 0$ pour tout $i = (1,2)$, $j = 1,2 \ldots m$.

Remarque 3.15. Dans un paragraphe ultérieur, nous étudierons les cas

$p_1 \geq 0 \quad p_2 \geq 0$ ou plus généralement $p_i^j \geq 0$

3.3.2. Les matrices $A^1(0)$ et $A^2(0)$ ne sont plus simultanément diagonalisables.

D'après le corollaire 3.2 , on peut supposer que

$$A^1(0) = \begin{pmatrix} A_1^1 & 0 & \cdots & 0 \\ 0 & A_2^1 & \cdots & \cdot \\ & & \ddots & 0 \\ 0 & & & A_m^1 \end{pmatrix}$$

$$A^2(0) = \begin{pmatrix} A_1^2 & 0 & \cdots & 0 \\ 0 & A_2^2 & 0 \cdots & 0 \\ \vdots & & & 0 \\ 0 & \cdots & 0 & A_m^2 \end{pmatrix}$$

avec $A_j^1 = \lambda_i^1 I + N_i^1 \qquad A_j^2 = \lambda_i^2 I + N_i^2$

$$[N_i^1 , N_i^2] = 0$$

où les N_i^1 , N_i^2 sont nilpotentes sous forme triangulaire supérieure.

Alors les équations intégrales prennent la forme suivante par exemple

$$\tilde{\wp}_{12}(z) = \int_{\tilde{\Gamma}_1} \exp\left(-\frac{(\Lambda^1+N^1)}{p_1}\left(\frac{1}{x_1^{p_1}} - \frac{1}{t_1^{p_1}}\right)\right) t_1^{-p_1-1} P^1(t_1,x_2,z)dt_1$$

$$+\exp\left(-\frac{(\Lambda^1+N^1)}{p_1}\left(\frac{1}{x_1^{p_1}} - \frac{1}{a_1^{p_1}}\right)\right)\int_{\tilde{\Gamma}_2}\exp\left(-\frac{(\Lambda^2+N^2)}{p_2}\left(\frac{1}{x_2^{p_2}} - \frac{1}{t_2^{p_2}}\right)\right)t_2^{-p_2-1}P^2(a_2,t_2,z)dt_2$$

LEMME 3.16. <u>Soit</u> N <u>une matrice nilpotente, alors pour tout</u> α <u>vérifiant</u> $0 < \alpha < 1$ <u>il existe une constante</u> C_α <u>telle que</u>

$$\|\exp(-Nu)\| \leq C_\alpha e^{\alpha|u|}$$

La démonstration de ce lemme est laissée en exercice et résulte du fait que $\exp(-Nu)$ est un polynôme en u . On en déduit

$$\|\exp(-\frac{(\Lambda_j^1+N_j^1)}{p_1}(\xi_1-\tau_1))\| \leq \|\exp(-\frac{\Lambda_j^1}{p_1}(\xi_1-\tau_1))\|.\|\exp -\frac{N_j^1}{p_1}(\xi_1-\tau_1)\|$$

$$\leq \exp(-\frac{|\lambda_j^2|\mu_j|\xi_1-\tau_1|}{p_1})C_\alpha\exp(\frac{\alpha\|N_j^1\|\xi_1-\tau_1\|}{p_1})$$

$$\leq \exp(-\frac{|\lambda_j^1|}{p_1}|\xi_1-\tau_1|(\mu_1-\frac{\alpha\|N_j^1\|}{|\lambda_j^1|}))$$

Comme α est arbitraire, on peut le choisir assez petit pour que

$$\mu_1^* = \mu_1 - \frac{\alpha\|N_j^1\|}{|\lambda_j^1|} > 0$$

Vu ceci et l'étude faite ci-dessus ainsi que les inégalités du chapitre I , on vérifie aisément que le théorème 3.12 s'étend à ce cas plus général ; il en est d'ailleurs de même des résultats énoncés dans les remarques 3.13 et 3.14 .

§ 4. Cas où les fonctions f^1 et f^2 admettent des développements asymptotiques en x_1 uniformes en (x_2,y) .

Soient $S_1 \times S_2$ un secteur de $\mathbb{C}^2$ et U un polydisque centré à l'origine de $\mathbb{C}^m$. On suppose dans ce paragraphe que

1) f^1 et f^2 sont holomorphes dans $S_1 \times S_2 \times U$.

2) pour $i = 1,2$

$$f^i(x_1,x_2,y) \underset{u.S_2\times V}{\overset{S_1}{\sim}} \sum_{m\geq o} f^i_{1,m}(x_2,y)x_1^m$$

$$f^i(x_1,x_2,y) \underset{u.S_1\times V}{\overset{S_2}{\sim}} \sum_{m\geq o} f^i_{2,m}(x_1,y)x_2^m$$

où pour tout m

$$f^i_{1,m}(x_2,y) \underset{u.V}{\overset{S_2}{\sim}} \sum_{\ell\geq o} f^i_{1,m,\ell}(y)x_2^\ell$$

$$f^i_{2,m}(x_1,y) \underset{u.V}{\overset{S_1}{\sim}} \sum_{\ell\geq o} f^i_{2,m,\ell}(y)x_1^\ell$$

Les coefficients étant holomorphes dans U , vu ces hypothèses, nous avons

$$f^i(x_1,x_2,y) = f^i_o(x_1,x_2) + A^i(x_1,x_2)y + \sum_{|p|\geq 2}^{+\infty} f^i_p(x_1,x_2)y^p$$

avec

$$A^i(x_1,x_2) \underset{u.\ S_2}{\overset{S_1}{\sim}} \sum_{m\geq o} A^i_m(x_2)\ x_1^m$$

et

$$A^i_m(x_2) \overset{S_2}{\sim} \sum_{m\geq o} A^i_{m;\ell}\ \ x_2^m$$

On suppose de plus

3) $f^1_{1,o}(0,x_2) = o(x_2)$

4) A^1_{oo} inversible

5) Si $\lambda_j^1 (j = 1,2,\dots m)$ sont les valeurs propres de A_{oo}^1

$$|\arg(-\lambda_j^1) - p_1 \arg x_1| \leq \frac{3\pi}{2} \quad \text{dans} \quad S_1$$

pour tout $j = 1,2,\dots m$.

THEOREME 4.1. Si l'ouverture de S_1 est strictement supérieure à $\frac{\pi}{p_1}$, il existe deux nombres strictement positifs R_1, R_2 et une solution φ de (1) holomorphe dans $\Sigma_1 \times \Sigma_2$ où $\Sigma_i = S_i \cap \{|x_i| < R_i\}$ telle que

$$\varphi(x_1,x_2) \underset{\text{u. } S_2}{\overset{S_1}{\sim}} \sum_{m \geq o} \varphi_m(x_2) x_1^m$$

avec

$$\varphi_m(x_2) \overset{S_2}{\sim} \sum_{\ell \geq o} \varphi_{m,\ell} \, x_2^m$$

et

$$\varphi_o(x_2) = O(x_2) .$$

Preuve : D'après le théorème 1.1 $(\sigma = 0)$ de ce chapitre, il existe une solution $\varphi(x_1,x_2)$ holomorphe sur $\Sigma_1 \times \Sigma_2$ de l'équation différentielle

$$x_1^{p_1+1} \frac{dy}{dx_1} = f^1(x_1,x_2,y)$$

la variable x_2 étant considérée comme étant un paramètre. Alors en utilisant les hypothèses $A^1(0,0)$ inversible et $\text{ouv}(S_1) > \frac{\pi}{p_1}$, on montre comme dans le § 2 que φ est également solution de l'équation

$$x_2^{p_2+1} \frac{dy}{dx_2} = f^2(x_1,x_2,y)$$

THEOREME 4.2. Si l'ouverture de S_1 est strictement supérieure à $\frac{\pi}{p_1}$, il existe deux constantes strictement positives R_1 , R_2 et une solution ψ de (1) holomorphe sur $\Sigma_1 \times \Sigma_2$ où $\Sigma_i = S_i \cap \{|x_i| < R_i\}$ telle que

$$\psi(x_1,x_2) \underset{u.\ S_1}{\overset{S_2}{\sim}} \sum_{\ell=o}^{+\infty} \psi_\ell(x_1)x_2^\ell$$

avec pour tout ℓ

$$\psi_\ell(x_1) \overset{S_1}{\sim} \sum_{m\geq o} \psi_{\ell,m}\, x_1^m$$

et

$$\psi_o(x_1) = O(x_1) .$$

La démonstration se fait comme ci-dessus, en utilisant le théorème 1.2 $(\sigma = 0)$.

Mais alors, en utilisant le théorème 1.3 , nous avons

$$\varphi(x_1,x_2) = \psi(x_1,x_2) \quad \text{sur} \quad \Sigma_1 \times \Sigma_2 .$$

La solution trouvée vérifie donc

$$\varphi(x_1,x_2) \overset{S_1\times S_2}{\sim} \sum_{m+\ell\geq o} \varphi_{m,\ell}\, x_1^m x_2^\ell$$

$$\varphi(x_1,x_2) \underset{u.\ S_2}{\overset{S_1}{\sim}} \sum_{m\geq o} \varphi_m(x_2)\, x_1^m$$

$$\varphi(x_1,x_2) \underset{u.\ S_1}{\overset{S_2}{\sim}} \sum_{\ell\geq o} \varphi_\ell(x_1)\, x_2^\ell$$

où pour tout m

$$\varphi_m(x_2) \overset{S_2}{\sim} \sum_{\ell\geq o} \psi_{m,\ell}\, x_2^\ell$$

et tout ℓ

$$\psi_\ell(x_1) \overset{S_1}{\sim} \sum_{m\geq o} \varphi_{m,\ell}\, x_1^m$$

Remarque 4.3. Les hypothèses de ce paragraphe entraînent celles du § 3 et la série formelle $\sum_{m+\ell\geq 1} \varphi_{m,\ell}\, x_1^m x_2^\ell$ vérifie le système formel (1^*) associé à (1) . Il en résulte que si Φ est la solution obtenue au § 3 , nous avons

$$\Phi(x_1,x_2) - \varphi(x_1,x_2) \underset{u.\ S_2}{\overset{S_1}{\sim}} 0$$

et si l'ouverture du secteur S_1 est supérieure strictement à π/p_1 , nous avons

$$\Phi = \varphi .$$

§ 5. Applications aux systèmes de Pfaff linéaires.

Nous allons ici étudier les systèmes de Pfaff complètement intégrables de la forme $dy = \omega y$ avec

(1) $$\omega = \frac{A_1(x_1,x_2)}{x_1^{p_1+1}}\, dx_1 + \frac{A_2(x_1,x_2)}{x_2^{p_2+1}}\, dx_2$$

avec $p_1 > 0$ et $p_2 > 0$.

Les hypothèses sur les matrices A_1 et A_2 seront données dans les divers sous-paragraphes.

5.1. Le cas scalaire.

On considère les systèmes complètement intégrables de la forme

(1') $$dy = \left(\frac{a_1(x_1,x_2)}{x_1^{p_1+1}}\, dx_1 + \frac{a_2(x_1,x_2)}{x_2^{p_2+1}}\, dx_2\right)y$$

où a_1 et a_2 sont des séries formelles ou des séries convergentes à l'origine.

La condition de complète intégrabilité est

(C.I.) $$x_2^{p_2+1}\frac{\partial a_1}{\partial x_2} = x_1^{p_1+1}\frac{\partial a_2}{\partial x_1}$$

On peut supposer que $p_1 \leq p_2$.

LEMME 5.1. La condition (C.I) entraîne que

$$a_1(x_1,x_2) = x_1^{p_1+1}\left[\int_{h_2}^{x_2}\varphi(x_1,t_2)dt_2+h_1(x_1)\right]+x_1^{p_1}\alpha_1^{p_1}+\ldots+\alpha_1^{o}$$

$$a_2(x_1,x_2) = x_2^{p_2+1}\left[\int_{h_1}^{x_1}\varphi(t_1,x_2)dt_1+ h_2(x_2)\right]+x_2^{p_2}\alpha_2^{p_2}+\ldots+\alpha_2^{o}$$

où

φ <u>est une série formelle</u> (ou <u>convergente</u>) <u>en</u> x_1, x_2 <u>arbitraire</u>.

h_1 (resp. h_2) <u>une série formelle</u> (ou <u>convergente</u>) <u>en</u> x_1 (resp. x_2) <u>arbitraire</u>.

$\alpha_1^o, \alpha_1^1, \ldots \alpha_1^{p_1}, \alpha_2^o, \alpha_2^1, \ldots \alpha_2^{p_2}$ <u>sont des constantes arbitraires.</u>

<u>Preuve</u> : Posons

$$\frac{\partial a_1}{\partial x_2} = x_1^{p_1+1} C_{12}(x_1, x_2)$$

$$\frac{\partial a_2}{\partial x_1} = x_2^{p_2+1} C_{21}(x_1, x_2)$$

la condition (C.I) est alors $C_{12} = C_{21}$, et

$$a_1 = x_1^{p_1+1} \int_o^{x_2} C_{12}(x_1, t_2) dt_2 + \alpha_1(x_1)$$

$$a_2 = x_2^{p_2+1} \int_o^{x_1} C_{12}(t_1, x_2) dt_1 + \alpha_2(x_2)$$

où α_1 et α_2 sont des séries arbitraires.

En posant

$$\alpha_1(x_1) = \alpha_1^o + x_1 \hat{\alpha}_1(x_1)$$

$$\alpha_2(x_2) = \alpha_2^o + x_2 \hat{\alpha}_2(x_2)$$

on peut écrire

$$a_1(x_1, x_2) = x_1 a_1^1(x_1, x_2) + \alpha_1^o$$

$$a_2(x_1, x_2) = x_2 a_2^1(x_1, x_2) + \alpha_2^o$$

avec

$$a_1^1(x_1, x_2) = x_1^{p_1} \int_o^{x_2} C_{12}(x_1, t_2) dt_2 + \hat{\alpha}_1(x_1)$$

$$a_2^1(x_1, x_2) = x_2^{p_2} \int_o^{x_1} C_{12}(t_1, x_2) dt_1 + \hat{\alpha}_2(x_2) \ .$$

La condition (C.I) est alors

$$x_2^{p_2}\frac{\partial a_1^1}{\partial x_2} = x_1^{p_1}\frac{\partial a_2^1}{\partial x_1} .$$

En procédant alors avec a_1^1 et a_2^1 comme nous l'avons fait ci-dessus avec a_1 et a_2, nous obtenons par récurrence $(p_1 \le p_2)$

$$a_1(x_1,x_2) = x_1^{p_1+1} a_1^{p_1+1}(x_1,x_2) + x_1^{p_1}\alpha_1^{p_1} + \ldots + \alpha_1^o$$

$$a_2(x_1,x_2) = x_2^{p_1+1} a_2^{p_1+1}(x_1,x_2) + x_2^{p_1}\alpha_2^{p_1} + \ldots + \alpha_2^o$$

avec

$$x_2^{p_2-p_1}\frac{\partial a_1^{p_1+1}}{\partial x_2} = \frac{\partial a_2^{p_1+1}}{\partial x_1}$$

Posons

$$\varphi(x_1,x_2) = \frac{\partial a_1^{p_1+1}}{\partial x_2} \quad \text{alors,}$$

$$\frac{\partial a_2^{p_1+1}}{\partial x_1} = x_2^{p_2-p_1}\varphi(x_1,x_2) .$$

Et

$$a_1^{p_1+1}(x_1,x_2) = \int_{h_2}^{x_2}\varphi(x_1,t_2)dt_2 + h_1(x_1)$$

$$a_2^{p_1+1}(x_1,x_2) = x_2^{p_2-p_1}\int_{h_1}^{x_1}\varphi(t_1,x_1)dt_1 + k(x_2)$$

où h_1 et k sont des séries arbitraires, et

$$a_1(x_1,x_2) = x_1^{p_1+1}\left[\int_{h_2}^{x_2}\varphi(x_1,t_2)dt_2 + h_1(x_1)\right] + x_1^{p_1}\alpha_1^{p_1} + \ldots + \alpha_1^o$$

$$a_2(x_1,x_2) = x_2^{p_2+1}\left[\int_{h_1}^{x_1}\varphi(t_1,x_2)dt_1 + h_2(x_2)\right] + x_2^{p_2}\alpha_2^{p_2} + \ldots + \alpha_2^o$$

ce qui prouve le lemme 5.1.

PROPOSITION 5.2. <u>Les solutions du système</u> (1') <u>sont de la forme</u>

$$C\, U(x_1,x_2)x_1^{\rho_1}x_2^{\rho_2}\exp P_1\left(\frac{1}{x_1}\right)\exp P_2\left(\frac{1}{x_2}\right)$$

<u>où</u>

C, ρ_1, ρ_2 <u>sont des constantes</u>,

U <u>une série formelle ou convergente suivant</u>

que a_1 et a_2 <u>sont formelles ou convergentes</u>.

$P_i\left(\frac{1}{x_i}\right)$ <u>un polynôme de degré</u> p_i <u>en</u> $\frac{1}{x_i}$.

<u>Preuve</u> : Le système (1') a la forme suivante :

$$dy = (\omega_1 + \omega_2)y$$

avec

$$\omega_1 = \left(\int_{h_2}^{x_2}\varphi(x_1,t_2)dt_2+h_1(x_1)\right)dx_1+\left(\int_{h_1}^{x_1}\varphi(t_1,x_2)dt_1+h_2(x_2)\right)dx_2$$

$$\omega_2 = \left(\frac{\alpha_1^{p_1}}{x_1}+\dots\frac{\alpha_1^{o}}{x_1^{p_1+1}}\right)dx_1+\left(\frac{\alpha_2^{p_2}}{x_2}+\dots+\frac{\alpha_2^{o}}{x_2^{p_2+1}}\right)dx_2$$

et les deux systèmes

$$(1_1') \qquad dz = \omega_1 z \quad \text{et} \quad (1_2')\ dz = \omega_2 z$$

sont séparément complètement intégrables. Le système $(1_2')$ admet une matrice fondamentale de la forme :

$$V(x_1,x_2) = \exp\left\{\int_{h_1}^{x_1}\left(\frac{\alpha_1^{p_1}}{t_1}+\dots+\frac{\alpha_1^{o}}{t_1^{p_1+1}}\right)dt_1\right\}$$
$$\exp\left\{\int_{h_2}^{x_2}\left(\frac{\alpha_2^{p_2}}{t_2}+\dots+\frac{\alpha_2^{o}}{t_2^{p_2+1}}\right)dt_2\right\}$$

En posant $y = Vu$ dans (1') il vient

$$du = \omega_1 u$$

c'est-à-dire

$$\frac{\partial u}{\partial x_1} = \left(\int_{h_2}^{x_2} \varphi(x_1,t_2)dt_2 + h_1(x_1)\right) u_1, \frac{\partial u}{\partial x_2} = \left(\int_{h_1}^{x_1} \varphi(t_1,x_2)dt_1 + h_2(x_2)\right)$$

Par intégration, on obtient

$$u = K \exp\left\{\int_{h_1}^{x_1} h_1(t_1)dt_1\right\} \exp\left\{\int_{h_2}^{x_2} h_2(t_2)dt_2\right\} \exp\left\{\int_{h_1}^{x_1}\int_{h_2}^{x_2} \varphi(t_1,t_2)dt_1dt_2\right\}$$

où K est une constante.

Finalement

$$y = \hat{K} \exp\left\{\int_{h_1}^{x_1} h_1(t_1)dt_1\right\} \exp\left\{\int_{h_2}^{x_2} h_2(t_2)dt_2\right\} \exp\left\{\int_{h_1}^{x_1}\int_{h_2}^{x_2} \varphi(t_1,t_2)dt_1dt_2\right\}$$

$$\times\, x_1^{\alpha_1^{p_1}}\, x_2^{\alpha_2^{p_2}} \times \exp(P_1(\tfrac{1}{x_1}))\, \exp(P_2(\tfrac{1}{x_2}))$$

où $\hat{K}$ est une autre constante, qui est une forme un peu plus précise que celle qui est indiquée dans la proposition. Si les données sont des séries convergentes, alors les séries obtenues dans le résultat sont également convergentes.

5.2. Des lemmes de réduction formelle.

On suppose maintenant que le système (1) est un système formel, c'est-à-dire que les éléments des matrices $A_i(x_1,x_2)$ sont des séries formelles. Pour ne pas avoir à écrire trop d'indices, nous noterons

$$\omega = \frac{A(x_1,x_2)}{x_1^{p_1+1}}\, dx_1 + \frac{B(x_1,x_2)}{x_2^{p_2+1}}\, dx_2$$

$p_1 > 0$ et $p_2 > 0$.

Lemme de réduction totale.

Si $A(0,0) = \begin{pmatrix} A_{oo}^{11} & 0 \\ 0 & A_{oo}^{22} \end{pmatrix}$ et $B(0,0) = \begin{pmatrix} B_{oo}^{11} & 0 \\ 0 & B_{oo}^{22} \end{pmatrix}$

<u>où l'un des couples</u> $(A^{11}_{oo}, A^{22}_{oo})$, $(B^{11}_{oo}, B^{22}_{oo})$ <u>est sans valeurs propres communes</u>, <u>il existe une transformation formelle unique</u> T <u>de la forme</u>

$$T = \begin{pmatrix} I & T^{12} \\ T^{21} & I \end{pmatrix}$$

<u>qui transforme le système</u> (1) <u>en</u>

$$dz = \omega' z$$

<u>avec</u>

$$\omega' = \frac{\begin{pmatrix} \mathcal{A}^{11} & 0 \\ 0 & \mathcal{A}^{22} \end{pmatrix}}{x_1^{p_1+1}} dx_1 + \frac{\begin{pmatrix} \mathcal{B}^{11} & 0 \\ 0 & \mathcal{B}^{22} \end{pmatrix}}{x_2^{p_2+1}} dx_2$$

<u>et</u>

$$\mathcal{A}^{ii}(0,0) = A^{ii}_{oo} \qquad \mathcal{B}^{ii}(0,0) = B^{ii}_{oo}$$

<u>Preuve</u> : Ecrivons

$$A = \begin{pmatrix} A^{11} & A^{12} \\ A^{21} & A^{22} \end{pmatrix} \qquad B = \begin{pmatrix} B^{11} & B^{12} \\ B^{21} & B^{22} \end{pmatrix}$$

et cherchons une transformation

$$T = \begin{pmatrix} I & T^{12} \\ T^{21} & I \end{pmatrix} \qquad I = \text{identité}$$

qui mette le système sous la forme suivante :

$$\mathcal{A} = \begin{pmatrix} \mathcal{A}^{11} & 0 \\ 0 & \mathcal{A}^{22} \end{pmatrix} \qquad \mathcal{B} = \begin{pmatrix} \mathcal{B}^{11} & 0 \\ 0 & \mathcal{B}^{22} \end{pmatrix}$$

Un calcul facile nous donne alors pour déterminer T^{12} et T^{21}

$$\left\{\begin{array}{l} x_1^{p_1+1}\dfrac{\partial T^{12}}{\partial x_1} = A^{12}+A^{11}T^{12}-T^{12}A^{22}-T^{12}A^{21}T^{12} \\ x_2^{p_2+1}\dfrac{\partial T^{12}}{\partial x_2} = B^{12}+B^{11}T^{12}-T^{12}B^{22}-T^{12}B^{21}T^{12} \end{array}\right.$$

$$\left\{\begin{array}{l} x_1^{p_1+1}\dfrac{\partial T^{21}}{\partial x_1} = A^{21}+A^{22}T^{21}-T^{21}A^{11}-T^{21}A^{12}T^{21} \\ x_2^{p_2+1}\dfrac{\partial T^{21}}{\partial x_2} = B^{21}+B^{22}T^{21}-T^{21}B^{11}-T^{21}B^{12}T^{21} \end{array}\right.$$

Considérons seulement le système en T^{12}, pour l'autre le raisonnement est identique. Si on range les éléments de T^{12} en une seule colonne $\tilde{T}^{12}$, par exemple en commençant par les éléments de la première ligne de T^{12}, on voit aisément que $\tilde{T}^{12}$ est donné par un système de Pfaff non linéaire et complètement intégrable de la forme suivante :

$$x_1^{p_1+1}\frac{\partial z}{\partial x_1} = f_o^1(x_1,x_2)+ \mathbb{C}_1(x_1,x_2)z + f_2^1(x_1,x_2,z)$$

$$x_2^{p_2+1}\frac{\partial z}{\partial x_2} = f_o^2(x_1,x_2)+ \mathbb{C}_2(x_1,x_2)z + f_2^2(x_1,x_2,z)$$

où $\mathbb{C}_1$ et $\mathbb{C}_2$ proviennent respectivement de $A^{11}T^{12}-T^{12}A^{22}$, $B^{11}T^{12}-T^{12}B^{22}$, comme un des couples $(A_{oo}^{11}, A_{oo}^{22})$, $(B_{oo}^{11}, B_{oo}^{22})$ est sans valeurs propres communes, il résulte que l'une des matrices $\mathbb{C}_1(0,0)$, $\mathbb{C}_2(0,0)$ est non singulière et le lemme 3.3 affirme l'existence de la solution $\tilde{T}_{12}$ cherchée. On obtient ainsi T^{12} et de la même manière T^{21}. L'unicité de T résulte alors du fait que $T(0,0) = Id.$, ce qui prouve le lemme de réduction.

Nous allons maintenant en donner une autre démonstration qui est plus pratique et permet d'énoncer un résultat un peu plus précis.

Notons

$$H(x_1,x_2) = x_2^{p_2+1}\frac{\partial A}{\partial x_2} - x_1^{p_1+1}\frac{\partial B}{\partial x_1} + [A,B]$$

alors

$$H(x_1,x_2) = \sum_{p_1+p_2\geq 0}^{+\infty} H_{p_1,p_2}$$

La condition de complète intégrabilité du système (1) est

$$H(x_1,x_2) \equiv 0$$

c'est-à-dire $H_{p_1,p_2} = 0$ pour tout (p_1,p_2).

Nous dirons que le système (1) <u>est complètement intégrable jusqu'à l'ordre</u> ℓ si

$$\sum_{p_1+p_2 \geq 0}^{\ell} H_{p_1,p_2} x_1^{p_1} x_2^{p_2} = 0$$

On suppose maintenant que le système formel (1) est seulement complètement intégrable jusqu'à <u>l'odre ℓ</u>.

<u>LEMME de réduction partielle. Si</u>

$$A(0,0) = \begin{pmatrix} A_{oo}^{11} & 0 \\ 0 & A_{oo}^{22} \end{pmatrix} \quad \underline{\text{et}} \quad B(0,0) = \begin{pmatrix} B_{oo}^{11} & 0 \\ 0 & B_{oo}^{22} \end{pmatrix}$$

<u>où l'un des couples</u> $(A_{oo}^{11}, A_{oo}^{22})$, $(B_{oo}^{11}, B_{oo}^{22})$ <u>est sans valeurs propres communes, il existe une transformation formelle unique</u> T <u>de la forme</u>

$$T = \begin{pmatrix} I & T^{12} \\ T^{21} & I \end{pmatrix}$$

<u>qui transforme le système</u> (1) <u>en</u>

$$dz = \omega_\ell^1 z$$

<u>avec</u>

$$\omega_\ell^1 = \frac{\begin{pmatrix} \mathfrak{A}^{11} & \mathfrak{A}^{12} \\ \mathfrak{A}^{21} & \mathfrak{A}^{22} \end{pmatrix}}{x_1^{p_1+1}} dx_1 + \frac{\begin{pmatrix} \mathfrak{B}^{11} & \mathfrak{B}^{12} \\ \mathfrak{B}^{21} & \mathfrak{B}^{22} \end{pmatrix}}{x_2^{p_2+1}} dx_2$$

<u>et</u> $\mathfrak{A}_{p_1,p_2}^{12} = \mathfrak{A}_{p_1,p_2}^{21} = \mathfrak{B}_{p_1,p_2}^{12} = \mathfrak{B}_{p_1,p_2}^{21} = 0$ <u>pour tout</u> (p_1,p_2) <u>vérifiant</u> $p_1+p_2 \leq \ell$

De plus $\mathcal{A}^{ii}(0,0) = A^{ii}_{oo}$; $\mathcal{B}^{ii}(0,0) = B^{ii}_{oo}$ pour $i = 1,2$.

Preuve : Supposons que

$$A = \begin{pmatrix} A^{11} & A^{12} \\ A^{21} & A^{22} \end{pmatrix} ; \quad B = \begin{pmatrix} B^{11} & B^{12} \\ B^{21} & B^{22} \end{pmatrix}$$

avec $A^{12}_{p_1,p_2} = A^{21}_{p_1,p_2} = B^{12}_{p_1,p_2} = B^{21}_{p_1,p_2} = 0$ pour tout couple (p_1,p_2) vérifiant $p_1+p_2 < m \leq \ell$ et montrons qu'il existe une transformation unique de la forme

$$T_m = \begin{pmatrix} I & T^{12} \\ T^{21} & I \end{pmatrix}$$

avec

$$T^{12} = \sum_{p+q=m} T^{12}_{p,q} x_1^p x_2^q , \quad T^{21} = \sum_{p+q=m} T^{21}_{p,q} x_1^p x_2^q$$

qui transforme (1) en un système

$$dz = \left(\frac{\mathcal{A} dx_1}{x_1^{p_1+1}} + \frac{\mathcal{B} dx_2}{x_2^{p_2+1}} \right) z$$

où

$$\mathcal{A}^{12}_{p,q} = \mathcal{A}^{21}_{p,q} = \mathcal{B}^{12}_{p,q} = \mathcal{B}^{21}_{p,q} = 0$$

pour tout couple (p,q) vérifiant $p+q \leq m$.

Nous avons pour déterminer T_m

(1) $$A^{11} + A^{12} T^{21} - \mathcal{A}^{11} - T^{12} \mathcal{A}^{21} = 0$$

(1') $$B^{11} + B^{12} T^{21} - \mathcal{B}^{11} - T^{12} \mathcal{B}^{21} = 0$$

(2) $$A^{22} + A^{21} T^{12} - \mathcal{A}^{22} - T^{21} \mathcal{A}^{12} = 0$$

(2') $$B^{22} + B^{21} T^{12} - \mathcal{B}^{22} - T^{21} \mathcal{B}^{12} = 0$$

$$(3)\quad \begin{cases} x_1^{p_1+1}\dfrac{\partial T^{12}}{\partial x_1} = A^{11}T^{12} + A^{12} - T^{12}\mathfrak{a}^{22} - \mathfrak{a}^{12} \\ x_2^{p_2+1}\dfrac{\partial T^{12}}{\partial x_2} = B^{11}T^{12} + B^{12} - T^{12}\mathfrak{B}^{22} - \mathfrak{B}^{12} \end{cases}$$

$$(3')\quad \begin{cases} x_1^{p_1+1}\dfrac{\partial T^{21}}{\partial x_1} = A^{22}T^{21} + A^{21} - T^{21}\mathfrak{a}^{11} - \mathfrak{a}^{21} \\ x_2^{p_2+1}\dfrac{\partial T^{21}}{\partial x_2} = B^{22}T^{21} + B^{21} - T^{21}\mathfrak{B}^{11} - \mathfrak{B}^{21} \end{cases}$$

Avec les équations (1) (1') (2) et (2') on obtient :

$$\mathfrak{a}^{11}_{r,s} = A^{11}_{r,s} \qquad \mathfrak{a}^{22}_{r,s} = A^{22}_{r,s}$$

$$\mathfrak{B}^{11}_{r,s} = B^{11}_{r,s} \qquad \mathfrak{B}^{22}_{r\,s} = B^{22}_{r,s} .$$

pour tout couple (r,s) vérifiant $r+s = m$.

Pour déterminer les $T^{12}_{r,s}$ pour $r+s = m$, nous avons le système

$$(s)\quad \begin{cases} A^{11}_{oo}\, T^{12}_{r,s} - T^{12}_{r,s}\, A^{22}_{oo} = - A^{12}_{r,s} \\ B^{11}_{oo}\, T^{12}_{r,s} - T^{12}_{r,s}\, B^{22}_{oo} = - B^{12}_{r,s} . \end{cases}$$

PROPOSITION 5.3. <u>Soient</u> A, B, A', B' <u>quatre matrices carrées qui vérifient</u>

$$[A,A'] = 0 \quad [B,B'] = 0 .$$

<u>Alors si un des couples</u> (A,B) <u>où</u> (A',B') <u>est sans valeur propre commune le système</u>

$$Ax - xB = C \quad A'x - xB' = C'$$

<u>admet une solution et une seule si et seulement si</u> $A'C - CB' = AC' - C'B$.

La preuve est laissée au lecteur.

Appliquons ce résultat au système (s) , ce système admet une solution unique si et seulement si

$$B^{12}_{r,s}\, A^{22}_{oo} - A^{11}_{oo}\, B^{12}_{r,s} = A^{12}_{r,s}\, B^{22}_{oo} - B^{11}_{o}\, A^{12}_{r,s}$$

Or, cette condition est :

$$H_{r,s} = 0$$

Comme $r+s \leq \ell$ et que le système est complètement intégrable jusqu'à l'ordre ℓ , elle est satisfaite.

Un raisonnement par récurrence nous donne alors le résultat annoncé dans le lemme, la transformation cherchée étant

$$T = T_{\ell} \circ \dots\dots \circ T_2 \circ T_1$$

qui est d'ailleurs polynômiale et vérifie $T(0) = \mathrm{id}$.

5.3. <u>Le cas convergent</u>. Le système (1) est complètement intégrable.

On suppose maintenant que les matrices A et B sont holomorphes à l'origine, elles sont donc représentables par des séries convergentes :

$$A = \sum_{p+q \geq o} A_{pq}\, x_1^p\, x_2^p \qquad B = \sum_{p+q \geq o} B_{pq}\, x_1^p\, x_2^q \,.$$

<u>LEMME de réduction totale</u>.

<u>Si</u> $A(0,0) = \begin{pmatrix} A^{11}_{oo} & 0 \\ 0 & A^{22}_{oo} \end{pmatrix}$ et $B(0,0) = \begin{pmatrix} B^{11}_{oo} & 0 \\ 0 & B^{22}_{oo} \end{pmatrix}$

<u>où les deux couples</u> $(A^{11}_{oo} , A^{22}_{oo})$, $(B^{11}_{oo} , B^{22}_{oo})$ <u>sont sans valeurs propres communes</u>, <u>il existe une transformation convergente unique</u> T <u>de la forme</u>

$$T = \begin{pmatrix} I & T^{12} \\ T^{21} & I \end{pmatrix}$$

<u>qui transforme le système</u> (1) <u>en</u>

$$dz = \omega' z$$

avec

$$\omega' = \frac{\begin{pmatrix} \mathcal{A}^{11} & 0 \\ 0 & \mathcal{A}^{22} \end{pmatrix}}{x_1^{p_1+1}} dx_1 + \frac{\begin{pmatrix} \mathcal{B}^{11} & 0 \\ 0 & \mathcal{B}^{22} \end{pmatrix}}{x_2^{p_2+1}} dx_2$$

et $\mathcal{A}^{ii}(0,0) = A^{ii}_{00}$ $\quad \mathcal{B}^{ii}(0,0) = B^{ii}_{00}$.

Preuve : En reprenant la démonstration du lemme de réduction totale dans le cas formel, l'hypothèse supplémentaire faite ci-dessus entraîne que $\mathcal{C}_1(0,0)$ et $\mathcal{C}_2(0,0)$ sont non singulières et le théorème 2.1 implique que la transformation formelle donnée par le lemme de réduction formelle est convergente.

Remarque 5.4. Le lemme de réduction partielle nous montre que la réduction est possible à tout ordre par une transformation polynômiale.

De ce lemme, on déduit :

THEOREME 5.5. Si les deux matrices $A(0,0)$ et $B(0,0)$ ont des valeurs propres distinctes, le système de Pfaff

$$dy = \left(\frac{A(x_1,x_2)}{x_1^{p_1+1}} dx_1 + \frac{B(x_1,x_2)}{x_2^{p_2+1}} dx_2 \right) y$$

supposé complètement intégrable, admet une matrice fondamentale de la forme :

$$U(x_1,x_2) x_1^{\Lambda_1} x_2^{\Lambda_2} \exp P_1\left(\frac{1}{x_2}\right) \exp P_2\left(\frac{1}{x_2}\right)$$

où : $U(x_1,x_2)$ est une matrice holomorphe à l'origine

Λ_1 et Λ_2 des matrices disgonales constantes

$P_i\left(\frac{1}{x_i}\right)$ des polynômes en $\frac{1}{x_i}$ à coefficients matriciels.

En effet, ce résultat est une conséquence du lemme de réduction totale qui entraîne la diagonalisation de notre système de Pfaff et des résultats du § 5.1 sur le cas scalaire.

5.4. Le cas asymptotique.

Soient $S = S_1 \times S_2$ un secteur de $\mathbf{C}^2$ et supposons que

$$A(x_1,x_2) \overset{S}{\sim} \sum_{|r|=o}^{+\infty} A_{r_1,r_2} x_1^{r_1} x_2^{r_2}$$

$$B(x_1,x_2) \overset{S}{\sim} \sum_{|r|=o}^{+\infty} B_{r_1,r_2} x_1^{r_1} x_2^{r_2}$$

$$\frac{\partial A}{\partial x_1} \overset{S}{\sim} \sum_{|r|=o}^{+\infty} r_1 A_{r_1,r_2} x_1^{r_1-1} x_2^{r_2}$$

$$\frac{\partial A}{\partial x_2} \overset{S}{\sim} \sum_{|r|=o}^{+\infty} r_2 A_{r_1,r_2} x_1^{r_1} x_2^{r_2-1}$$

$$\frac{\partial B}{\partial x_1} \overset{S}{\sim} \sum_{|r|=o}^{+\infty} r_1 B_{r_1,r_2} x_1^{r_1-1} x_2^{r_2}$$

$$\frac{\partial B}{\partial x_2} \overset{S}{\sim} \sum_{|r|=o}^{+\infty} r_2 B_{r_1,r_2} x_1^{r_1} x_2^{r_2-1}$$

et désignons par $(\hat{1})$ le système de Pfaff formel obtenu en remplaçant dans (1) A et B par leurs développements asymptotiques dans S .

Alors en utilisant les résultats du § 3 , on voit facilement que toute réduction formelle du système $(\hat{1})$ nous donne dans les conditions indiquées au § 3 une réduction asymptotique du système (1) .

En particulier, on a sous des hypothèses faciles à expliciter le résultat du théorème 5.5 sous forme asymptotique.

CHAPITRE III

ETUDE DES SYSTEMES DE PFAFF COMPLETEMENT INTEGRABLES DE LA FORME

$$(1) \qquad dy = \frac{f^1(x_1,x_2,y)}{x_1^{p_1+1}}\, dx_1 + \frac{f^2(x_1,x_2,y)}{x_2^{p_2+1}}\, dx_2$$

lorsque $p_1 = p_2 = 0$ et lorsque $p_1 > 0$, $p_2 = 0$.

§ 1. Préliminaires sur les systèmes différentiels ordinaires.

§ 2. Les applications f_1 et f_2 sont holomorphes à l'origine.

§ 3. Les applications f_1 et f_2 admettent des développements asymptotiques.

§ 4. Applications aux systèmes de Pfaff linéaires.

§ 1. Préliminaires sur les systèmes différentiels ordinaires.

1.1. On considère ici des systèmes différentiels de la forme

$$x \frac{du}{dx} = f(x,y,u) \tag{1}$$

où y est un paramètre et f une application à valeurs dans $\mathbb{C}^n$ holomorphe au voisinage de l'origine de $\mathbb{C}^2 \times \mathbb{C}^n$.

LEMME 1.1. Toute solution formelle de (1) de la forme

$$\sum_{m=0}^{+\infty} a_m(y)x^m$$

où :

1) pour tout m, a_m est holomorphe dans $|y| < \delta$

2) $a_o(0) = 0$

est convergente.

Preuve : Posons $\varphi_N(x,y) = \sum_{m=0}^{N} a_m(y)x^m$, alors le changement de fonctions $u = \varphi_N(x,y) + v$ nous donne

$$x \frac{dv}{dx} = f(x,y,\varphi_N(x,y)+v) - x \frac{d\varphi_N}{dx}$$

et

$$x \frac{dv}{dx} = f(x,y,\varphi_N(x,y)) - x \frac{d\varphi_N}{dx} + f(x,y,\varphi_N(x,y)+v) - f(x,y,\varphi_N(x,y))$$

ce qui peut s'écrire

$$x \frac{dv}{dx} = g_N(x,y) + A_N(x,y)v + R_N(x,y,v) \tag{2}$$

où

$$g_N(x,y) = f(x,y,\varphi_N(x,y)) - x \frac{d\varphi_N}{dx}$$

$$A_N(x,y) = \left(\frac{\partial f}{\partial u}\right)(x,y,\varphi_N(x,y))$$

$$R_N(x,y,v) = O(v^2)$$

De plus le fait que $\sum_{m=0}^{+\infty} a_m(y)x^m$ soit une solution formelle de (1) entraîne que

$$|g_N(x,y)| \leq K_N|x|^{N+1}$$

dans $$\{|x| \leq \delta_1\} \times \{|y| \leq \delta_2\}$$

ce que nous venons de faire est valable pour tout $N \geq 0$, fixons maintenant N assez grand pour que

$$\frac{\|A(0,0)\|}{N+1} \leq \frac{1}{4}$$

où $A(0,0) = (\frac{\partial f}{\partial u})(0,0,0)$.

A l'équation (2) est associée l'équation intégrale

$$(E) \qquad v(x,y) = \int_0^x \{g_N(\xi,y)+A_N(\xi,y)v(\xi,y)+R_N(\xi,y,v(\xi,y))\}\frac{d\xi}{\xi} .$$

Il est possible de choisir δ_1, δ_2, δ_3 tels que :

$$|R_N(\xi,y,v)| \leq L\ |v^2| \quad \text{sur} \quad \{|\xi| \leq \delta_1\} \times \{|y| \leq \delta_2\} \times \{|v| \leq \delta_3\}$$

$$\frac{\|A_N(\xi,y)\|}{N+1} \leq \frac{1}{2} \quad \text{sur} \quad \{|\xi| \leq \delta_1\} \times \{|y| \leq \delta_2\}$$

Soit $\varphi(x,y)$ une fonction vectorielle holomorphe dans $\{|x| \leq \delta_1\} \times \{|y| \leq \delta_2\}$ telle que

$$|\varphi(x,y)| \leq M\ |x|^{N+1} < \delta_3$$

Prenons δ_1 et M tel que

$$\frac{K_N + L\,M^2\,\delta_1^{N+1}}{N+1} \leq \frac{1}{2}M$$

Alors la fonction vectorielle

$$\psi(x,y) = \int_0^x \{g_N(\xi,y) + A_N(\xi,y)\ \varphi(\xi,y) + R_N(\xi,y,\varphi(\xi,y))\}\ \frac{d\xi}{\xi}$$

vérifie

$$|\psi(x,y)| \leq M|x|^{N+1} \quad \text{sur} \quad \{|x| \leq \delta_1\} \times \{|y| \leq \delta_2\}$$

On montre alors par le procédé classique d'itération déjà utilisé dans le chap. II, § 3 , qu'il existe une solution $\varphi(x,y)$ de (E) holomorphe à l'origine et vérifiant

$$|\varphi(x,y)| \leq M|x|^{N+1}$$

D'autre part $\sum_{m=N+1}^{+\infty} a_m(y)x^m$ est une solution formelle de (2) , en écrivant

$$\varphi(x,y) = \sum_{m=N+1}^{+\infty} \varphi_m(y)x^m$$

il est alors facile de montrer que

$$a_m(y) = \varphi_m(y) \quad \text{pour tout} \quad m \geq N+1$$

ce qui prouve la convergence de la série

$\sum_{m=N+1}^{+\infty} a_m(y)x^m$ et donc aussi le lemme . (cf.[5] et aussi [6]).

Remarque 1.2. Si les coefficients $a_m(y)$ sont également des séries formelles, le résultat ci-dessus n'est plus vrai comme le montre l'exemple

$$\frac{du}{dx} = (1+y)u$$

qui a pour solution $u = c(y)\exp(1+y)x$ où $c(y)$ est arbitraire et qui,en particulier, pourrait être une série divergente.

Par contre, on a :

LEMME 1.3. Si le système (1) admet une solution formelle de la forme $\sum_{m=o}^{+\infty} a_m(y)x^m$ où les $a_m(y)$ sont des séries formelles et $a_o(0) = 0$ alors le système (1) admet une solution convergente de la même forme, où les $a_m(y)$ sont des séries convergentes.

Preuve : Considérons

$$f(x,y, \sum_{\ell=o}^{N} \alpha_\ell x^\ell) = \sum_{m=o}^{+\infty} f_m(y,\alpha)x^m$$

où $\alpha_o, \alpha_1, \alpha_2, \dots \alpha_N$ sont des paramètres.

Pour tout $m \geq 0$, $f_m(y,\alpha)$ est une fonction holomorphe de y, $\alpha = (\alpha_o, \alpha_1, \dots \alpha_N)$ dans un voisinage de l'origine de $\mathbb{C}^{N+2}$.

Comme $\sum_{m=o}^{+\infty} a_m(y)x^m$ est une solution formelle de

$$x \frac{du}{dx} = f(x,y,u)$$

les séries formelles $a_j(y)$ $j = 0,1,\dots N$, sont des solutions formelles du système d'équations

$$m\alpha_m = f_m(y,\alpha) \quad m = 0,1,\dots,N .$$

Mais d'après un théorème d'Artin [1], si un tel système admet des solutions formelles, il admet ainsi des solutions convergentes.

Notons $a_j^*(y)$ $j = 0,1,2 \dots N$ ces solutions convergentes. Ceci étant vrai pour tout N , nous pouvons supposer que N est fixé assez grand pour que

$$\left\| \frac{A(0,0)}{N+1} \right\| = \frac{\left\| \frac{\partial f}{\partial u}(0,0,0) \right\|}{N+1} \leq \frac{1}{4}$$

Posons alors

$$u = v + \varphi_N^*(x,y)$$

où

$$\varphi_N^*(x,y) = \sum_{m=o}^{N} a_m^*(y)x^m$$

alors

(2) $$x \frac{dv}{dx} = g_N(x,y) + A_N(x,y)v + R_N(x,y,v)$$

avec

$$g_N(x,y) = 0(x^{N+1})$$

$$R_N(x,y,v) = 0\ (v^2)$$

Cherchons pour (2) une solution formelle de la forme

$$v = \sum_{m=N+1}^{+\infty} \alpha_m(y)x^m$$

Ceci nous donne pour déterminer les coefficients $\alpha_m(y)$ le système infini

$$m\alpha_m(y) = A(0,y)\,\alpha_m(y) + \mathcal{P}_m(y)$$

$m = N+1,\ N+2,\ \ldots$

où $\mathcal{P}_m(y)$ est connu.

Or, le choix de N implique que la série $m\,I - A(0,Y)$ est holomorphiquement invisible à l'origine pour tout $m \geq N+1$. Donc le système (2) admet une solution formelle de la forme $\sum_{m=N+1}^{+\infty} \alpha_m(y)x^m$ où les $\alpha_m(y)$ sont holomorphes à l'origine. La convergence de cette série est alors une conséquence du lemme 1.1.

1.2. Soient

S_1 un secteur dans le plan de la variable x

S_2 un secteur dans le plan du paramètre y

$$U = \{u \in \mathbb{C}^n \mid\ |u| < \delta_o\}$$

et

(1) $$x\,\frac{du}{dx} = f(x,y,u)$$

un système différentiel où :

$f(x,y,u)$ est holomorphe dans $S_1 \times S_2 \times U$

$$f(x,y,u) \underset{u.S_2\times U}{\overset{S_1}{\sim}} \sum_{m=o}^{+\infty} f_m(y,u)x^m$$

pour tout $m \geq 0$

$$f_m(y,u) \underset{u.\ U}{\overset{S_2}{\sim}} \sum_{\ell=o}^{+\infty} f_{m,\ell}(u)y^{\ell}$$

$f_{o,o}(0) = 0$.

Désignons par $(\hat{1})$ le système obtenu à partir de (1) en remplaçant f par son développement asymptotique $\hat{f}$ en (x,y,u) .

Une solution formelle de (1) est par définition une série formelle en (x,y) qui est solution de $(\hat{1})$.

Désignons par $(\hat{1}_x)$ le système obtenu à partir de (1) en remplaçant f par son développement asymptotique $\hat{f}_x$ en x.

Une solution <u>formelle en</u> x de (1) est par définition une série formelle $\Sigma\, a_m(y)x^m$ qui vérifie $(\hat{1}_x)$ comme série en x.

<u>Exemple</u> :

(1)
$$x\frac{du}{dx} = xu + f_o(y)$$

où
$$f_o(y) \underset{}{\overset{S_2}{\sim}} 0$$

alors

$(\hat{1})$
$$x\frac{du}{dx} = xu\,,$$

$(\hat{1}_x)$
$$x\frac{du}{dx} = f_o(y) + ux\,.$$

LEMME 1.4. <u>Si</u> $\hat{\varphi}(x,y) = \sum_{m=o}^{+\infty} \varphi_m(y)x^m$ <u>est une solution formelle en</u> x <u>de</u> (1) <u>telle que pour tout</u> m, φ_m <u>soit holomorphe dans</u> S_2 <u>et</u>

$$\varphi_m(y) \overset{S_2}{\sim} \sum_{\ell=o}^{+\infty} a_{m,\ell}\, y^{\ell}\,.$$

<u>Alors il existe une solution</u> $\varphi(x,y)$ <u>de</u> (1) <u>holomorphe dans</u> $S_1 \times S_2$ <u>telle que</u>

$$\varphi(x,y) \underset{u.\ S_2}{\overset{S_1}{\sim}} \sum_{m=o}^{+\infty} \varphi_m(y)x^m\,.$$

La transformation $u = v + \hat{\varphi}$ nous ramène au cas où

$$f(x,y,u) = f_o(x,y) + A(x,y)u + R(x,y,u)$$

avec
$$f_o(x,y) \underset{u.\ S_2}{\overset{S_1}{\sim}} 0$$

$$R(x,y,u) = O(u^2)\,.$$

Considérons alors comme toujours l'équation intégrale associée

$$(E) \qquad u(x,y) = \int_0^x \{f_0(\xi,y) + A(\xi,y)\,u(\xi,y) + R(\xi,y,u(\xi,y))\} \frac{d\xi}{\xi}$$

Comme dans la démonstration du lemme 1.1 , on montre que si N est assez grand, l'équation (E) admet une solution $u(x,y)$ d'ordre x^{N+1} .
Si cette solution u est unique, alors

$$u \underset{u.\ S_2}{\overset{S_1}{\sim}} 0$$

ce qui prouve le lemme 1.4.

Montrons que cette solution est unique.

Soient $u_1(x,y)$ et $u_2(x,y)$ deux solutions de (E) telle que

$$|u_1(x,y)| \leq K|x|^{N+1}$$

$$|u_2(x,y)| \leq K|x|^{N+1}$$

sur $S_1 \times S_2$.

Alors

$$u_1(x,y) - u_2(x,y) = \int_0^x \{A(\xi,y)(u_1(\xi,y) - u_2(\xi,y))$$

$$+ R(\xi,y,u_1(\xi,y)) - R(\xi,y,u_2(\xi,y))\} \frac{d\xi}{\xi} .$$

Posons $\quad u_1(x,y) - u_2(x,y) = x^{N+1} w(x,y)$.

Par une majoration facile de l'équation intégrale ci-dessus, nous obtenons

$$M_0 \leq \frac{(\alpha+\delta)}{N+1} M_0$$

où

$$M_0 = \sup_{S_1 \times S_2} |w(x,y)|$$

$$\alpha = \sup_{S_1 \times S_2} \|A(x,y)\|$$

δ une constante qui peut être choisie aussi petite que l'on veut en restreignant éventuellement le secteur S_1 .

Alors si $N > 2(\alpha+\delta)-1$, on a $M_o = 0$, ce qui prouve l'unicité d'une solution d'ordre en x assez élevé.

Remarque 1.5. Le résultat de ce lemme est faux lorsqu'on suppose seulement que $\hat{\varphi}$ est simplement une solution formelle. En effet, reprenons l'exemple ci-dessus :

$$x \frac{du}{dx} = xu + f_o(y)$$

avec

$$f_o(y) \overset{S_2}{\sim} 0$$

$u = 0$ est une solution formelle, mais n'est pas une solution formelle en x . La solution générale de cette équation est

$$u = C(y)e^x + f_o(y)\{e^x \log x + e^x \int_0^x \frac{e^{-\xi}-1}{\xi} d\xi\}$$

Comme $e^x \log x$ n'est pas borné à l'origine, on ne va pas avoir le résultat du lemme pour la solution formelle $u = 0$.

§ 2. Les applications f^1 et f^2 sont holomorphes à l'origine.

2.1. $$P_1 = P_2 = 0 .$$

On considère donc des systèmes de Pfaff complètement intégrables de la forme

$$(1) \qquad \begin{cases} x_1 \dfrac{\partial y}{\partial x_1} = f^1(x_1,x_2,y) \\ x_2 \dfrac{\partial y}{\partial x_2} = f^2(x_1,x_2,y) \end{cases}$$

où f^1 et f^2 sont holomorphes dans

$$\{|x_1| < \delta_1\} \times \{|x_2| < \delta_2\} \times \{\|y\| < \delta_3\}$$

Ecrivons

$$x_i \frac{\partial y}{\partial x_i} = f_o^i(x_1,x_2) + A^i(x_1,x_2)y + R^i(x_1,x_2,y)$$

où $R^i(x_1,x_2,y)$ est d'ordre au moins deux en y .

LEMME 2.1. Si une des matrices $A^i(0,0)$ n'a pas de valeur propre entière positive ou nulle, alors le système (1) admet une solution formelle et une seule de la forme

$$\varphi = \sum_{r_1+r_2>0} \varphi_{r_1,r_2} x_1^{r_1} x_2^{r_2}$$

Preuve : Supposons par exemple que $A^1(0,0)$ a la propriété indiquée, alors on voit facilement que

$$x_1 \frac{\partial y}{\partial x_1} = f^1(x_1,x_2,y)$$

admet une solution formelle et une seule φ . Les mêmes calculs que dans la démonstration du lemme 3.3 du chapitre II utilisant la complète intégrabilité, nous montrent que

$$v = x_2 \frac{\partial \varphi}{\partial x_2} - f^2(x_1,x_2,\varphi)$$

est solution du système linéaire

$$x_1 \frac{\partial u}{\partial x_1} = \frac{\partial f^1}{\partial y}(x_1,x_2,\varphi(x_1,x_2))u$$

Or
$$\frac{\partial f^1}{\partial y}(x_1,x_2,\varphi(x_1,x_2)) = A^1(x_1,x_2) + O(\varphi)$$

et la condition sur les valeurs propres, entraîne que ce système n'a pas d'autre solution formelle que la solution triviale, c'est-à-dire que l'unique solution formelle de la première des équations est aussi solution de la seconde.

Remarque 2.2. Si l'hypothèse sur les matrices $A^i(0,0)$ n'est pas satisfaite, il se peut quand même que (1) ait des solutions formelles .

THEOREME 2.3. <u>Si</u> $f^i(0,0,0) = 0 \quad i = 1,2$

<u>alors toute solution formelle</u>

$$\sum_{r_1+r_2>0} a_{r_1,r_2} x_1^{r_1} x_2^{r_2}$$

<u>de</u> (1) <u>est convergente</u>.

<u>Preuve</u> : Posons $$a_{r_1}(x_2) = \sum_{r_2=0}^{+\infty} a_{r_1,r_2} x_2^{r_2}$$

et

$$u = \sum_{r_1=0}^{+\infty} a_{r_1}(x_2) x_1^{r_1}$$

Mais u est une solution formelle de

$$x_2 \frac{\partial u}{\partial x_2} = f^2(x_1,x_2,y)$$

donc $$x_2 \frac{\partial u}{\partial x_2} = f^2(x_1,x_2,u) \text{ (formellement)}$$

$$x_2 \sum_{r_1=0}^{+\infty} \frac{d}{dx_2}(a_{r_1}(x_2))\, x_1^{r_1} = f^2(x_1,x_2,\sum_{r_1=0}^{+\infty} a_{r_1}(x_2)x_1^{r_1})$$

c'est-à-dire que

$$x_2 \frac{d\, a_o(x_2)}{dx_2} = f^2(0,x_2,a_o(x_2))$$

et le lemme 1.1 entraîne que la série formelle $a_o(x_2)$ est convergente .

Posons $u = v + a_o(x_2)$, alors

$$x_2 \frac{\partial v}{\partial x_2} = h(x_1,x_2,v)$$

$$= h_o(x_1,x_2) + B(x_1,x_2)v + O(v^2)$$

et $\sum_{m=1}^{+\infty} a_m(x_2)x_1^m$ est une solution formelle en x_1 de ce système ; on a donc formellement pour tout $m = 1,2,\ldots.$

$$x_2 \frac{dam(x_2)}{dx_2} = B(0,x_2)a_m(x_2) + Q_m(x_2)$$

où Q_m est connu comme fonction de x_2, dès que l'on connaît les $a_p(x_2)$ pour $p < m$. Il en résulte que pour tout m, $a_m(x_2)$ est une série convergente à l'origine, d'autre part, comme les $a_m(x_2)$ sont solutions des systèmes linéaires, il existe un disque centré à l'origine du plan de la variable x_2 tel que pour tout m, $a_m(x_2)$ soit convergente dans ce disque.

La série formelle $\sum_{m=o}^{+\infty} a_m(x_2)x_1^m$ est une solution formelle en x_1 à coefficient holomorphe comme de plus $a_o(0) = 0$; le lemme 1.1 entraîne que cette série est convergente, ce qui prouve le théorème .

COROLLAIRE 2.4. Si $f^i(0,0,0) = 0$ $(i = 1,2)$ et si une des matrices $A^i(0,0)$ n'a pas de valeurs propres entières positives ou nulles, alors le système (1) admet une solution holomorphe à l'origine et une seule .

2.2. Par exemple $p_1 = 0$, $p_2 > 0$.

Le système que nous considérons maintenant est le suivant :

$$(1) \qquad \begin{cases} x_1 \dfrac{\partial y}{\partial x_1} = f^1(x_1,x_2,y) \\ x_2^{p_2+1} \dfrac{\partial y}{\partial x_2} = f^2(x_1,x_2y) \end{cases}$$

avec toujours les mêmes hypothèses sur f^1 et f^2 .

On écrit encore :

$$f^i(x_1,x_2,y) = f_o^i(x_1,x_2) + A^i(x_1,x_2)y + R^i(x_1,x_2,y) .$$

LEMME 2.5. Si $A^1(0,0)$ n'a pas de valeurs propres entières positives ou nulles, ou si $A^2(0,0)$ est inversible, alors le système (1) admet une solution formelle et une seule de la forme

$$\sum_{r_1+r_2>o} \varphi_{r_1,r_2} x_1^{r_1} x_2^{r_2}$$

La démonstration est suivant le cas, analogue à celle des lemmes 2.1 de ce chapitre ou 3.3 du chapitre II .

Remarque 2.6. Analogue à la remarque 2.2 .

Théorème 2.7. Si $A^1(0,0)$ n'a pas de valeurs propres entières positives ou nulles, alors le système (1) admet une solution holomorphe et une seule nulle à l'origine.

Preuve : L'hypothèse sur $A^1(0,0)$ entraîne l'existence d'une solution formelle de (1) de la forme

$$\hat{\varphi} = \sum_{r_1+r_2>0} \varphi_{r_1,r_2} x_1^{r_1} x_2^{r_2}$$

et une seule .

Ecrivons cette solution sous la forme

$$\hat{\varphi} = \sum_{r_1=0}^{+\infty} \varphi_{r_1}(x_2) x_1^{r_1}$$

avec

$$\varphi_{r_1}(x_2) = \sum_{r_2=0}^{+\infty} \varphi_{r_1,r_2} x_2^{r_2}$$

Nous avons formellement

$$x_1 \frac{\partial \hat{\varphi}}{\partial x_1} = f^1(x_1,x_2,\hat{\varphi})$$

ou encore

$$x_1 \frac{\partial \hat{\varphi}}{\partial x_1} = f_0^1(x_1,x_2) + A^1(x_1,x_2)\hat{\varphi} + O((\hat{\varphi})^2) \ .$$

Donc pour déterminer les coefficients $\varphi_{r_1}(x_2)$ les équations

$$f^1(0,x_2,\varphi_0(x_2)) = 0$$

$$(\frac{\partial f^1}{\partial u}(0,x_2,\varphi_o(x_2)) - I)\varphi_1(x_1) = H_1(x_2)$$

$$(\frac{\partial f^1}{\partial u}(0,x_2,\varphi_o(x_2)) - 2I)\ \varphi_2(x_2) = H_2(x_2)$$

- -

$$(\frac{\partial f^2}{\partial u}(0,x_2,\varphi_o(x_2)) - r_1 I)\varphi_{r_1}(x_2) = H_{r_1}(x_2)$$

- -

où $H_{r_1}(x_2)$ est connu dès que l'on connaît $\varphi_r(x_2)$ pour $r < r_i$.
Le théorème des fonctions implicites nous donne $\varphi_o(x_2)$ comme série convergente.

D'autre part, il existe un disque D centré à l'origine du plan de la variable x_2 tel que pour tout $r_1 > 0$, $\frac{\partial f^1}{\partial u}(0,x_2,\varphi_o(x_2)) - r_1 I$ soit inversible dans D ; ce qui nous donne par récurrence des séries convergentes $\varphi_1,\varphi_2,\dots\ \varphi_{r_1}\dots$. Comme $\varphi_o(0) = \varphi_{oo} = 0$ le lemme 1.1 entraîne la convergence de la série $\hat{\varphi}$.

§ 3. <u>Les applications</u> f^1 <u>et</u> f^2 <u>admettent des développements asymptotiques.</u>

3.1. $$P_1 = P_2 = 0 .$$

On considère maintenant un système de Pfaff, <u>complètement intégrable</u> de la forme

$$(1)\qquad \begin{cases} x_1 \dfrac{\partial y}{\partial x_1} = f^1(x_1,x_2,y) \\[2ex] x_2 \dfrac{\partial y}{\partial x_2} = f^2(x_1,x_2,y) \end{cases}$$

où f^1 et f^2 sont holomorphes dans $S_1 \times S_2 \times U$, S_1(resp. S_2) étant un secteur dans le plan de la variable x_1(resp. x_2) et $U = \{y \in C^n |\ \|y\| < \delta_o\}$.
On suppose que

$$f^1(x_1,x_2,y) \underset{u.S_2 \times U}{\overset{S_1}{\sim}} \sum_{m=o}^{+\infty} f^1_m(x_2,y)x_1^m$$

et pour tout m , f^1_m holomorphe dans $S_2 \times U$.

$$\frac{\partial f^1}{\partial x_2}(x_1,x_2,y) \underset{u.S_2\times U}{\overset{S_1}{\sim}} \sum_{m=o}^{+\infty} \frac{\partial f^1_m}{\partial x_2}(x_2,y)x_1^m$$

$$f^2\,(x_1,x_2,y) \underset{u.S_2\times U}{\overset{S_1}{\sim}} \sum_{m=o}^{+\infty} f^2_m\,(x_2,y)x_1^m$$

et pour tout m f^2_m holomorphe dans $S_2\times U$.

pour tout $m \geq 0$

$$f^1_m\,(x_2,y) \underset{u.\ U}{\overset{S_1}{\sim}} \sum_{\ell=o}^{+\infty} f^1_{m,\ell}(y)\ x_2^{\ell}$$

où $f^1_{m,\ell}$ est holomorphe dans U et $f^1_{oo}(0) = 0$.

pour tout $m \geq 0$

$$f^2_m\,(x_2,y) \underset{u.\ U}{\overset{S_2}{\sim}} \sum_{\ell=o}^{+\infty} f^2_{m,\ell}(y)\ x_2^{\ell}$$

où $f^2_{m,\ell}$ est holomorphe dans U et $f^2_{oo}(0) = 0$.

Ces hypothèses entraînent que

$$f^i(x_1,x_2,y) \underset{u.U}{\overset{S_1\times S_2}{\sim}} \sum_{\ell+m\geq o} f^i_{m,\ell}(y)x_1^m x_2^{\ell}$$

Le système

$$(\hat{1})\qquad \begin{cases} x_1\dfrac{\partial y}{\partial x_1} = \displaystyle\sum_{\ell+m\geq o} f^1_{m,\ell}(y)x_1^m x_2^{\ell} \\[2ex] x_2\dfrac{\partial y}{\partial x_2} = \displaystyle\sum_{\ell+m\geq o} f^2_{m,\ell}(y)x_1^m x_2^{\ell} \end{cases}$$

est par définition le système formel associé à (1) .

THEOREME 3.1. <u>Si</u> $\hat{\varphi} = \sum_{m+\ell\geq 1} \varphi_{m,\ell}x_1^m x_2^{\ell}$ <u>est une solution formelle de</u> (1), <u>il existe une solution</u> φ <u>de</u> (1) <u>holomorphe sur</u> $S_1\times S_2$ <u>et telle que</u>

$$\varphi \underset{u.\ S_2}{\overset{S_1}{\sim}} \sum_{m=o}^{+\infty} \varphi_m(x_2)x_1^m$$

<u>où pour tout</u> $m \geq 0$, φ_m <u>est holomorphe sur</u> S_2 <u>et</u>

$$\varphi_m \overset{S_2}{\sim} \sum_{\ell=o}^{+\infty} \varphi_{m,\ell}\, x_2^\ell$$

<u>Remarque</u> 3.2. On a, comme conséquence, que

$$\varphi \overset{S_1 \times S_2}{\sim} \sum_{m+\ell \geq 1} \varphi_{m,\ell} x_1^m x_2^\ell$$

<u>Démonstration</u> : Ecrivons

$$\hat{\varphi} = \sum_{m=o}^{+\infty} \hat{\varphi}_m(x_2)x_1^m$$

avec

$$\hat{\varphi}_m = \sum_{\ell=o}^{+\infty} \varphi_{m,\ell}\, x_2^\ell .$$

La démonstration se fait en plusieurs étapes .

<u>1ère étape : Il existe une solution formelle en</u> x_1
$\hat{\varphi}(x_1,x_2) = \sum_{m=o}^{+\infty} \varphi_m(x_2)x_1^m$ <u>de</u> $(\hat{1}_2)$ <u>telle que pour tout</u> m,φ_m <u>soit holomorphe</u> <u>dans</u> S_2 <u>et</u> $\varphi_m \overset{S_2}{\sim} \hat{\varphi}_m$.

Remplaçons dans l'équation formelle

$(\hat{1}_2)$ $x_2 \dfrac{\partial y}{\partial x_2} = f^2(x_1,x_2,y)$, y par $\hat{\varphi}$, on voit alors que $\hat{\varphi}_o(x_2)$ est une solution formelle du système différentiel ordinaire

$$x_2 \frac{du}{dx_2} = f^2(0,x_2,u)$$

Il existe donc une solution φ_o de ce système holomorphe dans S_2 telle que

$$\varphi_o \overset{S_2}{\sim} \hat{\varphi}_o$$

Posons alors dans (1_2) $y = v + \varphi_o$ il vient

$$x_2 \frac{\partial v}{\partial x_2} = g(x_1,x_2,v) = g_o(x_1,x_2) + B(x_1,x_2)v + O(v^2)$$

et $\hat{\varphi} = \sum_{m=1}^{+\infty} \hat{\varphi}_m(x_2)x_1^m$ est une solution formelle de

$$x_2 \frac{\partial v}{\partial x_2} = g(x_1,x_2,v)$$

Comme

$$B(x_1,x_2) \underset{u.\ S_2}{\overset{S_1}{\sim}} \sum_{m=o}^{+\infty} B_m(x_2)x_1^m$$

il en résulte que $\hat{\varphi}_m$ est une solution formelle d'une équation de la forme

(E_m) $$x_2 \frac{dz}{dx_2} = B_o(x_2)z + b_m(x_2)$$

où b_m est connu .

Il existe donc une solution φ_m de (E_m) holomorphe dans S_2 et telle que

$$\varphi_m \overset{S_2}{\sim} \hat{\varphi}_m$$

Mais alors si on pose

$$\hat{\psi} = \sum_{m=o}^{+\infty} \varphi_m(x_2)x_1^m ,$$

$\hat{\psi}$ est une série formelle en x_1 qui vérifie

$$x_2 \frac{\partial \hat{\psi}}{\partial x_2} - f^2(x_1,x_2,\hat{\psi}) = 0$$

comme série formelle en x_1 .

<u>2° étape</u> : $\hat{\psi}$ <u>vérifie</u> $x_1 \frac{\partial \hat{\psi}}{\partial x_1} - f^1(x_1,x_2,\hat{\psi}) = 0$ <u>en tant que série formelle en</u> x_1 .

Ecrivons formellement

$$x_1 \frac{\partial \hat{\psi}}{\partial x_1} - f^1(x_1,x_2,\hat{\psi}) = \sum_{m=o}^{+\infty} \mu_m(x_2)x_1^m$$

Comme $\sum_{m+\ell \geq 1} \varphi_{m,\ell}\, x_1^m x_2^\ell$ est une solution formelle du système de Pfaff (1) , nous avons pour tout $m \geq 0$

$$\mu_m \overset{S_2}{\sim} 0$$

La condition de complète intégrabilité nous donne :

$$x_2 \frac{\partial f^1}{\partial x_2}(x_1,x_2,\hat{\psi}) + [\frac{\partial f^1}{\partial y}(x_1,x_2,\hat{\psi})]f^2(x_1,x_2,\hat{\psi})$$

$$= x_1 \frac{\partial f^2}{\partial x_1}(x_1,x_2,\hat{\psi}) + [\frac{\partial f^2}{\partial y}(x_1,x_2,\hat{\psi})]f^1(x_1,x_2,\hat{\psi})$$

en tant que séries formelles en x_1

Donc

$$x_2 \frac{\partial f^1}{\partial x_2}(x_1,x_2,\hat{\psi}) + [\frac{\partial f^1}{\partial y}(x_1,x_2,\hat{\psi})]x_2 \frac{\partial \hat{\psi}}{\partial x_2}$$

$$= x_1 \frac{\partial}{\partial x_1}(f^2(x_1,x_2,\psi)) - [\frac{\partial f^2}{\partial y}(x_1,x_2,\hat{\psi})]x_1 \frac{\partial \hat{\psi}}{\partial x_1} + [\frac{\partial f^2}{\partial y}(x_1,x_2,\hat{\psi})]f^1(x_1,x_2,\hat{\psi})$$

et

$$x_2 \frac{\partial f^1}{\partial x_2}(x_1,x_2,\hat{\psi}) + [\frac{\partial f^1}{\partial y}(x_1,x_2,\hat{\psi})]x_2 \frac{\partial \hat{\psi}}{\partial x_2}$$

$$= x_2 \frac{\partial}{\partial x_2}(x_1 \frac{\partial \hat{\psi}}{\partial x_1}) + [\frac{\partial f^2}{\partial y}(x_1,x_2,\hat{\psi})][f^1(x_1,x_2,\hat{\psi}) - x_1 \frac{\partial \hat{\psi}}{\partial x_1}]$$

ce qui donne :

$$x_2 \frac{\partial}{\partial x_2}[x_1 \frac{\partial \hat{\psi}}{\partial x_1} - f^1(x_1,x_2,\hat{\psi})] = [\frac{\partial f^2}{\partial y}(x_1,x_2,\hat{\psi})][x_1 \frac{\partial \hat{\psi}}{\partial x_1} - f^1(x_1,x_2,\hat{\psi})]$$

Donc en tant que série formelle en x_1 , $x_1 \frac{\partial \hat{\psi}}{\partial x_1} - f^1(x_1,x_2,\hat{\psi})$ est une solution formelle du système

$$x_2 \frac{\partial v}{\partial x_2} = [\frac{\partial f^2}{\partial y}(x_1,x_2,\hat{\psi}(x_1,x_2))]v$$

Ecrivons

$$\frac{\partial f^2}{\partial y}(x_1,x_2,\hat{\psi}) = \sum_{m=0}^{+\infty} \alpha_m(x_2)x_1^m$$

c'est une série formelle en x_1, à coefficients holomorphes.

Alors pour tout $m \geq 0$, nous avons

$$x_2 \frac{d\mu_m}{dx_2} = \alpha_o(x_2)\,\mu_m + \sum_{\substack{p+q=m \\ p \geq 1}} \alpha_p(x_2)\mu_q(x_2)$$

en particulier

$$x_2 \frac{d\mu_o}{dx_2} = \alpha_o(x_2)\mu_o$$

Comme $\mu_o \overset{S_2}{\sim} 0$ on a $\mu_o = 0$.

Par récurrence, il est alors facile de montrer en utilisant ci-dessus que $\mu_m(x_2) = 0$ dans S_2 , c'est-à-dire que

$$x_1 \frac{\partial \hat{\psi}}{\partial x_1} - f^1(x_1,x_2,\hat{\psi}) = 0$$

en tant que série formelle en x_1 .

<u>3° étape</u> : <u>Il existe une solution</u> φ <u>de</u> (1) <u>holomorphe sur</u> $S_1 \times S_2$ <u>ayant les propriétés voulues</u> .

En effet, d'après le lemme 1.4 , il existe une fonction φ holomorphe sur $S_1 \times S_2$ telle que :

1. $$\varphi \underset{u.\ S_2}{\overset{S_1}{\sim}} \sum_{m=o}^{+\infty} \varphi_m(x_2)x_1^m$$

2. $$x_1 \frac{\partial \varphi}{\partial x_1} = f^1(x_1,x_2,\varphi)$$

Alors

$$\Phi = x_2 \frac{\partial \varphi}{\partial x_2} - f^2(x_1,x_2,\varphi)$$

vérifie

1. $$\Phi \underset{u.\ S_2}{\overset{S_1}{\sim}} 0$$

2. par la complète intégrabilité

$$x_1 \frac{\partial \Phi}{\partial x_1} = \left[\frac{\partial f^1}{\partial y}(x_1,x_2,\varphi)\right]\Phi$$

ce qui implique que $\Phi = 0$, c'est-à-dire que φ est la solution cherchée du système de Pfaff (1) .

Remarque 3.3. Si une des matrices $A^i(0,0)$ n'a pas de valeurs propres entières positives ou nulles, alors le système formel $(\hat{1})$ admet une solution formelle et une seule, alors la solution φ de (1) donnée par le théorème 3.1 est unique modulo une fonction asymptotique à zéro dans un sens facile à préciser. En particulier, si $A^1(0,0)$ n'a pas de valeurs propres entières positives ou nulles, la solution φ est vraiment unique.

3.2. $p_1 > 0$, $p_2 = 0$.

Soient

$S = S_1 \times S_2$ un secteur de $\mathbb{C}^2$

U un polydisque centré à l'origine de $\mathbb{C}^m$.

$f^i (i = 1,2)$ deux fonctions holomorphes dans $S \times U$ telles que :

$$f^i \underset{\text{u. } U}{\overset{S}{\sim}} \sum_{|r|=0}^{+\infty} f^i_{r_1,r_2}(y)\, x_2^{r_1} x_2^{r_2}$$

$$\frac{\partial f^i}{\partial x_1} \underset{\text{u. } U}{\overset{S}{\sim}} \sum_{|r|=0}^{+\infty} f^i_{r_1,r_2}\, r_1 x_1^{r_1-1} x_2^{r_2}$$

$$\frac{\partial f^i}{\partial x_2} \underset{\text{u. } U}{\overset{S}{\sim}} \sum_{|r|=0}^{+\infty} f^i_{r_1,r_2}\, r_2 x_1^{r_1} x_2^{r_2-1}$$

Nous avons de plus

$$f^i(x_1,x_2,y) = \sum_{|p|=0}^{+\infty} \hat{f}^i_p\,(x_1,x_2) y^p \quad \text{dans } S \times U$$

et on supposera que $\hat{f}^i_o(0,0) = 0$ pour $i = 1,2$.

On se propose maintenant d'étudier le système de Pfaff complètement intégrable :

$$(1) \qquad dy = \frac{f^1(x_1,x_2,y)}{x_2^{p_1+1}}\, dx_1 + \frac{f^2(x_1,x_2,y)}{x_2}\, dx_2$$

Ecrivons

$$f^i(x_1,x_2,y) = f_o^i(x_1,x_2) + A^i(x_1,x_2)y + R^i(x_1,x_2,y)$$

avec
$$R^i(x_1,x_2,y) = O(y^2) .$$

La complète intégrabilité du système entraîne encore $[A^1(0,0), A^2(0,0)] = 0$

On a encore :

LEMME 3.4. <u>Si</u> $A^1(0,0)$ <u>est non singulière ou si</u> $A^2(0,0)$ <u>n'a pas de valeur propre entière positive ou nulle, le système</u> (1) <u>admet une solution formelle et une seule.</u>

THEOREME 3.5. <u>Si</u> $A^1(0,0)$ <u>est régulière et si les parties réelles des valeurs propres de</u> $A^2(0,0)$ <u>sont différentes de zéro, alors pour toute solution formelle</u> $\hat{\varphi} = \sum_{|r|>0} \varphi_{r_1,r_2} x_1^{r_1} x_2^{r_2}$ de (1) , <u>il existe une solution</u> φ <u>de</u> (1) <u>holomorphe dans un secteur</u> $S' \subset S$ <u>telle que</u>

$$\varphi \overset{S'}{\sim} \hat{\varphi} .$$

<u>Idée de la démonstration.</u>

Reprendre les développements du §3 du chapitre II avec les hypothèses actuelles $p_1 > 0$, $p_2 = 0$.

On est ainsi amené à considérer des équations intégrales de la forme

$$z = \int_{\gamma_1(x_1)} \exp\left(-\frac{\lambda}{p_1}\left(\frac{1}{x_1^{p_1}} - \frac{1}{t_1^{p_1}}\right)\right) t_1^{-p_1-1} P(t_1,x_2,z)\,dt_1$$

$$+ \exp\left(-\frac{\lambda}{p_1}\left(\frac{1}{x_1^{p_1}} - \frac{1}{a_1^{p_1}}\right)\right) \int_{\gamma_2(x_2)} \left(\frac{x_2}{t_2}\right)^{\mu} Q(a_1,t_2,z)\, \frac{dt_2}{t_2} .$$

Les raisonnements sont alors identiques pour un choix convenable des chemins d'intégration. Le choix des chemins $\gamma_1(x_1)$ est indiqué dans le § 6.1 du chapitre I, et celui des chemins $\gamma_2(x_2)$ dans le § 6.2 du même chapitre.

Les considérations développées dans le § 3 du chapitre II sur le choix de ces chemins, montrent qu'un choix précis pour $\gamma(x_2)$ est nécessaire que lorsque S_1 est un "petit" secteur.

Remarque 3.6. Si S_1 est un "grand" secteur, le résultat du théorème 3.5 est encore valable sans aucune hypothèse sur les valeurs propres de $A^2(0,0)$.

Si S_1 est un "petit"secteur, et si toutes les valeurs propres de $A^2(0,0)$ ont une partie réelle strictement négative, alors le résultat du théorème 3.5 reste valable sans aucune hypothèse sur $A^1(0,0)$.

Remarque 3.7. La méthode utilisée s'étend à d'autres systèmes de Pfaff. En particulier, le résultat ci-dessus et les résultats un peu plus généraux indiqués dans la remarque 3.6 s'étendent avec des hypothèses faciles à donner à des systèmes de Pfaff complètement intégrables de la forme

$$dy = (x_1^{p_1+1})^{-1} f^1(x_1,x_2,y)dx_1 + (x_2^{p_2+1})^{-1} f^2(x_1,x_2,y)dx_2$$

où

$$x_1^{p_1+1} = \begin{pmatrix} x_1^{p_1^1+1} & 0 & \cdots & 0 \\ 0 & x_1^{p_1^2+1} & 0 \cdots & 0 \\ \vdots & & \ddots & \\ 0 & \cdots & \cdots & x_1^{p_1^n+1} \end{pmatrix} \qquad x_2^{p_2+1} = \begin{pmatrix} x_2^{p_2^1+1} & 0 & \cdots & 0 \\ 0 & x_2^{p_2^2+1} & 0 \cdots & 0 \\ \vdots & & \ddots & \\ 0 & \cdots & \cdots & x_2^{p_2^n+1} \end{pmatrix}$$

avec $p_i^j \geq 0$ et $p_1^i + p_2^j > 0$.

Mais en utilisant les résultats obtenus dans le paragraphe 3.1 , on voit comment obtenir également certains résultats dans l'hypothèse où l'on a seulement $p_i^j \geq 0$ c'est-à-dire que pour certains j on pourrait avoir $p_1^j = p_2^j = 0$.

§ 4. Applications aux systèmes de Pfaff linéaires.

Considérons des systèmes de Pfaff complètement intégrables, de la forme $dy = \omega y$ avec

$$(1) \qquad \omega = \frac{A_1(x_1,x_2)}{x_1^{p_1+1}}\, dx_1 + \frac{A_2(x_1,x_2)}{x_2^{p_2+1}}\, dx_2 \, .$$

dans les deux cas suivants :

$$(I) \quad p_1 = p_2 = 0$$

$$(II) \quad p_1 > 0 \quad p_2 = 0$$

Les hypothèses sur les matrices A_1 et A_2 seront précisées dans la suite.

4.1. Le cas scalaire.

La proposition 5.2 du chapitre II reste vraie dans les cas considérés ici.

4.2. Des lemmes de réduction formelle.

On suppose maintenant que le système (1) est un système formel, c'est-à-dire que les éléments des matrices $A_i(x_1,x_2)$ sont des séries formelles. Pour éviter l'introduction d'indice en surnombre, nous noterons

$$\omega = \frac{A(x_1,x_2)}{x_1^{p_1+1}}\, dx_1 + \frac{B(x_1,x_2)}{x_2^{p_2+1}}\, dx_2 \, .$$

Supposons que

$$A(0,0) = \begin{pmatrix} A_{oo}^{11} & 0 \\ 0 & A_{oo}^{22} \end{pmatrix} \qquad B(0,0) = \begin{pmatrix} B_{oo}^{11} & 0 \\ 0 & B_{oo}^{22} \end{pmatrix}$$

et notons $\alpha_j^{11} (j = 1,2 \ldots s)$, $\alpha_j^{22} (j = s+1,\ldots n)$ respectivement les valeurs propres de A_{oo}^{11} et A_{oo}^{22} . De même $\beta_j^{11} (j = 1,2 \ldots s)$ $\beta_j^{22} (j = s+1,\ldots n)$ celles de B_{oo}^{11} et B_{oo}^{22} .

LEMME DE REDUCTION TOTALE.

Cas $p_1 = p_2 = 0$ Si $\alpha_j^{11} - \alpha_k^{22} \notin \mathbb{Z}$ pour tout $j = 1,2 \dots s$, $k = s+1, \dots n$ ou si $\beta_j^{11} - \beta_k^{22} \notin \mathbb{Z}$ pour tout $j = 1,2 \dots s$, $k = s+1, \dots n$.

Cas $p_1 > 0$, $p_2 = 0$ Si $\alpha_j^{11} - \alpha_k^{22} \neq 0$ pour tout $j = 1,2 \dots s$; $k = s+1, \dots n$ ou si $\beta_j^{11} - \beta_k^{22} \notin \mathbb{Z}$ pour tout $j = 1,2 \dots s$: $k = s+1, \dots n$.

Il existe une transformation formelle unique T de la forme

$$T = \begin{pmatrix} I & T^{12} \\ T^{21} & I \end{pmatrix}$$

qui transforme le système (1) en

$$dz = \omega' z$$

avec

$$\omega' = \frac{\begin{pmatrix} \mathcal{G}^{11} & 0 \\ 0 & \mathcal{G}^{22} \end{pmatrix}}{x_1^{p_1+1}} dx_1 + \frac{\begin{pmatrix} \mathcal{B}^{11} & 0 \\ 0 & \mathcal{B}^{22} \end{pmatrix}}{x_2^{p_2+1}} dx_2$$

et $\mathcal{G}^{ii}(0,0) = A_{oo}^{ii}$ $\quad \mathcal{B}^{ii}(o,o) = \mathcal{B}_{oo}^{ii}$

Preuve : Ecrivons

$$A = \begin{pmatrix} A^{11} & A^{12} \\ A^{21} & A^{22} \end{pmatrix} \quad B = \begin{pmatrix} B^{11} & B^{12} \\ B^{21} & B^{22} \end{pmatrix}$$

et chercons une transformation

$$T = \begin{pmatrix} I & T^{12} \\ T^{21} & I \end{pmatrix} \quad I = \text{identité},$$

qui mette le système sous la forme suivante :

$$\mathcal{G} = \begin{pmatrix} \mathcal{G}^{11} & 0 \\ 0 & \mathcal{G}^{22} \end{pmatrix} \quad \mathcal{B} = \begin{pmatrix} \mathcal{B}^{11} & 0 \\ 0 & \mathcal{B}^{22} \end{pmatrix}$$

Un calcul facile nous donne alors pour déterminer par exemple T^{12}

$$\begin{cases} x_1^{p_1+1} \dfrac{\partial T^{12}}{\partial x_1} = A^{12} + A^{11}T^{12} - T^{12}A^{22} - T^{12}A^{21}T^{12} \\[2ex] x_2^{p_2+1} \dfrac{\partial T^{12}}{\partial x_2} = B^{12} + B^{11}T^{12} - T^{12}B^{22} - T^{12}B^{21}T^{12} \end{cases}$$

Pour démontrer le lemme de réduction, on procède alors comme indiqué au § 5.2 du chapitre II en utilisant dans le cas $p_1 = p_2 = 0$ le lemme 2.1 et dans le cas $p_1 > 0$, $p_2 = 0$ le lemme 2.5 .

<u>Remarque 4.1</u>. Nous avons également un lemme de réduction partielle . L'énoncé ci-dessus indique la modification à faire sur les hypothèses du lemme de réduction partielle donné dans le § 5.2 du chapitre II .

4.3. <u>Le cas convergent.</u>

On suppose maintenant que les matrices A et B sont holomorphes à l'origine.

Le théorème 2.3 montre que le lemme de réduction totale dans le cas $p_1 = p_2 = 0$ reste valable dans le cadre des séries convergentes, c'est-à-dire que si les données sont holomorphes, la transformation formelle donnée par le lemme de réduction formelle est convergente.

Dans le cas $p_1 > 0$, $p_2 = 0$ on a, en utilisant le théorème 2.7

LEMME DE REDUCTION. <u>Si</u> $A(0,0) \neq \begin{pmatrix} A_{oo}^{11} & 0 \\ 0 & A_{oo}^{22} \end{pmatrix}$ <u>et</u> $B(0,0) = \begin{pmatrix} B_{oo}^{11} & 0 \\ 0 & B_{oo}^{22} \end{pmatrix}$

<u>où</u> $\beta_j^{11} - \beta_k^{22} \notin \mathbb{Z}$ <u>pour tout</u> $j = 1,\dots s$, $k = s+1,\dots n$,

<u>il existe une transformation convergente unique</u> T <u>de la forme</u>

$$T = \begin{pmatrix} I & T^{12} \\ T^{21} & I \end{pmatrix}$$

<u>qui transforme le système</u> (1) <u>en</u>

$$dz = \omega' z$$

<u>avec</u>

$$\omega' = \frac{\begin{pmatrix} \mathfrak{A}^{11} & 0 \\ 0 & \mathfrak{A}^{22} \end{pmatrix}}{x_1^{p_1+1}} dx_1 + \frac{\begin{pmatrix} \mathfrak{B}^{11} & 0 \\ 0 & \mathfrak{B}^{22} \end{pmatrix}}{x_2} dx_2$$

et $\mathfrak{A}^{ii}(0,0) = A^{ii}_{oo}$ $\mathfrak{B}^{ii}(0,0) = B^{ii}_{oo}$.

A l'aide de ces lemmes de réduction, il est maintenant facile, en utilisant le § 4.1 , de donner pour les cas $p_1 = p_2 = 0$ et $p_1 > 0$, $p_2 = 0$, un énoncé analogue au théorème 5.5 du chapitre II . Les modifications apportées aux hypothèses ont été plusieurs fois explicitées clairement ci-dessus.

4.4. Le cas asymptotique.

En procédant comme dans le chapitre II § 5.4 , on obtient, en utilisant les résultats du § 3 , des théorèmes de réduction valables asymptotiquement.

Les hypothèses sont faciles à expliciter et il en est de même des énoncés.

CHAPITRE IV

ETUDE DES SYSTEMES DE PFAFF COMPLETEMENT INTEGRABLES DE LA FORME

$$dy = \sum_{j=1}^{n} \frac{f_j(x,y)}{x_j^{p_j}} dx_j \qquad p_j \geq 0 .$$

§ 1. Etude formelle.

On considère dans ce paragraphe des systèmes de Pfaff complètement intégrables de la forme :

(1) $$dy = \sum_{j=1}^{y} \frac{f_j(x,y)}{x_j^{p_j}} dx_j$$

où :

pour tout j, p_j est un entier positif ou nul.

$$x = (x_1, x_2, \ldots, x_n) \ , \ y = (y_1, y_2, \ldots, y_m) \ ;$$

$$f_j(x,y) = (f_j^{\ell}(x,y))_{\ell = 1,2 \ldots m}$$

avec pour tout j et tout ℓ

$f_j^{\ell} \in \mathbb{C}[[x,y]]$ (anneau des séries formelles).

On écrira simplement $f_j \in (\mathbb{C}[[x,y]])^m$.

La condition de complète intégrabilité de ce système formel (1) s'écrit :

Pour tout $k = 1,2,\ldots,n$; $j = 1,2,\ldots,n$

$$x_k^{p_k} \frac{\partial f_j}{\partial x_k} + \left(\frac{\partial f_j}{\partial y}\right) f_k = x_j^{p_j} \frac{\partial f_k}{\partial x_j} + \left(\frac{\partial f_k}{\partial y}\right) f_j$$

ou $\left(\frac{\partial f_j}{\partial y}\right)$ désigne la matrice $\left(\frac{\partial f_j^{\ell}}{\partial y_q}\right)$.

On supposera dans toute la suite que pour tout $j = 1,2,\ldots,n$

$$f_j(0,0) = 0 \quad \text{lorsque} \quad p_j > 0 .$$

Le système de Pfaff (1) peut également s'écrire

$$(1') \left\{ (1_j) \quad x_j^{p_j} \frac{\partial y}{\partial x_j} = f_j(x,y) \qquad j = 1,2\ldots n \right.$$

et de manière explicite pour tout j

$$(1_j) \quad \left\{ \; x_j^{p_j} \frac{\partial y_k}{\partial x_j} = f_j^k(x,y) \qquad k = 1,2\ldots m \; . \right.$$

Remarque 1.1. On pourrait supposer que les p_j sont des matrices diagonales à éléments entiers.

LEMME 1.2. S'il existe $j_o \in \{1,2,\ldots,n\}$ et une solution formelle φ du système (1_{jo}) vérifiant $\varphi(0,0) = 0$ alors les séries formelles

$$v_j = x_j^{p_j} \frac{\partial \varphi}{\varphi x_j} - f_j(x,\varphi) \qquad j = 1,2,\ldots,n$$

sont solutions du système

$$x_{jo}^{p_{jo}} \frac{\partial u}{\partial x_{jo}} = (\frac{\partial f_{jo}}{\partial y})(x,\varphi)u \; .$$

Preuve : Dans le cas $n = 2$, elle a été donnée au cours de la démonstration du lemme 3.3 du chap. II.

On peut évidemment supposer que $j_o = 1$. Nous avons pour tout j :

$$x_1^{p_1} \frac{\partial}{\partial x_1} (x_j^{p_j} \frac{\partial \varphi}{\partial x_j}) = x_j^{p_j} \frac{\partial}{\partial x_j} (x_1^{p_1} \frac{\partial \varphi}{\partial x_1})$$

$$= x_j^{p_j} \frac{\partial}{\partial x_j} (f_1(x,\varphi))$$

$$= x_j^{p_j} \frac{\partial f_1}{\partial x_j} (x,\varphi) + \frac{\partial}{\partial y}(f_1)(x,\varphi).x_j^{p_j} \frac{\partial \varphi}{\partial x_j} \; .$$

La signification de l'écriture condensée utilisée est facile à deviner.

La condition de complète intégrabilité du système (1) nous donne en particulier :

$$x_j^{p_j} \frac{\partial f_1}{\partial x_j} (x,\varphi) + \frac{\partial f_1}{\partial y} (x,\varphi).f_j(x,\varphi) = x_1^{p_1} \frac{\partial f_j}{\partial x_1} (x,\varphi) + \frac{\partial f_i}{\partial x_1} (x,\varphi) f_1(x,\varphi)$$

pour tout $j = 1,2\ldots n$

c'est-à-dire que

$$x_1^{p_1} \frac{\partial}{\partial x_1} (x_j^{p_j} \frac{\partial \varphi}{\partial x_j} - f_j(x,\varphi)) = \frac{\partial f_1}{\partial y} (x,\varphi)(x_j^{p_j} \frac{\partial \varphi}{\partial x_j} - f_j(x,\varphi))$$

ou encore

$$x_1^{p_1} \frac{\partial v_j}{\partial x_1} = \frac{\partial f_1}{\partial y}(x,\varphi)v_j$$

ce qui prouve le lemme 1.2.

Remarque 1.3. La condition de complète intégrabilité n'a été que partiellement utilisée.

1.1. Un des entiers p_i est nul.

Supposons par exemple que $p_1 = 0$ et posons

$$\hat{x}_1 = (x_2, x_3, \dots, x_n) \quad \text{et} \quad \hat{f}(\hat{x}_1, y) = f(x,y)\big|_{x_1 = 0} .$$

LEMME 1.4. Il existe $\varphi \in (\mathbb{C}[[\hat{x}_1]][[x_1]])^m$ telle que

$$\frac{d\varphi}{dx_1} = f_1(x,\varphi) \quad \text{et} \quad \varphi(0) = 0$$

si $\varphi = \sum_{p=0}^{+\infty} \varphi_p(\hat{x}_1)x_1^p$ où pour tout p, $\varphi_p(\hat{x}_1) \in (\mathbb{C}[[\hat{x}_1]])^m$ alors φ est entièrement déterminée par la donnée de $\varphi_0(\hat{x}_1)$.

La démonstration de ce résultat se fait par identification et en remarquant que la série formelle φ est entièrement déterminée par la donnée de $\varphi_0(\hat{x}_1)$.

Remarque 1.5. Ce lemme nous dit également que l'on a une solution unique $\varphi \in (\mathbb{C}[[x]])^m$ dès que l'on se donne $\varphi_0(\hat{x}_1)$.

PROPOSITION 1.6. Soit $\varphi_0 \in (\mathbb{C}[[\hat{x}_1]])^m$ vérifiant

1) $\varphi_0(0) = 0$

2) pour tout $j = 2,3,\dots,n$

$$x_j^{p_j} \frac{\partial \varphi_0}{\partial x_j} = \hat{f}_j(\hat{x}_1, \varphi_0) .$$

Alors la solution unique $\psi(x) \in (\mathbb{C}[[x]])^m$ de

$$\frac{\partial y}{\partial x_1} = f_1(x,y)$$

<u>qui vérifie</u> $\psi|_{x_1=o} = \varphi_o$ <u>est une solution du système de Pfaff</u> (1).

<u>Preuve</u> : Posons pour tout $j = 2,3,\ldots,n$

$$v_j = x_j^{p_j} \frac{\partial \psi}{\partial x_j} - f_j(x,\psi) .$$

Comme $\psi|_{x_1=o} = \varphi_o$

et

$$x_j^{p_j} \frac{\partial \varphi_o}{\partial x_j} = \hat{f}_j(\hat{x}_1,\varphi_o) \qquad j = 2,3,\ldots,n$$

on a pour tout $j = 2,3,\ldots,n$

$$v_j = O(x_1) .$$

Le lemme 1.2. dit que

$$\frac{\partial v_j}{\partial x_1} = \frac{\partial f_1}{\partial y}(x,\psi)v_j \qquad j = 2,3,\ldots,n$$

ce qui implique $v_j = 0$ et la proposition est démontrée.

1.2. <u>Il existe</u> $j_o \in \{1,2,\ldots,n\}$ <u>tel que</u> $p_{j_o} = 1$.

On supposera par exemple que $p_1 = 1$.

THEOREME 1.7. <u>Si</u> $A_1 = \frac{\partial f_1}{\partial y}(0,0)$ <u>n'a pas de valeur propre entière positive ou nulle alors le système de Pfaff</u> (1) <u>admet une solution</u> $\varphi \in (\mathbb{C}[[x]])^m$ <u>et une seule vérifiant</u>

$$\varphi(0) = 0 .$$

<u>Preuve</u> : Cherchons pour le système

$$x_1 \frac{\partial y}{\partial x_1} = f_1(x,y)$$

une solution formelle de la forme

$$y = \sum_{p=o}^{+\infty} y_p(\hat{x}_1)x_1^p .$$

Par identification nous obtenons d'abord

$$(s_o) \quad \hat{f}_1(\hat{x}_1, y_o) = 0$$

et ensuite par un calcul de dérivation pour tout $p \geq 1$

$$(s_p) \quad \left(\frac{\partial \hat{f}_1(\hat{x}_1, y_o)}{\partial y} - pI\right) y_p = h_p(\hat{x}_1)$$

où $h_p(\hat{x}_1)$ est connu et déterminé par les solutions des systèmes (s_q) avec $q < p$.

Comme $A_1 = \frac{\partial f_1}{\partial y}(0,0)$ est inversible le système (s_o) nous donne $y_o(\hat{x}_1)$ et l'hypothèse sur les valeurs propres de A_1 permet par récurrence de résoudre les systèmes (s_p).

Le système de Pfaff (1) admet donc une solution unique

$$\varphi \in (\mathbb{C}[[x]])^m$$

telle que

$$\varphi(0) = 0$$

$$x_1 \frac{\partial \varphi}{\partial x_1} = f_1(x, \varphi) .$$

D'après le lemme 1.2. pour tout $j = 2,3,\dots,n$,

$$v_j = x_j^{p_j} \frac{\partial \varphi}{\partial x_j} - f_j(x, \varphi)$$

est solution de

$$x_1 \frac{du}{dx_1} = \frac{\partial f_1}{\partial y}(x, \varphi) v$$

et l'hypothèse faite sur A_1 entraîne que $v_j = 0$ pour tout $j = 2,3,\dots,n$.

1.3. <u>Pour tout</u> j, $p_j > 1$.

THEOREME 1.8. <u>Si pour</u> $j_o \in \{1,2,\dots,n\}$ $A_{j_o} = \frac{\partial f_{j_o}}{\partial y}(0,0)$ <u>est inversible alors le système de Pfaff</u> (1) <u>admet une solution formelle</u> $\varphi \in (\mathbb{C}[[x]])^m$ <u>et une seule vérifiant</u> $\varphi(0) = 0$.

On suppose par exemple que $j_o = 1$. La démonstration se fait alors d'une manière tout à fait analogue au cas $n = 2$ (lemme 3.3 chap. II).

§ 2. Solutions convergentes à l'origine.

Dans ce paragraphe on considère des systèmes de Pfaff analytiques complètement intégrable de la forme

(1) $$dy = \sum_{j=1}^{n} \frac{f_j(x,y)}{x_j^{p_j}} dx_j$$

p_j entier positif ou nul

où

$$x = (x_1, x_2, \ldots, x_n) \ , \ y = (y_1, y_2 \ldots y_m)$$

$f_j = (f_j^{\ell})_{\ell = 1,2\ldots m}$ avec pour tout j et tout ℓ , $f_j^{\ell} \in C\{x,y\}$ c'est-à-dire que pour tout $(j,\ell), f_j^{\ell}(x,y)$ est une série convergente.

On écrira $f_j \in (C\{x,y\})^m$.

On supposera dans toute la suite que $f_j(0,0) = 0$. La condition de complète intégrabilité du système (1) a la même forme que dans le cas formel.

Les systèmes de Pfaff considérés dans ce paragraphe peuvent évidemment être considérés comme étant des systèmes formels.

On a comme dans le cas formel :

LEMME 2.1. S'il existe $j_o \in \{1,2\ldots n\}$ et une solution convergente φ du système (1_{j_o}) vérifiant $\varphi(0,0) = 0$ alors les séries convergentes

$$v_j = x_j^{p_j} \frac{\partial \varphi}{\partial x_j} - f_j(x,\varphi) \qquad j = 1,2,\ldots,n$$

sont solutions du système

$$x_{jo}^{p_{jo}} \frac{\partial u}{\partial x_{jo}} = (\frac{\partial f_{jo}}{\partial y})(x,\varphi)u \ .$$

2.1. Un des entiers p_i est nul.

Par exemple $p_1 = 0$.

C'est un exercice facile de généraliser au cas convergent les résultats du 1.1 de ce chapitre.

2.2. Pour tout $j = 1,2,\ldots,n$, $p_j = 1$.

THEOREME 2.2. Toute solution formelle φ du système de Pfaff (1) qui vérifie $\varphi(0) = 0$ est convergente.

La démonstration de ce théorème se fait par récurrence sur le nombre des variables il est vrai pour $n = 2$ (théorème 2.3 du chapitre III).
Soit φ une solution formelle de (1) vérifiant $\varphi(0) = 0$. On peut l'écrire

$$\varphi(x) = \sum_{p=0}^{+\infty} \varphi_p(\hat{x}_1)x_1^p$$

où pour tout p , $\varphi_p(\hat{x}_1) \in (\mathbb{C}[[\hat{x}_1]])^m$.

LEMME 2.3. Pour tout p , $\varphi_p(\hat{x}_1)$ converge dans un polydisque D centré à l'origine de $\mathbb{C}^{n-1}$.

Preuve : Nous avons pour tout $j = 2,3,\ldots,n$

$$x_j \frac{\partial \varphi_0}{\partial x_j} = \hat{f}_j(\hat{x}_1, \varphi_0(\hat{x}_1))$$

donc par notre hypothèse de récurrence $\varphi_0(\hat{x}_1)$ est une série convergente.

Posons $\varphi = v + \varphi_0(\hat{x}_1)$, il vient pour tout $j = 2,3,\ldots,n$.

$$x_j \frac{\partial v}{\partial x_j} + x_j \frac{\partial \varphi_0(\hat{x}_1)}{\partial x_j} = f_j(x, v + \varphi_0(\hat{x}_1))$$

qui s'écrit

$$\begin{aligned} x_j \frac{\partial v}{\partial x_j} &= F_j(x,v) \\ &= F_j^0(x) + A_j(x)v + O(v^2) \ . \end{aligned}$$

Or ce système admet la solution formelle

$$\sum_{p=1}^{+\infty} \varphi_p(\hat{x}_1)x_1^p \ .$$

On en déduit que pour tout $j = 2,3,\dots,n$ et $p = 2,3,\dots$

$$x_j \frac{\partial \varphi_p}{\partial x_j} = A_j(\hat{x}_1)\varphi_p(\hat{x}_1) + Q_j(\hat{x}_1)$$

où Q_j est une fonction entièrement connue dès que l'on connaît les φ_q pour tout $q < p$.

D'après notre hypothèse de récurrence tous les φ_p convergent mais comme ce système est linéaire, il existe un polydisque D centré à l'origine de $\mathbb{C}^{n-1}$ tel que tous les $\varphi_p (p = o,1,\dots)$ convergent dans ce polydiquque.

Preuve du théorème 2.2. : La solution formelle du système de Pfaff (1) est donc de la forme

$$\varphi = \sum_{p=o}^{+\infty} \varphi_p(\hat{x}_1)x_1^p$$

avec $\varphi(0) = 0$ et pour tout $p, \varphi_p(\hat{x}_1)$ converge dans D.

Cette série formelle vérifie

$$x_1 \frac{d\varphi}{dx_1} = f_1(x,\varphi) = f_1(x_1,\hat{x}_1,\varphi)$$

et en utilisant une généralisation facile du lemme 1.1 du chap. III on conclut que la série φ est convergente ce qui prouve le théorème 2.2.

2.3. Un des p_j est égal à un $(p_j \geq 1)$.

Par exemple $p_1 = 1$.

THEOREME 2.3. Si $A_1 = \frac{\partial f_1}{\partial y}(0,0)$ n'a pas de valeur propre entière positive ou nulle alors le système de Pfaff (1) admet une solution φ holomorphe à l'origine et une seule telle que $\varphi(0) = 0$.

Preuve : D'après le théorème 1.7, il existe une solution formelle unique φ vérifiant $\varphi(0) = 0$ il suffit donc de prouver que cette solution converge

$$\varphi(x) = \sum_{p=o}^{+\infty} \varphi_p(\hat{x}_1)x_1^p$$

et les coefficients φ_p sont donnés par

$$\begin{cases} \hat{f}_1(\hat{x}_1,\varphi_o) = 0 \\ \left(\dfrac{\partial \hat{f}_1}{\partial y}(\hat{x}_1,\varphi_o) - pI\right)\varphi_p = h_p(\hat{x}_1) \quad p \geq 1 \,. \end{cases}$$

Avec nos hypothèses on déduit que tous les φ_p ont un domaine de convergence commun et la forme généralisée du lemme 1.1 du chap. III nous donne le résultat.

2.4. Pour tout $j = 1,2,\ldots,n$ $p_j > 1$.

THEOREME 2.4. S'il existe j et k $(j \neq k)$ tels que les matrices

$$A_j = \frac{\partial f_j}{\partial y}(0,0) \quad \text{et} \quad A_k = \frac{\partial f_k}{\partial y}(0,0)$$

soient inversibles alors le système de Pfaff (1) admet une solution φ et une seule holomorphe à l'origine telle que $\varphi(0,0) = 0$.

La preuve de ce théorème se fait en remarquant que le théorème 2.1 du chap. II reste valable avec paramètres. C'est-à-dire pour un système de la forme

$$x_1^{p_1} \frac{\partial y}{\partial x_1} = f^1(x_1,x_2,z,y)$$

$$x_2^{p_2} \frac{\partial y}{\partial x_2} = f^2(x_1,x_2,z,y)$$

où $z = (z_1,z_2\ldots z_p)$ est un paramètre.

Les seconds membres étant holomorphes au voisinage de $0 \in \mathbb{C}^2 \times \mathbb{C}^p \times \mathbb{C}^n$.

La méthode utilisée pour la démonstration reste alors la même avec cette petite complication supplémentaire. Voir également les théorèmes 4.1 et 4.2 du chapitre II.

§ 3. Etude asymptotique.

Notations :

- $x = (x_1,x_2,\ldots,x_n)$ $y = (y_1,y_2,\ldots,y_m)$;

- pour tout $j = 1,2,\ldots,n$, S_j désignera un secteur de sommet l'origine dan dans le plan de la variable x_j .

- pour tout $j = 1,2,\dots,m$, U_j désignera un disque centré à l'origine dans le plan de la variable y_j .

$S = S_1 \times S_2 \times \dots \times S_n$

$U = U_1 \times U_2 \times \dots \times U_m$

$\hat{x}_k = (x_1, x_2, \dots, x_{k-1}, x_{k+1}, \dots, x_n)$ $k = 1,2,\dots,n$

$\hat{S}_k = S_1 \times S_2 \times \dots \times S_{k-1} \times S_{k+1} \times \dots \times S_n$ $k = 1,2,\dots,n$.

Nous allons définir par <u>récurrence une classe de fonctions notée</u> $\mathcal{G}(S \times U)$.

Si $n = 1$ une fonction f définie sur $S \times U$ $(S = S_1)$ appartient à la classe $\mathcal{G}(S \times U)$ si et seulement si :

1) f est holomorphe sur $S \times U$

2) $f \underset{u.U}{\overset{S_1}{\sim}} \sum_{p=0}^{+\infty} f_p(y) x_1^p$

où pour tout p , f_p est holomorphe sur U .

Si $n > 1$ une fonction f définie sur $S \times U$ appartient à la classe $\mathcal{G}(S \times U)$ si et seulement si :

1) f est holomorphe sur $S \times U$

2) pour tout $k = 1,2,\dots,n$;

$$f \underset{u.\hat{S}_k \times U}{\overset{S_k}{\sim}} \sum_{p=0}^{+\infty} f_p^{(k)}(\hat{x}_k, y) x_k^p$$

$$\frac{\partial f}{\partial x_j} \underset{u.\hat{S}_k \times U}{\overset{S_k}{\sim}} \sum_{p=0}^{+\infty} \frac{\partial f_p^{(k)}}{\partial x_j} (\hat{x}_k, y)\, x_k^p$$

pour tout $j \in \{1,2,\dots,n\}$ et $j \neq k$

où pour tout p

$$f_p^{(k)} \in \mathcal{G}(\hat{S}_k \times U)$$

$$\frac{\partial f_p^k}{\partial x_j} \in \mathcal{G}(\hat{S}_k \times U) \quad (j = 1,2\dots n \;,\; j \neq k) .$$

Dans ce chapitre nous nous proposons d'étudier les systèmes de Pfaff complètement intégrables de la forme

(E) $$dy = \sum_{j=1}^{n} \frac{f_j(x,y)}{x_j^{p_j}} dx_j$$

où pour tout $j = 1,2,\dots,n$,

$f_j \in (\mathcal{G}(S \times U))^m$ et où pour tout j , p_j est un entier positif ou nul.

On suppose de plus que lorsque $p_j > 0$ on a $f_j(0,0) = 0$.

§ 3.1. Un des entiers p_j est nul.

Supposons par exemple que $p_1 = 0$.

THEOREME 3.1. Si le système de Pfaff

$(\hat{E}_1)$ $$dy = \sum_{j=2}^{n} \frac{\hat{f}_j(\hat{x}_1,y)}{x_j^{p_j}} dx_j$$

admet une solution $\varphi_o(\hat{x}_1)$ holomorphe dans $\hat{S}_1$ telle que

$$\varphi_o(\hat{x}_1) \overset{\hat{S}_1}{\sim} \sum_{|p|=o}^{+\infty} \tilde{\varphi}_{o,p}\, \hat{x}_1^p$$

$$\frac{\partial \varphi_o}{\partial x_j}(\hat{x}_1) \overset{\hat{S}_1}{\sim} \sum_{|p|=o}^{+\infty} \tilde{\varphi}_{o,p} \frac{\partial(\hat{x}_1^p)}{\partial x_j}$$

pour $j = 2,3,\dots,n$.

Alors le système de Pfaff (E) admet une solution φ et une seule telle que

$$\varphi(x) \underset{u.\hat{S}_1}{\overset{S_1}{\sim}} \sum_{p=o}^{+\infty} \varphi_p(\hat{x}_1) x_1^p$$

et pour tout

$$\varphi_p(\hat{x}_1) \overset{\hat{S}_1}{\sim} \sum_{|q|=o}^{+\infty} \tilde{\varphi}_{p,q}(\hat{x}_1)^q .$$

Démonstration : Considérons l'équation différentielle ordinaire

$$\frac{dy}{dx_1} = f_1(x_1, \hat{x}_1, y)$$

dépendant du paramètre $\hat{x}_1$.

Cette équation admet une solution $\varphi(x_1, \hat{x}_1)$ et une seule holomorphe dans $S = S_1 \times \hat{S}_1$ vérifiant la condition initiale

$$\varphi(0, \hat{x}_1) = \varphi_o(\hat{x}_1)$$

de plus

$$\varphi(x_1, \hat{x}_1) \underset{u.S_1}{\overset{S_1}{\sim}} \sum_{p=o}^{+\infty} \varphi_p(\hat{x}_1) x_1^p$$

où pour tout

$$\varphi_p(\hat{x}_1) \overset{\hat{S}_1}{\sim} \sum_{|q|=o}^{+\infty} \widetilde{\varphi}_{p,q}(\hat{x}_1)^q .$$

Il reste simplement à voir que $\varphi(x_1, \hat{x}_1)$ vérifie le système $(\hat{E}_1)$.

Pour cela considérons pour tout $j = 2,3,\ldots,n$

$$v_j = x_j^{p_j} \frac{\partial \varphi}{\partial x_j} - f_j(x, \varphi) .$$

En utilisant la condition de complète intégrabilité comme nous l'avons déjà fait plusieurs fois on constate que pour tout $j = 2,3,\ldots,n$, v_j est une solution du système linéaire

$$\frac{dv}{dx_1} = \frac{\partial f_1}{\partial y} (x_1, \hat{x}_1, \varphi(x_1, \hat{x}_1))v$$

Or

$$v_j(0, \hat{x}_1) = x_j^{p_j} \frac{\partial \varphi_o}{\partial x_j} - \hat{f}_j(\hat{x}_1, \varphi_o) = 0$$

donc v_j est la solution du système linéaire ci-dessus qui prend la valeur zéro à l'origine on a donc $v_j = 0$ pour tout $j = 2,3,\ldots,n$ ce qui prouve le théorème 3.1.

§ 3.2. Pour tout $j = 1,2,\dots,n$, $p_j = 1$.

THEOREME 3.2. Si le système de Pfaff (E) admet une solution formelle $\varphi \in (\mathbb{C}[[x]])^m$ et si on pose pour tout $k = 1,2,\dots,n$

$$\varphi = \sum_{p=0}^{+\infty} \varphi_p(\hat{x}_k) x_k^p$$

où pour tout p , $\varphi_p \in (\mathbb{C}[[\hat{x}_k]])^m$.

Alors il existe une solution $y = \Phi_k$ de (E) telle que

$$\Phi_k \underset{u.\hat{S}_k}{\overset{S_k}{\sim}} \sum_{p=0}^{+\infty} \tilde{\varphi}_p(\hat{x}_k) x_k^p$$

où pour tout p , $\tilde{\varphi}_p$ est holomorphe dans $\hat{S}_k$ et

$$\tilde{\varphi}_p(\hat{x}_k) \overset{\hat{S}_k}{\sim} \varphi_p(\hat{x}_k) .$$

Preuve : Ce théorème a été démontré dans le cas $n = 2$ dans le chapitre III (théorème 3.1).

On va en faire une démonstration par récurrence sur le nombre des variables.

Faisons l'étude pour $k = 1$.

Le système de Pfaff

$$(\hat{E}_1) \qquad x_j \frac{\partial y}{\partial x_j} = f_j(x,y) \qquad j = 2,3,\dots,n$$

est complètement intégrable et admet par hypothèse une solution formelle de la forme

$$y = \sum_{p=0}^{+\infty} \varphi_p(\hat{x}_1) x_1^p$$

où pour tout p , $\varphi_p \in (\mathbb{C}[[\hat{x}_1]])^m$.

En utilisant l'hypothèse de récurrence et en procédant comme dans la démonstration du théorème 3.1 du chapitre III, on montre que pour tout p , il existe une fonction $\tilde{\varphi}_p(\hat{x}_1)$ holomorphe dans $\hat{S}_1$ telle que :

1°) $\tilde{\varphi}_p(\hat{x}_1) \overset{\hat{S}_1}{\sim} \varphi_p(\hat{x}_1)$

2°) La série formelle $\sum_{p=0}^{+\infty} \tilde{\varphi}_p(\hat{x}_1)x_1^p$ soit une solution formelle en x_1 du système $(\hat{E}_1)$.

Montrons maintenant que

$$\tilde{\varphi} = \sum_{p=0}^{+\infty} \tilde{\varphi}_p(\hat{x}_1)x_1^p$$

est encore une solution formelle de

$$(1) \qquad x_1 \frac{\partial y}{\partial x_1} = f_1(x_1,\hat{x}_1,y) .$$

Pour cela considérons

$$\psi = x_1 \frac{\partial \tilde{\varphi}}{\partial x_1} - f_1(x_1,\hat{x}_1,\tilde{\varphi})$$

$$= \sum_{p=0}^{+\infty} \psi_p(\hat{x}_1)x_1^p$$

où pour tout p, $\psi_p(\hat{x}_1)$ est holomorphe dans $\hat{S}_1$.

Comme $\varphi = \sum_{p=0}^{+\infty} \varphi_p(\hat{x}_1)x_1^p$ est une solution formelle de (1) on a pour tout $p \geq 0$

$$\psi_o(\hat{x}_1) \overset{\hat{S}_1}{\sim} 0 .$$

Toujours de la même manière la condition de complète intégrabilité entraîne que pour tout $j = 2,3,\ldots,n$ on a formellement

$$x_j \frac{\partial \psi}{\partial x_j} = \frac{\partial f_j}{\partial y}(x,\tilde{\varphi})\psi$$

en tant que série formelle en x_1.

L'identification des deux membres considérés comme séries formelles en x_1, nous montre que chaque $\psi_p(\hat{x}_1)$ est solution d'un système de Pfaff à singularités régulières sur $x_2 = x_3 = \ldots\ x_n = 0$. Chaque ψ_p étant déterminé par un système de Pfaff connu dès que l'on connaît ψ_q pour tout $q<p$. Mais ceci et le fait que $\psi_p(\hat{x}_1) \overset{\hat{S}_1}{\sim} 0$ entraîne que l'on a pour tout p

$$\psi_p(\hat{x}_1) = 0 .$$

Donc $\psi = 0$ c'est-à-dire que

$$x_1 \frac{\partial \tilde{\varphi}}{\partial x_1} = f_1(x, \tilde{\varphi}) .$$

Or il existe une solution Φ holomorphe sur S de l'équation

$$x_1 \frac{\partial y}{\partial x_1} = f_1(x,y)$$

vérifiant

$$\Phi \underset{u.\hat{S}_1}{\overset{S_1}{\sim}} \tilde{\varphi} = \sum_{p=0}^{+\infty} \tilde{\varphi}_p(\hat{x}_1) x_1^p .$$

Il reste à montrer que Φ vérifie également

$$x_j \frac{\partial \Phi}{\partial x_j} = f_j(x,\Phi) \quad \text{pour} \quad j = 2,3,\dots,n ;$$

pour cela posons

$$\psi_j = x_j \frac{\partial \Phi}{\partial x_j} - f_j(x,\Phi) .$$

Par construction de $\tilde{\varphi}$, nous avons pour tout $j = 2,3,\dots,n$;

$$\psi_j \underset{u.\hat{S}_1}{\overset{S_1}{\sim}} 0$$

et toujours de la même manière en utilisant la condition de complète intégrabilité

$$x_1 \frac{\partial \psi_j}{\partial x_1} = \frac{\partial f_1}{\partial y}(x,\Phi)\psi_j$$

pour tout $j = 2,3,\dots n$.

Comme $\psi_j \underset{u.\hat{S}_1}{\overset{S_1}{\sim}} 0$ nous avons $\psi_j = 0$. Ce qui prouve le théorème.

§ 3.3. <u>Il existe</u> $j_o \in \{1,2,\dots,n\}$ <u>tel que</u> $p_{j_o} = 1$. On peut supposer que $j_o = 1$ donc $p_1 = 1$.

THEOREME 3.3. Si $A_1 = \frac{\partial f_1}{\partial y}(0,0)$ n'a pas de valeur propre entière positive ou nulle alors le système de Pfaff (E) admet une solution φ holomorphe dans S telle que

$$\varphi \underset{u.\hat{S}_1}{\overset{S_1}{\sim}} \sum_{p=0}^{+\infty} \varphi_p(\hat{x}_1)x_1^p$$

où pour tout p φ_p est holomorphe dans $\hat{S}_1$ et $\varphi_p \overset{\hat{S}_1}{\sim} \sum_{|q|=0}^{+\infty} \varphi_{p,q}(\hat{x}_1)^q$.

Preuve : La condition sur A_1 entraîne l'existence d'une solution formelle de la forme

$$\sum_{p=0}^{+\infty} \varphi_p(\hat{x}_1)x_1^p$$

de l'équation

(1) $$x_1 \frac{\partial y}{\partial x_1} = f_1(x_1,\hat{x}_1,y)$$

où pour tout p , φ_p est holomorphe dans $\hat{S}_1$ et admet un développement asymptotique

$$\varphi_p(\hat{x}_1) \overset{\hat{S}_1}{\sim} \sum_{|q|=0}^{+\infty} \varphi_{p,q}(\hat{x}_1)^q .$$

D'après le lemme 1.4 du chapitre III il existe une solution φ de l'équation (1) holomorphe dans $S = S_1 \times \hat{S}_1$ telle que

$$\varphi \underset{u.\hat{S}_1}{\overset{S_1}{\sim}} \sum_{p=0}^{+\infty} \varphi_p(\hat{x}_1)x_1^p$$

et

$$\frac{\partial \varphi}{\partial x_j} \underset{u.\hat{S}_1}{\overset{S_1}{\sim}} \sum_{p=0}^{+\infty} \frac{\partial \varphi_p}{\partial x_j}(\hat{x}_1)x_1^p$$

pour tout $j = 2,3,\ldots,n$.

Pour tout $j \in \{2,3,\ldots,n\}$ considérons

$$v_j = x_j^{p_j} \frac{\partial \varphi}{\partial x_j} - f_j(x,\varphi) \underset{u.\hat{S}_1}{\overset{S_1}{\sim}} \sum_{p=0}^{+\infty} \psi_{j,p}(\hat{x}_1)x_1^p .$$

En utilisant la condition de complète intégrabilité on a toujours

$$x_1 \frac{\partial v_j}{\partial x_1} = \frac{\partial f_1}{\partial y}(x,\varphi)vj$$

ce qui entraîne par identification que pour tout j et tout p

$$\psi_{j,p}(\hat{x}_1) = 0$$

c'est-à-dire que

$$v_j \underset{u.\hat{S}_1}{\overset{S_1}{\sim}} 0 .$$

Comme l'équation (1) est à singularité régulière on a pour tout $j = 2,3,\dots,n$,

$$v_j = 0 .$$

Ce qui prouve le théorème.

§ 3.4. Pour tout $j \in \{1,2,\dots,n\}$ $p_j > 1$.

THEOREME 3.4. Si $A_1 = \frac{\partial f_1}{\partial y}(0,0)$ est inversible et si l'ouverture du secteur S_1 est supérieure à π/p_1 alors (E) admet une solution $y = \varphi$ holomorphe dans S telle que pour tout $k \in \{1,2,\dots,n\}$

$$\varphi \underset{u.\hat{S}_k}{\overset{S_k}{\sim}} \sum_{p=o}^{+\infty} \varphi_p^{(k)}(\hat{x}_k)x_k^p$$

ou pour tout p

$$\varphi_p^{(k)}(\hat{x}_k) \overset{\hat{S}_k}{\sim} \sum_{|q|=o}^{+\infty} \varphi_{p,q}^{(k)}(\hat{x}_k)^q .$$

La démonstration se fait de la même manière que celle du théorème 3.3.

§ 3.5. Cas général.

Considérons le système de Pfaff complètement intégrable

(E)
$$dy = \sum_{j=1}^{n} \frac{f_j(x,y)}{x_j^{p_j}} dx_j$$

où

1) pour tout $j \in \{1,2,\dots,n\}$

$$f_j \underset{u.U}{\overset{S}{\sim}} \sum_{|q|=0}^{+\infty} f_{j,q}^{(y)} x^q$$

et pour tout $k \in \{1,2,\dots,n\}$

$$\frac{\partial f_j}{\partial x_k} \underset{u.U}{\overset{S}{\sim}} \sum_{|q|=0}^{+\infty} f_{j,q}(y) \frac{\partial (x)^q}{\partial x_k} .$$

2) pour tout j, tel que $p_j > 0$ la matrice $A_j = \frac{\partial f_j}{\partial y}(0,0)$ est inversible et pour les j tel que $p_j = 1$ la matrice A_j n'a pas de valeurs propres imaginaires pures.

3) pour tout j, tel que $p_j > 0$

$$f_j(0,0) = 0 .$$

THEOREME 3.5. Le système de Pfaff (E) admet une solution formelle $\hat{\varphi}$ et il existe une solution φ de (E) holomorphe dans S et telle que

$$\varphi \overset{S}{\sim} \hat{\varphi} .$$

Remarque 3.6. Dans tous les énoncés que nous avons donnés dans ce paragraphe il est parfois nécessaire de restreindre le rayon du secteur donné initialement. Mises à part les complications d'écriture, la démonstration se fait comme dans le cas de deux variables, voir les § 3 des chapitres II et III.

§ 4. Applications aux systèmes de Pfaff linéaires.

Les résultats que l'on obtient sont tout à fait analogues à ceux qui ont été donnés dans le cas de deux variables dans chap. II § 5 et chap. III § 4.

BIBLIOGRAPHIE

[1] ARTIN M. On the solutions of analytic equations, Inventiones Math., 5(1968) 277-291.

[2] HUKUHARA M. Sur les points singuliers des équations différentielles linéaires, II, J. Fac. Sci. Hokkaido Univ., 5(1937) 157-166.

[3] HUKUHARA M. Sur les points singuliers des équations différentielles linéaires III, Mem. Fac. Sci. Kyushu Univ., 2(1942) 125-137.

[4] HUKUHARA M. and IWANO M. Etude de la convergence des solutions formelles d'un système différentiel ordinaire linéaire, Funkcialaj Ekvacioj 2(1959) 1-18.

[5] HARRIS W.A.Jr. Holomorphic solutions of non linear differential equations at singular points, Advances in Differential and Integral Equations, SIAM, Studies in Applied Math., N° 5 (1969) 184-187.

[6] HARRIS W.A.Jr., SIBUYA Y. and WEINBERG L. Holomorphic solutions of linear differential systems at singular points, Arch. Rational Mech. Anal., 35 (1969) 245-248.

[7] JURKAT W.B. Meromorphe Differentialgleichungen, Lecture Notes, Ulm, 1977.

[8] MALGRANGE B. Sur les points singuliers des équations différentielles, l'Enseignement mathématique, 20 (1974) 147-176.

[9] MALMQUIST J. Sur l'étude analytique des solutions d'un système des équations différentielles dans le voisinage d'un point singulier d'indétermination, I,II,III, Acta Math. 73 (1940) 87-129, 74((1941) 1-64, 109-128.

[10] SIBUYA Y. Simplification of a system of linear ordinary differential equations about a singular point, Funkcialaj Ekvacioj, 4(1962) 29-56.

[11] SIBUYA Y. Perturbation of linear ordinary differential equations at irregular singular points, ibid., 11(1968) 235-246.

[12] SIBUYA Y. Perturbation at an irregular singular point, Proc. of Japan-US Seminar on Ordinary Differential and Functional Equations, Kyoto, Sept. 6-11, 1971, Lecture Notes in Math., N° 243, 148-168, Springer, 1971.

[13] TURRITTIN H.L. Convergence solutions of ordinary linear homogeneous differential equations in the neighborhood of an irregular singular point, Acta Math., 93 (1955) 27-66.

[14] WASOW W. Asymptotic Expansions for Ordinary Differential Equations, John Wiley, 1976 (revised).

A PROPOS DU THÉORÈME DE BOREL-RITT A PLUSIEURS VARIABLES

(Appendice à l'article "Etude de certains systèmes de Pfaff avec singularités" de R. GÉRARD et Y. SIBUYA)

par J. P. RAMIS

Nous renvoyons pour les notations et définitions à l'article de GÉRARD et SIBUYA.

THÉORÈME 1. (Borel-Ritt à plusieurs variables). - Soit $\varphi = \sum_{|p|=0}^{+\infty} a_p x^p \in \mathbb{C}[[x_1, \dots, x_n]]$. Soit $S = S_1 \times \dots \times S_n$ un secteur strict ($S_i = \{x_i / \theta_{1i} < \arg x_i < \theta_{2i}$ et $0 < |x_i| < r_i\}$; avec $0 < \theta_{2i} - \theta_{1i} < 2\pi$; $i = 1, \dots, n$). Alors il existe une fonction Φ, holomorphe dans S, telle que :

(i)
$$\Phi(x) \overset{S}{\sim} \sum_{|p|=0}^{+\infty} a_p x^p = \varphi ,$$

et

(ii) Pour tout opérateur différentiel d'ordre fini D à coefficients constants, on a :

$$D\Phi(x) \overset{S}{\sim} D\varphi = \sum_{|p|=0}^{+\infty} a_p Dx^p .$$

Ce Théorème améliore le Corollaire 2.2.3 du Théorème 2.2.2 de GÉRARD-SIBUYA [1] (et fournit une autre démonstration du Théorème 2.2.2 [1]) . Cette amélioration devrait être fondamentale pour l'extension à plusieurs variables des résultats de MALGRANGE [2] (puisqu'il faut passer par les fonctions C^∞) ; Cf. RAMIS [4] .

<u>Notations</u> : Si X est un ouvert de $\mathbb{C}^n$ et Y un sous-ensemble analytique complexe de X , on note $\mathcal{O}_{\widehat{X|Y}}$ le complété formel du faisceau structural $\mathcal{O}_X$ le long de Y : $\mathcal{O}_{\widehat{X|Y}} = \varprojlim_k \mathcal{O}_X / I_Y^k$ (limite indépendante de I_Y si $V(I_Y) = Y$). Si $0 \in X$ et si F est un faisceau sur X , on désigne par

F_o la fibre de F en 0 .

La démonstration du Théorème 1 utilise (au choix) l'une des deux Propositions :

PROPOSITION 2. - Soient $Y_1, \dots, Y_n$ des sous-variétés analytiques complexes (ou plus généralement des sous-espaces analytiques complexes) d'un voisinage ouvert X de 0 dans $\mathbb{C}^n$. On suppose que $Y_1 \cap \dots \cap Y_n = \{0\}$. Alors l'application naturelle

$$(\mathcal{O}_{X}\hat{|}Y_1)_o \oplus \dots \oplus (\mathcal{O}_{X}\hat{|}Y_n)_o \longrightarrow (\mathcal{O}_{X}\hat{|}\{0\})_o = \mathbb{C}[[x_1, \dots, x_n]]$$

$$(f_i)_{i=1,\dots,n} \longmapsto \sum_{i=1,\dots,n} (-1)^i f_i$$

est surjective.

Soit $Y_i = \{x_i = 0\} \cap X$ $(i = 1, \dots, n)$; on a évidemment $Y_1 \cap \dots \cap Y_n = \{0\}$.

PROPOSITION 3.-L'application naturelle $(\mathbb{C}[x_2, \dots, x_n])[[x_1]] \oplus \dots$ $\dots \oplus (\mathbb{C}[x_1, \dots, x_{n-1}])[[x_n]] \longrightarrow \mathbb{C}[[x_1, \dots, x_n]]$ est surjective.

La Proposition 2 est "bien connue" ; elle s'établit par récurrence à partir de la Proposition 4.1 de RAMIS [3]. La démonstration de la Proposition 3 est élémentaire, nous l'écrirons pour $n = 2$, laissant le cas général au lecteur :

Soit $\varphi = \Sigma a_{p_1 p_2} x_1^{p_1} x_2^{p_2}$. On pose $f_1 = \sum_{p_1 \geq p_2} a_{p_1 p_2} x_1^{p_1} x_2^{p_2}$ et $f_2 = \sum_{p_1 < p_2} a_{p_1 p_2} x_1^{p_1} x_2^{p_2}$. On peut écrire de façon évidente f_1 comme élément de $(\mathbb{C}[x_2])[[x_1]]$ et f_2 comme élément de $(\mathbb{C}[x_1])[[x_2]]$, ce qui répond à la question.

Nous allons maintenant établir pour chacun des f_i de la Proposition 2 (ou 3) un Théorème de Borel-Ritt en la variable x_i (pour le secteur propre S_i) paramétré par un polydisque ouvert P_i de $\mathbb{C}^{n-1}$ (espace des $(x_1, \ldots, \hat{x}_i, \ldots, x_n))$, avec dérivation par rapport à l'ensemble des variables. Comme $S_1 \times \ldots \times S_n \subset S_i \times P_i$ $(i = 1, \ldots, n)$, il en résultera que le Théorème 1 est vrai pour les f_i , donc pour φ .

Soit $f_n = \sum_k a_k(x_1, \ldots, x_{n-1})\, x_n^k$, avec $a_i \in O(p)$ et borné sur P (pour un polydisque ouvert P de $\mathbb{C}^{n-1}$ indépendant de k). Tout élément de $(\mathcal{O}_{\widehat{X|Y_n}})_o$ (resp. $(\mathbb{C}[X_1, \ldots, X_{n-1}])[[X_n]]$) s'écrit ainsi pour P assez petit (resp. pour tout P).

THÉORÈME 4. - Soit f_n comme ci-dessus :

(i) Soit S_n un secteur strict de $\mathbb{C}$. Alors il existe $\Phi \overset{S_n}{\sim} \sum_k a_k x_n^k$ uniformément sur P' , pour tout polydisque ouvert $P' \subset\subset P$. $(\Phi \in \mathcal{O}(P \times S_n))$.

(ii) Soit $P' \subset P$. Soit $\Phi \overset{S_n}{\sim} \sum_k a_k x_n^k$ uniformément sur P' $(\Phi \in \mathcal{O}(P \times S_n))$. Soient D , D' , D'' des opérateurs différentiels d'ordre fini à coefficients constants respectivement en $(\partial/\partial x_1, \ldots, \partial/\partial x_n)$, $(\partial/\partial x_1, \ldots, \partial/\partial x_{n-1})$, $(\partial/\partial x_n)$. Alors

(a) $D'\Phi \overset{S_n}{\sim} \sum_k D' a_k x_n^k$ uniformément sur P'' , pour tout $P'' \subset\subset P'$.

(b) $D''\Phi \overset{S_n}{\sim} \sum_k a_k D'' x_n^k$ uniformément sur P'' , pour tout $P'' \subset\subset P'$.

(c) $D\Phi \overset{S_n}{\sim} \sum_k D a_k x_n^k$ uniformément sur P'' , pour tout $P'' \subset\subset P'$.

L'uniformité en $(x_1, \ldots, x_{n-1})$ est pour un sous-secteur strict arbitraire S_n' de S_n fixé.

L'assertion (i) est une généralisation triviale de WASOW [5], Théorème 9.6.

L'assertion (ii)(c) est une conséquence immédiate de (ii)(a) et (ii)(b), puisque D peut s'écrire $D'D''$. L'assertion (ii)(a) est une généralisation triviale de WASOW [5], Théorème 9.4. Enfin l'assertion (ii)(b) est une généralisation triviale de WASOW [5], Théorème 8.8.

BIBLIOGRAPHIE

[1] GÉRARD R., SIBUYA Y. : Etude de certains systèmes de Pfaff avec singularités. Dans ce volume.

[2] MALGRANGE B. : Remarques sur les équations différentielles à points singuliers irréguliers. Dans ce volume.

[3] RAMIS J. P. : Variations sur le thème "GAGA". Séminaire P. LELONG 76-77 (Lecture Notes ; Springer).

[4] RAMIS J. P. : Appendice I à [3].

[5] WASOW W. : Asymptotic expansions for ordinary differential equations (J. Wiley. Interscience publishers, 1965).

SUR LA MONODROMIE DES SYSTEMES DE PFAFF DU TYPE DE FUCHS SUR $\mathbb{P}_m(\mathbb{C})$

par

B. KLARÈS

§ 0. - INTRODUCTION.

Le problème de Riemann a conduit L. Schlesinger à étudier les systèmes de Fuchs (e) sur $\mathbb{P}_1(\mathbb{C})$ dont "la monodromie" est indépendante des points singuliers de (e) [1]. Les matrices résidus associées à (e) sont alors des fonctions des points singuliers qui satisfont à un système d'équations différentielles appelées équations de Schlesinger. Ces équations ont de plus la propriété remarquable d'être à points critiques fixes [1] et [2].

R. Gérard ayant généralisé la théorie de Fuchs à une variété analytique complexe [3] et étudié le problème de Riemann-Hilbert correspondant [4], il devenait naturel de rechercher les systèmes de Fuchs sur une variété analytique complexe dont la monodromie était indépendante des singularités.

Nous allons résoudre ce problème dans le cas où la variété considérée est $\mathbb{P}_2(\mathbb{C})$. L'étude faite ci-après se généralise immédiatement à $\mathbb{P}_m(\mathbb{C})$ $m \geq 2$ et les résultats obtenus sont identiques.

Plus précisément, soient $\mathcal{U}$ un ouvert simplement connexe de $\mathbb{C}^r$, $(M,\pi,\mathcal{U})$ une fibration analytique triviale, de fibre isomorphe à $\mathbb{P}_2(\mathbb{C})$, S une hypersurface analytique de M réunion de n composantes irréductibles $S_1, S_2, \ , S_n$ d'équations homogènes $F_i(u,X,Y,Z) = 0$ $i = 1,2, \ ,n$ et telle que $(S,\pi/_S,\mathcal{U})$ soit triviale.

Si $d_v f = f(\sum_{i=1}^{n} A_i(u) \frac{d_v F_i}{F_i})$ (e) est un système de Fuchs associé, avec $A_i(u)$ application matricielle $p \times p$, définie sur $\mathcal{U}$ et $d_v F_i$ la différentielle verticale dans $\mathcal{U} \times (\mathbb{C}^3 - \{0\})$, on montre qu'une condition nécessaire et suffisante pour qu'il existe une matrice fondamentale Φ de (e) dont la monodromie associée soit indépendante de u dans $\mathcal{U}$, est que les applications matricielles $A_i(u)$ vérifient les équations différentielles (E) suivantes :

$$dA_i(u) = \tilde{\varepsilon}_i \qquad i = 1,2,\ldots,n$$

où $\tilde{\varepsilon}_i$ est une forme sur $\mathcal{U}$ définie dans le § 2.

La connaissance de ce théorème permet de montrer que s'il existe une droite projective (D) telle que $\mathcal{U} \times (D)$ soit transverse à S, la propriété ci-dessus est vraie, si et seulement si elle est vérifiée pour le système (e') restriction de (e) à $\mathcal{U} \times (D)$.

On peut aussi montrer que le système (E) possède quelques propriétés remarquables, par exemple d'être complètement intégrable et à points critiques fixes.

On donne enfin une application du théorème ci-dessus aux systèmes de Fuchs associés aux fonctions hypergéométriques F_1 sur $\mathbb{P}_2(\mathbb{C})$, qui permet de déterminer explicitement ceux qui possèdent une matrice fondamentale dont la monodromie associée est indépendante de la position des singularités.

§ 1. - SYSTEME DE FUCHS SUR M .

1) Notations.

Soient :

- $\mathcal{U}$ un domaine de C^r , $(M,\pi,\mathcal{U})$ une fibration analytique triviale de fibre isomorphe à $\mathbb{P}_2(C)$, φ l'isomorphisme de M sur $\mathcal{U}\times\mathbb{P}_2(C)$, θ la surjection canonique de $\mathcal{U}\times(C^3-\{0\})$ sur $\mathcal{U}\times\mathbb{P}_2(C)$ qui à (u,X,Y,Z) associe le point correspondant de $\mathcal{U}\times\mathbb{P}_2(C)$.

- S une hypersurface analytique réunion de n composantes irréductibles $S_1,\dots,S_n$ d'équations homogènes $F_i(u,X,Y,Z) = 0$ $i = 1,2,\dots,n$ où les $F_i(u,X,Y,Z)$ sont des polynômes homogènes de degré k_i à coefficients holomorphes en u . Nous supposerons pour plus de simplicité que :

a) le coefficient de X^{k_i} est égal à 1 pour tous les F_i $i = 1,2,\dots,n$.

b) $F_i|_{\theta^{-1}(S_j)} = R_j^i$ $j \neq i$ est holomorphe par rapport à u dans $\mathcal{U}$.

c) $(S,\pi/_S,\mathcal{U})$ est triviale. s sera la fibre type correspondante dans $\mathbb{P}_2(C)$ et $s_1, ,s_n$ les composantes irréductibles associées.

On note :

- $x = \frac{X}{Z}$ $y = \frac{Y}{Z}$ les coordonées locales habituelles dans la carte O_1 de $\mathbb{P}_2(C)$ correspondant à $C^3-\{(X,Y,Z)\,|Z = 0\}$.

- $\mathbb{P}_2(u) = \pi^{-1}(u)$, $S_i(u) = S_i\cap\pi^{-1}(u)$, $S(u) = S\cap\pi^{-1}(u)$

$\mathbb{P}_2^*(u) = \mathbb{P}_2(u) - S(u)$

- $\pi_1(M-S)$, $\pi_1(\mathbb{P}_2(C)-s)$, $\pi_1(\mathbb{P}_2^*(u))$ les groupes fondamentaux de $M-S$, $\mathbb{P}_2(C)-s$ et $\mathbb{P}_2^*(u)$.

- $\mathcal{R}(M-S)$, $\mathcal{R}(\mathbb{P}_2(C)-s)$, $\mathcal{R}(\mathbb{P}_2^*(u))$ les revêtements universels de $M-S$, $\mathbb{P}_2(C)-s$, $\mathbb{P}_2^*(u)$. ψ sera la projection de $\mathcal{R}(M-S)$ sur $M-S$ et ψ_u celle de $\mathcal{R}(\mathbb{P}_2^*(u))$ sur $\mathbb{P}_2^*(u)$. Si g est une application différentiable de M dans C , d_hg et d_vg sont respectivement les différentielles horizontales et verticales de g sur M.

2) Remarques 1-1.

D'après les hypothèses faites ci-dessus, φ induit des isomorphismes :

φ_u de $\mathbb{P}_2^*(u)$ sur $\mathbb{P}_2(\mathbb{C})-s$, quel que soit u dans $\mathcal{U}$

$\tilde{\varphi}$ de $\mathbb{R}(M-S)$ sur $\mathcal{U}\times\mathbb{R}(\mathbb{P}_2(\mathbb{C})-s)$

φ_u^* de $\pi_1(\mathbb{P}_2^*(u))$ sur $\pi_1(\mathbb{P}_2(\mathbb{C})-s)$, quel que soit u dans $\mathcal{U}$

$\tilde{\varphi}_u$ de $\mathbb{R}(\mathbb{P}_2^*(u))$ sur $\mathbb{R}(\mathbb{P}_2(\mathbb{C})-s)$, quel que soit u dans $\mathcal{U}$.

3) Formes de Fuchs relatives sur M.

On appelle $\Omega_V^{p\times p}(M,S)$ la classe des 1-formes différentielles matricielles (p,p) sur M complètement intégrables, verticales, qui sont du type de Fuchs en restriction à chaque fibre verticale $\mathbb{P}_2(u)$, l'ensemble singulier associé étant $S(u)$. D'après [3] si $\omega\in\Omega_V^{p\times p}(M,S)$ il existe n applications matricielles $A_i(u)$ de $\mathcal{U}$ dans $\mathcal{M}(p,\mathbb{C})$ (espace vectoriel des matrices carrées $p\times p$ à coefficients dans $\mathbb{C}$) telles que

1) $$(\varphi^{-1}\circ\theta)^*(\omega) = \sum_{i=1}^{n} A_i(u)\,\frac{d_V F_i(u,X,Y,Z)}{F_i(u,X,Y,Z)}$$

2) $$\sum_{k=1}^{n} k_i . A_i(u) = 0 .$$

La condition de complète intégrabilité s'écrit $\omega\wedge\omega = 0$.
La classe des systèmes de Pfaff de la forme $d_V f = f.\omega(e)$ où $\omega\in\Omega_V^{p\times p}(M,S)$ et où f est un vecteur ligne $(f_1,\dots,f_p)$ sera notée $\mathfrak{F}_V^{p\times p}(M,S)$ et la restriction de (e) à $\mathbb{P}_2^*(u)$ sera notée $(e)_u$. On suppose dans la suite les $A_i(u)$ holomorphes sur $\mathcal{U}$, $i=1,2,\ ,n$ et ayant des valeurs propres ne différant pas 2 à 2 d'un entier. Soit Φ une matrice fondamentale de (e), c'est-à-dire une application de $\mathbb{R}(M-S)$ dans $\mathcal{G}\ell(p,\mathbb{C})$, différentiable verticalement et telle que quel que soit u dans $\mathcal{U}$ $\Phi_u = \Phi|_{\psi^{-1}(\mathbb{P}_2^*(u))}$ soit une matrice fondamentale de $(e)_u$.
Remarquons que puisque $A_i(u)$ est holomorphe par rapport à u, Φ est elle aussi holomorphe par rapport à u (théorème de Cauchy avec paramètre).

Considérons un point $m_i \in S_i - \bigcup_{\substack{j=1 \\ j \neq i}}^{n} S_j$. Il existe un voisinage V_i de m_i dans M tel que $V_i \cap S_j = \emptyset$ $\forall j \neq i$. On peut supposer de plus que V_i est un voisinage de coordonnées locales (u, z_i, t_i) contenu dans $\mathcal{U} \times \theta_1$ par exemple et tel que :

1) $z_i = F_i(u,x,y,1)|_{V_i}$

2) m_i corresponde à $u = u_o$, $z_i = 0$, $t_i = 0$.

Soient C une composante connexe de $\psi^{-1}(V_i - S_i)$ dans $\mathcal{R}(M - S)$ et (u, Z_i, T_i) les points de C qui se projettent en (u, z_i, t_i) dans V_i alors :

4) PROPOSITION 1-2.- <u>Il existe une application matricielle holomorphe</u> $R_i(u)$ <u>de</u> $\pi(V_i)$ <u>dans</u> $\mathcal{M}(p, \mathbb{C})$ <u>et une application matricielle</u> Φ_i <u>holomorphe par rapport à</u> u <u>et holomorphe inversible par rapport à</u> z_i, t_i <u>de</u> V_i <u>dans</u> $\mathcal{Gl}(p, \mathbb{C})$ <u>telles que</u> :

$$\Phi|_C = Z_i^{R_i} \cdot \Phi_i \, .$$

<u>Démonstration</u>.- D'après les hypothèses faites précédemment et les résultats contenus dans [3] et [7] il existe une matrice fondamentale qui dans C est de la forme :

$$\varphi = Z_i^{r_i(u)} \cdot \varphi_i$$

où r_i est une application matricielle de $\pi(V_i)$ dans $\mathcal{M}(p, \mathbb{C})$ et φ_i une application matricielle de V_i dans $\mathcal{Gl}(p, \mathbb{C})$ holomorphe inversible par rapport à z_i, t_i. Il existe donc une application matricielle $P(u)$ de $\pi(V_i)$ dans $\mathcal{Gl}(p, \mathbb{C})$ telle que :

$$\Phi|_C = P(u) \cdot \varphi \, .$$

Par conséquent :

$$\Phi|_C = Z_i^{R_i(u)} \, \Phi_i \quad \text{avec} \quad R_i(u) = P(u) r_i(u) P(u)^{-1}$$

$$\Phi_i = P \cdot \varphi_i \, .$$

De plus comme ω et Φ sont holomorphes par rapport à u , $P(u)$, $R_i(u)$, Φ_i sont eux aussi holomorphes par rapport à u . Cqfd.

Soient : $\Phi_i(u,z_i,t_i) = B_i(u,t_i) + C_i(u,t_i)z_i + \dots$

$$F_j(u,x,y,1)\big|_{V_i} = r^i_j(u,t_i) + s^i_j(u,t_i)z_i + \dots \qquad j \neq i$$

les développements en série entière en fonction de z_i dans V_i de Φ_i et F_j . Vu le choix de V_i $r^i_j(u,t_i) \neq 0$ dans V_i .

5) PROPOSITION 1-3.- <u>On a</u>

$$1)\quad B_i^{-1}.R_i.B_i = A_i$$

$$2)\quad R_i C_i + C_i - C_i.A_i = B_i.\left(\sum_{\substack{j=1\\ j\neq i}}^{n} A_j . \frac{s^i_j}{r^i_j}\right)$$

$$3)\quad d_v B_i = B_i.\left(\sum_{\substack{j=1\\ j\neq i}}^{n} A_j . \frac{d_v r^i_j}{r^i_j}\right).$$

<u>Démonstration</u>.- Ecrivons que $\Phi|_C$ est une matrice fondamentale de (e) dans C i.e.

$d_v(\Phi|_C) = (\Phi|_C).(\omega|_C)$. On a alors

$$R_i\Phi_i \frac{d_v z_i}{z_i} + d_v\Phi_i = \Phi_i . \sum_{j=1}^{n} A_j \frac{d_v F_j}{F_j} .$$

En utilisant les développements en série précédents il vient :

$$R_i(B_i + C_i z_i + \dots) \frac{d_v z_i}{z_i} + d_v B_i + C_i d_v z_i =$$

$$(B_i + C_i z_i + \dots).\left(\sum_{\substack{j=1\\ j\neq i}}^{n} A_j \frac{d_v r^i_j + s^i_j d_v z_i + \dots}{r^i_j + B_i s^i_j + \dots} + A_i \frac{d_v z_i}{z_i}\right).$$

On identifie alors les termes ayant z_i comme pôle et l'on a :

$$R_i.B_i\, d_v z_i = B_i\, A_i\, d_v z_i \quad \text{d'où 1)} .$$

Si l'on identifie les termes constants par rapport à z_i il vient :

$$R_i C_i \cdot d_v z_i + d_v B_i + C_i d_v z_i = B_i \left(\sum_{\substack{j=1 \\ j \neq i}}^{n} A_j \frac{d_v r_j^i + s_j^i d_v z_i}{r_j^i} \right) + C_i A_i d_v z_i$$

d'où 2) et 3).

§ 2. - FORMES HORIZONTALES ASSOCIEES.

Rappelons que $R_j^i(u,X,Y,Z) = F_j(u,X,Y,Z)|_{\theta^{-1}(S_i)}$ $j \neq i$ et que l'on a supposé $R_j^i(u,X,Y,Z)$ holomorphe par rapport à u.

Soit alors :

$$\tilde{\varepsilon}_i(u,X,Y,Z) = \sum_{\substack{j=1 \\ j \neq i}}^{n} [A_i, A_j] \frac{d_h R_j^i(u,X,Y,Z)}{R_j^i(u,X,Y,Z)} .$$

Comme $\tilde{\varepsilon}_i(u,\lambda X,\lambda Y,\lambda Z) = \tilde{\varepsilon}_i(u,X,Y,Z)$ $\forall\ \lambda \in \mathbb{C} - \{0\}$, $\tilde{\varepsilon}_i$ induit une forme horizontale sur S_i notée encore $\tilde{\varepsilon}_i$ et l'on a :

1) PROPOSITION 2-1.- Les coefficients de $\tilde{\varepsilon}_i$ ne dépendent que de u.

Démonstration.- Montrons que pour tout u_o fixé dans $\mathcal{U}$, les coefficients de $\tilde{\varepsilon}_i$ sont des fonctions holomorphes sur $S_i(u_o)$ et par conséquent sont constants sur $S_i(u_o)$.

En tout point $m_i \in S_i - \bigcup_{\substack{j=1 \\ j \neq i}}^{n} S_j$ contenu dans V_i voisinage de coordonnées locales (u,z_i,t_i) choisi comme dans le § 1 on a :

$$z_i = F_i(u,x,y,1)|_{V_i}$$

$$F_j(u,x,y,1)|_{V_i} = r_j^i(u,t_i) + s_j^i(u,t_i)z_i + \dots \quad j \neq i .$$

Par conséquent :

$$R_j^i(u,x,y,1)|_{S_i \cap V_i} = r_j^i(u,t_i) \quad \text{et}$$

$$\tilde{\varepsilon}_i|_{V_i} = \sum_{\substack{j=1 \\ j\neq i}}^{n} [A_i, A_j] \frac{d_h r_j^i(u,t_i)}{r_j^i(u,t_i)}$$

et $\tilde{\varepsilon}_i|_{V_i}$ a ses coefficients holomorphes par rapport à t_i pour tout u_o fixé puisque $r_j^i(u,t_i)$ n'est pas nul au voisinage de m_i. Il reste à étudier ce qui se passe au voisinage d'un point $m_{j_o}^i$ appartenant à $S_i \cap S_{j_o}$ et à montrer que les coefficients de $\tilde{\varepsilon}_i$ sont encore holomorphes en ce point pour tout u_o fixé dans $\mathcal{U}$. Comme précédemment V_i sera un voisinage de coordonnées locales (u, z_i, t_i)

et $r_j^i(u,t_i) = R_j^i(u,x,y,1)|_{V_i \cap S_i}$. Mais contrairement au cas précédent

$r_j^i(u_o,0) = 0$ et par conséquent il y a éventuellement un pôle au point $m_{j_o}^i$ pour les coefficients de $\tilde{\varepsilon}_i$.

Soient j_k $k = 0,1, \ ,s$ les indices tels que $r_{j_k}^i(u_o,0) = 0$, c'est-à-dire les S_{j_k} passant par $m_{j_o}^i$. On a :

$$\tilde{\varepsilon}_i|_{V_i} = \sum_{\substack{\ell=1 \\ \ell\neq j_k \\ \ell\neq i}}^{n} [A_i, A_\ell] \frac{d_h r_\ell^i}{r_\ell^i} + \sum_{k=o}^{s} [A_i, A_{j_k}] \frac{d_h r_{j_k}^i}{r_{j_k}^i}$$

$\sum_{\substack{\ell=1 \\ \ell\neq j_k \\ \ell\neq i}}^{n} [A_i, A_\ell] \frac{d_h r_\ell^i}{r_\ell^i}$ a ses coefficients holomorphes au voisinage de $m_{j_o}^i$ pour u_o fixé puisque $r_\ell^i(u_o,0) \neq 0$.

Il reste à étudier :

$$\alpha_i = \sum_{k=o}^{s} [A_i, A_{j_k}] \frac{d_h r_{j_k}^i}{r_{j_k}^i}.$$

Pour cela posons :

$$r_{j_k}^i(u,t_i) = b_k^1(u) t_i^{s_k} + b_k^2(u) t_i^{s_k+1} + \ldots.$$

Vu les hypothèses faites au départ on a $b_k^1(u) \neq 0$ pour $u \in \mathcal{U}$ et

$$d_h r_{j_k}^i = t_i^{s_k} db_k^1 + s_k b_k^1 t_i^{s_k-1} d_h t_i + \ldots.$$

D'où :

$$\alpha_i = \sum_{k=o}^{s} [A_i, A_{j_k}] \frac{d\, b_k^1 + \dots}{b_k^1 + \dots} + \sum_{k=o}^{s} [A_i, A_{j_k}] \left(\frac{s_k b_k^1 + \dots}{b_k^1 + \dots}\right) \frac{d_h t_i}{t_i}$$

$\sum_{k=o}^{s} [A_i, A_{j_k}] \frac{d\, b_k^1 + ..}{b_k^1 + ..}$ est holomorphe en $m_{j_o}^i$ puisque $b_k^1 \neq 0$.

Pour $\sum_{k=o}^{s} [A_i, A_{j_k}] \left(\frac{s_k b_k^1 + \dots}{b_k^1 + \dots}\right) \frac{d_h t_i}{t_i}$ on va utiliser la complète intégrabilité de ω et montrer que cette forme a ses coefficients holomorphes en $m_{j_o}^i$.

On a :

$$\omega \wedge \omega = 0 \quad \text{c'est-à-dire} \quad \sum_{i<j} [A_i, A_j] \frac{d_v F_i \wedge d_v F_j}{F_i \cdot F_j} = 0 \; .$$

Ecrivons que la partie polaire relative à z_i de cette expression est nulle. Il vient :

$$\sum_{\substack{j=1 \\ j \neq i}}^{n} [A_i, A_j] \frac{d_v r_j^i \wedge d_v z_i}{r_j^i} = 0 \; .$$

$r_{j_k}^i(u_o, 0)$ est un pôle pour cette expression, écrivons que la partie polaire correspondante est nulle.

Comme $d_v r_{j_k}^i = (s_k b_k^1 t_i^{s_k - 1} + \dots) d_v t_i$ on a :

$$\sum_{k=o}^{s} ([A_i, A_{j_k}] s_k)\, d_v\, t_i \wedge d_v z_i = 0 \quad \text{soit :}$$

$$\sum_{k=o}^{s} s_k [A_i, A_{j_k}] = 0 \; .$$

Par conséquent :

$$\left(\sum_{k=o}^{s} [A_i, A_{j_k}] \frac{s_k b_k^1 + (s_k+1) b_k^2 t_i + \dots}{b_k^1 + b_k^2 t_i + \dots} \right) \frac{d_h t_i}{t_i} =$$

$$\sum_{k=o}^{s} \left([A_i, A_{j_k}] \frac{s_k b_k^1 + (s_k+1) b_k^2 t_i + ..}{b_k^1 + b_k^2 t_i + \dots} - [A_i, A_{j_k}] s_k \right) \frac{d_h t_i}{t_i}$$

D'où :

$$\left(\sum_{k=o}^{s} [A_i, A_{j_k}] \frac{s_k b_k^1 + \cdots}{b_k^1 + \cdots}\right) \frac{d_h t_i}{t_i} = \left(\sum_{k=o}^{s} [A_i, A_{j_k}] \frac{b_k^2 + \cdots}{b_k^1 + \cdots}\right) d_h t_i \,.$$

Les coefficients de cette forme sont donc eux aussi holomorphes en $m^i_{j_o}$ et la proposition est démontrée en remarquant que les seules fonctions holomorphes de $S_i(u_o)$ dans $\mathbb{C}$ sont les constantes.

Remarques 2-2.- Il suffit d'écrire $\tilde{\varepsilon}_i$ en un point de $S_i(u)$ pour l'obtenir sur tout $S_i(u)$, en tenant compte de la complète intégrabilité de ω.

$\tilde{\varepsilon}_i$ est une forme holomorphe sur $\mathcal{U}$.

2) DEFINITION 2-3.- Les $\tilde{\varepsilon}_i$, formes horizontales associées à (e) seront appelées formes de Schlesinger dans la suite.

Elles généralisent en effet au cas des systèmes de Fuchs sur $\mathbb{P}_2(\mathbb{C})$, les formes rencontrées par L. Schlesinger dans [1].

§ 3. - PROBLEME DE SCHLESINGER GENERALISE.

Rappelons une propriété citée dans [4] :

Soit Φ_u une matrice fondamentale de $(e)_u$, alors Φ_u définit une représentation $\chi_u^{\Phi_u}$ de $\pi_1(\mathbb{P}_2^*(u))$ dans $\mathcal{G}\ell(p,\mathbb{C})$. Plus précisément si $g(u) \in \pi_1(\mathbb{P}_2^*(u))$, $g^*(u)\Phi_u$ est une nouvelle matrice fondamentale et par conséquent $g^*(u)\Phi_u = P_{g(u)} \cdot \Phi_u$ avec $P_{g(u)}$ appartenant à $\mathcal{G}\ell(p,\mathbb{C})$.

On pose $\chi_u^{\Phi_u}(g(u)) = P_{g(u)}$ et on vérifie que $\chi_u^{\Phi_u}$ est une représentation de $\pi_1(\mathbb{P}_2^*(u))$ dans $\mathcal{G}\ell(p,\mathbb{C})$. Cette représentation est appelée monodromie associée à Φ_u. A deux matrices fondamentales différentes sont associées des représentations semblables.

Soit $g(u) = (\varphi_u^*)^{-1} g$ $g \in \pi_1(\mathbb{P}_2(\mathbb{C})-s)$ (cf remarque 1-1). On peut alors définir pour tout u dans $\mathcal{U}$ une représentation $\tilde{\chi}_u^{\Phi_u}$ de $\pi_1(\mathbb{P}_2(\mathbb{C})-s)$ dans

$\mathcal{G}\ell(p,\mathbb{C})$ par :

$$\tilde{\chi}_u^{\Phi_u}(g) = \chi_u^{\Phi_u}(g(u)) = P_{g(u)} .$$

1) DEFINITION 3-1.- On dit que la monodromie relative à Φ matrice fondamentale de (e) est indépendante de u si pour tout g appartenant à $\pi_1(\mathbb{P}_2(\mathbb{C})-s)$ $\tilde{\chi}_u^{\Phi_u}(g)$ est constant quand u appartient à $\mathcal{U}$.

Remarque 3-2.- Si la monodromie associée à Φ est indépendante de u, il n'est pas vrai en général que la monodromie associée à toute autre matrice fondamentale soit indépendante de u. Il suffit de remarquer que si $P(u) \in \mathcal{G}\ell(p,\mathbb{C})$, $P(u)\Phi$ est une autre matrice fondamentale, la représentation associée étant $P(u)\tilde{\chi}_u^{\Phi_u} P(u)^{-1}$. Il est alors clair, qu'en général, cette représentation va varier avec u, si $P(u)$ varie.

2) Problème de Schlesinger généralisé.

Soit μ_o le point de $\mathbb{P}_2(\mathbb{C})$ correspondant à $(1,0,0)$ et $m_o(u)$ les points correspondants de M pour $u \in \mathcal{U}$. Trouver une condition nécessaire et suffisante pour qu'il existe une matrice fondamentale de (e) dont la monodromie associée soit indépendante de u et telle que $\Phi(m_o(u)) = Id \quad \forall\, u \in \mathcal{U}$.

Soient V_i défini dans le § 1, (u,z_i,t_i) un point de V_i et (u,z_i,T_i) un point de C tel que $\psi(u,z_i,T_i) = (u,z_i,t_i)$. D'après la proposition 1-2, il existe une application matricielle holomorphe $R_i(u)$ de $\pi(V_i)$ dans $\mathcal{M}(p,\mathbb{C})$ et Φ_i application matricielle holomorphe de V_i dans $\mathcal{G}\ell(p,\mathbb{C})$ tel que l'on ait :

$$\Phi|_C = Z_i^{R_i}\, \Phi_i(u,z_i,t_i) .$$

2) PROPOSITION 3-3.- Si la monodromie relative à Φ est indépendante de u alors $d R_i(u) = 0$ pour tout u dans $\pi(V_i)$.

Démonstration.- Soit $\gamma(u)$ le chemin de $V_i \cap \mathbb{P}_2^*(u)$ défini par :

$$\gamma(u) : [0,1 \longrightarrow V_i \cap \mathbb{P}_2^*(u) \qquad z_i(u) \text{ choisi pour que}$$
$$t \longmapsto (u,z_i(u)e^{2\pi i t},0) \qquad \gamma(u)(t) \in V_i \cap \mathbb{P}_2^*(u) .$$

Soit $g(u)$ la classe de $\gamma(u)$ dans $\pi_1(\mathbb{P}_2^*(u))$ et $g = \varphi_u^*(g(u)) \in \pi_1(\mathbb{P}_2(\mathbb{C})-s)$

$$g^* \Phi = g^*(u)\,\Phi = P_{g(u)} \cdot \Phi \;.$$

De plus :

$g^*(u) \log z_i = \log z_{i+2\pi}$ et par conséquent :

$g^* \Phi = e^{2\pi i R_i} Z_i^{R_i} \cdot \Phi_i = P_{g(u)} \cdot \Phi$ c'est-à-dire

$$P_{g(u)} = e^{2\pi i R_i} \;.$$

Comme $P_{g(u)} = \tilde{\chi}_u^{\Phi_u}(g)$ est constant par hypothèse on a :

$$d\,R_i(u) = 0 \;. \qquad \underline{\text{Cqfd.}}$$

Posons :

$$\tilde{\omega}(u,X,Y,Z) = \sum_{i=1}^{n} A_i(u) \frac{d_h F_i(u,X,Y,Z)}{F_i(u,X,Y,Z)} \;.$$

$\tilde{\omega}(u,\lambda X,\lambda Y,\lambda Z) = \tilde{\omega}(u,X,Y,Z)$ $\lambda \in \mathbb{C}\{0\}$ et par conséquent $\tilde{\omega}$ induit une forme horizontale sur M. On note encore $\tilde{\omega}$ cette forme induite.

3) PROPOSITION 3-4.- Si la monodromie associée à Φ est indépendante de u, $\tilde{\Omega}_\Phi = \Phi^{-1} d_h \Phi - \tilde{\omega}$ est une forme horizontale sur M dont les coefficients ne dépendent que de $u \in \mathcal{U}$.

Démonstration.- Soit u_o fixé. Montrons que les coefficients de $\tilde{\Omega}_\Phi$ sont des fonctions définies sur $\mathbb{P}_2^*(u)$ c'est-à-dire sont uniformes. Pour cela il faut montrer que $\tilde{\Omega}_\Phi$ est invariant par opération de $\pi_1(\mathbb{P}_2^*(u_o))$.

Soit $g(u_o) \in \pi_1(\mathbb{P}_2^*(u_o))$ $\quad g = \varphi_{u_o}^*(u_o))$

$$g^*(u_o)\tilde{\Omega}_\Phi = g^*(u_o)(\Phi^{-1} d_h \Phi) - g^*(u_o)\tilde{\omega}$$

$g^*(u_o)\,\tilde{\omega} = \tilde{\omega}$ puisque les coefficients de $\tilde{\omega}$ sont uniformes dans $\mathbb{P}_2^*(u)$.

De plus :

$$g^*(u_o)(d_h\Phi)_{u=u_o} = g^*(d_h\Phi)_{u=u_o} = d_h(g^*\Phi)_{u=u_o} = d_h(P_{g(u)}\cdot\Phi)_{u=u_o} = (d_hP_{g(u)})_{u=u_o}$$

$$+ P_{g(u_o)}(d_h\Phi)_{u=u_o}$$

car g est indépendant de u. Comme $dP_{g(u)} = 0$ (hypothèse)

$$g^*(u_o)(d_h\Phi)_{u=u_o} = P_{g(u_o)}\cdot(d_h\Phi)_{u=u_o}.$$

Par conséquent :

$$g^*(u_o)(\Phi^{-1} d_h\Phi) = \Phi^{-1}\cdot d_h\Phi$$

et $\tilde{\Omega}_\Phi$ est invariant par opération du $\pi_1(\mathbb{P}_2^*(u_o))$.

Montrons maintenant que les coefficients de $\tilde{\Omega}_\Phi$ se prolongent holomorphiquement sur $\mathbb{P}_2(u_o)$.

Etudions $\tilde{\Omega}_\Phi$ au voisingage du point $m_i(u_o) \in S_i(u_o) - \bigcup_{\substack{j=1 \\ j\neq i}}^{n} S_j(u_o)$.

En utilisant la forme de Φ donnée précédemment il vient :

$$\tilde{\Omega}_\Phi(u_o)|_{V_i(u_o)} = \Phi_i^{-1} R_i \Phi_i \frac{d_h z_i}{z_i} + \Phi_i^{-1} d_h\Phi_i - \sum_{j=1}^{n} A_j(u) \frac{d_h F_j}{F_j}$$

en tenant compte du fait que : $dR_i(u) = 0$.

On a éventuellement un pôle en $z_i = 0$ car Φ_i est holomorphe par rapport à z_i, t_i ainsi que Φ_i^{-1}. De plus

$$\Phi_i(u_o,z_i,t_i) = B_i(u_o,t_i) + C_i(u_o,t_i)z_i + \dots$$

$$\Phi^{-1}(u_o,z_i,t_i) = B_i^{-1}(u_o,t_i) - B_i^{-1}(u_o,t_i)C_i(u_o,t_i)B_i^{-1}(u_o,t_i)z_i + \dots$$

$$F_j(u_o,x,y,1)|_{V_i(u_o)} = r_j^i(u_o,t_i) + s_j^i(u_o,t_i)z_i + \dots$$

Ce qui donne pour coefficient de $\frac{1}{z_i}$.

$B_i(u_o,t_i)R_i B_i^{-1}(u_o,t_i)d_h z_i - A_i d_h z_i$ et cette expression est nulle d'après la proposition 1-3.

$\tilde{\Omega}_\Phi$ se prolonge donc holomorphiquement en $m_i(u_o) \in S_i - \bigcup_{\substack{j=1 \\ j \neq i}}^{n} S_j$.

$\tilde{\Omega}_\Phi$ a des coefficients holomorphes sur $\mathbb{P}_2(u_o)$ sauf peut-être aux points d'intersection de $S_i(u_o)$ et $S_j(u_o)$ $(i \neq j)$. Ces points étant en nombre fini, les coefficients de $\tilde{\Omega}_\Phi$ se prolongent holomorphiquement sur tout $\mathbb{P}_2(u)$ et sont donc constants.

Remarque 3-5.- Φ étant holomorphe par rapport à u , ainsi que $\tilde{\omega}$, $\tilde{\Omega}_\Phi$ l'est aussi. Supposons de plus $\Phi(m_o(u)) = Id$ pour tout u dans $\mathcal{U}$. Φ est holomorphe au voisinage de $m_o(u)$ et par conséquent si :

$$x' = \frac{Y}{X} \quad y' = \frac{Z}{X} \quad \text{on a :} \quad \Phi = \Phi^o(u) + x'\Phi^1(u) + y'\Phi^2(u) + \dots$$

avec $\Phi^o(u) = Id$ d'où :

$$d_h\Phi = x'd_h\Phi^1 + y'd_h\Phi^2 + \dots \quad \text{car} \quad d_hx' = 0 \quad d_hy' = 0$$

et par suite :

$$(d_h\Phi)(m_o(u)) = 0 .$$

De même comme $F_i(u,X,Y,Z) = X^{k_i} + \dots$. on vérifie immédiatement que $(d_hF_i)(m_o(u)) = 0$ et on en déduit que :

$$\tilde{\Omega}_\Phi = 0 .$$

4) THEOREME 3-6.- Une condition nécessaire et suffisante pour qu'il existe une matrice fondamentale de (e) dont la monodromie associée soit indépendante de u et telle que $\Phi(m_o(u)) = Id$ est que les applications matricielles A_i vérifient les équations différentielles (E) suivantes :

$$dA_i = \tilde{\varepsilon}_i \qquad i = 1,2,\dots,n \quad (E)$$

les $\tilde{\varepsilon}_i$ étant les formes de Schlesinger associées à (e) et définies dans le § 2.

Démonstration.- Démontrons d'abord le lemme suivant :

5) LEMME 3-7.- Si la monodromie associée à Φ est indépendante de u, les applications matricielles A_i vérifient :

$$dA_i = [A_i, B_i^{-1}(u,t_i) d_h B_i(u,t_i)] .$$

Démonstration.- On a d'après la proposition 1-3 : $B_i^{-1} R_i B_i = A_i$. D'où en tenant compte de $dR_i = 0$:

$$dA_i = -B_i^{-1} d_h B_i B_i^{-1} R_i B_i + B_i^{-1} R_i d_h B_i = -B_i^{-1} d_h B_i \circ A_i + A_i B_i^{-1} d_h B_i$$

et le lemme est démontré.

6) Conditions nécessaires.

D'après le lemme précédent, il suffit de déterminer $B_i^{-1} d_h B_i$.
Pour cela revenons à : $\widetilde{\Omega}_\Phi = \Phi^{-1}.d_h \Phi - \widetilde{\omega}$ qui s'écrit en restriction à $V_i(u_o)$:

$$\widetilde{\Omega}_\Phi |_{V_i(u_o)} - \Phi_i^{-1} R_i \Phi_i \frac{d_h z_i}{z_i} - \Phi_i^{-1} d_h \Phi_i + \sum_{j=1}^{n} A_j(u) \frac{d_h F_j}{F_j} = 0 .$$

Ecrivons que le terme constant du développement en série par rapport à z_i des différents termes de cette expression est nul. Il vient avec les notations utilisées précédemment :

$$\left[B_i^{-1}(R_i C_i - C_i A_i + C_i) - \sum_{\substack{j=1 \\ j \neq i}}^{n} A_j \frac{s_j^i}{r_j^i}\right] d_h z_i + B_i^{-1} d_h B_i - \sum_{\substack{j=1 \\ j \neq i}}^{n} A_j \frac{d_h r_j^i}{r_j^i} - \widetilde{\Omega}_\Phi = 0 .$$

D'après la proposition 1-3

$$B_i^1(R_i C_i - C_i A_i + C_i) - \sum_{\substack{j=1 \\ j \neq i}}^{n} A_j \frac{s_j^i}{r_j^i} = 0$$ et par conséquent :

$$B_i^{-1} d_h B_i = \sum_{\substack{j=1 \\ j \neq i}}^{n} A_j \frac{d_h r_j^i}{r_j^i} + \widetilde{\Omega}_\Phi .$$

Si l'on tient compte de la remarque 3-5 et du lemme 3-7 on a :

$$dA_i = \sum_{\substack{j=1 \\ j\neq i}}^{n} [A_i, A_j] \frac{d_h r_j^i}{r_j^i} = \tilde{\varepsilon}_i \qquad i = 1,2,\dots,n \qquad (E)$$

et les conditions nécessaires sont établies.

Montrons que les équations (E) constituent des conditions suffisantes.

7) LEMME 3-8.- <u>Si les</u> A_i <u>vérifient</u> (E) <u>il existe une matrice fondamentale</u> Φ <u>de</u> (e) <u>telle que</u> :

(1) $\Phi^{-1}.d_h\Phi = \tilde{\omega}$

(2) $\Phi(m_o(u)) = \mathrm{Id} \quad \forall\, u \in \mathcal{U}$.

<u>Démonstration</u>.- Pour démontrer le lemme, nous allons prouver que le système différentiel suivant est complètement intégrable :

$$df = f(\omega + \tilde{\omega}) \quad (f) .$$

Remarquons que $\omega + \tilde{\omega} = \sum_{i=1}^{n} A_i \frac{dF_i}{F_i}$ et que la condition de complète intégrabilité pour (f) s'écrit :

$$d(\omega + \tilde{\omega}) + (\tilde{\omega} + \omega) \wedge (\tilde{\omega} + \omega) = 0 \text{ soit en remplaçant :}$$

$$\sum_{i=1}^{n} dA_i \wedge \frac{dF_i}{F_i} + \sum_{i<j} [A_i, A_j] \frac{dF_i \wedge dF_j}{F_i . F_j} = 0 .$$

Comme $dF_i = d_h F_i + d_v F_i$ il vient :

$$\sum_{i=1}^{n} \frac{dA_i \wedge d_h F_i}{F_i} + \sum_{i=1}^{n} \frac{dA_i \wedge d_v F_i}{F_i} +$$

$$\sum_{i<j} [A_i, A_j] \frac{d_h F_i \wedge d_h F_j}{F_i . F_j} + \sum_{i<j} [A_i, A_j] \frac{d_h F_i \wedge d_v F_j}{F_i . F_j} +$$

$$\sum_{i<j} [A_i, A_j] \frac{d_v F_i \wedge d_h F_i}{F_i F_j} + \sum_{i<j} [A_i, A_j] \frac{d_v F_i \wedge d_v F_j}{F_i F_j} = 0 .$$

Montrons que ces différentes expressions sont nulles. Remarquons d'abord que

$\omega \wedge \omega = 0$ entraîne :

$$\sum_{i<j} [A_i, A_j] \frac{d_v F_i \wedge d_v F_j}{F_i F_j} = 0 .$$

Il reste à montrer que :

$$R_\alpha = \sum_{i=1}^{n} \frac{dA_i \wedge d_h F_i}{F_i} + \sum_{i<j} [A_i, A_j] \frac{d_h F_i \wedge d_h F_j}{F_i F_j}$$

et

$$R_\beta = \sum_{i=1}^{n} \frac{dA_i \wedge d_v F_i}{F_i} + \sum_{i<j} [A_i, A_j] \frac{d_h F_i \wedge d_v F_j}{F_i F_j} + \sum_{i<j} [A_i, A_j] \frac{d_v F_i \wedge d_h F_i}{F_i F_j}$$

sont deux formes nulles.

Fixons u_o dans $\mathcal{U}$ et montrons que les coefficients de R_α et R_β se prolongent holomorphiquement sur $\mathbb{P}_2(u_o)$ et par conséquent sont constants.

R_α a éventuellement des pôles sur $S_i(u_o)$. Soit $m_i(u_o)$ un point de $S_i(u_o) - \bigcup_{\substack{j=1 \\ j \neq i}}^{n} S_j(u_o)$. Montrons que les coefficients de R_α se prolongent holomorphiquement en $m_i(u_o)$. On a avec les notations précédentes :

$$d_h F_j = d_h r_j^i + s_j^i d_h z_i + z_i d_h s_j^i + \ldots$$

$$d_v F_j = d_v r_j^i + s_j^i d_v z_i + z_i d_v s_j^i + \ldots$$

Le coefficient de $\frac{1}{z_i}$ dans R_α est alors :

$$dA_i \wedge d_h z_i + \sum_{\substack{j=1 \\ j \neq i}}^{n} [A_i, A_j] \frac{d_h z_i \wedge d_h r_j^i}{r_j^i} = d_h z_i \wedge (\tilde{\varepsilon}_i - dA_i) .$$

Il est donc nul d'après les équations (E) et les coefficients de R_α se prolongent holomorphiquement en $m_i(u_o)$. Il se prolongent de même sur tout $\mathbb{P}_2(u_o)$ puisque les points appartenant à $S_i(u_o) \cap S_j(u_o)$ $i \neq j$ sont en nombre fini. Ces coefficients sont donc constants.

Il reste à montrer qu'ils sont nuls. Pour cela écrivons R_α au point

$m_o(u_o)$. Comme $d_h F_i(u,1,0,0) = 0$ on a immédiatement :

$$R_\alpha(m_o(u_o)) = 0$$

et par conséquent R_α est nul partout.

Procédons de même pour R_β .

Au voisinage de m_i, le coefficient de $\frac{1}{z_i}$ dans R_β est :

$$R_\beta^o = dA_i \wedge d_v z_i + \sum_{\substack{j=1 \\ j \neq i}}^{n} [A_i, A_j] \frac{d_h z_i \wedge (d_v r_j^i + s_j^i d_v z_i)}{r_j^i} +$$

$$\sum_{\substack{j=1 \\ j \neq i}}^{n} [A_i, A_j] \frac{d_v z_i \wedge (d_h r_j^i + s_j^i d_h z_i}{r_j^i} .$$

Soit en développant et en simplifiant :

$$R_\beta^o = d_v z_i \wedge (\widetilde{\varepsilon}_i - dA_i) + d_h z_i \wedge \left(\sum_{\substack{j=1 \\ j \neq i}}^{n} [A_i, A_j] \frac{d_v r_j^i}{r_j^i} \right) .$$

Le premier terme de cette somme est nul d'après les équations (E).

Le second l'est aussi car d'après la proposition 1-3 on a :

$$\sum_{\substack{j=1 \\ j \neq i}}^{n} [A_i, A_j] \frac{d_v r_j^i}{r_j^i} = [A_i, B_i^{-1} d_v B_i] = d_v R_i = 0 \text{ .}$$

Les coefficients de R_β sont eux aussi constants. Montrons qu'ils sont nuls.

Soient (u,x,y) un point de la carte correspondant à $Z \neq 0$ dans $\mathbb{P}_2(u)$ alors :

$$R_\beta(u,x,y) = \sum_{k=o}^{r} R_\beta^{1k} du_k \wedge dx + \sum_{k=o}^{r} R_\beta^{2,k} du_k \wedge dy$$

$$(u_1, \ldots, u_r) \in \mathcal{U} \qquad R_\beta^{1,k} \text{ , } R_\beta^{2,k} \text{ sont constants (} u \text{ fixé) .}$$

Ecrivons R_β dans la carte correspondant à $X \neq 0$ c'est-à-dire (u,x',y') avec $x' = \frac{1}{x}$ $y' = \frac{y}{x}$ et :

$$R_\beta(u,x',y') = -\sum_{k=o}^{r} \left(\frac{R_\beta^{1,k}}{x'^2} + \frac{y'}{x'} R_\beta^{2,k}\right) du_k \wedge dx' + \sum_{k=o}^{r} \frac{R_\beta^{2,k}}{x'} du_k \wedge dy' .$$

$R_\beta(u,x',y')$ est à coefficients constants et par conséquent :

$$R_\beta^{1,k} = R_\beta^{2,k} = 0 \quad \text{pour tout} \quad k = 1, \ ,r .$$

R_β est nulle et la première partie du lemme est démontrée, puisque Φ matrice fondamentale de (f) vérifie :

$$d_h\Phi = \Phi\widetilde{\omega} \qquad d_v\Phi = \Phi\omega ,$$

si l'on montre de plus que Φ peut être choisie telle que $\Phi(m_o(u)) = Id$ pour tout u dans $\mathcal{U}$.

Choisissons alors Φ telle que $\Phi(m_o(u_o)) = Id$ pour u_o fixé dans $\mathcal{U}$. Comme Φ vérifie $d_h\Phi = \Phi.\widetilde{\omega}$ et $(d_h\Phi)(m_o(u)) = d_h(\Phi(m_o(u))$ on a en restriction à $\varphi^{-1}(\mathcal{U}\times\{\mu_o\})$:

$$d_h\Phi|_{\Phi^{-1}(\mathcal{U}\times\{\mu_o\})} = \Phi\widetilde{\omega}(m_o(u)) = 0 \quad \text{puisque} \quad \widetilde{\omega}(m_o(u)) = 0$$

et

$$\Phi(m_o(u)) = \text{Cste} = \Phi(m_o(u_o)) = Id \quad \text{pour tout} \quad u \quad \text{dans} \quad \mathcal{U} \qquad \text{C.Q.F.D.}$$

8) <u>Conditions suffisantes.</u>

D'après le lemme précédent, il existe une matrice fondamentale Φ de (e) qui vérifie :

$$d_h\Phi = \Phi.\widetilde{\omega} \quad \text{et} \quad \Phi(m_o(u)) = Id \qquad \forall\, u\in\mathcal{U} .$$

Montrons que la monodromie associée est indépendante de $u\in\mathcal{U}$.

Soit $g\in\pi_1(\mathbb{P}_2(\mathbb{C})-s)$ $\quad g(u) = (\varphi_u^*)^{-1}(g)$. On a

$$g^*\Phi = g^*(u)\,\Phi = P_{g(u)}\Phi \quad \text{et}$$

$$g^*d_h\,\Phi = d_h(g^*\Phi) = dP_{g(u)}\,\Phi + P_{g(u)}.\,d_h\,\Phi .$$

En tenant compte de l'équation vérifiée par Φ :

$g^*(d_h\Phi) = g^*(\Phi.\widetilde{\omega}) = (g^*.\Phi).\widetilde{\omega}$ puisque les coefficients de $\widetilde{\omega}$ sont uniformes,

et :

$$dP_{g(u)}\,\Phi + P_{g(u)}\,d_h\,\Phi - P_{g(u)}\,\Phi\,\widetilde{\omega}.$$

D'où

$$dP_{g(u)} = 0 .$$

$P_{g(u)}$ étant holomorphe par rapport à u , $P_{g(u)}$ est constant et le théorème est démontré.

9) Remarque 3-9.- Les équations (E) ainsi obtenues ne sont pas compatibles avec la relation de similitude sur les matrices A_i , à moins de choisir une matrice de passage indépendante de u .

10) Remarque 3-10.- Si l'on ne fait plus l'hypothèse $\Phi(m_o(u)) = \mathrm{Id}\ \ \forall\, u \in \mathcal{U}$ et si l'on suppose qu'il existe une courbe fixe (Γ) de $\mathbb{P}_2(\mathbb{C})$ (indépendante de u) d'équation $T_n(x,y) = 0$ dans la carte 0_1 de $\mathbb{P}_2(\mathbb{C})$ et telle que $\varphi^{-1}(\mathcal{U}\times\Gamma)$ soit transverse à S_n , on peut exprimer $\widetilde{\Omega}_\Phi$ (qui n'est plus nul) au voisinage d'un point p_o appartenant à $S_n \cap \varphi^{-1}(\mathcal{U}\times\Gamma)$.

Dans un voisinage V_n de ce point, voisinage de coordonnées locales (u,z_n,t_n) avec $z_n = F_n(u,x,y,1)|_{V_n}$ $t_n = T_n|_{V_n}$ on a $d_h t_n = 0$ et :

$$(B_n^{-1}(u,t_n).d_h B_n(u,t_n))_{t_n=o} = B_n^{-1}(u,o)d_h B_n(u,o) .$$

Comme : $\quad \widetilde{\Omega}_\Phi|_{V_n} = B_n^{-1}\,d_h\,B_n - \sum\limits_{j=1}^{n-1} A_j\,\dfrac{d_h r_j^n}{r_j^n}$ il vient

$$\widetilde{\Omega}_\Phi(p_o) = B_n^{-1}(u,o)\,d_h\,B_n(u,0) - \left(\sum_{j=1}^{n-1} A_j\,\frac{d_h r_j^n}{r_j^n}\right)(p_o) .$$

Multiplions (e) à droite par $B_n^{-1}(u,0)$ pour obtenir un nouveau système de Fuchs $(\hat{e})$:

$$d_v(f B_n^{-1}(u_o)) = (f.B_n^{-1}) \left(\sum_{i=1}^{n} B_n A_i B_n^{-1} \frac{d_v F_i}{F_i} \right)$$

$$d_v \hat{f} = \hat{f} \left(\sum_{i=1}^{n} \hat{A}_i \frac{d_v F_i}{F_i} \right)$$ et pour ce système la matrice

fondamentale : $\hat{\Phi} = \Phi.B_n^{-1}(u,0)$ vérifie $\hat{B}_n(u,0) = Id \quad \forall\, u \in \mathcal{U}$.

On peut donc quitte à transformer (e) en $(\hat{e})$ supposer que $B_n(u,0) = Id$ quel que soit u dans $\mathcal{U}$ et dans ces conditions :

$$\widetilde{\Omega}_\Phi = -\left(\sum_{j=1}^{n-1} A_j \frac{d_h r_j^n}{r_j^n} \right)(p_o)$$

et l'on montre comme précédemment :

11) THEOREME 3-11.- <u>Une condition nécessaire et suffisante pour qu'il existe une matrice fondamentale</u> Φ <u>de</u> (e) <u>dont la monodromie associée soit indépendante de</u> u <u>et telle que</u> $B_n(u,0) = Id$ <u>est que les matrices</u> A_i <u>vérifient</u> :

$$(E^*) \begin{cases} dA_i = \widetilde{\varepsilon}_i + [A_i, \widetilde{\Omega}_\Phi] & i = 1,2,\ldots,n-1 \\ dA_n = 0 \end{cases}$$

avec

$$\widetilde{\Omega}_\Phi = -\left(\sum_{j=1}^{n-1} A_j \frac{d_h r_j^n}{r_j^n} \right)(p_o) .$$

On peut donc, quitte à modifier (e) supposer qu'une des matrices A_i est constante. On retrouve ainsi les résultats énoncés dans [1] pour $\mathbb{P}_1(\mathbb{C})$, généralisés à $\mathbb{P}_2(\mathbb{C})$.

§ 4. - ETUDE DU PROBLEME EN RESTRICTION A UNE DROITE PROJECTIVE.

Supposons dans cette partie qu'il existe une droite projective (D) de $\mathbb{P}_2(\mathbb{C})$ telle que $\varphi^{-1}(\mathcal{U} \times D)$ soit en position générale par rapport aux

S_i $i = 1,2,\dots,n$. La restriction de (e) à $\varphi^{-1}(\mathcal{U}\times D)$ est un système de Fuchs (e').

Supposons de plus que (D) passe par m_o.

1) THEOREME 4-1.- Pour qu'il existe une matrice fondamentale Φ de (e) dont la monodromie associée soit indépendante de u et telle que $\Phi(m_o(u)) = \mathrm{Id}$ il faut et il suffit qu'il en existe une vérifiant cette propriété pour le système restreint (e').

Démonstration.- Nous supposerons pour plus de simplicité que (D) a pour équation $y = 0$ dans la carte O_1. Remarquons que si $\Phi(m_o(u)) = \mathrm{Id}$, $\Phi' = \Phi|_{\varphi^{-1}(\mathcal{U}\times D)}$ vérifie $\Phi'(m_o(u)) = \mathrm{Id}$ et réciproquement.

Le théorème 4-1 est prouvé si l'on démontre que les équations (E) et (E') associées à (e) et (e') sont identiques.

Les équations (E) associées à (e) sont d'après 3-6 :

$$dA_i = \tilde{\varepsilon}_i \qquad i = 1,2,\dots,n \quad \text{avec} \quad \tilde{\varepsilon}_i = \sum_{\substack{j=1\\ j\neq i}}^{n} [A_i,A_j]\, \frac{d_h R^i_j}{R^i_j} .$$

Comme les coefficients de $\tilde{\varepsilon}_i$ sont constants sur $S_i(u)$ il suffit d'écrire $\tilde{\varepsilon}_i$ en un point quelconque de $S_i(u)$. Choisissons pour ce point m_i un élément de $S_i(u)\cap(D)$: $x = \alpha_i$ $y = 0$ $(F_i(\alpha_i,0,1) = 0)$

alors :

$$\tilde{\varepsilon}_i = \left(\sum_{\substack{j=1\\ j\neq i}}^{n} [A_i,A_j]\, \frac{d_h r^i_j}{r^i_j} \right)(m_i)$$

avec puisque $d_h y = 0$: $\quad \dfrac{d_h r^i_j}{r^i_j}(m_i) = \dfrac{d_h F_j(\alpha_i,0,1)}{F_j(\alpha_i,0,1)}$.

Posons $\quad F_j(x,y,1) = \prod_{\ell=1}^{k_j} (x-\alpha^j_\ell) + G_j(x,y) \qquad G_j(x,0) = 0 \quad j = 1,2,\dots,n$

et $\alpha^i_1 = \alpha_i$.

Il vient :

$$\frac{d_h F_j(\alpha_i,0,1)}{F_j(\alpha_i,0,1)} = \sum_{\ell=1}^{k_j} \frac{d\alpha_i - d\alpha_\ell^j}{\alpha_i - \alpha_\ell^j} \quad \text{et} \quad \tilde{\varepsilon}_i = \sum_{\substack{j=1\\ j\neq i}}^{n} [A_i,A_j]\left(\sum_{\ell=1}^{k_j} \frac{d\alpha_i - d\alpha_\ell^j}{\alpha_i - \alpha_\ell^j}\right) .$$

Les équations (E) s'écrivent :

$$dA_i = \sum_{\substack{j=1\\ j\neq i}}^{n} [A_i,A_j]\left(\sum_{\ell=1}^{k_j} \frac{d\alpha_i - d\alpha_\ell^j}{\alpha_i - \alpha_\ell^j}\right) .$$

Ecrivons maintenant (e') :

$$F_j(x,y,1)\big|_{y=o} = \prod_{\ell=1}^{k_j} (x-\alpha_\ell^j) \quad \text{soit}$$

$$d_v f = f\left[\sum_{i=1}^{n} A_i\left(\sum_{\ell=1}^{k_i} \frac{dx}{x-\alpha_\ell^i}\right)\right] \quad (e') .$$

Les équations (E') associées sont alors :

$$dA_i = \sum_{\substack{j=1\\ j\neq i}}^{n} [A_i,A_j]\left(\sum_{\ell=1}^{k_j} \frac{d\alpha_1^i - d\alpha_\ell^j}{\alpha_1^i - \alpha_\ell^j}\right)$$

$$dA_i = \sum_{\substack{j=1\\ j\neq i}}^{n} [A_i,A_j]\left(\sum_{\ell=1}^{k_j} \frac{d\alpha_2^i - d\alpha_\ell^j}{\alpha_i - \alpha_\ell^j}\right)$$

$$dA_i = \sum_{\substack{j=1\\ j\neq i}}^{n} [A_i,A_j]\left(\sum_{\ell=1}^{k_j} \frac{d\alpha_{k_i}^i - d\alpha_\ell^j}{\alpha_{k_i}^i - \alpha_\ell^j}\right) . \qquad i = 1,2,\dots,n$$

Ces équations sont en fait toutes identiques et ceci grâce à la complète intégrabilité de (e) qui a permis de montrer que $\tilde{\varepsilon}_i$ était à coefficients constants (u fixé) et donc :

$$\tilde{\varepsilon}_i(u,\alpha_1^i,0) = \tilde{\varepsilon}_i(u,\alpha_2^i,0) \quad \text{c'est-à-dire :}$$

$$\sum_{\substack{j=1\\ j\neq i}}^{n} [A_i,A_j]\left(\sum_{\ell=1}^{k_j} \frac{d\alpha_1^i - d\alpha_\ell^j}{\alpha_1^i - \alpha_\ell^j}\right) = \sum_{\substack{j=1\\ j\neq i}}^{n} [A_i,A_j]\left(\sum_{\ell=1}^{k_j} \frac{d\alpha_2^i - d\alpha_\ell^j}{\alpha_2^i - \alpha_\ell^j}\right) .$$

Les équations (E') s'écrivent donc :

$$dA_i = \sum_{j=1}^{n} [A_i, A_j] \left(\sum_{\ell=1}^{k_j} \frac{d\alpha_i - d\alpha_\ell^j}{\alpha_i - \alpha_\ell^j} \right)$$

elles sont identiques à (E) et le théorème est démontré.

2. Remarque 4-2.- On a un résultat identique à partir du théorème 3-11, la démonstration étant légèrement plus difficile.

Les équations (E) possèdent des propriétés analogues à celles étudiées par L. Schlesinger dans [1], en particulier on a :

3. PROPOSITION 4-3.- *Le système (E) est complètement intégrable.*

4. PROPOSITION 4-4.- *Les solutions de (E) n'ont pas de singularités critiques mobiles.*

Il suffit de remarquer que vers les hypothèses prises au départ, les $\tilde{\varepsilon}_i$ n'ont pas de singularité sur u, et d'utiliser les résultats contenus dans [1] et [2] ainsi que le théorème 4-1.

5. PROPOSITION 4-5.- *Les valeurs caractéristiques des matrices A_i sont invariantes le long d'une solution.*

Démonstration.- On a d'après la proposition 1-3 : $B_i R_i B_i^{-1} = A_i$ avec $R_i(u) = \text{Cste}$. La proposition en résulte immédiatement.

6. Remarque 4-6.- On peut vérifier de plus que le système (E) vérifie

$$\sum_{i=1}^{n} k_i \, dA_i = 0 .$$

On vérifierait de même qu'il est compatible avec les conditions de complète intégrabilité de ω.

Nous allons maintenant étudier un exemple :

§ 5. - APPLICATIONS AUX FONCTIONS HYPERGEOMETRIQUES F_1 sur $\mathbb{P}_2(\mathbb{C})$.

Nous allons étudier dans ce paragraphe le problème de Schlesinger associé aux fonctions hypergéométriques F_1 sur $\mathbb{P}_2(\mathbb{C})$, plus précisément le problème de Schlesinger associé au système de Fuchs possédant les singularités suivantes :

$$F_1(u_1,u_2,X,Y,Z) = X \qquad F_2(u_1,u_2,X,Y,Z) = Y \qquad F_3(u_1,u_2,X,Y,Z) = X - u_1 Z$$

$$F_u(u_1,u_2,X,Y,Z) = Y - \mathcal{U}_2 Z \quad F_5(u_1,u_2,X,Y,Z) = \frac{1}{u_2-u_1}(u_2 X - u_1 Y) \quad F_6(u_1,u_2,X,Y,Z) = Z$$

$$(u_1,u_2) \in \mathcal{U} \subset \mathbb{C}^2 - [\{(u_1,u_2) \mid u_1 = u_2\} \cup \{u_1 = 0\} \cup \{u_2 = 0\}]$$

($\mathcal{U}$ ouvert simplement connexe) .

Le système de Fuchs associé s'écrit :

(e) $$d_v f = f \left[A_1 \frac{dX}{X} + A_2 \frac{dY}{Y} + A_3 \frac{dX-u_1 dZ}{X-u_1 Z} + A_4 \frac{dY-u_2 dZ}{Y-u_2 Z} + A_5 \frac{u_2 dX-u_1 dY}{u_2 X-u_1 Y} + A_6 \frac{dZ}{Z} \right]$$

avec $\sum_{i=1}^{6} A_i = 0$.

Dans la carte 0_1 (e) s'écrit :

$$d_v f = f \left[A_1 \frac{dx}{x} + A_2 \frac{dy}{y} + A_3 \frac{dx}{x-u_1} + A_4 \frac{dy}{y-u_2} + A_5 \frac{u_2 dx-u_1 dy}{u_2 x-u_1 y} \right] .$$

Remarque 5-1.- La configuration des singularités est la suivante :

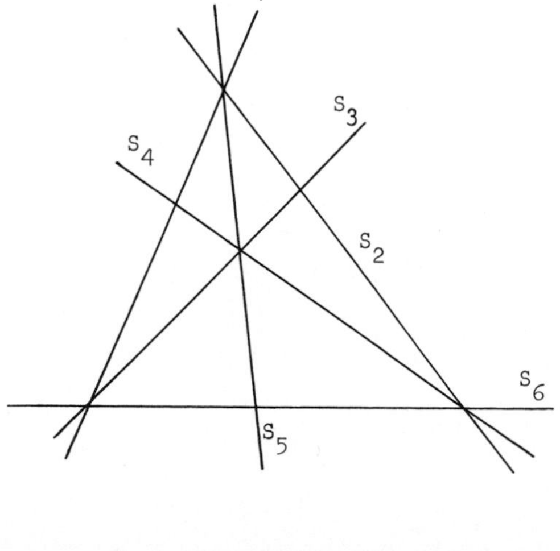

Nous allons écrire les équations $(E)^*$ énoncées dans le théorème 3-11 avec $B_6(u_1,u_2,1,0) = Id$. D'après le théorème 4-1 il suffit de les écrire pour le système restreint à une droite (D) passant par (1,1,0) par exemple la droite $y = x-1$, en tenant compte des relations de complète intégrabilité.

Le système restreint s'écrit :

$$d_V f = f[A_1 \frac{dx}{x} + A_2 \frac{dx}{x-1} + A_3 \frac{dx}{x-u_1} + A_4 \frac{dx}{x-(1+u_2)} + A_5 \frac{dx}{x - \frac{u_1}{u_2-u_1}}] .$$

Ecrivons aussi les conditions de complète intégrabilité :

2) PROPOSITION 5-2.- <u>Les conditions de complète intégrabilité pour</u> (e) <u>s'écrivent</u> :

$$[A_1,A_4] = [A_5,A_6] = [A_2,A_3] = 0$$

$$[A_1,A_3] = [A_3,A_6] = [A_6,A_1] \qquad [A_1,A_5] = [A_2,A_1] = [A_5,A_2]$$

$$[A_2,A_4] = [A_6,A_2] = [A_4,A_6] \qquad [A_3,A_5] = [A_4,A_3] = [A_5,A_4] .$$

<u>Démonstration</u>.- On a $\omega \wedge \omega = 0$ et en particulier $(X.(\omega\wedge\omega))|_{X=0} = 0$ soit :

$$[A_1,A_2] \frac{dX\wedge dY}{Y} + [A_1,A_3] \frac{dX\wedge dZ}{Z} + [A_1,A_4] \frac{dX\wedge dY - u_2 dX\wedge dZ}{Y-u_2 Z}$$

$$+ [A_1,A_5] \frac{dX\wedge dY}{Y} + [A_1,A_6] \frac{dX\wedge dZ}{Z} = 0 .$$

D'où $[A_1,A_4] = 0 \qquad [A_1,A_3]+[A_1,A_5] = 0 \qquad [A_1,A_3]+[A_1,A_6] = 0$.

On procède de même pour les autres relations.

3) <u>Equation relative à</u> A_1 .-

Il vient d'après (E') :

$$dA_1 = [A_1,A_2] \frac{0}{1} + [A_1,A_3] \frac{du_1}{u_1} + [A_1,A_4] \frac{du_2}{1+u_2} + [A_1,A_5] (\frac{du_1}{u_1} - \frac{du_2-du_1}{u_2-u_1})$$

qui compte tenu de la complète intégrabilité s'écrit :

$$dA_1 = [A_6,A_1]\,\frac{du_1}{u_1} + [A_2,A_1]\left(\frac{du_1}{u_2} - \frac{du_2-du_1}{u_2-u_1}\right).$$

4) <u>Système</u> (E^*) <u>associé</u> :

On procède de même pour les autres et finalement on a :

$$(E^*)\quad \begin{cases} dA_1 = [A_6,A_1]\,\dfrac{du_1}{u_1} + [A_2,A_1]\left(\dfrac{du_1}{u_1} - \dfrac{du_2-du_1}{u_2-u_1}\right) \\[2ex] dA_2 = [A_6,A_2]\,\dfrac{du_2}{u_2} + [A_1,A_2]\left(\dfrac{du_2}{u_2} - \dfrac{du_2-du_1}{u_2-u_1}\right) \\[2ex] dA_3 = [A_6,A_3]\,\dfrac{du_1}{u_1} + [A_3,A_5]\left(\dfrac{du_1}{u_1} - \dfrac{du_2-du_1}{u_2-u_1}\right) \\[2ex] dA_4 = [A_6,A_4]\,\dfrac{du_2}{u_2} + [A_4,A_5]\left(\dfrac{du_2}{u_2} - \dfrac{du_2-du_1}{u_2-u_1}\right) \\[2ex] dA_5 = [A_5,A_1]\left(\dfrac{du_1}{u_1} - \dfrac{du_2}{u_2}\right) + [A_5,A_4]\left(\dfrac{du_2}{u_2} - \dfrac{du_1}{u_1}\right) \\[2ex] dA_6 = 0\,. \end{cases}$$

<u>Remarque 5-3</u>.- On pourra vérifier que les équations obtenues sont compatibles avec les relations de complète intégrabilité, c'est-à-dire définissent un feuilletage de codimension 2 sur le sous espace associé aux matrices $A_1,\dots,A_6$ vérifiant les conditions de complète intégrabilité.

De plus $dA_1 + dA_2 + \quad + dA_5 = 0$.

<u>Remarque 5-4</u>.- Si les matrices A_i $i = 1,2,\dots,6$ sont indépendantes de u_1 et u_2 et vérifient (E^*) , le système de Fuchs associé ne définit que des fonctions élémentaires quel que soit (u_1, u_2) dans $\mathcal{U}$.

En effet, on a :

$dA_1 = 0$ ce qui entraîne immédiatement compte tenu de (E^*) :

$$[A_1, A_6] = 0 \qquad [A_1,A_2] = 0\,.$$

On procède de même pour A_2,A_3,A_4,A_5,A_6 et l'on constate que toutes les matrices commutent deux à deux ce qui entraîne d'après [5] que le système de Fuchs associé ne définit que des fonctions élémentaires.

Rappelons un théorème démontré dans [5] :

Si le sextuple $H = (A_1,A_2,A_3,A_4,A_5,A_6)$ n'est pas élémentaire et vérifie les conditions (I) et (S) alors ou bien H est décomposable ou bien modulo certaines permutations des matrices A_i , il existe une base de V telle que dans cette base les matrices des endomorphismes de H aient la forme :

$$A_1 = \begin{pmatrix} \alpha'_1 & 0 & 0 \\ -b_2 & \alpha_1 & 0 \\ -b_3 & 0 & \alpha_1 \end{pmatrix} \qquad A_2 = \begin{pmatrix} \alpha_2 & b_1 & 0 \\ 0 & \alpha'_2 & 0 \\ 0 & -b_3 & \alpha_2 \end{pmatrix} \qquad A_3 = \begin{pmatrix} b_1+\beta'_2 & 0 & b_1 \\ 0 & \beta_2 & 0 \\ b_3 & 0 & b_3+\beta'_2 \end{pmatrix}$$

$$A_4 = \begin{pmatrix} \beta_1 & 0 & 0 \\ 0 & b_2+\beta'_1 & b_2 \\ 0 & b_3 & b_3+\beta'_1 \end{pmatrix} \qquad A_5 = \begin{pmatrix} b_1+\beta'_1 & b_1 & 0 \\ b_2 & b_2+\beta'_3 & 0 \\ 0 & 0 & \beta_3 \end{pmatrix} \qquad A_6 = \begin{pmatrix} \alpha_3 & 0 & -b_1 \\ 0 & \alpha_3 & -b_2 \\ 0 & 0 & \alpha'_3 \end{pmatrix}$$

où $b_1 = \frac{1}{2}(-\beta_1+\beta'_1+\beta_2-\beta'_2+\beta_3-\beta'_3)$ $\quad b_2 = \frac{1}{2}(\beta_1-\beta'_1-\beta_2+\beta'_2+\beta_3-\beta'_3)$

$b_3 = \frac{1}{2}(\beta_1-\beta'_1+\beta_2-\beta'_2-\beta_3+\beta'_3)$ $\quad \alpha'_1+\alpha_2+\alpha_3+\beta'_1+\beta_2+\beta_3 = 0$

$\alpha_1+\alpha'_2+\alpha_3+\beta'_2+\beta_1+\beta_3 = 0$ $\quad \alpha_1+\alpha_2+\alpha'_3+\beta_1+\beta_2+\beta'_3 = 0$.

On a alors :

5) PROPOSITION 5-5.- Si les matrices définies ci-dessus vérifient les équations (E^*) , les solutions du système de Fuchs associé (u_1,u_2) fixé dans $\mathcal{U}$, sont toutes élémentaires.

Démonstration.- On a vu dans la proposition 4-5 que si les matrices A_i vérifiaient (E) (ou (E^*)) les valeurs propres étaient constantes le long d'une solution. Or ici les valeurs propres des matrices A_i , $i = 1,2,\dots,n$, sont :

$$\alpha_1,\alpha'_1,\alpha_2,\alpha'_2,\alpha_3,\alpha'_3,\beta_1,\beta'_1,\beta_2,\beta'_2,\beta_3,\beta'_3 .$$

Tous ces termes sont donc constants et par suite b_1, b_2, b_3 et donc les matrices A_i. D'après la remarque précédente les matrices A_i commutent et les fonctions définies par le système de Fuchs associé, sont élémentaires.

Conséquences. Dans les deux cas particuliers étudiés ci-dessus, si les matrices A_i vérifient (E^*) les fonctions solutions du système de Fuchs associé sont élémentaires. Le problème de savoir s'il en est toujours ainsi se pose donc naturellement et l'on a :

6) PROPOSITION 5-6.-

Il existe des fonctions hypergéométriques associées au système de Fuchs défini par :

$$df = f[B_1 \frac{dX}{X} + B_2 \frac{dY}{Y} + B_3 \frac{dX-u_1dZ}{X-u,Z} + B_4 \frac{dY-u_2dZ}{Y-u_2Z} + B_5 \frac{u_2dX-u,dY}{u_2X-u,Y} + B_6 \frac{dZ}{Z}]$$

où :

1. $B_i = e^P.A_i.e^{-P}$ $\quad A_i$ matrices définies dans la proposition 5-5

2. $P = \begin{pmatrix} a & b & c \\ d & e & f \\ g & h & i \end{pmatrix}$ avec

$$a = \mathrm{Log}[u_1^{\alpha_3-\alpha_3'} (\frac{u_1}{u_2-u_1})^{b_2}] \qquad b = \mathrm{Log}(\frac{u_2-u_1}{u_1})^{b_1}$$

$$c = \mathrm{Log}(u_1^{-b_1}) \qquad d = \mathrm{Log}(\frac{u_2-u_1}{u_2})^{b_1} \qquad e = \mathrm{Log}[u_2^{(\alpha_3-\alpha_3')} (\frac{u_2}{u_2-u_1})^{b_1}]$$

$$f = \mathrm{Log}(u_2^{-b_2}) \qquad g = h = i = 0$$

qui ont leur monodromie indépendante de u_1 et u_2 (et sont bien sûr non élémentaires).

Démonstration : Ecrivons les équations (E^*) associées aux B_i en remarquant que dA_i puisque les valeurs propres de B_i donc de A_i sont constantes.

$$dB_1 = e^P\, dP\, A_i.e^{-P} - e^P A_1 e^{-P}.dP = e^P[A_6, A_1]e^{-P} \frac{du_1}{u_1} + e^P[A_1, A_2]e^{-P}(\frac{du_2-du_1}{u_2-u_1} - \frac{du_2}{u_1})$$

d'où :

$$[dP,A_1] = [A_6,A_1]\,\frac{du_1}{u_1} + [A_1,A_2]\left(\frac{du_2-du_1}{u_2-u_1} - \frac{du_2}{u_1}\right) .$$

On procède de même pour les autres équations, en particulier :

$$[dP,A_2] = [A_6,A_2]\,\frac{du_2}{u_2} + [A_1,A_2]\left(\frac{du_2}{u_2} - \frac{du_2-du_1}{u_2-u_1}\right)$$

$$[dP,A_6] = 0 .$$

Comme $dP = \begin{pmatrix} da & db & dc \\ dd & de & df \\ dh & di & dj \end{pmatrix}$ il vient :

$$[dP,A_6] = \begin{pmatrix} b_1\,dg & b_1\,dh & (di-da)b_1 - (\alpha_3-\alpha_3')\,dc - b_2\,db \\ b_2\,dg & b_2\,dh & (di-de)b_2 - (\alpha_3-\alpha_3')\,df - b_1\,dd \\ (\alpha_3-\alpha_3')dg & (\alpha_3-\alpha_3')dh & -b_1\,dg - b_2\,dh \end{pmatrix}$$

Soit :

$$(1)\qquad \begin{cases} dg = 0 \qquad dh = 0 \\ (da-di)b_1 + (\alpha_3-\alpha_3')dc + b_2\,db = 0 \\ (de-di)b_2 + (\alpha_3-\alpha_3')df + b_1\,dd = 0 . \end{cases}$$

De même

$$[dP,A_1] = \begin{pmatrix} -b_2\,db - b_3\,dc & (\alpha_1-\alpha_1')db & (\alpha_1-\alpha_1')dc \\ (\alpha_1'-\alpha_1)dd + (da-de)b_2 - b_3\,df & b_2\,db & b_2\,dc \\ (da-di)b_3 - b_3\,dh & b_3\,db & b_3\,dc \end{pmatrix}$$

$$[A_6,A_1] = \begin{pmatrix} b_1 b_3 & 0 & (\alpha_1'-\alpha_1)b_1 \\ b_2 b_3 & 0 & b_1 b_2 \\ (\alpha_3-\alpha_3')b_3 & 0 & -b_1 b_3 \end{pmatrix}$$

$$[A_1,A_2] = \begin{pmatrix} -b_1b_2 & -(\alpha_1' - \alpha_1)b_1 & 0 \\ -(\alpha_2 - \alpha_2')b_2 & b_1b_2 & 0 \\ -b_2b_3 & b_1b_3 & 0 \end{pmatrix}$$

ce qui entraîne

$$(2) \quad \begin{cases} dc = b_1 \dfrac{du_1}{u_1} \quad db = -b_1\left(\dfrac{du_1}{u_1} - \dfrac{du_2-du_1}{u_2-u_1}\right) \\[2ex] da - di = (\alpha_3 - \alpha_3') \dfrac{du_1}{u_1} + b_2\left(\dfrac{du_1}{u_1} - \dfrac{du_2-du_1}{u_2-u_1}\right) . \end{cases}$$

De même en utilisant l'équation relative à $[dP, A_2]$ il vient :

$$(3) \quad \begin{cases} dd = -b_2\left(\dfrac{du_2}{u_2} - \dfrac{du_2-du_1}{u_2-u_1}\right) \quad df = -b_2 \dfrac{du_2}{u_2} \\[2ex] dc - di = (\alpha_3 - \alpha_3') \dfrac{du_2}{u_2} + b_1\left(\dfrac{du_2}{u_2} - \dfrac{du_2-du_1}{u_2-u_1}\right) . \end{cases}$$

Toutes les autres équations se ramènent à celles-ci et la proposition est démontrée.

§ 6. - CONCLUSION.

A partir des équations (E^*) associées au système de Fuchs sur $\mathbb{P}_1(\mathbb{C})$:

$$df = f\left(A \frac{dx}{x} + B \frac{dx}{x-1} + C \frac{dx}{x-t}\right) .$$

R. Fuchs a pu former l'équation VI de Painlevé qui elle-même "engendre" toutes les autres.

L'étude analogue faite pour l'exemple étudié ci-dessus, ne conduit, du moins dans le cas traité dans la proposition 5-6, qu'à des équations linéaires. Il serait peut être intéressant d'augmenter l'ordre des matrices pour obtenir des résultats plus intéressants, dans le cadre de la recherche d'équations à singularités fixes généralisant l'équation VI à plusieurs variables.

§ 7. - BIBLIOGRAPHIE.

[1] L. SCHLESINGER — Differential systeme mit festen kritischen Punkten. Journal für M. und angew. Math., t. 129, 1905.

[2] K. AOMOTO — Une remarque sur la solution des équations de L. Schlesinger et dappo. Danilewsky. J. Fac. Sciences Univ. Tokyo, t. 17, 1970.

[3] R. GERARD — Théorie de Fuchs sur une variété analytique complexe. Journal de Math. pures et appliquées, 47, 1968.

[4] R. GERARD — Le problème de Riemann-Hilbert sur une variété analytique complexe, Ann. Inst. Fourier, Tome XIX, 1970.

[5] R. GERARD et A.H.M. LEVELT — Etude d'une classe particulière de système de Pfaff du type de Fuchs sur l'espace projectif complexe. Journ. Math. Pures et Appliq. 51, 1972.

[6] R. GARNIER — Solution du problème de Riemann. Ann. Ec. Normale XLIII, 1926.

[7] P. DELIGNE — Equations Différentielles à points singuliers réguliers. Lect. Notes in Math. 163, 1970.

The Problems of Riemann and Hilbert and the relations of Fuchs in several complex variables

By

Osamu SUZUKI*

§ Introduction

In the theory of ordinary differential equations some results on the problem of Riemann and Hilbert and the relation of Fuchs are well known. The purpose of the present paper is to extend these results to the theory of several complex variables. It seems to me that these results give also main parts of the general theory of differential equations of regular singularity in the theory of several complex variables(as for the definition of regular singularity, see § 1).

Let M be a Riemann surface and let Y be a set of discrete points $\{p_j\}$ in M. We consider a differential equation which admits regular singularities at most on Y:

$$(0,1) \qquad d\Phi = \Phi\Omega ,$$

where Ω is a matrix valued meromorphic 1-form on M. Fix a point p in M - Y and consider an analytic continuation of a solution along a closed path through p. Then we obtain the following monodromy representation of the homotopy group $\pi_1(M-Y,p)$ to the

* The auther is supported by the Humboldt foundation during a part of the period of preparation of this work.

general linear group of rank r, GL(r, $\mathbb{C}$), where r is a rank of Ω:

(0,2) $\rho_{\Phi} : \pi_1(M-Y, p) \dashrightarrow GL(r, \mathbb{C})$.

Conversely assume that the following representation is given:

(0,3) $\rho : \pi_1(M-Y, p) \dashrightarrow GL(r, \mathbb{C})$.

Then the problem of Riemann and Hilbert asks the following question: Can we find a differential equation(0,1) so that the monodromy representation ρ_{Φ} of Φ is identical with the given ρ ?

When Y is empty,i.e., Y $\neq \emptyset$, the above problem is affirmatively solved by A.Weil [9]. There he solved the problem by using well known Theta-Fuchs series. More generally, when Y $\neq \emptyset$, the problem was solved by H.Röhrl in his famous paper [6]. Also it is well known that a necessary and sufficient condition to be a differential equation with regular singularity,i.e., the relation of Fuchs is given(for example, see T.Saito [7]).

Now we shall extend the above results to the theory of several complex variables. Let Y be an analytic set of codimension 1 which have the following two assumptions: (1) The singularities of Y are at most of normal crossing and (2) Every irreducible component of Y is non-singular. In view of the book of P.Deligne,[1] the above restrictions never lose the generalities of considerations. First following P.Deligne, we shall give the definition of regular singularities(§ 1). Then we can formulate the problem of Riemann and Hilbert as in the case of one variable. In what follows, this problem is called problem I when Y is empty and in the remained case, this problem is called problem II. Following the idea of H.Röhrl, we shall reduce the problems to the exsitence problems of meromorphic sections of the following two holomorphic vector bundles. The one is the flat vector bundle E_{ρ} on M-Y which is induced from the representation ρ (§ 2) and the other is the one which is obtained by extending E_ρ to the holomorphic vector bundle E_ρ^* on M(§ 3). The essential step in obtaining the solutions of the problem II is to construct the vector bundle E_ρ^* . In the one variable case, the singularity Y is of isolated points and there occurs no difficulty. But in our case, the situation seems rather difficult. In § 3 we shall devote ourselves to make E_ρ^* . Manin[4] has already treat this extension problem and given an affirmative answer. Therefore combining this with the results in P.Deligne[1], we may think that the problem II is already solved implicitly*. In this paper we shall treat the extension problem by using the idea of H.Röhrl and give an result which includes the result of Manin. By using this result and cohomology vanishing theorems, we can give the solutions for the problem II on Stein manifolds and projective algebraic manifolds respectively(§ 4). We remark that our results include the ones of R.Gerard[2] as a special case. Now we proceed to the relations of Fuchs. By using the results in § 3 and applying the residue theorem which is due to M.Otuki[5], we shall give the relations of Fuchs in several complex variables in terms of the monodromy representation ρ . At the end of § 5, in the case of one variable this result is nothing but the well known the relation of Fuchs(see T.Saito[7]).

Finally we shall give some comment on a relation between differntial equations and several complex variables. From the view point of differential equations we shall consider pseudoconvex manifolds which admit only constant holomorphic functions(§ 5).

In the appendix we give some propositions on matrixs which are used in § 3.

The auther would like to express his hearty thanks to Professors K.Kasahara and I.Wakabayashi and my friends M.Kita and M.Otuki for many corrections and for their encouragements during the preparation of this paper.

* After preparation of this paper, Prof. Deligne communicated me that the solution is given in N.M.Katz[11] explicitly.

§ 1 The Definition of Differential Equations of regular singularities

The purpose of this section is to define the regular singularities of differntial equations in several complex variables. Let M be a complex manifold and let Y be an analytic set with the assumptions stated in Introduction. By $\pi_1(M-Y,p)$ we denote the fundamental group with respect to the base point p. We assume that the following representation is given:

$$\rho : \pi_1(M-Y,p) \dashrightarrow GL(r,\mathbb{C}).$$

Defintion(1,1). The matrix valued function Φ is called ρ-multiplicative function if there exists a branch Φ_0 of Φ at p such that the following holds for any closed path γ :

$$\gamma^* \Phi_0 = \rho([\gamma])\Phi_0,$$

where $[\gamma]$ denotes the homotopy class of γ and γ^* denotes the analytic continuation of Φ_0 along γ. Moreover, we assume that det $\Phi_0(p^*) \neq 0$ for some point $p^* \in M-Y$.

If Φ is a ρ-multiplicative function, then we obtain the following matrix valued meromorphic 1-form on M-Y:

$$\Omega = \Phi^{-1}d\Phi. \tag{1,2}$$

Here we remark that Ω satisfies the following integrabilty condition:

$$d\Omega - \Omega\wedge\Omega = 0. \tag{1,3}$$

Conversely, take a 1-form Ω on M-Y with the condition(1,3) and the differential equation (1,2). Then we obtain a multivalued function .

By the assumptions stated in Introduction, the singularities of Y are of normal crossing. Hence for any point p Y, there exists a system of local coordinates $z^1, z^2, \cdots, z^n$ on some neighborhood U of p such that

$$Y = \bigcup_{j=1}^{N} Y_j , \qquad U \cap Y_j = \{ z_j = 0 \} \ (j=1,2,\cdots,N).$$

Now we shall define the regular singularities of Φ . We assume that there exist a constant matrix $\underline{M}_j$ for each j such that

$$[\underline{M}_j, \underline{M}_k] = \underline{M}_j\underline{M}_k - \underline{M}_k\underline{M}_j = 0 \quad \text{for all j and k.}$$

Letting

$$z^{\underline{M}} = \exp(\underline{M} \log z) \qquad \text{for} \quad z \in \mathbb{C} ,$$

we set

$$\Phi^* = z_1^{\underline{M}_1} \cdot z_2^{\underline{M}_2} \cdots z_N^{\underline{M}_N} \qquad \text{on} \quad U.$$

Definition(1,4). The ρ -multiplicative function Φ has regular singularities on Y, if for any point $p \in Y$, there exists a neighborhood U of p and Φ^* on U such that $\Phi^{*-1}\Phi$ is a single valued meromorphic function on U.

It is easily seen that the definition does not depend on the choices of defining equations of Y_j and the branchs of log z_j. It must be remarked that Φ has the regularsingularities on Y, then Ω is a meromorphic 1-form on M.

Next we shall define accessary singularities of Φ : By P_Φ and Z_Φ we denote the analytic sets of pole sets of Φ and the analytic set defined by $\{ \det\Phi = 0 \}$.

Definition(1,5). The analytic set $Z = P_{\Phi} \cup Z_{\Phi}$ is called accessary singularities of Φ.

Finally we remark that the definition of the regular singularities does not depend on the forming of monoidal transforms. Let A be a non-singular analytic set which is contained in Y. Let $Q: M^* \dashrightarrow M$ be a monoidal transform with the center A. We write $\rho^* = Q^*\rho$ and $Y^* = Q^*Y$. Then we obtain

Proposition(1,6). If there exists a ρ^*-multiplicative function Φ^* which admits regular singularities on Y^*, then there exists a ρ-multiplicative function Φ such that Φ admits regular singularities on Y. Moreover, $\Phi^* = Q^*\Phi$.

§ 2 H.Röhrl's Formulation of Problem I

In this section, following H.Röhrl[6], we shall deduce the problem I to an existence problem of sections of a flat vector bundle. Let γ_1, γ_2 be two closed paths through p. We define the product of γ_1 and γ_2 as follows:

$$\gamma_1 \gamma_2 = \begin{cases} \gamma_1(2t) & 0 \leqq t \leqq 1/2 \\ \gamma_2(2t-1) & 1/2 \leqq t \leqq 1 \end{cases}$$

Hence we see that $\rho([\gamma_1][\gamma_2]) = \rho([\gamma_1])\,\rho([\gamma_2])$ holds, where $[\gamma]$ denotes the homotopy class of γ, i.e, $[\gamma] \in \pi_1(M,p)$.

In a well known manner, from the representation ρ, we make the flat vector bundle E_ρ as follows: Let $\{U_\lambda\}$ be a simple covering of M, i.e., every intersection $U_{i_1} \cap U_{i_2} \cap \ldots \cap U_{i_k}$ is connected and simply connected. We may assume that $p \in U_0$.

For each U_λ, we choose a point $p_\lambda \in U_\lambda$ and join p and p_λ by a path γ_λ' starting at p and ending at p_λ. For a point $q \in U_\lambda$, we choose a path $D_\lambda(q)(\subset U_\lambda)$ which starts at p_λ and ends at q and set $\gamma_\lambda(q) = \gamma'.D_\lambda(q)$. Consider

$$\gamma_{\lambda\mu}(q) = \gamma_\lambda(q)\cdot\gamma^{-1}(q) \qquad \text{for } q \in U_\lambda \cap U_\mu .$$

It is easily seen that $[\gamma_{\lambda\mu}(q)] \in \pi_1(M,p)$ and that it does not depend on the choice of q. Hence we see that

$$c_{\lambda\mu} = \rho\,([\gamma_{\lambda\mu}(q)])$$

determines an element in $GL(r,\mathbb{C})$. Moreover, we see that

$$c_{\lambda\mu} = c_{\lambda\tau}\cdot c_{\tau\mu} \qquad \text{on } U_\lambda \cap U_\mu \cap U_\tau .$$

Hence from this cocycle $\{c_{\lambda\mu}\}$ we obtain a flat vector bundle, which is denoted by E_ρ. The following Proposition is due to H.Röhrl:

Proposition(2,1). For a given representation ρ, there exists a ρ-multiplicative function if and only if E_ρ admits a system of meromorphic sections which are linearly independent.

Proof. Suppose that a ρ-multiplicative function Φ is given. Then there exists a branch Φ_0 of Φ on U_0 so that

$$\gamma^* \Phi_0 = \rho([\gamma])\Phi_0$$

holds for every loop γ. We choose a covering $\{U_\lambda\}$ and paths $\{\gamma'_\lambda\}$ in the manner above mentioned. We set

$$\gamma_\lambda^{*} \Phi_0 = \Phi_\lambda$$

for each λ. Since Φ_λ satisfies (1,3) on U_λ, we can find a constant matrix $c'_{\lambda\mu}$ $(\det c'_{\lambda\mu} \neq 0)$ such that

$$\Phi_\lambda = c'_{\lambda\mu}\Phi_\mu \qquad \text{on } U_\lambda \cap U_\mu .$$

By the definition of Φ_λ and Φ_μ, it is easily seen that

$$(2,2) \qquad c'_{\lambda\mu} = \rho([\gamma_\lambda(q)\cdot\gamma_\mu(q)^{-1}]) \qquad \text{for} \quad q \in U_\lambda \cap U_\mu .$$

Hence, letting $\Phi_\lambda = (\varphi_\lambda^{(1)}, \cdots, \varphi_\lambda^{(r)})$, where $\varphi_\lambda^{(j)}(j=1,2,\cdots,r)$ are column vectors, we see that $\{\varphi_\lambda^{(j)}\}$ gives a meromorphic sections of E_ρ for each j. From det $\Phi \neq 0$, $\varphi^{(1)},\cdots,\varphi^{(r)}$ are linearly independent. Conversly we consider a meromorphic section φ of E . Choosing a path σ which starts at p, we define an analytic continuation of φ . We choose a finite covering elements $\{U_j\}_{j=o,1,\ldots,m}$ of σ so that $U_i \cap U_{i+1} \neq \emptyset (i=o,1,\cdots,m-1)$. Let $\varphi = \{\varphi_\lambda\}$. Then we see that $\varphi_i = c_{i,i+1}\ \varphi_{i+1}$ on $U_i \cap U_{i+1}$ $(i=o,1,\cdots,m-1)$. For each i, we define ϕ_i on U_i as follows:

$$\phi_i = c_{o,1}\cdot c_{1,2}\cdots c_{i-1,i}\ \varphi_i \ .$$

Since $\{c_{i,i+1}\}$ are constant matrixs, ϕ_i are defined on U_i and $\phi_i = \phi_{i+1}$ on $U_i \cap U_{i+1}$. Hence we obtain a function ϕ on some neighborhood of σ which is defined by $\phi = \phi_i$ on U_i. We call ϕ the analytic continuation of φ along σ . Making the continuation of φ for every path starting at p, we obtain a multivalued function Φ on M. It is easily seen that Φ may be considered as a single valued function on the universal covering manifold of M. Now we shall show that

$$(2,3) \qquad \Phi(\gamma^* p) = \rho([\sigma])\,\Phi(p)$$

for every $[\sigma] \in \pi_1(M,p)$. To prove (2,3), we consider the continuation of φ along σ . We choose covering elements $\{U_i\}_{i=o,1,\cdots,m+1}$, where $U_{m+1} = U_o$ as in the manner above mentioned. Choose a point p_{i+1} on $\sigma \cap U_i \cap U_{i+1}$ and denote by σ_i the part of σ between p_i and p_{i+1} for i=o,1,...,m-1 and by σ_m the remained part of σ from p_m to p_o. Then we see that

$\sigma = \sigma_o \cdot \sigma_1 \cdot \cdots \sigma_m$. From

$$\sigma = \sigma_o : \gamma_1^{-1}(p_1)\cdot(\gamma_1(p_1)\cdot\sigma_1\cdot\gamma_2^{-1}(p_2))\cdot(\gamma_2(p_2)\cdot\sigma_2\cdot\gamma_3^{-1}(p_3))$$

$$\cdots(\gamma_{m-1}(p_{m-1})\cdot\sigma_{m-1}\cdot\gamma_m^{-1}(p_m))\cdot\gamma_m(p_m)\cdot\sigma_m$$

and from(2,2), we obtain

$$\rho(\sigma) = c_{o,1}\cdot c_{1,2}\cdot\cdots c_{m,o}$$

which proves (2,3). From this we can easily the converse of Proposition(2,1).

In § 4, we shall give a method of obtaining ρ-multiplicative functions.

§ 3 Röhrl's Formulation of Problem II

Let M be a complex manifold and let Y be a divisor in M. Suppose that a representation $\rho : \pi_1(M-Y,p) \dashrightarrow GL(r,\mathbb{C})$ is given. For this ρ, we shall consider the problem II. Following the idea due to Röhrl, we shall reduce this problem to the existence problems of meromorphic sections of two vector bundles. The one is the flat vector bundle E_ρ on M-Y which is obtained in §2 and the other is a holomorphic vector bundle E_ρ^* on M which is a holomorphic extension of E_ρ. The purpose of this section is to prove the existence of E_ρ^* under the following assumptions:

(A-1): Y has at most singularities of normal crossing and every irreducible component of Y is non-singular,

(A-2): There exists a divisor S with $p \notin S$, where S may be not assumed to have singularities of normal crossing,

(A-3): From ρ, we obtain $\rho' : \pi_1(M-(Y\cup S),p) \dashrightarrow GL(r,\mathbb{C})$. Then there exists a ρ'-multiplicative function Φ on $M-(Y\cup S)$.

Let $\{U_\lambda\}$ be a simple covering of M. Take U_λ with $U_\lambda \cap Y \neq \emptyset$. We may assume that the origin of the local coordinates $z_\lambda^1, z_\lambda^2, \cdots, z_\lambda^n$ is in Y and the following is satisfied:

$$(3,1) \qquad U \cap Y = \bigcup_{\alpha=1}^{N_\lambda} Y_\alpha \quad \text{and} \quad Y_\alpha = \{ z_\lambda^\alpha = 0 \}.$$

In what follows we may assume that

$$U_\lambda \subset D_\lambda, \text{ where } D_\lambda = \{ (z_\lambda^1, z_\lambda^2, \cdots, z_\lambda^n) : |z_\lambda^j| < 1 \ (j=1,2,\cdots,n) \}.$$

Restricting U_λ on $M-(Y \cup S)$, we obtain a covering $\{U_\lambda'\}$ of $M-(Y \cup S)$. Refining this covering, we obtain also a simple covering $\{U_\lambda^{(j)}\}$ of $M-(Y \cup S)$, where $U_\lambda^{(j)} \subset U_\lambda'$ (see, A.Weil [10]). We may assume that $p \in U_0$. In the same manner as in §2, we can construct $E_{\rho'}$ on $M-(Y \cup S)$: For each λ, we fix an arbitrary covering element $U_\lambda^{(j)}$, which is denoted by $U_\lambda^{(j_\lambda)}$. For each $U_\lambda^{(j_\lambda)}$, we choose a point $p_\lambda^{(j_\lambda)}$ in $U_\lambda^{(j_\lambda)}$ and a path $\gamma_\lambda^{(j_\lambda)'} (\subset M-(Y \cup S))$ which starts at p_0 and ends at $p_\lambda^{(j_\lambda)}$. We take another $U_\lambda^{(j)}$ ($j \neq j_\lambda$). We choose a point $p_\lambda^{(j)}$ in $U_\lambda^{(j)}$ and a path $\sigma_\lambda^{(j)} (\subset U_\lambda-(Y \cup S))$ which starts at $p_\lambda^{(j_\lambda)}$ and ends at $p_\lambda^{(j)}$. We set $\gamma_\lambda^{(j)'} = \gamma_\lambda^{(j_\lambda)'} \cdot \sigma_\lambda^{(j)}$. As in §2, we denote a path in $U_\lambda^{(j)}$ joining $p_\lambda^{(j)}$ and $q \in U_\lambda^{(j)}$ by $D_\lambda^{(j)}(q)$. Finally we write $\gamma_\lambda^{(j)}(q) = \gamma_\lambda^{(j)'} \cdot D_\lambda(q)$ and we set

$$c_{\lambda\mu}^{(j,k)} = \rho([\gamma_\lambda^{(j)}(q) \cdot \gamma_\mu^{(k)^{-1}}(q)]) \qquad \text{on } U_\lambda^{(j)} \cap U_\mu^{(k)}.$$

Then we obtain a flat vector bundle $E_{\rho'}$ on $M-(Y \cup S)$.

Here we assemble basic properties concerning monodromy representations. Corresponding a loop γ ($\gamma \subset U_\lambda-(Y \cup S)$) starting $p_\lambda^{(j)}$ to a loop $\gamma_\lambda^{(j)'} \cdot \gamma \cdot \gamma_\lambda^{(j)'-1}$, we obtain the following representation:

$$\rho_\lambda^{(j)} : \pi_1(U_\lambda - (S \cup Y)) \dashrightarrow GL(r, \mathbb{C}).$$

For U_λ with $U_\lambda \cap Y \neq \emptyset$, we choose a loop $\gamma^{(j)}_{\lambda|\alpha}$ which winds a time clockwise along an irreducible component Y_α. Then from the condition(A-1), we see that

$$[\gamma^{(j)}_{\lambda|\alpha}][\gamma^{(j)}_{\lambda|\beta}] = [\gamma^{(j)}_{\lambda|\beta}]\,[\gamma^{(j)}_{\lambda|\alpha}] \qquad \text{in } \pi_1(D_\lambda - Y, p^{(j)}_\lambda).$$

We write

$$\rho^{(j)}_\lambda([\gamma^{(j)}_{\lambda|\alpha}]) = M^{(j)}_{\lambda|\alpha}.$$

Then from the definition of $\rho^{(j)}_\lambda$, we see that

$$(3,2) \qquad M^{(j)}_{\lambda|\alpha} \cdot M^{(j)}_{\lambda|\beta} = M^{(j)}_{\lambda|\beta} \cdot M^{(j)}_{\lambda|\alpha}.$$

We prove the following Proposition:

Proposition(3,3). Let $U^{(j)}_\lambda$ and $U^{(k)}_\mu$ be two covering elements with $U^{(j)}_\lambda \cap U^{(k)}_\mu \neq \emptyset$. Then for Y_α with $Y_\alpha \cap U_\lambda \cap U_\mu \neq \emptyset$, we have

$$M^{(j)}_{\lambda|\alpha} = c^{(j,k)}_{\lambda,\mu}\, M^{(k)}_{\mu|\alpha}\, c^{(j,k)\,-1}_{\lambda,\mu}.$$

proof. Since $\{U_\lambda\}$ is a simple covering, we can find a loop γ $(\subset U_\lambda \cap U_\mu - (Y \cup S))$ starting at a point $q \in U^{(j)}_\lambda \cap U^{(k)}_\mu$ which winds a time along Y_α in the anticrock direction. By the definition

$$M^{(j)}_{\lambda|\alpha} = \rho([\gamma^{(j)'}_\lambda \cdot D^{(j)}_\lambda(q) \cdot \gamma \cdot D^{(j)-1}_\lambda(q) \cdot \gamma^{(j)'-1}_\lambda])$$

$$M^{(k)}_{\mu|\alpha} = \rho([\gamma^{(k)'}_\lambda \cdot D^{(k)}_\lambda(q) \cdot \gamma \cdot D^{(k)-1}_\mu(q) \cdot \gamma^{(j)'-1}_\mu])$$

and

$$c^{(j,k)}_{\lambda,\mu} = \rho([\gamma^{(j)'}_\lambda \cdot D^{(j)}_\lambda(q) \cdot D^{(k)-1}_\mu(q)\, \gamma^{(k)'-1}_\mu]).$$

From this we can get the conclusion easily.

Corollary. $M^{(j)}_{\lambda|\alpha} = M^{(k)}_{\lambda|\alpha}$ for every j and k.

proof. From the choices of $\{\gamma^{(j)'}_\lambda\}$, $c^{(j,k)}_{\lambda,\lambda}$ commuts with

$M^{(j)}_{\lambda|\alpha}$. Then from(3,3) and from this, the Corollary follows.

Hence, in what follows we write $M_{\lambda|\alpha}$ for $M^{(j)}_{\lambda|\alpha}$.

Now we define the logarithm of matrixs in a well known manner and set

$$(3,4) \qquad \underline{M}_{\lambda|\alpha} = \frac{1}{2\pi\sqrt{-1}} \operatorname{Log} M_{\lambda|\alpha},$$

where Log denotes the special branches of loarithms of $M_{\lambda|\alpha}$ (see (A,5) in Appendix). Referring to (3,3) and (A,8) in Appendix, We can choose the same branches of logarithms for each irreducible component Y_α (see (A,7) in Appendix). Therefore in the following, we choose the same branch for each Y_α. Then from (A,9) and (3,2), we see that

$$\underline{M}_{\lambda|\alpha} \cdot \underline{M}_{\lambda|\beta} = \underline{M}_{\lambda|\beta} \cdot \underline{M}_{\lambda|\alpha} .$$

Moreover, if $U^{(j)}_\lambda \cap U^{(k)}_\mu \cap Y_\alpha \neq \emptyset$, from(A,8) and(3,3), we see that

$$(3,5) \qquad \underline{M}_{\lambda|\alpha} = c^{(j,k)}_{\lambda\mu} \cdot \underline{M}_{\mu|\alpha} \cdot c^{(j,k)-1}_{\lambda\mu} .$$

As for the detail discussions of the logarithm of matrixs, see Appendix.

We consider the ρ'-multiplicative function which is given in (A-3). By the definition(1,1), for a suitable branch Φ_0 of Φ at p, we see that

$$\gamma^* \Phi_0 = \rho([\gamma])\, \Phi_0 .$$

Now we set

$$\gamma^{(j)}_\lambda(q)^* \, \Phi_0 = \Phi^{(j)}_\lambda ,$$

which is a single valued function on $U_\lambda^{(j)}$. From(2,2), we see that

(3,6) $$\Phi_\lambda^{(j)} = c_{\lambda\mu}^{(j,k)} \ \Phi_\mu^{(k)}.$$

Also we see that

(3,7) $$\gamma_{\lambda|\alpha}^{(j)*} \ \Phi_\lambda^{(j)} = M_{\lambda|\alpha} \cdot \Phi_\lambda^{(j)}.$$

The proof is easy and may be omitted.

First we solve the problemII for the representation(3,7) on U_λ: For this we set

$$\Phi_\lambda^{*} = (z_\lambda^1)^{\underline{M}\lambda|1} . (z_\lambda^2)^{\underline{M}\lambda|2} \cdots (z_\lambda^N)^{\underline{M}\lambda|N} .$$

Then this gives a solution for (3,7) whose singularities are clearly regular.

Now we proceed to consider the problemII on M. We set on $U_\lambda^{(j)}$ with $U_\lambda \cap Y \neq \emptyset$

(3,8) $$\Phi_\lambda^{(j)*} = \sigma_\lambda^{(j)*}(\Phi_\lambda^{*}).$$

Then from(2,1), we see that

(3,9) $$\Phi_\lambda^{(j)*} = c_{\lambda.\lambda}^{(j,k)} \ \Phi_\lambda^{(k)*} \qquad \text{on} \quad U_\lambda^{(j)} \cap U_\lambda^{(k)}.$$

For $U_\lambda^{(j)}$ with $U_\lambda \cap Y = \emptyset$, we set $\Phi_\lambda^{(j)*} = E$ on $U_\lambda^{(j)}$, where E is the unit matrix. From this cochain $\{\Phi_\lambda^{(j)*}\}$, we set

$$Y_\lambda^{(j)} = \Phi_\lambda^{(j)*-1} . \ \Phi_\lambda^{(j)} \qquad \text{on} \quad U_\lambda^{(j)}.$$

From (3,6) and (3,9), we see that

$$Y_\lambda^{(j)} = Y_\lambda^{(k)} \qquad \text{on} \quad U_\lambda^{(j)} \cap U_\lambda^{(k)}.$$

Hence we get a function Y_λ on $U_\lambda - Y \cup S$ by defining $Y_\lambda |_{U_\lambda^{(j)}} = Y_\lambda^{(j)}$. Here we remark on $\{\Phi_\lambda^{(k)}\}$ that $\Phi_\lambda^{(k)} = \Phi_\lambda^{(l)}$ holds on $U_\lambda^{(k)} \cap U_\lambda^{(l)}$ with $U_\lambda \cap S \neq \emptyset$ and $U_\lambda \cap Y = \emptyset$. This follows from the fact that ρ' is induced from ρ. We may assume that $U_\lambda^{(j)} = U_\lambda$ for $U_\lambda \cap S = \emptyset$ and $U_\lambda \cap Y = \emptyset$. We set $Y = \Phi_\lambda^{(j)}$ for these two kinds of U_λ. From this we get a cochain $\{Y_\lambda\}$ with respect to the covering $\{U'_\lambda\}$ on $M - Y \cup S$. From this we set

$$H_{\lambda\mu} = Y_\lambda \cdot Y_\mu^{-1} \qquad \text{on } U_\lambda \cap U_\mu - Y \cup S.$$

Then we get the following

Proposition(3,10). $H_{\lambda\mu}$ are defined on $U_\lambda \cap U_\mu$ and $\{H_{\lambda\mu}\}$ defines a holomorphic vector bundle on M.

proof. At first we consider $H_{\lambda\mu}$ on $U_\lambda \cap U_\mu$ with $Y \cap U_\lambda \cap U_\mu \neq \emptyset$. We may assume the following

$$Y \cap U_\lambda = \bigcup_{\alpha=1}^{N_\lambda} Y_{\lambda|\alpha}$$

$$Y \cap U_\mu = \bigcup_{\beta=1}^{N_\mu} Y_{\mu|\beta}$$

$$Y \cap U_\lambda \cap U_\mu = \bigcup_{\gamma=1}^{N_{\lambda\mu}} Y_{\lambda|\gamma} = \bigcup_{\gamma=1}^{N_{\lambda\mu}} Y_{\mu|\gamma}.$$

The coordinate transforms are given as follows:

$$(3,11) \qquad \begin{aligned} z_\lambda^{(j)} &= z_\mu^{(j)} \cdot \phi_{\lambda\mu}^{(j)}(z_\mu^1, z_\mu^2, \cdots, z_\mu^n) \qquad j=1,2,\cdots,N_{\lambda\mu} \\ &\qquad (\phi_{\lambda\mu}^{(j)} \neq 0) \\ z_\lambda^{(j)} &= \phi_{\lambda\mu}^{(j)}(z_\mu^1, z_\mu^2, \cdots, z_\mu^n) \qquad j=N_{\lambda\mu}+1,\cdots,n. \end{aligned}$$

Now we calculate $H_{\lambda\mu}$ on $U_\lambda^{(k)} \cap U_\mu^{(l)}$.

$$(3,12) \qquad \begin{aligned} H_{\lambda\mu} &= Y_\lambda^{(k)} \; Y_\mu^{(l)-1} \\ &= \Phi_\lambda^{(k)*-1} \cdot \Phi_\lambda^{(k)} \cdot \Phi_\mu^{(l)-1} \cdot \Phi_\mu^{(l)*} \\ &= \Phi_\lambda^{(k)*-1} \; c_{\lambda\mu}^{(k,l)} \; \Phi_\mu^{(l)*}. \end{aligned}$$

We choose a slit Γ_λ (resp. Γ_μ) on U_λ (resp. U_μ) with $U_\lambda^{(k)} \cap \Gamma_\lambda = \emptyset$ (resp. $U_\mu^{(l)} \cap \Gamma_\mu = \emptyset$) so that the log z^j (resp. log z^j) $(j=1,2,\cdots,n)$ are single valued functions on $U_\lambda^{(k)}$ (resp. $U_\mu^{(l)}$). These functions are denoted by Log $z_\lambda^{(j)}$ (resp. Log $z_\mu^{(j)}$). With these Log $z_\lambda^{(j)}$, we define

$$\Psi_\lambda^{(j)} = \prod_{j=1}^{N} (z_\lambda^{(j)})^{\underline{M}_\lambda | j} .$$

Then we can find matrixs $M_\lambda^{(k)}$ and $M_\mu^{(l)}$ such that

$$(3,13) \qquad \begin{cases} \Phi_\lambda^{(k)*} = \Psi_\lambda^{(k)} M_\lambda^{(k)} \\ \Phi_\mu^{(l)*} = \Psi_\mu^{(l)} M_\mu^{(l)}. \end{cases}$$

From (3,11) and (A,1), we see that

$$\Psi_\lambda^{(k)} = (z_\mu^1)^{\underline{M}_\lambda | 1} \cdots (z_\mu^{N_{\lambda\mu}})^{\underline{M}_\lambda | N_{\lambda\mu}} E_\lambda^{(k)} \qquad \text{on } U_\lambda^{(k)} \cap U_\mu^{(l)},$$

where

$$E_\lambda^{(k)} = (\phi_{\lambda\mu}^{(1)})^{\underline{M}_\lambda | 1} \cdots (\phi_{\lambda\mu}^{(N_{\lambda\mu})})^{M_\lambda | N_{\lambda\mu}}.$$

By using (3,5) for $\alpha = 1,2,\cdots,N_{\lambda\mu}$, we get

$$(3,14) \quad \Psi_\lambda^{(k)} = c_{\lambda\mu}^{(k,l)} (z_\mu^{(1)})^{\underline{M}_\mu | 1} \cdots (z_\mu^{N_{\lambda\mu}})^{\underline{M}_\mu | N_{\lambda\mu}} \cdot c_{\lambda\mu}^{(k,l)-1} E_\lambda^{(k)} \qquad \text{on } U_\lambda^{(k)} \cap U_\mu^{(l)}.$$

From (3,12),(3,13) and (3,14), we obtain that

$$H_{\lambda\mu} = M_\lambda^{(k)-1} E_\lambda^{(k)-1} c_{\lambda\mu}^{(k,l)} E_\mu^{(l)} M_\mu^{(l)} \qquad \text{on } U_\lambda^{(k)} \cap U_\mu^{(l)}.$$

Since $E_\lambda^{(k)}$ and $E_\mu^{(l)}$ are holomorphic on $U_\lambda \cap U_\mu$, $H_{\lambda\mu}$ is also holomorphic on $U_\lambda \cap U_\mu$. By chainging λ and μ, we see that $H_{\lambda\mu}^{-1}$ is also holomorphic on $U_\lambda \cap U_\mu$. On the other $U_\lambda \cap U_\mu$ with $U_\lambda \cap Y = \emptyset$ or $U_\mu \cap Y = \emptyset$, the assertion is easily proved. Hence we complete the proof of the Prosition.

Definition(3,15). The holomorphic vector bundle which is defined by $\{H_{\lambda\mu}\}$ is denoted by E_ρ^*.

Remark. From(3,12), it is easily seen that E_ρ^* is a holomorphic extension of E_ρ.

With these preliminaries we formulate our problem II:

Proposition(3,16). Under the condition(A-1) $\sim$ (A-3), the problem II can be solved(with admitting accessory singularities) if E^* admits r linearly independent meromorphic sections.

proof. Let $\{\phi^{(j)}\}$ ($j=1,2,\cdots,r$) be linearly independent meromorphic sections. We consider the following matrix $\phi = \{\phi_\lambda\}$,

$$\phi_\lambda = (\phi_\lambda^{(1)}, \phi_\lambda^{(2)}, \cdots, \phi_\lambda^{(r)}).$$

Then we see that

$$\phi_\lambda = H_{\lambda\mu} \cdot \phi_\mu \qquad \text{on } U_\lambda \cap U_\mu.$$

From $H_{\lambda\mu} = Y_\lambda \cdot Y_\mu^{-1}$, we obtain a single valued meromorphic function

$$F = Y_\lambda^{-1} \phi_\lambda \qquad \text{on } M - (Y \cup S).$$

Set $\Phi^* = \Phi \cdot F$. Then it is easily seen that Φ^* is also a ρ-multiplicative function on $M-(Y \cup S)$. Now we show that Φ^* admits at most regular singularity along Y. For this it is sufficient to show that $\Phi_\lambda^{(k)} \cdot F$ admits a regular singularity along Y. From

$$\begin{aligned} \Phi_\lambda^{(k)} \cdot F &= \Phi_\lambda^{(k)} \cdot Y_\lambda^{-1} \phi_\lambda \\ &= \Phi_\lambda^{(k)*} \phi_\lambda, \end{aligned}$$

we get the conclusion. Next we show that Φ^* has only accessory singularities along S. Since $\Phi^* = C \phi_\lambda$ holds on U_λ with $U_\lambda \cap S \neq \emptyset$, where C is a constant matrix, it is easily seen that Φ^* is defined on M - Y. Hence we complete the proof of Proposition (3,15).

§ 4 The problem of Riemann and Hilbert in several complex variables

The purpose of this section is to solve the problem of Riemann and Hilbert (i.e., problems I and II in Introduction) on Stein manifolds and projective algebraic manifolds. The results can be stated as follows:

Theorem(4,1). On projective algebraic manifolds and Stein manifolds, the problem I can be solved.

Theorem(4,2) On projective algebraic manifolds and Stein manifolds, the problem II can be solved.

proof of Theorem(4,1). For the proof, it is sufficient to show that E_ρ admits r linearly independent meromorphic sections (see Proposition(2,1)). This follows easily by using Kodaira and Serre's cohomology vanishing theorem(resp. Oka and Cartan's cohomology vanishing theorem) on projective algebraic manifolds (resp. Stein manifolds).

proof of Theorem(4,2). (i) In the case where M is a Stein manifold. Since Y is a divisor, therefore M-Y is also Stein. Now we construct E^*_ρ from E_ρ. From Theorem(4,1), we see that there exists a ρ'-multiplicative function on M-Y. Hence choosing S as empty set, we can satisfy the conditions(A-1)$\sim$(A-3) in Proposition(3,16). Therefore we get E^*_ρ (see (3,15)). Hence, in order to prove the assertion, it is sufficient to show Proposition(3,16). This follows from Oka and Cartan's vanishing theorem.

(ii) In the case where M is a projective algebraic manifold. Let S be a positive divisor in M. Then $M-(Y \cup S)$ is a Stein manifold. Therefore, by using Oka and Cartan's thorem, we get a ρ'-multiplicative function on $M-(Y \cup S)$ as in (i). Hence in this case the conditions(A-1)$\sim$(A-3) can be also satisfied. Hence we may only prove Proposition(3,16) on M. This follows from Kodaira and Serre's vanishing theorem.

Remark. The solutions in Theorems(4,1) and(4,2) have always accessory singularities.

§ 5 The Relations of Fuchs in several complex variables

In this section we shall deduce the relations of Fuchs on projective algebraic manifolds of high dimensions by calculating the characteristic polynomials of E^*_ρ . We beginn with assembling basic notations concerning holomorphic vector bundles.

Let M be a complex manifold and let $\pi : E \dashrightarrow M$ be a holomorphic vector bundle of rank r. E may be expressed as $\{H_{\lambda\mu}\}$ with respect to some covering $\{U_\lambda\}$ of M. The fibre coordinate ζ_λ on U_λ is written as

$$\zeta_\lambda = \begin{pmatrix} \zeta^{(1)} \\ \vdots \\ \zeta^{(r)} \end{pmatrix}.$$

Then $\zeta_\lambda = H_{\lambda\mu}\zeta_\mu$ holds on $U_\lambda \cap U_\mu$. The adoint vector bundle Ad(E) of E, $\tilde{\pi} : Ad(E) \dashrightarrow M$ is a holomorphic vector bundle of rank r^2 which is defined in the following manner: The transition matrixs between the fibre coordinates $\tilde{\zeta}_\lambda$ and $\tilde{\zeta}_\mu$ are given by

$$\tilde{\zeta}_\lambda = H_{\lambda\mu}\tilde{\zeta}_\mu H^{-1}_{\lambda\mu} \qquad \text{on } U_\lambda \cap U_\mu .$$

A 0-cochain $\omega = \{\omega_\lambda\}$ is called a connection of E, if the following hold

$$(5,1) \qquad \omega_\lambda H_{\lambda\mu} = -dH_{\lambda\mu} + H_{\lambda\mu}\omega_\mu \qquad \text{on } U_\lambda \cap U_\mu .$$

If ω_λ is holomorphic(or meromorphic) 1-form on each U_λ , then ω is called a holomorphic(resp. meromorphic) connection. We set $\Lambda = \frac{1}{2\pi\sqrt{-1}}\bar{\partial}\omega$. Then Λ is an Ad(E)-valued (1,1)-form. Λ is called the curvature of ω . Let Y be a divisor with the assumptions(1),(2) in Introduction. On U_λ with $U_\lambda \cap Y \neq \emptyset$,

Y is expressed as in (3,1). Following P.Deligne[1], we make the following

Definition(5,2). A meromorphic connection $\omega = \{\omega_\lambda\}$ has a simple pole along Y if ω_λ is expressed on $U_\lambda (U_\lambda \cap Y \neq \emptyset)$ as

$$\omega_\lambda = \sum_{j=1}^{N_\lambda} \frac{A_\lambda^{(j)}}{z_\lambda^j} dz_\lambda^j + B_\lambda,$$

where $A_\lambda^{(j)}$ are holomorphic functions on U_λ and B_λ are holomorphic 1-forms.

Then we see that

$$(5,3) \qquad \{ A_\lambda^{(j)}|_{Y^j} \} \in \Gamma(Y_j, \mathcal{O}(\mathrm{Ad}\, E|_{Y^j})).$$

We write

$$\mathrm{Re}\, \omega|_{Y^j} = \{ A_\lambda^{(j)}|_{Y^j} \}.$$

A positive definite matrixs valued 0-cochain $\{h_\lambda\}$ is called a metric of E, if

$$(5,4) \qquad {}^t\overline{H}_{\lambda\mu}\, h_\lambda\, H_{\lambda\mu} = h_\mu \qquad \text{on } U_\lambda \cap U_\mu .$$

Let $h = \{h_\lambda\}$ be a metric of E of C^∞-class. Then $\omega = h^{-1}\partial h$ gives a C^∞-connection of E. The curvature form of the metric h is denoted by Ω . Let $P(X_1,\cdots,X_l)$ be a function of matrix variables X_i. $P(X_1,\cdots,X_l)$ is called $\mathbb{C}$-linear if

$$P(X_1,\cdots,X_l) = \sum a_{j_1,k_1}\cdots a_{j_l,k_l}\, X^{(1)}_{j_1,k_1} \cdots X^{(l)}_{j_l,k_l},$$

where $X_{(i)} = (X^{(i)}_{j,l})$. $P(X_1,X_2,\cdots,X_l)$ is called E-invariant if

$$P(H_{\lambda\mu} X_1 H_{\lambda\mu}^{-1}, \cdots, H_{\lambda\mu} X_l H_{\lambda\mu}^{-1}) = P(X_1, \cdots, X_l).$$

We call invariant $\mathbb{C}$-linear polynomials characteristic polynomials. Then we see that for a characteristic polynomial, $P(\Omega, \cdots, \Omega)$ is a well defined (l,l)-form on M. In the following $P(\Omega, \cdots, \Omega)$ is written as $P(\Omega)$ simply.

Now we return to the complex manifold M with the divisor Y which is considered in § 3. We also assume that the following representation is given:

$$\rho : \pi_1(M-Y, p) \dashrightarrow GL(r, \mathbb{C}).$$

We follow the notations in § 3. Let Y_α be an irreducible component of Y. By $[Y_\alpha]$, we denote the complex line bundle which is defined by Y_α. By $[Y_\alpha]^{-1}$ we denote the dual bundle of $[Y_\alpha]$. We choose a metric of $[Y_\alpha]^{-1}$. From (3,11) and (5,4) the metric $h^{(\alpha)} = \{h_\lambda^{(\alpha)}\}$ satisfies

$$h_\lambda^{(\alpha)} | \phi_{\lambda\mu}^{(\alpha)} |^{-2} = h_\mu^{(\alpha)} \qquad \text{on } U_\lambda \cap U_\mu .$$

By $\theta^{(\alpha)} = h^{(\alpha)-1} \partial h^{(\alpha)}$ we denote the connection form of $h^{(\alpha)}$. We write the chern form of $[Y_\alpha]^{-1}$ by

$$(5,5) \qquad c_1([Y_\alpha]^{-1}) = \frac{\sqrt{-1}}{2\pi} \partial\bar{\partial} \log h^{(\alpha)}.$$

From (3,11) we get

$$(5,6) \qquad \begin{aligned} \partial\phi_{\lambda\mu}^{(\alpha)} \cdot \phi_{\lambda\mu}^{(\alpha)-1} &= \theta_\lambda^{(\alpha)} - \theta_\mu^{(\alpha)} \\ &= dz_\lambda^\alpha z_\lambda^{\alpha-1} - dz_\mu^\alpha z_\mu^{\alpha-1} \end{aligned} \qquad \text{on } U_\lambda \cap U_\mu .$$

We set

$$Y_{\alpha_1 \cdots \alpha_l} = \bigcap_{j=1}^{l} Y_{\alpha_j} .$$

and the inclusion mapping from $Y_{\alpha_1 \cdots \alpha_l}$ into M is denoted by $\iota_{\alpha_1 \cdots \alpha_l}$. Moreover, we set $\varphi_{\alpha_1 \cdots \alpha_l} = \iota^*_{\alpha_1 \cdots \alpha_l} \varphi$ for a form φ on M. Here we put the following assumption:

(5,7) Every $Y_{\alpha_1 \cdots \alpha_l}$ is connected.

This condition can be satisfied by forming monoidal transforms $Q: M^* \dashrightarrow M$ with the center in Y and by replacing ρ by $Q^*\rho$. In the following we restrict our considerations to a projective algebraic manifold M with the assumption(5,7). As we have shown in § 4, E^*_ρ can be constructed. We consider $\Phi^{(k)*}_\lambda$ which is defined in (3,8). We set

$$\Theta^{(k)}_\lambda = \Phi^{(k)*-1}_\lambda d \Phi^{(k)*}_\lambda \quad \text{on} \quad U^{(k)}_\lambda .$$

From (3,9) it follows that $\Theta^{(k)}_\lambda = \Theta^{(l)}_\lambda$ on $U^{(k)}_\lambda \cap U^{(l)}_\lambda$. Hence we get the following 1-form Θ^*_λ on U_λ:

$$\text{(5,8)} \qquad \Theta^*_\lambda = \sum_{\alpha=1}^{N_\lambda} \frac{\underline{M}_{\lambda|\alpha}}{z^\alpha_\lambda} dz^\alpha_\lambda \quad \text{on} \quad U_\lambda .$$

The following Proposition is essential in this section:

Proposition(5,9). $\Theta^* = \{\Theta^*_\lambda\}$ defines a meromorphic connection of E^*_ρ with simple poles along Y. Hence we see that the residue of Θ^*, $\operatorname{Re} \Theta^*|_{Y_\alpha}$ is constant on $U_\lambda \cap Y_\alpha$.

Proof. From(3,6), we see that

$$\Phi^{(k)-1}_\lambda d \Phi^{(k)}_\lambda = \Phi^{(l)-1}_\mu d \Phi^{(l)}_\mu \quad \text{on} \quad U^{(k)}_\lambda \cap U^{(l)}_\mu .$$

From $\Phi^{(k)}_\lambda = \Phi^{(k)*}_\lambda Y^{(k)}_\lambda$, we obtain

$$\Phi^{(k)-1}_\lambda d \Phi^{(k)}_\lambda = Y^{(k)-1}_\lambda \Theta^*_\lambda Y^{(k)}_\lambda + Y^{(k)}_\lambda dY^{(k)}_\lambda$$

and

$$\Phi_{\mu}^{(l)-1}\, d\,\Phi_{\mu}^{(l)} = Y_{\mu}^{(l)-1}\, \Theta_{\mu}^{*}\, Y_{\mu}^{(l)} + Y_{\mu}^{(l)}\, dY_{\mu}^{(l)}.$$

Hence we obtain on $U_{\lambda}^{(k)} \cap U_{\mu}^{(l)}$

$$\Theta_{\lambda}^{*} - H_{\lambda\mu}\Theta_{\mu}^{*} H_{\lambda\mu}^{-1} = - dY_{\lambda}^{(k)}\, Y_{\lambda}^{(k)-1} + Y_{\lambda}^{(k)} Y_{\mu}^{(l)-1}\, dY_{\mu}^{(l)} Y_{\lambda}^{(k)-1}$$

It is easily seen that the right side is nothing but $-dH_{\lambda\mu} H_{\lambda\mu}^{-1}$. Hence we get the conclusion.

Now we shall prove our Theorem:

Theorem(5,10). Let M be a projective algebraic manifold with the assumption(5,7). Suppose that $\rho : \pi_1(M - Y, p) \dashrightarrow GL(r, \mathbb{C})$ is given. Then for a characteristic polynomial P of E_{ρ}^{*}, the following holds:

$$P(\Omega) = \sum_{1 \leqq \alpha_1 \leqq \alpha_2 \cdots \leqq \alpha_s \leqq N} P(\underline{M}_{\alpha_1}, \underline{M}_{\alpha_2}, \cdots, \underline{M}_{\alpha_s}) \prod_{j=1}^{s} c_1([Y_{\alpha_j}]^{-1}),$$

where Ω is a curvature form of a metrical connection which is defined by a C^{∞}-metric and $\underline{M}_{\alpha}$ is defined in (3,4).

Following M.Otuki, we shall give the proof of Theorem. For this we prepare some propositions. For $\Phi_{\lambda}^{(l)*}$ in (3,8), we set

$$\Phi^{(l)*}_{\lambda\,|\alpha_1, \cdots, \alpha_t} = \Phi_{\lambda}^{(l)*} (z_{\lambda}^{\alpha_1})^{-\underline{M}_{\lambda|\alpha_1}} \cdots (z^{\alpha_t})^{-\underline{M}_{\lambda|\alpha_t}},$$

where $(z_{\lambda}^{\alpha_l})^{-\underline{M}_{\lambda|\alpha_l}}$ ($l=1,2,\cdots,t$) are defined by using the same branches of $\log z_{\lambda}^{\alpha_l}$ ($l=1,2,\cdots,t$) which appeare in $\Phi_{\lambda}^{(k)*}$. We set

$$\tilde{\Theta}^{(l)}_{\lambda|\alpha_1, \cdots, \alpha_t} = d\,\Phi^{(l)}_{\lambda|\alpha_1, \cdots, \alpha_t} \cdot \Phi^{(l)-1}_{\lambda|\alpha_1, \cdots, \alpha_t} \text{ on } U_{\lambda}^{(l)}.$$

Then it is easily seen that $\tilde{\Theta}^{(l)}_{\lambda|\alpha_1, \cdots, \alpha_t} = \tilde{\Theta}^{(k)}_{\lambda|\alpha_1, \cdots, \alpha_t}$

on $U_\lambda^{(1)} \cap U_\lambda^{(k)}$. So we obtain a form $\widetilde{\Theta}_{\lambda|\alpha_1,\dots,\alpha_t}$ on U_λ. By using metrics $h^{(\alpha)}$ of $[Y_\alpha]^{-1}$, we set

$$\Theta^*_{\lambda|\alpha_1,\dots,\alpha_t} = \widetilde{\Theta}_{\lambda|\alpha_1,\dots,\alpha_t} + \sum_{s=1}^{t} \underline{M}_{\lambda|\alpha_s}\, \theta_\lambda^{(\alpha_s)}.$$

Now we prove the following

Proposition(5,11). $\Theta^*{}_{\alpha_1,\dots,\alpha_t} = \{\Theta^*_{\lambda|\alpha_1,\dots,\alpha_t}\}$ defines a connection of $E^*_\rho|Y_{\alpha_1,\dots,\alpha_t}$.

Proof. For U_λ and U_μ with $U_\lambda \cap U_\mu \cap Y_{\alpha_1,\dots,\alpha_t} \neq \emptyset$, we consider

$$H = \Theta^*_{\lambda|\alpha_1,\dots,\alpha_t} - H_{\lambda\mu}\, \Theta^*_{\mu|\alpha_1,\dots,\alpha_t} \cdot H_{\lambda\mu}^{-1}.$$

From (5,3) and (5,9), we see that

$$\underline{M}_{\lambda|\alpha_s} = H_{\lambda\mu}\, \underline{M}_{\mu|\alpha_s}\, H_{\lambda\mu}^{-1} \qquad (s=1,2,\cdots,t). \tag{5,12}$$

Hence we obtain

$$H = \widetilde{\Theta}_{\lambda|\alpha_1,\dots,\alpha_t} - H_{\lambda\mu}\, \widetilde{\Theta}_{\mu|\alpha_1,\dots,\alpha_t}\, H_{\lambda\mu}^{-1} + \sum_{s=1}^{t} \underline{M}_{\lambda|\alpha_s}(\theta_\lambda^{(\alpha_s)} - \theta_\mu^{(\alpha_s)}).$$

From (5,6), we see that

$$H = \widetilde{\Theta}_{\lambda|\alpha_1,\dots,\alpha_t} - H_{\lambda\mu}\, \widetilde{\Theta}_{\mu|\alpha_1,\dots,\alpha_t} + \sum_{s=1}^{t} \left(\underline{M}_{\lambda|\alpha_s} \frac{dz_\lambda^{\alpha_s}}{z_\lambda^{\alpha_s}} - \underline{M}_{\lambda|\alpha_s} \frac{dz_\mu^{\alpha_s}}{z_\mu^{\alpha_s}} \right).$$

By using (5,12) again, we obtain

$$H = (\widetilde{\Theta}_{\lambda|\alpha_1,\dots,\alpha_t} + \sum_{s=1}^{t} \underline{M}_{\lambda|\alpha_s} \frac{dz_\lambda^{\alpha_s}}{z_\lambda^{\alpha_s}})$$

$$- H_{\lambda\mu}(\widetilde{\Theta}_{\mu}|_{\alpha_1,\dots,\alpha_t} + \sum_{s=1}^{t} \underline{M}_{\mu|\alpha_s} \frac{dz^{\alpha_s}}{z^{\alpha_s}}) H_{\lambda\mu}^{-1}.$$

From (5,8), we see that

$$H = \Theta_\lambda - H_{\lambda\mu}\Theta_\mu H_{\lambda\mu}^{-1} .$$

Hence we see that

$$\Theta^*_\lambda |_{\alpha_1,\dots,\alpha_t} - H_{\lambda\mu}\Theta^*_\mu|_{\alpha_1,\dots,\alpha_t} \cdot H_{\lambda\mu}^{-1}$$

$$= -dH_{\lambda\mu} H_{\lambda\mu}^{-1}$$

on some neighborhood of $Y_{\alpha_1,\dots,\alpha_t}$. Hence we get the conclusion.

Furthermore, we need the following well known Proposition:

Proposition(5,13). Let ϕ be a form of type (n-1,n-1). Then

$$\int_{Y_{\alpha_1,\dots,\alpha_t}} \phi = \int_M \prod_{j=1}^{t} c_1([Y_{\alpha_j}]^{-1}) \wedge \phi .$$

As for the proof, see A.Weil[4].

Now we shall give the proof of Theorem(5,10): Let $h = \{h_\lambda\}$ be a Hermitian metric of E^*_ρ and let $\omega = \{\omega_\lambda\}$ be the connection form of h. We set

$$L = \{L_\lambda\} , \qquad L_\lambda = \omega_\lambda - \Theta^*_\lambda,$$

where $\Theta^* = \{\Theta^*_\lambda\}$ is defined in (5,8). Then we see that $L \in \Gamma(M, Ad(E^*_\rho))$. We note that

$$\frac{1}{2\pi\sqrt{-1}}\bar{\partial}L = \Omega \qquad \text{on } M - Y,$$

where Ω is the curvature form of ω. We take a characteristic polynomial $P(X_1,\dots,X_l)$. In view of $\bar{\partial}\Omega = 0$ on M, we get the following equality on M - Y: For a $\bar{\partial}$-closed form ϕ of type(n-1,n-1),

$$\phi \wedge P(\Omega) = \frac{1}{2\pi\sqrt{-1}} d(P(L,\Omega,\cdots,\Omega)\wedge\phi).$$

Here we take a small tublar neighborhood V_ε of Y such that ∂V_ε is a real submanifold of M. By $\iota_\varepsilon : \partial V_\varepsilon \longrightarrow M$, we denote the inclusion mapping. By using Stoke's Theorem, we obtain

$$\int_{M-V_\varepsilon} P(\Omega)\wedge\phi = \frac{1}{2\pi\sqrt{-1}} \int_{\partial V_\varepsilon} P(L^\varepsilon,\Omega^\varepsilon,\cdots,\Omega^\varepsilon)\wedge\phi^\varepsilon,$$

where $L^\varepsilon = \iota_\varepsilon^* L$, $\Omega^\varepsilon = \iota_\varepsilon^*\Omega$ and $\phi^\varepsilon = \iota_\varepsilon^*\phi$. By making $\varepsilon \dashrightarrow 0$ and by using the residue theorem, we obtain

$$(5,14) \qquad \int_M P(\Omega)\wedge\phi = \sum_{\alpha_1=1}^{N} \int_{Y\alpha_1} P(\underline{M}_{\alpha_1},\Omega_{\alpha_1},\cdots,\Omega_{\alpha_1})\wedge\phi_{\alpha_1}.$$

Therefore, if l=1, the proof is completed. Hence we assume that $l \geq 2$. We set

$$L_{\alpha 1} = \omega_{\alpha 1} - \Theta^*_{\alpha 1} \qquad \text{on } Y_{\alpha 1}.$$

From (5,11), we see that $L_{\alpha 1} \in (Y_{\alpha 1}, Ad(E^*|_{Y_{\alpha_1}})$ and

$$\frac{1}{2\pi\sqrt{-1}}\bar{\partial}L_{\alpha_1} = \Omega_{\alpha_1} - \underline{M}_{\lambda|\alpha 1}\bar{\partial}\left(\frac{1}{2\pi\sqrt{-1}}\theta_{\alpha_1}\right)$$

$$\text{on } U_\lambda \cap Y_{\alpha 1} - \bigcup_{\alpha_1 \neq \beta} Y_{\beta\alpha 1}.$$

Therefore

$$(5,15)\quad P(\underline{M}_{\alpha_1}, \Omega_{\alpha_1}, \cdots, \Omega_{\alpha_1}) = P(\underline{M}_{\alpha_1}, \bar{\partial} L_{\alpha_1}, \Omega_{\alpha_1}, \cdots, \Omega_{\alpha_1})$$

$$+ P(\underline{M}_{\alpha_1}, \underline{M}_{\alpha_1} c_1([Y_{\alpha_1}]^{-1}), \Omega_{\alpha_1}, \cdots, \Omega_{\alpha_1})$$

$$\text{on } Y_{\alpha_1} - \bigcup_{\beta \neq \alpha_1} Y_{\beta\alpha_1}.$$

As we have done in the case l = 1, we choose a tublar neighborhood $V^{\varepsilon}_{\alpha_1\beta}$ of $Y_{\alpha_1\beta}$ and integrate(5,14). Then we obtain

$$\int_{Y_{\alpha_1} - \bigcup_{\alpha_1 \neq \alpha_2} V^{\varepsilon}_{\alpha_1\alpha_2}} P(\underline{M}_{\alpha_1}, \Omega^{\varepsilon}_{\alpha_1}, \ldots, \Omega^{\varepsilon}_{\alpha_1}) \wedge \phi^{\varepsilon}_{\alpha_1}$$

$$= \int_{Y_{\alpha_1} - \bigcup_{\alpha_1 \neq \alpha_2} V^{\varepsilon}_{\alpha_1\alpha_2}} P(\underline{M}_{\alpha_1}, \bar{\partial} L^{\varepsilon}_{\alpha_1}, \Omega^{\varepsilon}_{\alpha_1}, \cdots, \Omega^{\varepsilon}_{\alpha_1}) \wedge \phi^{\varepsilon}_{\alpha_1}$$

$$+ \int_{Y_{\alpha_1} - \bigcup_{\alpha_1 \neq \alpha_2} V^{\varepsilon}_{\alpha_1\alpha_2}} P(\underline{M}_{\alpha_1}, \underline{M}_{\alpha_2}, \Omega^{\varepsilon}_{\alpha_1}, \cdots, \Omega^{\varepsilon}_{\alpha_1})\; c_1([Y_{\alpha_1}]^{-1})^{\varepsilon} \wedge \phi^{\varepsilon}_{\alpha_1}.$$

The notations are used similarly in the case l = 1. Making $\varepsilon \longrightarrow 0$, we obtain

$$\int_{Y_{\alpha_1}} P(\underline{M}_{\alpha_1}, \Omega_{\alpha_1}, \cdots, \Omega_{\alpha_1}) \wedge \phi_{\alpha_1}$$

$$= \int_{Y_{\alpha_1\alpha_2}} P(\underline{M}_{\alpha_1}, \underline{M}_{\alpha_2}, \Omega_{\alpha_1\alpha_2}, \cdots, \Omega_{\alpha_1\alpha_2}) \wedge \phi_{\alpha_1\alpha_2}$$

$$+\int_{Y_{\alpha_1}} P(\underline{M}_{\alpha_1},\underline{M}_{\alpha_1},\Omega_{\alpha_1},\cdots,\Omega_{\alpha_1})\wedge c_1([Y_{\alpha_1}]^{-1})\wedge\phi_{\alpha_1}.$$

Repeating these process l-times, we can write the left side of (5,13) as the sum of the terms in the following form:

$$\int_{Y_{\alpha_1,\cdots,\alpha_s}} P(\underbrace{\underline{M}_{\alpha_1},\cdots,\underline{M}_{\alpha_1}}_{k_1},\underbrace{\underline{M}_{\alpha_2},\cdots,\underline{M}_{\alpha_2}}_{k_2},\cdots,\underbrace{\underline{M}_{\alpha_s},\cdots,\underline{M}_{\alpha_s}}_{k_s})$$

$$\wedge\prod_{t=1}^{l}\underbrace{c_1([Y_{\alpha_t}]^{-1})\cdots\wedge c_1([Y_{\alpha_t}]^{-1})}_{k_t-1}\wedge\phi_{\alpha_1,\cdots,\alpha_s}$$

$$(s=1,2,\cdots,l).$$

In the case where $k_i = 1$, we need not the exterior product of the chern form $c_1([Y_{\alpha_i}]^{-1})$. Hence by using (5,7), we take the constant terms $P(\underline{M}_{\alpha_1},\cdots,\underline{M}_{\alpha_1},\underline{M}_{\alpha_2},\cdots,\underline{M}_{\alpha_2},\cdots,\underline{M}_{\alpha_s},\cdots,\underline{M}_{\alpha_s})$ out side of the integrand and by using (5,12), we get the conclusion.

We enclose this section by proving that the above result on compact Riemann surfaces implies the well known relation of Fuchs. Let R be a compact Riemann surface and let $Y=\{p_j\}_{j=1}^{m}$ be points on R. Let $\rho:\pi_1(R-Y,p)\dashrightarrow GL(r,\mathbb{C})$ be given a monodromy representation. Let γ_j ($j=1,2,\cdots,m$) be loop as chosen for p_j in § 3. We write $\rho(\gamma_j) = M_j$. Define $\underline{M}_j$ by (3,4). Then from Theorem(5,10), we see that

$$c_1(E_\rho^*) = \sum_{j=1}^{m} \text{trace}\ \underline{M}_j. \qquad (5,16)$$

Consider a finite covering of R over $\mathbb{P}$, $\pi: R \dashrightarrow \mathbb{P}$. We assume that $\{p_j\}_{j=1}^{m}$ are not contained in the branch points of π and in $\pi^{-1}(\infty)$. Consider the following differential equation:

$$\frac{d^n w}{dz^n} + a_1 \frac{d^{n-1} w}{dz^{n-1}} + \dots + a_n w = 0, \tag{5,17}$$

where $a_1,\cdots,a_n$ are meromorphic functions on R and z denotes the local coordinate of $\mathbb{P} - \{\infty\}$. In the following we assume that (5,17) admits regular singularities at most on Y. Let $w_1,\dots,w_n$ be a system of non-trivial linearly independent solutions. We write $\pi(p_i) = \zeta_i$ and $\phi = \prod_{i=1}^{m} (z - \zeta_i)$ and we set

$$\Phi = \begin{pmatrix} w_1, & \phi\frac{dw_1}{dz}, & \phi^2\frac{d^2 w_1}{d^2 z}, & \dots\dots\dots, & \phi^{n-1}\frac{d^{n-1} w_1}{d^{n-1} z} \\ & & \dots\dots\dots\dots\dots\dots & & \\ w_n, & \phi\frac{dw_n}{dz}, & \phi^2\frac{d^2 w_n}{d^2 z}, & \dots\dots\dots, & \phi^{n-1}\frac{d^{n-1} w_n}{d^n z} \end{pmatrix}$$

and

$$\Phi^{-1}\, d\Phi = \Omega .$$

Then

$$\Omega = \begin{pmatrix} 0, & 0, & & 0 & & -\phi^{n-1} a_n \\ \phi^{-1}, & \omega, & & & & \vdots \\ & \phi^{-1}, & 2\omega, & & & \\ & & & \ddots & & \\ & 0 & & \phi^{-1}, & (n-2)\omega & -\phi^2 a_2 \\ & & & & \phi^{-1}, & (n-1)\omega - a_1 \end{pmatrix} dz,$$

where $\omega = \frac{d\phi}{dz}\phi^{-1}$. Hence we see that Ω admits only simple poles. We write

$$a_{i+1}^{*(j)} = \lim_{z\to\zeta_j}(z-\zeta_j)\,\phi^i\,a_{i+1} \quad \begin{pmatrix} i=1,2,\cdots,n-1 \\ j=1,2,\cdots,m \end{pmatrix}.$$

Then it is well known that the characteristic roots of (5,17) at p_j, $\lambda_j^{(k)}$ $(k=1,2,\cdots,n)$ satisfiy

$$(5,18) \qquad \sum_{k=1}^{n} \lambda_j^{(k)} = \frac{(n-1)(n-2)}{2} - a_1^*(j).$$

Here we consider the following differential equation on some neighborhood of p_j:

$$(5,19) \qquad \frac{d^n w^*}{dz^n} + \frac{a_1^{*(j)}}{\phi}\frac{d^{n-1}w^*}{dz^{n-1}} + \cdots + \frac{a_n^{*(n)}}{\phi^n} w^* = 0.$$

If we solve the initial value problem for (5,17) and (5,19) for the same initial conditions at a point in some neighborhood of p_j, the monodromy group of (5,19) which is induced by winding around p_j is identical with the one of (5,17). As we have defined Φ from $w_1, w_2, \cdots, w_n$, we define Φ^* from $w_1^*, w_2^*, \ldots, w_n^*$ and $\Phi^{*-1} d\Phi^* = \Omega^*$. Then we see that

$$\operatorname{Re} \Omega^*|_{p_j} = \operatorname{Re} \Omega\,|_{p_j}.$$

Hence from Theorem(5,10), we see that

$$(5,20) \qquad c_1(E_\rho^*) = \sum_{j=1}^{m} \operatorname{trace} \Omega^*|_{p_j}$$

$$= \sum_{j=1}^{m} \frac{(n-1)(n-2)}{2} - a^*{}_1(j).$$

Hence we obtain

$$c_1(E^*) = \sum_{j,k} \lambda_j^{(k)} .$$

On the other hand, the right side of (5,20) can be written as follows:

$$c_1(E^*) = \frac{n(n-1)}{2}(m + 2(g-1)),$$

where g is the genus of R. Hence our Theorem(5,10) can be considered as a generalization of the relations of Fuchs in several complex variables.

§ 6 An aspect of the theory of differential equations in several complex variables.

The purpose of this section is to show that the theory of differential equations gives a new point of view in several complex variables.

Recently we have several examples of pseudoconvex manifolds which admit only constant holomorphic functions. We shall treat these examples by using the theory of holomorphic foliations which are defined by differential equations with regular singularities. As for the detail treatment, see O.Suzuki[8]. In the following we restrict our considerations to 2-dimensional complex manifolds. By $\mathcal{H}(M)$ we denote the algebra of holomorphic functions on a complex manifold M.

At first we shall consider general holomorphic foliations and state a proposition concerning global integrability condition of the foliation and degeneracy of non-constant holomorphic functions. Let $\mathcal{F}$ be a 1-dimensional holomorphic foliation on M.

For a point p in M, there exists the unique complex maximal integral manifold S_p in the sense of C.Chevally, which is called the leaf through p. In what follows, S(or S_p) denotes the leaf of $\mathcal{F}$.

Definition(6,1). $\mathcal{F}$ is called a compact foliation if the closure $\overline{S}$ of S is compact for every leaf S of $\mathcal{F}$.

Definition(6,2). (i) $\mathcal{F}$ is called (globally) integrable if every leaf S is a closed submanifold in M. (ii) Let $\mathcal{F}$ be a non-globally integrable foliation. A leaf is called nowhere integrable if (1) $\overline{S} \neq S$ and (2) for any point $q \in \overline{S} - S$, $\overline{S}_q \neq S_q$ holds. (iii) $\mathcal{F}$ is called nowhere integrable(resp. not integrable almost everywhere) if every leaf(resp. every non-closed leaf) is nowhere integrable.

Proposition(6,3). Let $\mathcal{F}$ be a compact foliation. Then (i) if $\mathcal{F}$ is integrable, then there exists an analytic curve C and a proper fibre connected holomorphic mapping $\Phi : M \dashrightarrow C$ such that $\mathcal{K}(M) \cong \mathcal{K}(C)$, (ii) if $\mathcal{F}$ has a nowhere integrable leaf, then $\mathcal{K}(M) \cong \mathbb{C}$.

As for the proof, see O.Suzuki[8].

Now we shall treat examples. The first one is due to H.Grauert:

Example 1.

Let $\mathbb{C}^2 = \{(z_1, z_2)\}$ and let $z_i = x_i + \sqrt{-1}\, y_i$ (i=1,2).

We consider the following properly discontinous group G which is generated by the following linear transforms on $\mathbb{C}^2$:

$$T_1 : \begin{cases} z_1' = z_1 + 1 \\ z_2' = z_2 \end{cases}, \qquad T_2 : \begin{cases} z_1' = z_1 \\ z_2' = z_2 + 1 \end{cases},$$

$$T_3 : \begin{cases} z_1' = z_1 + \sqrt{-1} \\ z_2' = z_2 \end{cases}, \qquad T_4 : \begin{cases} z_1' = z_1 + a\sqrt{-1} \\ z_2' = z_2 + \sqrt{-1} \end{cases},$$

where a is a real number. Then we obtain a complex torus $T = \mathbb{C}^2/G$. Let

$$\mathcal{D} = \{(z_1, z_2) : 1/4 < \mathrm{Re}\, z_1 < 3/4\}.$$

Then $\mathcal{D}$ is regarded as a domain on T. $\mathcal{D}$ is expressed as follows:

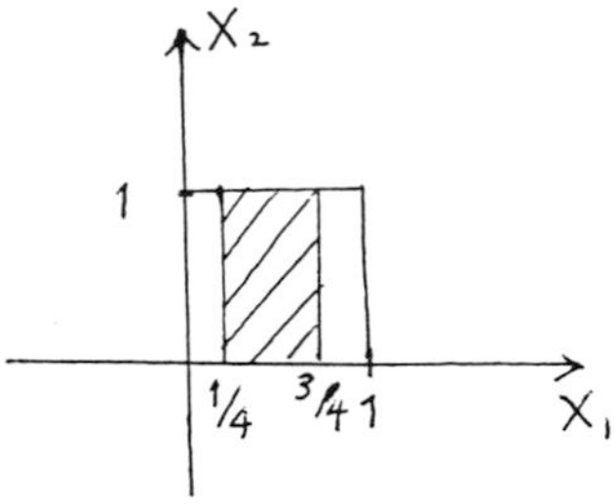

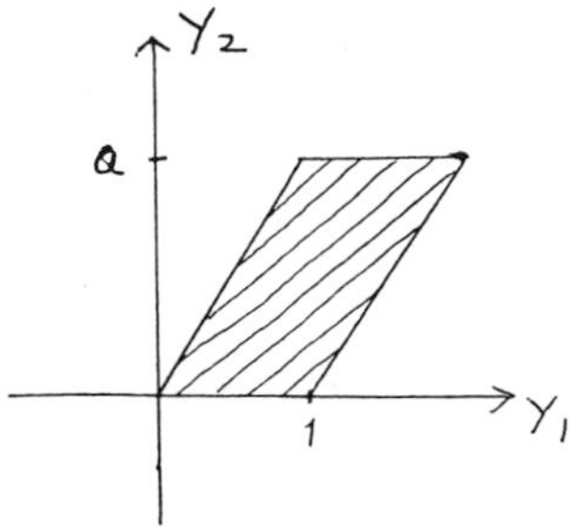

We set

$$\varphi = 1/(4\mathrm{Re}\, z_1 - 1) + 1/(3 - \mathrm{Re}\, z_1).$$

Then we see that φ is a complete pseudoconvex function, where φ is called complete if $\{\varphi < c\}$ is relatively compact for every $c \in \mathbb{R}$. Define a holomorphic foliation by

$$\omega = 0, \quad \omega = dz_1.$$

Since φ is a complete function, we get a compact foliation $\mathcal{F}$.

Propostion(6,4). (i) If a is a rational number, then $\mathcal{F}$ is integrable and Spec $\mathcal{H}(\mathcal{D})$(i.e., Remmert reduction of $\mathcal{D}$) is a non-compact analytic curve. (ii) If a is irrational, then is nowhere integrable. Thus we see that $\mathcal{H}(\mathcal{D}) \cong \mathbb{C}$.

Proof. Let π be the natural projection $\pi : \mathbb{C}^2 \dashrightarrow T$. Then the inverse image of an integral manifold by π is expressed as $S_c = \{z_1 = c\}$ with some c ($1/4 < \mathrm{Re}\, c < 3/4$). If a is a rational number, then $\pi(S_c)$ is a compact analytic curve in $\mathcal{D}$. So we prove (i). If a is irrational, then $\dim_{\mathbb{R}} \pi(\overline{S}_c) = 3$ for every c. So $\mathcal{F}$ is nowhere integrable. Then by Proposition(6,3) we prove (ii).

The second example is due to K.Kodaira [3]:

Example 2

Let M be a projective algebraic manifold and let D be a divisor with $c_1([D]) = 0$ on M. Then by K.Kodaira, we can find a differential equation with regular singularities along D

$$dY = \Omega Y$$

such that a solution Φ_D satisfies the following condition:

$$\gamma^* \Phi_D(z) = \alpha_\gamma \Phi_D(z),$$

where $\gamma \in H_1(M - D, \mathbb{Z})$ and α_γ satisfies $|\alpha_\gamma| = 1$. By using monoidal transforms succesively, if necessary, we may assume that Φ_D has no singularities of inderminancy. Let $\varphi = |\Phi_D|^2$. Then we obtain a pseudoconvex function. By construction of Φ_D there exist only finite values $c_1, c_2, \ldots, c_r$ such that the analytic continuation of the analytic set $\{\Phi_D = c_j\}$ contain singular points..For a positive ε, we set

$$\mathcal{D}_\varepsilon = \{\varphi < \varepsilon\} - \Sigma \quad , \text{ where } \Sigma = \bigcup_{j=1}^{r} \{\overline{\Phi_D = c_j}\} .$$

Define a holomorphic foliation $\mathcal{F}$ by

$$\omega = 0 , \quad \omega = d\Phi_D .$$

By construction, $\mathcal{F}$ is a compact foliation in $\mathcal{D}_\varepsilon$. Here we have the following

Proposition(6,5). (i) If $[D]^n$ is analytically trivial for some integer n ($n \neq 0$), then $\mathcal{F}$ is interable. Hence Spec$\mathcal{H}(\mathcal{D}_\varepsilon)$ is a non-compact analytic curve. (ii) Otherwise, $\mathcal{F}$ is not integrable almosteverywhere. Hence $\mathcal{H}(\mathcal{D}_\varepsilon) \cong \mathbb{C}$.

The proof is almost the same as the one of Proposition (6,4) and may be omitted.

Appendix

In this appendix we shall prove some results concerning the logarithm of matrixs which are used in § 3.

Let B be a matrix of type(r,r). We define exp B as follows:

$$\exp B = \sum_{n=0}^{\infty} B^n/n! .$$

exp B can be defined for every B and $\det(\exp B) \neq 0$.

Proposition(A,1). Let A be a matrix with $\det A \neq 0$. Then there exists a matrix(not unique) such that

$$A = \exp B.$$

Proof. Let A = S + N, where S is semi-simple and N is nipotent with SN = NS. We remark that N and S can be written as polynomials of A. In the following we say that A is decomposed into S and N. Now we assume that there exists B such that $\exp B = A$. The decomposition of B is denoted by $B = \underline{S} + \underline{N}$. Then from

$$A = \exp B = \exp(\underline{S} + \underline{N}) = \exp \underline{S} \cdot \exp \underline{N}$$
$$= \exp \underline{S} + \exp \underline{S} \cdot (\exp \underline{N} - I),$$

where I denotes the unit matrix, we see that

$$S = \exp \underline{S} \qquad \text{and} \qquad N = S(\exp \underline{N} - I) .$$

Let

$$(A,2) \qquad \underline{N} = \sum_{j=1}^{\infty} (-1)^{j-1}(S^{-1}N)^j/j .$$

Then in view of that $S^{-1}N$ is nilpotent, $\underline{N}$ is well defined and $N = S(\exp \underline{N} - I)$ holds. Now we determine $\underline{S}$. Since S is semi-simple, there exists a matrix $P(\det P \neq 0)$ such that

$$(A,3) \qquad P^{-1} S P = A , \qquad A = \begin{pmatrix} \alpha_1 & & 0 \\ & \ddots & \\ 0 & & \alpha_r \end{pmatrix}.$$

Hence letting

$$(A,4) \qquad \underline{S} = P \underline{A} P^{-1}, \qquad \underline{A} = \begin{pmatrix} \log \alpha_1 & & 0 \\ & \ddots & \\ 0 & & \log \alpha_r \end{pmatrix},$$

we see that $\exp \underline{S} = S$ holds. If we choose a branch of $\log \alpha_i$ by the following condition:

(*) For the same α_i, we choose the same branch of $\log \alpha_i$,

then we see that $\underline{S}\,\underline{N} = \underline{N}\,\underline{S}$ holds. Hence we complete the proof of Proposition(A,1).

Here we make the following definition:

Definition(A,5). The B defined by using $\underline{S}$ in (A,4) with the condition(*) is denoted by Log A.

Of course Log A is not determined uniquely. By using the following Proposition, the definition of Log A does not depend on the choice of P.

Proposition(A,6). Let A and A' be two matrixs with the following conditions: (1) There exists a matrix P(det P $\neq$ 0) such that $A' = P^{-1} A P$ and (2) A and A' can be written as follows:

$$A = \begin{pmatrix} \alpha_1 . & & 0 \\ & . & \\ 0 & & .\alpha_r \end{pmatrix} \quad \text{and} \quad A' = \begin{pmatrix} \alpha'_1 . & & 0 \\ & . & \\ 0 & & .\alpha'_r \end{pmatrix} .$$

Hence we see that $(\alpha'_1,\cdots,\alpha'_r)$ are a substitution of $(\alpha_1,\cdot \cdots,\alpha_r)$. Taking the same branch of $\log \alpha_i$ for the same α_i in A and A', we define Log A and Log A'. Then we see that

$$\text{Log } A' = P^{-1} \text{Log } A\ P.$$

Proof. We write $P = (p_{ij})$. Then $PA = A'P$ implies that $\alpha'_i\, p_{ij} = p_{ij}\, \alpha_j$. Then if $p_{ij} \neq 0$, then $\alpha'_i = \alpha_j$. Hence $\log \alpha'_i\, p_{ij} = p_{ij} \log \alpha_j$, which proves the assertion.

Let A and A' be two matrixs with det A $\neq$ 0 and det A' $\neq$ 0. We say that A and A' are equivalent if there exists a matix C (det C $\neq$ 0) satisfying $A' = C A C^{-1}$. If A and A' are euivalent, then the eigenvalues of A are identical to the ones of A'. Hence we make the following

Definition(A,7). Let A and A' be equivalent. We say that Log A and Log A' have the same branches if they are defined by the condition that we take the same branch of logarithm for

for the same eigenvalue.

Then we have the following

Proposition(A,8). If A is equivalent to A', i.e., $A' = C\,A\,C^{-1}$ with some C($\det C \neq 0$), then for the same branches of Log A and Log A', we have

$$\mathrm{Log}\,A' = C\,\mathrm{Log}\,A\,C^{-1}.$$

The assertion follows from (A,2) and (A,6). Finally we prove the following

Proposition(A,9). Let $\{A_i\}_{i\in I}$ be a set of matrixs with $\det A_i \neq 0$ for every $i \in I$. Suppose that $A_i\,A_j = A_j\,A_i$ for every pair i and j. Then for each $\underline{A}_i = \mathrm{Log}\,A_i$, we obtain $\underline{A}_i\,\underline{A}_j = \underline{A}_j\,\underline{A}_i$.

Proof. We write the decomposition of A_i(resp. $\underline{A}_i$) as $A_i = S_i + N_i$(resp. $\underline{A}_i = \underline{S}_i + \underline{N}_i$). Then we see that

$$(A,10)\qquad S_i\,S_j = S_j\,S_i,\quad N_i\,S_j = S_j\,N_i \quad\text{and}\quad N_i\,N_j = N_j\,N_i \quad \text{for } i \text{ and } j \text{ in } I.$$

Then from (A,2), we see that $\underline{N}_i\,\underline{N}_j = \underline{N}_j\,\underline{N}_i$. For the proof of the assertion, it is sufficient to show that $\underline{S}_i\,\underline{S}_j = \underline{S}_j\,\underline{S}_i$ and $\underline{N}_i\,\underline{S}_j = \underline{S}_j\,\underline{N}_i$. Now we fix an arbitrary suffix $i \in I$ and consider a Jordan form of S_i:

$$(A,11)\quad P_i^{-1} S_i\,P_i = A_i^*,\quad A_i^* = \left(\begin{array}{ccc|c|ccc} \alpha_1^{(i)} & & 0 & & & & \\ & \ddots & & & & 0 & \\ 0 & & \alpha_1^{(i)} & & & & \\ \hline & & & \ddots\ 0 & & & \\ & & & 0\ \ddots & & & \\ \hline & & & & \alpha_r^{(i)} & & 0 \\ & 0 & & & & \ddots & \\ & & & & 0 & & \alpha_r^{(i)} \end{array}\right)$$

From (A,10) we see that for each $j \in I$, the following holds:

$$P_i^{-1} S_j P_i = \begin{pmatrix} \boxed{*} & & & 0 \\ & \boxed{*} & & \\ & & \ddots & \\ 0 & & & \boxed{*} \end{pmatrix} \quad \text{and} \quad P_i^{-1} N_j P_i = \begin{pmatrix} \boxed{*} & & & 0 \\ & \boxed{*} & & \\ & & \ddots & \\ 0 & & & \boxed{*} \end{pmatrix},$$

where the size of eash brock is identical with the one of A_i^*. Hence $P_i^{-1}(S_j^{-1} N_j) P_i$ has the brock decomposition of the same size. Referring to (A,2), we find that $P_i^{-1} \underline{N}_j P_i$ has the same property. Now we define $\underline{S}_j$ by making the Jordan normal form for each brock. Then we see that $P_i^{-1} \underline{S}_j P_i$ has also the decomposition of the same type. Hence from (A,11), we get the assertion.

References

[1]. Deligne, P. Equations differentielles à points singuliers réguliers, Lecture notes in Mathematics, 163, Springer, 1970.

[2] Gerard, R. Le problème de Riemann Hilbert sur une variété analytique complex, Ann. Inst. Fourier, Grenoble 19, 2(1969), 1-12.

[3] Kodaira, K. Green's forms and meromorphic functions on compact analytic varieties, Canada. Jour. Math., vol 3 (1951), 108-128.

[4] Manin, Y. Moduli Fuchsiani, Annali Socola Normale Sup di Pisa Ser III 19 (1965), 113-126.

[5] Otuki, M. Chern class formula for a holomorphic vector bundle with an integrable logarithmic connection, to appear.

[6] Röhrl, H. Das Riemannsch-Hilbertsche Problem der Theorie der linieren Differentialgleichungen, Math. Ann., 133 (1957), 1-25.

[7] Saito, T. On Fuchs' relation for the differential equation with algebraic coefficients, Kodai Math. Sem. Rep., 10 (1958), 101-104.

[8] Suzuki, O. Remarks on examples of 2-dimensional weakly 1-complete manifolds which admit only constant holomorphic functions, to appear in J. Fac. Sci. Univ. Tokyo, Sec IA.

[9] Weil, A. Généralisation des fonctions abéliennes, Jour. Math. pure et appl, 17 (1938) 47-87.

[10] -------. Introduction a l'Etude des Varieties Kähleriennes, Hermann, Paris, 1958.

[11] Katz, N. M. An overview of Deligne's work on Hilbert's twenty-first problem, Proc. Sym. in Pure Math. 28 (1976), 537-557, Amer. Math. Soc.

Departments of Mathematics
College of Humanities and
Sciences,
Nihon University

Departments of Mathematics
University of Göttingen

Vol. 551: Algebraic K-Theory, Evanston 1976. Proceedings. Edited by M. R. Stein. XI, 409 pages. 1976.

Vol. 552: C. G. Gibson, K. Wirthmüller, A. A. du Plessis and E. J. N. Looijenga. Topological Stability of Smooth Mappings. V, 155 pages. 1976.

Vol. 553: M. Petrich, Categories of Algebraic Systems. Vector and Projective Spaces, Semigroups, Rings and Lattices. VIII, 217 pages. 1976.

Vol. 554: J. D. H. Smith, Mal'cev Varieties. VIII, 158 pages. 1976.

Vol. 555: M. Ishida, The Genus Fields of Algebraic Number Fields. VII, 116 pages. 1976.

Vol. 556: Approximation Theory. Bonn 1976. Proceedings. Edited by R. Schaback and K. Scherer. VII, 466 pages. 1976.

Vol. 557: W. Iberkleid and T. Petrie, Smooth S^1 Manifolds. III, 163 pages. 1976.

Vol. 558: B. Weisfeiler, On Construction and Identification of Graphs. XIV, 237 pages. 1976.

Vol. 559: J.-P. Caubet, Le Mouvement Brownien Relativiste. IX, 212 pages. 1976.

Vol. 560: Combinatorial Mathematics, IV, Proceedings 1975. Edited by L. R. A. Casse and W. D. Wallis. VII, 249 pages. 1976.

Vol. 561: Function Theoretic Methods for Partial Differential Equations. Darmstadt 1976. Proceedings. Edited by V. E. Meister, N. Weck and W. L. Wendland. XVIII, 520 pages. 1976.

Vol. 562: R. W. Goodman, Nilpotent Lie Groups: Structure and Applications to Analysis. X, 210 pages. 1976.

Vol. 563: Séminaire de Théorie du Potentiel. Paris, No. 2. Proceedings 1975–1976. Edited by F. Hirsch and G. Mokobodzki. VI, 292 pages. 1976.

Vol. 564: Ordinary and Partial Differential Equations, Dundee 1976. Proceedings. Edited by W. N. Everitt and B. D. Sleeman. XVIII, 551 pages. 1976.

Vol. 565: Turbulence and Navier Stokes Equations. Proceedings 1975. Edited by R. Temam. IX, 194 pages. 1976.

Vol. 566: Empirical Distributions and Processes. Oberwolfach 1976. Proceedings. Edited by P. Gaenssler and P. Révész. VII, 146 pages. 1976.

Vol. 567: Séminaire Bourbaki vol. 1975/76. Exposés 471–488. IV, 303 pages. 1977.

Vol. 568: R. E. Gaines and J. L. Mawhin, Coincidence Degree, and Nonlinear Differential Equations. V, 262 pages. 1977.

Vol. 569: Cohomologie Etale SGA $4\frac{1}{2}$. Séminaire de Géométrie Algébrique du Bois-Marie. Edité par P. Deligne. V, 312 pages. 1977.

Vol. 570: Differential Geometrical Methods in Mathematical Physics, Bonn 1975. Proceedings. Edited by K. Bleuler and A. Reetz. VIII, 576 pages. 1977.

Vol. 571: Constructive Theory of Functions of Several Variables, Oberwolfach 1976. Proceedings. Edited by W. Schempp and K. Zeller. VI. 290 pages. 1977

Vol. 572: Sparse Matrix Techniques, Copenhagen 1976. Edited by V. A. Barker. V, 184 pages. 1977.

Vol. 573: Group Theory, Canberra 1975. Proceedings. Edited by R. A. Bryce, J. Cossey and M. F. Newman. VII, 146 pages. 1977.

Vol. 574: J. Moldestad, Computations in Higher Types. IV, 203 pages. 1977.

Vol. 575: K-Theory and Operator Algebras, Athens, Georgia 1975. Edited by B. B. Morrel and I. M. Singer. VI, 191 pages. 1977.

Vol. 576: V. S. Varadarajan, Harmonic Analysis on Real Reductive Groups. VI, 521 pages. 1977.

Vol. 577: J. P. May, E_∞ Ring Spaces and E_∞ Ring Spectra. IV, 268 pages. 1977.

Vol. 578: Séminaire Pierre Lelong (Analyse) Année 1975/76. Edité par P. Lelong. VI, 327 pages. 1977.

Vol. 579: Combinatoire et Représentation du Groupe Symétrique, Strasbourg 1976. Proceedings 1976. Edité par D. Foata. IV, 339 pages. 1977.

Vol. 580: C. Castaing and M. Valadier, Convex Analysis and Measurable Multifunctions. VIII, 278 pages. 1977.

Vol. 581: Séminaire de Probabilités XI, Université de Strasbourg. Proceedings 1975/1976. Edité par C. Dellacherie, P. A. Meyer et M. Weil. VI, 574 pages. 1977.

Vol. 582: J. M. G. Fell, Induced Representations and Banach *-Algebraic Bundles. IV, 349 pages. 1977.

Vol. 583: W. Hirsch, C. C. Pugh and M. Shub, Invariant Manifolds. IV, 149 pages. 1977.

Vol. 584: C. Brezinski, Accélération de la Convergence en Analyse Numérique. IV, 313 pages. 1977.

Vol. 585: T. A. Springer, Invariant Theory. VI, 112 pages. 1977.

Vol. 586: Séminaire d'Algèbre Paul Dubreil, Paris 1975–1976 (29ème Année). Edited by M. P. Malliavin. VI, 188 pages. 1977.

Vol. 587: Non-Commutative Harmonic Analysis. Proceedings 1976. Edited by J. Carmona and M. Vergne. IV, 240 pages. 1977.

Vol. 588: P. Molino, Théorie des G-Structures: Le Problème d'Equivalence. VI, 163 pages. 1977.

Vol. 589: Cohomologie l-adique et Fonctions L. Séminaire de Géométrie Algébrique du Bois-Marie 1965–66, SGA 5. Edité par L. Illusie. XII, 484 pages. 1977.

Vol. 590: H. Matsumoto, Analyse Harmonique dans les Systèmes de Tits Bornologiques de Type Affine. IV, 219 pages. 1977.

Vol. 591: G. A. Anderson, Surgery with Coefficients. VIII, 157 pages. 1977.

Vol. 592: D. Voigt, Induzierte Darstellungen in der Theorie der endlichen, algebraischen Gruppen. V, 413 Seiten. 1977.

Vol. 593: K. Barbey and H. König, Abstract Analytic Function Theory and Hardy Algebras. VIII, 260 pages. 1977.

Vol. 594: Singular Perturbations and Boundary Layer Theory, Lyon 1976. Edited by C. M. Brauner, B. Gay, and J. Mathieu. VIII, 539 pages. 1977.

Vol. 595: W. Hazod, Stetige Faltungshalbgruppen von Wahrscheinlichkeitsmaßen und erzeugende Distributionen. XIII, 157 Seiten. 1977.

Vol. 596: K. Deimling, Ordinary Differential Equations in Banach Spaces. VI, 137 pages. 1977.

Vol. 597: Geometry and Topology, Rio de Janeiro, July 1976. Proceedings. Edited by J. Palis and M. do Carmo. VI, 866 pages. 1977.

Vol. 598: J. Hoffmann-Jørgensen, T. M. Liggett et J. Neveu, Ecole d'Eté de Probabilités de Saint-Flour VI – 1976. Edité par P.-L. Hennequin. XII, 447 pages. 1977.

Vol. 599: Complex Analysis, Kentucky 1976. Proceedings. Edited by J. D. Buckholtz and T. J. Suffridge. X, 159 pages. 1977.

Vol. 600: W. Stoll, Value Distribution on Parabolic Spaces. VIII, 216 pages. 1977.

Vol. 601: Modular Functions of one Variable V, Bonn 1976. Proceedings. Edited by J.-P. Serre and D. B. Zagier. VI, 294 pages. 1977.

Vol. 602: J. P. Brezin, Harmonic Analysis on Compact Solvmanifolds. VIII, 179 pages. 1977.

Vol. 603: B. Moishezon, Complex Surfaces and Connected Sums of Complex Projective Planes. IV, 234 pages. 1977.

Vol. 604: Banach Spaces of Analytic Functions, Kent, Ohio 1976. Proceedings. Edited by J. Baker, C. Cleaver and Joseph Diestel. VI, 141 pages. 1977.

Vol. 605: Sario et al., Classification Theory of Riemannian Manifolds. XX, 498 pages. 1977.

Vol. 606: Mathematical Aspects of Finite Element Methods. Proceedings 1975. Edited by I. Galligani and E. Magenes. VI, 362 pages. 1977.

Vol. 607: M. Métivier, Reelle und Vektorwertige Quasimartingale und die Theorie der Stochastischen Integration. X, 310 Seiten. 1977.

Vol. 608: Bigard et al., Groupes et Anneaux Réticulés. XIV, 334 pages. 1977.

Vol. 609: General Topology and Its Relations to Modern Analysis and Algebra IV. Proceedings 1976. Edited by J. Novák. XVIII, 225 pages. 1977.

Vol. 610: G. Jensen, Higher Order Contact of Submanifolds of Homogeneous Spaces. XII, 154 pages. 1977.

Vol. 611: M. Makkai and G. E. Reyes, First Order Categorical Logic. VIII, 301 pages. 1977.

Vol. 612: E. M. Kleinberg, Infinitary Combinatorics and the Axiom of Determinateness. VIII, 150 pages. 1977.

Vol. 613: E. Behrends et al., L^p-Structure in Real Banach Spaces. X, 108 pages. 1977.

Vol. 614: H. Yanagihara, Theory of Hopf Algebras Attached to Group Schemes. VIII, 308 pages. 1977.

Vol. 615: Turbulence Seminar, Proceedings 1976/77. Edited by P. Bernard and T. Ratiu. VI, 155 pages. 1977.

Vol. 616: Abelian Group Theory, 2nd New Mexico State University Conference, 1976. Proceedings. Edited by D. Arnold, R. Hunter and E. Walker. X, 423 pages. 1977.

Vol. 617: K. J. Devlin, The Axiom of Constructibility: A Guide for the Mathematician. VIII, 96 pages. 1977.

Vol. 618: I. I. Hirschman, Jr. and D. E. Hughes, Extreme Eigen Values of Toeplitz Operators. VI, 145 pages. 1977.

Vol. 619: Set Theory and Hierarchy Theory V, Bierutowice 1976. Edited by A. Lachlan, M. Srebrny, and A. Zarach. VIII, 358 pages. 1977.

Vol. 620: H. Popp, Moduli Theory and Classification Theory of Algebraic Varieties. VIII, 189 pages. 1977.

Vol. 621: Kauffman et al., The Deficiency Index Problem. VI, 112 pages. 1977.

Vol. 622: Combinatorial Mathematics V, Melbourne 1976. Proceedings. Edited by C. Little. VIII, 213 pages. 1977.

Vol. 623: I. Erdelyi and R. Lange, Spectral Decompositions on Banach Spaces. VIII, 122 pages. 1977.

Vol. 624: Y. Guivarc'h et al., Marches Aléatoires sur les Groupes de Lie. VIII, 292 pages. 1977.

Vol. 625: J. P. Alexander et al., Odd Order Group Actions and Witt Classification of Innerproducts. IV, 202 pages. 1977.

Vol. 626: Number Theory Day, New York 1976. Proceedings. Edited by M. B. Nathanson. VI, 241 pages. 1977.

Vol. 627: Modular Functions of One Variable VI, Bonn 1976. Proceedings. Edited by J.-P. Serre and D. B. Zagier. VI, 339 pages. 1977.

Vol. 628: H. J. Baues, Obstruction Theory on the Homotopy Classification of Maps. XII, 387 pages. 1977.

Vol. 629: W. A. Coppel, Dichotomies in Stability Theory. VI, 98 pages. 1978.

Vol. 630: Numerical Analysis, Proceedings, Biennial Conference, Dundee 1977. Edited by G. A. Watson. XII, 199 pages. 1978.

Vol. 631: Numerical Treatment of Differential Equations. Proceedings 1976. Edited by R. Bulirsch, R. D. Grigorieff, and J. Schröder. X, 219 pages. 1978.

Vol. 632: J.-F. Boutot, Schéma de Picard Local. X, 165 pages. 1978.

Vol. 633: N. R. Coleff and M. E. Herrera, Les Courants Résiduels Associés à une Forme Méromorphe. X, 211 pages. 1978.

Vol. 634: H. Kurke et al., Die Approximationseigenschaft lokaler Ringe. IV, 204 Seiten. 1978.

Vol. 635: T. Y. Lam, Serre's Conjecture. XVI, 227 pages. 1978.

Vol. 636: Journées de Statistique des Processus Stochastiques, Grenoble 1977, Proceedings. Edité par Didier Dacunha-Castelle et Bernard Van Cutsem. VII, 202 pages. 1978.

Vol. 637: W. B. Jurkat, Meromorphe Differentialgleichungen. VII, 194 Seiten. 1978.

Vol. 638: P. Shanahan, The Atiyah-Singer Index Theorem, An Introduction. V, 224 pages. 1978.

Vol. 639: N. Adasch et al., Topological Vector Spaces. V, 125 pages. 1978.

Vol. 640: J. L. Dupont, Curvature and Characteristic Classes. X, 175 pages. 1978.

Vol. 641: Séminaire d'Algèbre Paul Dubreil, Proceedings Paris 1976–1977. Edité par M. P. Malliavin. IV, 367 pages. 1978.

Vol. 642: Theory and Applications of Graphs, Proceedings, Michigan 1976. Edited by Y. Alavi and D. R. Lick. XIV, 635 pages. 1978.

Vol. 643: M. Davis, Multiaxial Actions on Manifolds. VI, 141 pages. 1978.

Vol. 644: Vector Space Measures and Applications I, Proceedings 1977. Edited by R. M. Aron and S. Dineen. VIII, 451 pages. 1978.

Vol. 645: Vector Space Measures and Applications II, Proceedings 1977. Edited by R. M. Aron and S. Dineen. VIII, 218 pages. 1978.

Vol. 646: O. Tammi, Extremum Problems for Bounded Univalent Functions. VIII, 313 pages. 1978.

Vol. 647: L. J. Ratliff, Jr., Chain Conjectures in Ring Theory. VIII, 133 pages. 1978.

Vol. 648: Nonlinear Partial Differential Equations and Applications, Proceedings, Indiana 1976–1977. Edited by J. M. Chadam. VI, 206 pages. 1978.

Vol. 649: Séminaire de Probabilités XII, Proceedings, Strasbourg, 1976–1977. Edité par C. Dellacherie, P. A. Meyer et M. Weil. VIII, 805 pages. 1978.

Vol. 650: C*-Algebras and Applications to Physics. Proceedings 1977. Edited by H. Araki and R. V. Kadison. V, 192 pages. 1978.

Vol. 651: P. W. Michor, Functors and Categories of Banach Spaces. VI, 99 pages. 1978.

Vol. 652: Differential Topology, Foliations and Gelfand-Fuks-Cohomology, Proceedings 1976. Edited by P. A. Schweitzer. XIV, 252 pages. 1978.

Vol. 653: Locally Interacting Systems and Their Application in Biology. Proceedings, 1976. Edited by R. L. Dobrushin, V. I. Kryukov and A. L. Toom. XI, 202 pages. 1978.

Vol. 654: J. P. Buhler, Icosahedral Golois Representations. III, 143 pages. 1978.

Vol. 655: R. Baeza, Quadratic Forms Over Semilocal Rings. VI, 199 pages. 1978.

Vol. 656: Probability Theory on Vector Spaces. Proceedings, 1977. Edited by A. Weron. VIII, 274 pages. 1978.

Vol. 657: Geometric Applications of Homotopy Theory I, Proceedings 1977. Edited by M. G. Barratt and M. E. Mahowald. VIII, 459 pages. 1978.

Vol. 658: Geometric Applications of Homotopy Theory II, Proceedings 1977. Edited by M. G. Barratt and M. E. Mahowald. VIII, 487 pages. 1978.

Vol. 659: Bruckner, Differentiation of Real Functions. X, 247 pages. 1978.

Vol. 660: Equations aux Dérivée Partielles. Proceedings, 1977. Edité par Pham The Lai. VI, 216 pages. 1978.

Vol. 661: P. T. Johnstone, R. Paré, R. D. Rosebrugh, D. Schumacher, R. J. Wood, and G. C. Wraith, Indexed Categories and Their Applications. VII, 260 pages. 1978.

Vol. 662: Akin, The Metric Theory of Banach Manifolds. XIX, 306 pages. 1978.

Vol. 663: J. F. Berglund, H. D. Junghenn, P. Milnes, Compact Right Topological Semigroups and Generalizations of Almost Periodicity. X, 243 pages. 1978.

Vol. 664: Algebraic and Geometric Topology, Proceedings, 1977. Edited by K. C. Millett. XI, 240 pages. 1978.

Vol. 665: Journées d'Analyse Non Linéaire. Proceedings, 1977. Edité par P. Bénilan et J. Robert. VIII, 256 pages. 1978.

Vol. 666: B. Beauzamy, Espaces d'Interpolation Réels: Topologie et Géometrie. X, 104 pages. 1978.

Vol. 667: J. Gilewicz, Approximants de Padé. XIV, 511 pages. 1978.

Vol. 668: The Structure of Attractors in Dynamical Systems. Proceedings, 1977. Edited by J. C. Martin, N. G. Markley and W. Perrizo. VI, 264 pages. 1978.

Vol. 669: Higher Set Theory. Proceedings, 1977. Edited by G. H. Müller and D. S. Scott. XII, 476 pages. 1978.